Holt School Mathematics

HOLT, RINEHART AND WINSTON, PUBLISHERS
NEW YORK • TORONTO • LONDON • SYDNEY

ABOUT THE AUTHORS

EUGENE D. NICHOLS is Professor of Mathematics Education and Lecturer in the Mathematics Department at Florida State University, Tallahassee, Florida.

PAUL A. ANDERSON is an elementary school teacher in the Clark County School District, Las Vegas, Nevada.

LESLIE A. DWIGHT is the former Head of the Department of Mathematics and Professor of Mathematics at Southeastern Oklahoma State University, Durant, Oklahoma.

FRANCES FLOURNOY is Professor of Elementary Education at the University of Texas, Austin, Texas.

ROBERT KALIN is Professor, Mathematics Education Program, at Florida State University, Tallahassee, Florida.

JOHN SCHLUEP is Professor of Mathematics at State University College, Oswego, New York.

LEONARD SIMON is Assistant Director, Planning and Curriculum, for the New York City Board of Education.

Photo Credits
Pages 11, 38, 54, 188, 249, 288, 295, 340 HRW Photo by Russell Dian
Page 81 HRW Photo By Kenneth Karp
Page 123 Weyer Photo Service, Courtesy Owens-Illinois
Page 144 HRW Photo by John Running
Page 172 Courtesy A. T. and T. Photo Unit
Page 241 Courtesy National Center for Atmospheric Research

ISBN 0–03–018576–9

7   032   9

CONTENTS

v

1 NUMERATION

Let's study how names of the whole numbers are written. Suppose we have a money-counting machine.

After Counting	It Shows	Reason
6 dollars	6 0 0	$6 \cdot 100 = 600$
2 dimes	0 2 0	$2 \cdot 10 = 20$
4 pennies	0 0 4	$4 \cdot 1 = 4$

The dot is used as a times sign ⟶

After counting 6 dollars + 2 dimes + 4 pennies: 6 2 4 .

$$624 = 600 + 20 + 4$$
$$624 = (6 \cdot 100) + (2 \cdot 10) + (4 \cdot 1)$$

1. Consider the number 798.

Standard Numeral

798

Expanded Numeral

$700 + 90 + 8$

or

$(7 \cdot 100) + (9 \cdot 10) + (8 \cdot 1)$

Write two expanded numerals for each.

a. 437   **b.** 986   **c.** 721   **d.** 1,421

2. Consider a large number like 7,342,015.

$$7,000,000 + 300,000 + 40,000 + 2,000 + 0 + 10 + 5$$

or

$$(7 \cdot 1,000,000) + (3 \cdot 100,000) + (4 \cdot 10,000) +$$
$$(2 \cdot 1,000) + (0 \cdot 100) + (1 \cdot 10) + (5 \cdot 1)$$

Write two expanded numerals for each.

a. 3,125,643   **b.** 4,306,257   **c.** 481,517,832,004

3. Tell the value of the underlined digit.

Example 5,4̲27 4 · 100 or 400

a. 25̲9 **b.** 8,4̲37 **c.** 92,5̲86 **d.** 5̲6,821,60̲1,500

Write standard numerals.

1. 700 + 30 + 6 **2.** (5 · 100) + (0 · 10) + (6 · 1)

3. (8 · 100) + (4 · 10) + (7 · 1) **4.** 3,000 + 400 + 70 + 2

5. 6,000,000 + 100,000 + 30,000 + 7,000 + 200 + 40 + 5

6. (4 · 10,000) + (2 · 1,000) + (3 · 100) + (2 · 10) + (1 · 1)

7. (8 · 1,000,000) + (7 · 100,000) + (6 · 10,000) +
(9 · 1,000) + (0 · 100) + (1 · 10) + (6 · 1)

Write expanded numerals.

Example 2,476 2,000 + 400 + 70 + 6

8. 27 **9.** 4,586 **10.** 82,523 **11.** 2,418

12. 2,483,001 **13.** 105,202 **14.** 11,243,576,018 **15.** 7,100

Write expanded numerals.

Example 671 (6 · 100) + (7 · 10) + (1 · 1)

16. 246 **17.** 8,279 **18.** 46,888 **19.** 813,333

20. 642,819 **21.** 5,842,911 **22.** 6,000 **23.** 7,007

Tell the value of the underlined digit.

Example 42̲,827 4 · 10,000 or 40,000

24. 827,5̲01 **25.** 24̲6 **26.** 8,421̲,000 **27.** 8̲01,548

28. 16̲,450 **29.** 791,31̲5 **30.** 56̲,809 **31.** 97̲,999

WORD NAMES FOR NUMBERS

The Brownville Nursery School budget is $239,000. The word name for this amount is two hundred thirty-nine thousand dollars.

Brownville Nursery School

periods	trillions			billions			millions			thousands			ones		
	hundred trillions	ten trillions	trillions	hundred billions	ten billions	billions	hundred millions	ten millions	millions	hundred thousands	ten thousands	thousands	hundreds	tens	ones
	2	3	9	0	0	0	0	0	0	0	0	0	0	0	0
				2	3	9	0	0	0	0	0	0	0	0	0
							2	3	9	0	0	0	0	0	0
										2	3	9	0	0	0
													2	3	9

two hundred thirty-nine
two hundred thirty-nine thousand
two hundred thirty-nine million
two hundred thirty-nine billion
two hundred thirty-nine trillion

1. One million is 1,000 thousand. One billion is 1,000 million. One trillion is 1,000 billion. Suppose you could spend $1,000 a day. How many days would it take to spend one trillion dollars? If you started at age 10, could you spend it by age 70?

2. In 12,805,076,940,947, numeral 947 is in the ones period. Name the numeral in these periods.

   a. thousands **b.** millions **c.** trillions

3. Read the full word name.

   Example   213,700,460,301,010: two hundred thirteen-trillion, seven hundred billion, four hundred sixty million, three hundred one thousand, ten

   a. 12,805,076,940,947 **b.** 27,425,862

   c. 843,562,045,666 **d.** 257,004,529,463

   e. 999,999,999,999,999 **f.** 821,562,287

Write standard numerals.

1. Nine billion, three hundred twenty-five million, eight hundred thirty-two thousand, five hundred ninety-two

2. Twenty-four billion, eight hundred thirty-eight million, four hundred sixty-two thousand, one hundred fifty-three

3. Seven hundred billion, seventy-seven million, seven thousand, seven hundred seventy-seven

4. Six hundred three trillion, four hundred twenty billion, sixty-five million, seventy thousand, eight hundred ten

Use a short way to write word names.

Example   12,805,076,940,000
12 trillion, 805 billion, 76 million, 940 thousand

5. 1,234,567,892

6. 33,458,924,651

7. 234,300,460,040,231

8. 57,426,007,573

9. 847,506,009,127,006

10. 27,843,200,743,806

11. 284,591,200,003,840

12. 1,321,562,027,041

13. 84,723,467,901

14. 83,276,855,733,500

Write standard numerals.

15. The Space program budget was five billion, one hundred million dollars.

16. The sun is about ninety-three million miles from Earth.

Write word names for the numbers.

17. A satellite sent an S.O.S. from 22,000,000 miles in space.

18. After a day, a satellite was 160,311 miles from Earth.

3

POWERS OF TEN

POWERS OF TEN			
Standard Numeral	Factored Form	Exponential Form	Read
100	10 · 10	10^2	10 to the 2nd power or 10 squared
1,000	10 · 10 · 10	10^3	10 to the 3rd power or 10 cubed
10,000	10 · 10 · 10 · 10	10^4	10 to the 4th power

exponent

base → 10^4

Exponents tell how many times a base is used as a factor.

$$10^5 = 10 \cdot 10 \cdot 10 \cdot 10 \cdot 10$$

1. How many times is 10 a factor in 10 · 10?

2. Complete.

   a. 100 = ____ · ____ so, 100 = 10?

   b. 1,000 = ____ · ____ · ____ so, 1,000 = 10?

   c. 10,000 = ____ · ____ · ____ · ____ so, 10,000 = 10?

   d. 100,000 = ____ · ____ · ____ · ____ · ____ so, 100,000 = 10?

   e. 1,000,000 = ____ · ____ · ____ · ____ · ____ · ____ so, 1,000,000 = 10?

3. We can write expanded numerals using exponential notation.

   $3,745 = (3 \cdot 1,000) + (7 \cdot 100) + (4 \cdot 10) + 5$
   $= (3 \cdot 10 \cdot 10 \cdot 10) + (7 \cdot 10 \cdot 10) + (4 \cdot 10) + 5$
   $= (3 \cdot 10^3) + (7 \cdot 10^2) + (4 \cdot 10) + 5$

   Write expanded numerals. Use exponential form.

   a. 145   **b.** 2,745   **c.** 12,463   **d.** 234,432

Write in exponential form.

1. $10 \cdot 10 \cdot 10 \cdot 10 \cdot 10$ **2.** $10 \cdot 10$ **3.** 1,000

4. 10,000   **5.** 1,000,000   **6.** 100,000

Copy and complete.

7. $10^? = 1,000$ **8.** $10^? = 100$ **9.** $10^6 = $ ____

10. $10^3 = $ ____   **11.** $10^4 = $ ____   **12.** $10^5 = $ ____

Write standard numerals.

13. 10^2 **14.** 10^3 **15.** 10^5 **16.** 10^7

17. 10^4 **18.** 10^6 **19.** $10^2 \cdot 10^3$ **20.** $10^5 \cdot 10$

Write expanded numerals. Use exponential form.

21. 1,234   **22.** 3,518   **23.** 7,231

24. 9,548   **25.** 12,987   **26.** 75,000

27. 234,957   **28.** 547,000   **29.** 725,456

★Solve.

30. Which power of 10 is 1,000,000,000?

31. Robert said that the product of 10^2 and 10^4 is one billion. Prove that he was either right or wrong.

Brainteaser

Jane doubled a whole number and added a second number to it. The result was 27. Susan guessed that the first number was 5 and the second, 17.

Is Susan correct? Name two more pairs of numbers for which this is true.

ROUNDING

Number		Nearest Ten
27	20 ⟵+++++++++++⟶ 25 27 30	30

$$27 \doteq 30$$

read: is approximately equal to

41	40 ⟵+++++++++++⟶ 41 45 50	40

$$41 \doteq 40$$

Number		Nearest Hundred
527	500 ⟵+++++++++++⟶ 527 550 600	500

$$527 \doteq 500$$

283	200 ⟵+++++++++++⟶ 250 283 300	300

$$283 \doteq 300$$

1. Round to the nearest ten.

    a. 42   **b.** 28   **c.** 77   **d.** 33

2. Round a "half-way" number to the larger multiple of 10.

        Round 25 to 30

    a. 15   **b.** 45   **c.** 85   **d.** 5

3. Round to the nearest hundred.

        Round 123 to 100
        Round 278 to 300
        Round 450 to 500

    a. 618   **b.** 842   **c.** 281   **d.** 350

4. Rounding to the nearest thousand is just as easy.

        Round 1,426 to 1,000
        Round 1,691 to 2,000
        Round 4,500 to 5,000

    a. 2,725   **b.** 1,734   **c.** 5,550   **d.** 6,500

5. Round to the nearest ten thousand.

    a. 42,625   **b.** 66,521   **c.** 84,000   **d.** 75,000

6. Round to the nearest hundred thousand.

    a. 476,821   **b.** 357,921   **c.** 450,000

7. Round these prices to the nearest ten cents.

Example   Round 29¢ to 30¢

    a. 49¢   **b.** 73¢   **c.** 88¢   **d.** 55¢

EXERCISES

Round to the nearest ten.

1. 28   **2.** 42   **3.** 55   **4.** 65

5. 37   **6.** 85   **7.** 82   **8.** 35

Round to the nearest hundred.

9. 275   **10.** 490   **11.** 250   **12.** 782

13. 882   **14.** 78   **15.** 155   **16.** 550

Round to the nearest thousand.

17. 1,430   **18.** 3,721   **19.** 6,400   **20.** 8,920

21. 2,950   **22.** 5,500   **23.** 7,100   **24.** 9,427

Round to the nearest ten thousand.

25. 26,400   **26.** 31,326   **27.** 42,560   **28.** 65,000

29. 71,344   **30.** 56,000   **31.** 83,901   **32.** 47,500

Round to the nearest hundred thousand.

33. 201,840   **34.** 576,000   **35.** 750,000   **36.** 421,311

37. 637,960   **38.** 896,514   **39.** 210,000   **40.** 850,000

MORE ABOUT ROUNDING

We can round a number several ways.

1. Study this chart.

	Number	Think	Round
nearest thousand	17,486	17,486 ↑ Is this digit 5 or greater? No!	17,000
nearest ten	9,368	9,368 ↑ Is this digit 5 or greater? Yes!	9,370
nearest hundred	42,352	42,352 ↑ Is this digit 5 or greater? Yes!	42,400
nearest ten thousand	461,810	461,810 ↑ Is this digit 5 or greater? No!	460,000

2. Let's round 38,713 to the nearest thousand.

    a. Find the thousands digit.   3 **8**,7 1 3

    b. Look at the digit to its right.   3 **8**,7 1 3
        Is it 5 or greater?   ↑

    c. Now round the number.   3 **9**,0 0 0

Round to the nearest hundred.

1. 3,416   **2.** 8,655   **3.** 1,763   **4.** 42,076

5. 33,450   **6.** 6,278   **7.** 122,519   **8.** 85,329

Round to the nearest thousand.

9. 73,910   **10.** 26,842   **11.** 51,001   **12.** 72,314

13. 127,547   **14.** 831,400   **15.** 93,007   **16.** 2,431,187

Round to the nearest ten.

17. 477   **18.** 1,263   **19.** 929   **20.** 4,856

21. 8,018   **22.** 23,427   **23.** 9,845   **24.** 62,511

Round to the nearest ten thousand.

25. 42,516   **26.** 127,683   **27.** 214,011   **28.** 89,674

29. 145,956   **30.** 911,842   **31.** 787,503   **32.** 148,212

Round to the nearest hundred thousand.

33. 498,521   **34.** 3,846,300   **35.** 4,927,351

36. 8,740,516   **37.** 2,372,642   **38.** 1,453,275

Round to the nearest million.

39. 62,543,018   **40.** 47,300,011   **41.** 64,851,021

FINITE AND INFINITE

Here are the whole numbers less than 10.

0, 1, 2, 3, 4, 5, 6, 7, 8, 9

We can use three dots to list them in shorter form.

0, 1, 2, 3, . . . 9

1. Use three dots to list these numbers in short form.

    a. Whole numbers less than 21

    b. Whole numbers between 45 and 76

2. How many numbers are listed?

    a. 5, 6, 7, 8, 9, 10, 11   **b.** 101, 102, 103, . . . 115

    A set with a definite number of members is finite.

3. We can write all whole numbers like this:

    0, 1, 2, 3, 4, . . .

    The numbers go on and on
    without end.

    A set with an unending number of members is infinite.

    Finite or infinite?

    a. 51, 52, 53, . . . , 1,520   **b.** 7, 8, 9, . . .

EXERCISES

Finite or infinite?

1. 24, 25, 26, 27   **2.** 51, 52, 53, . . .

3. 94, 95, 96 . . .   **4.** 64, 65, 66, . . . , 101

LONG DISTANCE TRUCK DRIVERS

1. A truck driver must travel 400 kilometers to deliver cargo. So far, he has traveled 263 kilometers. How many more kilometers does he have to go?

2. A truck is traveling at 45 kilometers per hour for 6 hours. What is the total number of kilometers traveled?

3. The gas tank of a large truck can hold 114 liters. The cost per liter is 16¢. How much would 114 liters of gas cost?

4. There are 25,000 truck drivers working for a nationwide trucking firm. In 1985, the number of drivers is expected to rise to 32,000. How many more truck drivers are expected to be working for that firm in 1985?

5. One driver's time card shows a total of 50 hours for the week. The driver is paid $7.00 per hour. How much did she make for the week?

★ 6. A truck begins in New York with 800 kilograms of cargo. In Philadelphia, 625 kilograms of the cargo are unloaded. In Chicago, the truck picks up 120 kilograms of additional cargo. How much is the truck carrying when it leaves Chicago?

11

ANCIENT EGYPTIAN NUMERATION

The Ancient Egyptians used a numeration system different from our Hindu-Arabic system.

Ancient Egyptian Symbol	Name of Symbol	Hindu-Arabic Symbol
|	tally	1
∩	heel bone	10
9	coil of rope	100
⚘	lotus flower	1,000
⌐	bent stick	10,000
𓆟	fish	100,000
𓀁	astonished man	1,000,000

The ancient Egyptians did not use place value. They repeated symbols.

Egyptian	||	|||	∩∩	9999	⌐⌐⌐
Hindu-Arabic	2	3	20	400	30,000

1. Write Hindu-Arabic Numerals.

a. \|\|\|\|\| **b.** ∩∩∩∩ **c.** 9 9 9 9 **d.** 𓀁 𓀁 𓀁 𓀁

2. Write Ancient Egyptian numerals.

a. 7   **b.** 50   **c.** 300   **d.** 50,000

3. Complete.

	Hindu-Arabic	Ancient Egyptian
	23	∩∩|||
	412	9999∩||
	2,141	⚘⚘9∩∩∩∩|
a.		⚘99∩∩∩||
b.	3,235	
c.	2,132,131	
d.		𓀁𓀁𓀁 999 ⌐ 99∩|||
e.	3,054	

True or false?

1. 41 = ∩∩∩∩I   **2.** 401 = 99991

3. 320 = 999∩∩I   **4.** 1,211,111 = ⚹♐♐⟋⟋⚹9∩I

5. 1,000 000 = ⟋I   **6.** 30,010 = ⟋ ⟋ ⟋ I

Write Hindu-Arabic numerals.

7. ∩∩II   **8.** 9 9∩III

9. 9∩∩   **10.** ♐♐⟋⟋99∩∩III

11. ⟋⟋⚹9∩∩I   **12.** ⚹⚹⟋⟋⟋⟋9999∩III

13. ⚹999∩∩∩   **14.** ♐♐♐♐∩∩∩∩∩III

Write Ancient Egyptian numerals.

15. 45   **16.** 312   **17.** 6,123

18. 500,001   **19.** 4,020,101   **20.** 2,300,219

21. 3,307   **22.** 402,510   **23.** 999

True or false?

24. 9 9 9 > ⟋⟋⟋   **25.** 9 9 9 > ⚹

26. 9II < ∩I   **27.** 9∩I < ♐∩

28. IIIIIIIIII = ∩   **29.** 9 < ∩∩∩∩∩

Answer these questions.

30. "The answer to 23 shows that Egyptian numerals are often hard to write," said Peg. Is she right?

31. Gene said, "The ancient Egyptians needed a new numeral for numbers larger than 9,999,999." Is he right?

13

ROMAN NUMERALS

Roman Numeral	I	V	X	L	C	D	M
Hindu-Arabic Numeral	1	5	10	50	100	500	1,000

Roman	Hindu-Arabic
VIII	8
XXV	25
MMCCC	2,300
CMXX	920

Repetition, addition, and subtraction are used.

1. Write Hindu-Arabic numerals.

   Example   M   CC   L   XX   III
                ↓   ↓   ↓   ↓   ↓
                1,000 + 200 + 50 + 20 + 3, or 1,273

   a. XXIII   **b.** LXXI   **c.** MCCCXII   **d.** MDCCLII

2. The Roman system used subtraction in these special cases.

   IV means 5 − 1, or 4
   XL means 50 − 10, or 40
   IX means 10 − 1, or 9
   XC means 100 − 10, or 90
   CD means 500 − 100, or 400
   CM means 1,000 − 100, or 900

   Write Hindu-Arabic numerals.

   a. CDVIII   **b.** XLIV   **c.** XCIV   **d.** CMXXI

3. A bar over a Roman numeral multiplies the value by 1,000.

   $\overline{C} = 100 \times 1,000$ $\overline{XXX} = 30 \times 1,000$
   $\phantom{\overline{C}} = 100,000$ $\phantom{\overline{XXX}} = 30,000$

   Write Hindu-Arabic numerals.

   a. $\overline{M}$ **b.** $\overline{MM}$ **c.** $\overline{XC}$ **d.** $\overline{XXX}MMCXIV$

14

Write Hindu-Arabic numerals.

1. III   **2.** VII   **3.** XIII   **4.** XIV

5. XIX   **6.** XLIV   **7.** XLVI   **8.** LXVI

9. CDVI   **10.** MMCCCXVI   **11.** CCXXIX   **12.** MCMLXXVI

13. MCMLXXIV   **14.** $\overline{\text{M}}$MXXI   **15.** $\overline{\text{CXX}}$CXX   **16.** $\overline{\text{XLM}}$CMXIV

Write Roman numerals.

17. 2   **18.** 4   **19.** 5   **20.** 6

21. 9   **22.** 11   **23.** 24   **24.** 41

25. 49   **26.** 51   **27.** 93   **28.** 117

29. 1,776   **30.** 1,976   **31.** 100,000   **32.** 10,526

Brainteaser

Study this way of finding the sum of the first ten counting numbers.

We have ten 11's to add. But this is twice our sum. So our answer is $\frac{10 \times 11}{2}$, or 55.

$$1(+10) = \quad 11$$
$$2(+\ 9) = \quad 11$$
$$3(+\ 8) = \quad 11$$
$$4(+\ 7) = \quad 11$$
$$5(+\ 6) = \quad 11$$
$$6(+\ 5) = \quad 11$$
$$7(+\ 4) = \quad 11$$
$$8(+\ 3) = \quad 11$$
$$9(+\ 2) = \quad 11$$
$$+10(+\ 1) = +11$$

Use this way to find these answers.

1. The sum of the first twenty counting numbers.

2. The sum of the first hundred counting numbers.

3. The sum of the first thousand counting numbers.

4. The sum of the first ten odd counting numbers.

BASE-FIVE NUMERATION

Other numbers besides ten can be used as a base.

Base Ten: 1 2 3 4 5 6 7 8 9 10

Base Five: 1 2 3 4 10 11 12 13 14 20

Compare place-value charts.

BASE TEN

ten·ten·ten	ten·ten	ten	one
		1	6	3

ten·ten·ten	ten·ten	ten	one
	1	6	3

BASE FIVE

five·five·five	five·five	five	one
1	1	2	3

$1123_{five} = (1 \cdot five \cdot five \cdot five) + (1 \cdot five \cdot five) + (2 \cdot five) + 3$

$= (1 \cdot one\ hundred\ twenty\text{-}five) + (1 \cdot twenty\text{-}five) + (2 \cdot five) + 3$

$= 125 + 25 + 10 + 3$

$= 163$

---

1. Here are 17 stars. We can group by 5's.

   a. How many groups of 5's are there?

   b. How many ones are left over?
   We can write $17 = 32_{five}$

2. Here are 70 dots. We can get at most two groups of 25 each.

   a. How many groups of 5's are there?

   b. How many ones are left over?
   We can write $70 = 240_{five}$

   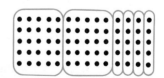

3. Group and write base-five numerals for each.

   a.  ★★★★★
      ★★★
      ★★★★★

   b.  ● ● ● ● ● ● ●
      ● ● ● ● ● ●
      ● ● ● ● ● ● ●

   c.  ▲▲▲▲▲▲▲▲▲▲▲
      ▲▲▲▲▲▲▲▲▲▲
      ▲▲▲▲▲▲▲▲▲▲

4. Let's rename 1432_{five} as a base-ten numeral.

$$1432_{\text{five}} = (1 \cdot \text{one hundred twenty-five}) +$$
$$(4 \cdot \text{twenty-five}) + (3 \cdot \text{five}) + 2$$
$$= 125 + 100 + 15 + 2$$
$$= 242$$

Complete.

$$2342_{\text{five}} = (\underline{\hphantom{XX}} \cdot \text{one hundred twenty-five}) +$$
$$(\underline{\hphantom{XX}} \cdot \text{twenty-five}) + (\underline{\hphantom{XX}} \cdot \text{five}) + \underline{\hphantom{XX}}$$
$$= 250 + \underline{\hphantom{XX}} + \underline{\hphantom{XX}} + \underline{\hphantom{XX}}$$
$$= \underline{\hphantom{XX}}$$

5. Rename as base-ten numerals.

a. 234_{five} **b.** 413_{five} **c.** 1342_{five} **d.** 1223_{five}

EXERCISES

1. Write 1 through 28 in base five. Complete.

$1 = 1$	$8 = 13_{\text{five}}$	$15 = 30_{\text{five}}$	$22 = \underline{\hphantom{XX}}$
$2 = 2$	$9 = 14_{\text{five}}$	$16 = 31_{\text{five}}$	$23 = \underline{\hphantom{XX}}$
$3 = 3$	$10 = \underline{\hphantom{XX}}$	$17 = \underline{\hphantom{XX}}$	$24 = 44_{\text{five}}$
$4 = 4$	$11 = 21_{\text{five}}$	$18 = \underline{\hphantom{XX}}$	$25 = \underline{\hphantom{XX}}$
$5 = 10_{\text{five}}$	$12 = \underline{\hphantom{XX}}$	$19 = 34_{\text{five}}$	$26 = 101_{\text{five}}$
$6 = 11_{\text{five}}$	$13 = \underline{\hphantom{XX}}$	$20 = 40_{\text{five}}$	$27 = \underline{\hphantom{XX}}$
$7 = \underline{\hphantom{XX}}$	$14 = 24_{\text{five}}$	$21 = \underline{\hphantom{XX}}$	$28 = \underline{\hphantom{XX}}$

Write base-five numerals for each.

2.
▲ ▲ ▲ ▲ ▲ ▲
▲ ▲ ▲ ▲ ▲ ▲
▲ ▲ ▲ ▲ ▲ ▲
▲ ▲ ▲ ▲

3.
● ● ● ● ● ● ● ●
● ● ● ● ● ● ● ●
● ● ●

4.
★ ★ ★ ★ ★ ★ ★ ★ ★
★ ★ ★ ★ ★ ★ ★ ★ ★
★ ★ ★ ★ ★ ★ ★ ★ ★
★ ★ ★ ★ ★ ★ ★ ★ ★
★ ★ ★ ★ ★ ★ ★ ★

Write base-ten numerals.

5. 23_{five} **6.** 32_{five} **7.** 44_{five} **8.** 222_{five}

9. 1234_{five} **10.** 4444_{five} **11.** 2321_{five} **12.** 3432_{five}

We can rewrite numerals like 44 in base five.

Find how many sets of twenty-fives there are.

$$\begin{array}{r} 1 \\ 25\overline{)44} \\ 25 \\ \hline 19 \end{array}$$

Fill in the twenty-five's place.

↓

| 1 | 3 | 4 |

Find how many sets of fives are left over.

$$\begin{array}{r} 3 \\ 5\overline{)19} \\ 15 \\ \hline 4 \end{array}$$

Fill in the fives

There are 4 ones left.

Fill in the ones.

$$44 = 134_{\text{five}}$$

1. Let's rename 98 in base five.

   a. How many sets of twenty-five are in 98? Divide.

   $$\begin{array}{r} 3 \\ 25\overline{)98} \\ 75 \\ \hline 23 \end{array}$$

   b. Write the answer in the twenty-five's place.

   c. What is the remainder? How many sets of five is this? Divide.

   $$\begin{array}{r} 4 \\ 5\overline{)23} \\ 20 \\ \hline 3 \end{array}$$

   d. Write this answer in the five's place.

   e. How many ones are left?

   f. Complete: 98 = ____

2. Rename in base five.

   a. 18   b. 37   c. 62   d. 86

   e. 57   f. 92   g. 48   h. 21

Write base-five numerals.

1. 23	**2.** 27	**3.** 34	**4.** 41
5. 59	**6.** 75	**7.** 76	**8.** 80
9. 99	**10.** 52	**11.** 83	**12.** 67
13. 39	**14.** 72	**15.** 50	**16.** 100
17. 124	**18.** 125	**19.** 200	**20.** 392
21. 446	**22.** 527	**23.** 593	**24.** 614

★ Solve.

25. Each of the numbers below is 4 greater than the previous number. Write the names for the next four numbers in the sequence.

$$0, 4, 13_{five}, 22_{five}, \ldots$$

ACTIVITY

Get some play money to do this money-changing activity with a friend.

1. Have your friend give you change of 32¢ from a dollar. What coins might be used? Think of at least two different ways that this can be done. Which way uses the fewest coins?

2. Suppose we did away with all the nickels. Find at least three ways to make change from a dollar for a 43¢ purchase. Find the way that uses the fewest coins.

3. Imagine a society that uses only pennies and dimes as coins. How would they make change for these purchases?

47¢	21¢	19¢	7¢

19

BASE-SIX NUMERATION

Six can also be used as a base.

Base Ten: 1   2   3   4   5   6   7   8   9   10

Base Six: 1   2   3   4   5   10   11   12   13   14

Compare place-value charts.

BASE TEN

ten · ten · ten	ten · ten	ten	one
	2	6	7

BASE SIX

six · six · six	six · six	six	one
1	1	2	3

1123_{six} = (1 · two hundred sixteen) + (1 · thirty-six) +
$$(2 \cdot six) + 3$$
$$= 216 + 36 + 12 + 3$$
$$= 267$$

1. Let's rename 1243_{six} as a base-ten numeral.

1243_{six} = (1 · two hundred sixteen) + (2 · thirty-six) +
$$(4 \cdot six) + (3 \cdot one)$$
$$= 216 + 72 + 24 + 3$$
$$= 315$$

Rename as base-ten numerals.

a. 24_{six} **b.** 543_{six} **c.** 1341_{six} **d.** 3111_{six}

EXERCISES

Write base-ten numerals.

1. 23_{six} **2.** 45_{six} **3.** 101_{six} **4.** 444_{six}

5. 1000_{six} **6.** 1234_{six} **7.** 4444_{six} **8.** 5432_{six}

1, 7, 13, 19, —, —, —

The rule is add 6. The next three numbers are 25, 31, and 37.

1. Let's look at this sequence.

$$1, 3, 9, 27, \ldots$$

   a. What is the rule that relates each number to the one before it?

   b. What is the next number in this sequence?

2. Find the rule and complete the sequence.

   a. 1, 4, 7, 10, ____ , ____ , ____ , ____

   b. 256, 128, 64, 32, ____ , ____ , ____ , ____

EXERCISES

Complete each sequence.

1. 7, 12, 17, 22, ____ , ____ , ____ , ____

2. 3, 9, 15, 21, ____ , ____ , ____ , ____

3. 4, 8, 12, 16, ____ , ____ , ____ , ____

4. 2, 6, 18, 54, ____ , ____ , ____

★ **5.** 1, 2, 4, 7, 11, ____ , ____ , ____

PICTURE PROBLEMS

Solve these picture problems.

1. How many more miles?

2. Groceries.
   Total cost?

3. Candy bars.
   10¢ each.
   Total cost?

4. How much change?

5. New buttons.
   20¢ each.
   Total cost?

6. How many tons?

7. Cookies.
   Shared equally.
   How many each?

8. Alarm set for 7:30.
   How much more time?

9. How many bunches of 6?

CHAPTER REVIEW

Consider 492, 364, 527.

1. Write the word name. [2]

2. Write an expanded numeral. Use exponential form. [4]

Round to the nearest million. [6]

3. 2,694,213   **4.** 25,532,962   **5.** 56,392,100

Round to the nearest hundred. [6]

6. 392   **7.** 4,624   **8.** 5,550   **9.** 365,694

Write standard numerals.

10. Fifty-nine billion, six hundred four thousand, seven.
[2]
11. Three hundred twenty-two million, three hundred twenty-
[2] two thousand, three hundred twenty-two.

12. 300 + 70 + 4   **13.** 6,000 + 600 + 60 + 6
[vi]   [vi]
14. $10^3 \cdot 10^4$ **15.** $(7 \cdot 1,000) + (4 \cdot 100) + (8 \cdot 1)$
[4]   [vi]

Finite or infinite? [10]

16. 99, 100, 101, . . . , 1,000   **17.** 1, 2, 3, 4, . . .

Write Hindu-Arabic numerals. [14]

18. MCXLVII   **19.** MMDCXXXII   **20.** $\overline{\text{MM}}$XIX

21. Complete this sequence: 2, 9, 16, 23, ____ , ____ , ____ [21]

Solve this problem. [11]

22. The odometer of a truck read 32,569 kilometers at the beginning of a trip, and 32,989 at the end. How many kilometers long was the trip?

23

CHAPTER TEST

Consider 701,425,839.

1. Write the word name.

2. Write an expanded numeral. Use exponential form.

Round to the nearest thousand.

3. 8,942   **4.** 64,521   **5.** 3,256,286

Round to the nearest ten thousand.

6. 64,622   **7.** 125,000   **8.** 4,927,431

Write standard numerals.

9. Five billion, two hundred twenty million, nine hundred thousand, four hundred six.

10. $7,000 + 400 + 60 + 3$ **11.** $(9 \cdot 1,000) + (0 \cdot 100) + (5 \cdot 10) + (6 \cdot 1)$

12. $10^3 \cdot 10^2$

Finite or infinite?

13. 74, 75, 76, . . . , 87   **14.** 2, 4, 6, 8, . . .

Write Hindu-Arabic numerals.

15. MDCCXLIV   **16.** MCMLXXIII

17. Complete this sequence: 3, 7, 11, 15, ____ , ____ , ____

Solve this problem.

18. A refrigerated long-distance truck weighed 3,500 kilograms before it was filled with vegetables. It weighed 4,876 kilograms afterwards. What should the truck driver write in the record for the weight of the vegetables?

Add.

1. 7
   +3

2. 8
   +4

3. 9
   +8

4. 38
   +21

5. 26
   +52

6. 56
   +21

7. 476
   +513

8. 267
   +331

9. 870
   +124

10. 39
    + 2

11. 54
    +39

12. 234
    +549

13. 672
    +281

14. 746
    +867

15. 32
     75
     81
     64
    +38

16. 198
     223
     410
     354
    +576

17. 176
     245
     283
     591
    +304

18. $21.37
    + 25.41

19. $84.92
    + 13.61

Subtract.

20. 76
    −25

21. 89
    −36

22. 48
    −26

23. 725
    −315

24. 409
    − 107

25. 73
    −29

26. 82
    −58

27. 63
    −38

28. 861
    −248

29. 971
    −438

30. 737
    −248

31. 614
    −359

32. 406
    −259

33. 600
    −357

34. 800
    −462

Brainteaser

Imagine that you are in another civilization. You find an unsolved addition table like the one shown. Copy the table. Fill in the missing sums. (*Hint:* Both the commutative property and the property of zero for addition hold.)

+	0	1	2	3	4	5	6
0	0	1	2				
1	1	2					
2	2		4				
3				6	10	11	12
4					11		
5						13	
6							15

2 ADDITION AND SUBTRACTION

A function machine helps to show how numbers are related.

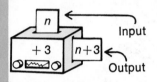

Input: n	0	1	2	9	40
Output: $n+3$	3	4	5	12	43

1. a. Complete.

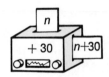

n	0	1	2	9	10	40
$n+30$	30					

b. Is each output a whole number?

2. a. Find the sums.

$$\begin{array}{cccc} 5 & 50 & 7 & 70 \\ +4 & +40 & +9 & +90 \\ \hline \end{array}$$

b. Is each sum a whole number?

The sum of two whole numbers is always a whole number.

3. a. Complete.

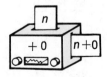

n	0	1	2	9	10	40
$n+0$						

b. Compare the input with the output. What pattern do you see?

26

Property of Zero for Addition

The sum of any number and 0 is the number itself.

4. Solve.

   a. $7 + 0 = n$ **b.** $7 + b = 7$ **c.** $12 + x = 12$

EXERCISES

Solve.

  1. $a + 0 = 17$ **2.** $c + 0 = 29$ **3.** $14 + 0 = x$

  4. $6 + 0 = n$ **5.** $8 + x = 8$ **6.** $13 + c = 13$

  7. $m + 0 = 18$ **8.** $n + 0 = 37$ **9.** $r + 5 = 5$

10. $p + 291 = 291$ **11.** $0 + n = 87$ **12.** $0 + n = 928$

13. $n + 0 = 384$ **14.** $842 + n = 842$ **15.** $200 + 0 = x$

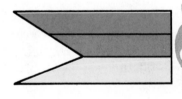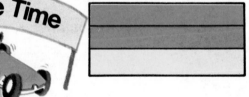

See how fast you can add without making errors.

1. $4 + 6$	**2.** $1 + 9$	**3.** $6 + 1$	**4.** $7 + 1$
5. $6 + 6$	**6.** $5 + 6$	**7.** $1 + 7$	**8.** $1 + 4$
9. $8 + 3$	**10.** $0 + 4$	**11.** $5 + 0$	**12.** $3 + 9$
13. $9 + 8$	**14.** $8 + 1$	**15.** $0 + 6$	**16.** $8 + 0$
17. $9 + 5$	**18.** $3 + 2$	**19.** $3 + 7$	**20.** $1 + 5$
21. $6 + 9$	**22.** $5 + 9$	**23.** $2 + 5$	**24.** $7 + 6$
25. $7 + 9$	**26.** $9 + 4$	**27.** $5 + 7$	**28.** $2 + 6$
29. $6 + 3$	**30.** $6 + 5$	**31.** $3 + 1$	**32.** $9 + 7$

PROPERTIES OF ADDITION

We can arrange the two blocks in these two orders. Is the sum the same in both orders?

sums the same

Commutative Property of Addition

For each pair of whole numbers, the order does not change the sum.

$$a + b = b + a$$

Arrange three blocks. Will the sums be the same?

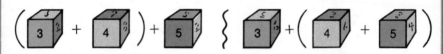

sums the same

Associative Property of Addition

For all whole numbers, the grouping does not change the sum.

$$(a + b) + c = a + (b + c)$$

1. Solve without computing.

   a. $4 + 5 = 5 + n$ b. $19 + 37 = 37 + n$

   c. $a + 20 = 20 + 6$ d. $42 + c = 19 + 42$

2. Solve without computing.

   a. $(4 + 6) + 9 = 4 + (6 + n)$

   b. $(6 + 2) + 98 = 6 + (n + 98)$

28

3. Often we rearrange to pair addends whose sum we recognize.

$$(8 + 14) + 2 \qquad 14 + (8 + 2)$$

Rearrange to find the sum.

a. $7 + 9 + 3$ **b.** $15 + 21 + 5$

c. $17 + 4 + 3$ **d.** $25 + 72 + 75$

Rearrangement Property

We can add whole numbers in any order and grouping. The sum is always the same.

EXERCISES

Without adding, tell which sums are the same.

1. $75 + 93$ $57 + 39$ $93 + 75$

2. $(27 + 35) + 12$ $27 + (12 + 35)$ $27 + (35 + 12)$

Solve without computing.

3. $7 + 9 = 9 + a$ **4.** $18 + 7 = n + 18$

5. $32 + 19 = 19 + x$ **6.** $45 + a = 27 + 45$

7. $39 + n = 12 + 39$ **8.** $x + 13 = 13 + 27$

9. $(7 + 8) + 9 = x + (8 + 9)$

10. $30 + (70 + 8) = (30 + 70) + p$

11. $(19 + 35) + 12 = 19 + (r + 12)$

12. $(40 + 7) + 60 = (40 + 60) + n$

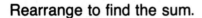

Rearrange to find the sum.

13. $25 + 6 + 5$ **14.** $13 + 20 + 7$ **15.** $4 + 85 + 96$

16. $9 + 47 + 91$ **17.** $20 + 59 + 80$ **18.** $87 + 17 + 3$

USING ADDITION PROPERTIES

The Rearrangement Property explains the way we add.

$$26 + 53 = (20 + 6) + (50 + 3)$$
$$= (20 + 50) + (6 + 3)$$

```
  2 6
+ 5 3
-----
  7 9
```

1. Add

a. 46	**b.** 70	**c.** 32	**d.** 74
+ 3	+26	+47	+21

2. Compare the two forms. Complete.

$$47 + 28 = (40 + 7) + (20 + 8)$$
$$= (40 + 20) + (\underline{} + 8)$$
$$= \underline{} + 15$$
$$= 60 + (10 + 5)$$
$$= (60 + 10) + 5$$
$$= \underline{} + 5$$
$$= 75$$

```
    1
  4 7
+ 2 8
-----
    5
```

3. Complete.

a. $\overset{1\ 1}{498}$	**b.** $\overset{1}{2,460}$	**c.** $\overset{1}{97,531}$
+207	+7,345	+40,782
0 5	0 5	1 3

4. Add.

a. 24	**b.** 273	**c.** 562
+68	+157	+ 89

d. 4,561	**e.** 47,602	**f.** 1,362
8,270	1,476	541
+3,400	+53,998	8,498
		+6,205

Add.

1. 36 + 28	**2.** 27 + 34	**3.** 46 + 36	**4.** 45 + 39
5. 73 + 92	**6.** 83 + 55	**7.** 73 + 98	**8.** 87 + 55
9. 352 + 491	**10.** 427 + 237	**11.** 497 + 231	**12.** 256 + 831
13. 842 + 501	**14.** 521 + 873	**15.** 620 + 456	**16.** 753 + 847
17. 624 + 57	**18.** 581 + 14	**19.** 622 + 50	**20.** 6,215 + 4,199
21. 7,185 + 1,092	**22.** 6,984 + 1,864	**23.** 4,689 + 1,753	**24.** 5,280 + 576
25. 17,469 + 6,511	**26.** 14,246 + 23,908	**27.** 62,946 + 53,018	**28.** 146,587 + 351,009

29. 317 238 + 142	**30.** 6,428 1,956 87 + 742	★ **31.** 11,492 20,134 32,105 64,208 + 74,185	★ **32.** 86,501 43,210 34,567 52,963 15,948 + 29,630

33. 850,400 + 5,287 + 56,902 + 4,820,000

Solve these mini-problems.

34. Football game.
Our team got 6 points.
Theirs got 7 points.
We got 7 more points.
Final score?

35. Groceries.
2 cans of peas, 29¢ each.
1 box cereal, 89¢.
1 liter milk, 69¢.
Total cost?

SELECTING NUMBER SENTENCES FOR PROBLEMS

Pick two number sentences that can help solve each problem.

1. Two classes sold 100 football game tickets. One class sold 27 tickets. How many did the other class sell?

$$27 + n = 100$$
$$n - 27 = 100$$
$$27 + 100 = n$$
$$100 - 27 = n$$

2. John has 28 cents. Together he and Richard have 92 cents. How much does Richard have?

$$92 + n = 28 \qquad 28 + n = 92$$
$$28 - n = 92 \qquad 92 - 28 = n$$

3. Alan picked a record that cost $4.95. His father will let him spend $10. How much more may he spend?

$$\$10 + n = \$4.95 \qquad \$4.95 + n = \$10$$
$$\$10 - \$4.95 = n \qquad n - \$4.95 = \$10$$

4. Sue traveled by car for 75 kilometers. Then she traveled 235 kilometers by train. How many kilometers was her whole trip?

$$235 - 75 = n$$
$$n - 75 = 235$$
$$n + 235 = 75$$
$$235 + 75 = n$$

5. Joan worked 40 hours last week. She worked 29 hours on Monday through Thursday. How long did she work Friday?

$$40 + 29 = n \qquad 40 - 29 = n$$
$$n + 40 = 29 \qquad n + 29 = 40$$

SUBTRACTION: OPPOSITE OF ADDITION

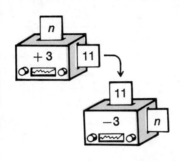   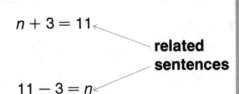

$n + 3 = 11$

$11 - 3 = n$

related sentences

Subtraction and addition are **opposite** operations.
Related sentences have the same solution.

1. Write number sentences. Solve.

a.    **b.**    **c.**

2. Find the solution for each pair of related sentences.

a. $x + 5 = 6$ **b.** $n + 9 = 11$ **c.** $n - 6 = 7$
  $6 - 5 = x$ $11 - 9 = n$ $6 + 7 = n$

3. Write related sentences. Solve.

a. $x + 5 = 6$ **b.** $4 + n = 10$ **c.** $c + 5 = 12$

d. $n + 7 = 9$ **e.** $x - 5 = 3$ **f.** $x - 4 = 2$

Write number sentences. Solve.

1.   **2.**   **3.**

4. **5.** 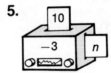 **6.**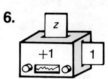

7. **8.** **9.**

Write related sentences. Solve.

10. $1 + n = 6$ **11.** $x + 2 = 6$ **12.** $9 + y = 18$

13. $z + 2 = 10$ **14.** $a - 4 = 11$ **15.** $x + 3 = 12$

16. $8 + x = 12$ **17.** $y + 0 = 5$ **18.** $z - 4 = 10$

19. $y - 3 = 8$ **20.** $6 + a = 10$ **21.** $x - 7 = 8$

22. $7 + p = 12$ **23.** $b + 9 = 11$ **24.** $4 + x = 15$

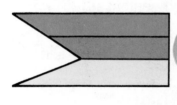  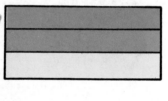

Race Time

See how fast you can subtract without making errors.

1. $13 - 4$	**2.** $17 - 0$	**3.** $16 - 8$	**4.** $17 - 4$
5. $15 - 3$	**6.** $18 - 7$	**7.** $11 - 4$	**8.** $15 - 7$
9. $11 - 3$	**10.** $15 - 1$	**11.** $16 - 5$	**12.** $14 - 3$
13. $9 - 6$	**14.** $18 - 3$	**15.** $11 - 1$	**16.** $12 - 9$
17. $16 - 7$	**18.** $13 - 2$	**19.** $17 - 6$	**20.** $17 - 3$
21. $14 - 9$	**22.** $18 - 4$	**23.** $14 - 4$	**24.** $14 - 8$
25. $11 - 9$	**26.** $15 - 8$	**27.** $15 - 9$	**28.** $18 - 5$
29. $14 - 5$	**30.** $9 - 3$	**31.** $12 - 4$	**32.** $12 - 7$
33. $12 - 5$	**34.** $13 - 3$	**35.** $14 - 7$	**36.** $15 - 6$
37. $8 - 3$	**38.** $15 - 2$	**39.** $18 - 9$	**40.** $9 - 7$

Using money can help you understand subtraction with regrouping.

$$
\begin{array}{l}
\$7.43 \longrightarrow 7 \text{ dollars} + 4 \text{ dimes} + 3 \text{ pennies} \\
-4.27 \longrightarrow 4 \text{ dollars} + 2 \text{ dimes} + 7 \text{ pennies} \\
\hline
 3 \text{ dollars} + 1 \text{ dime} + 6 \text{ pennies}
\end{array}
$$

$$
\begin{array}{r}
{}^{3}{}^{13} \\
\$7.43 \\
-4.27 \\
\hline
\$3.16
\end{array}
$$

We can compute 743 − 427 in a similar way.

$$
\begin{array}{l}
743 \longrightarrow 7 \text{ hundreds} + 4 \text{ tens} + 3 \\
-427 \longrightarrow 4 \text{ hundreds} + 2 \text{ tens} + 7 \\
\hline
 3 \text{ hundreds} + 1 \text{ ten} + 6
\end{array}
$$

$$
\begin{array}{r}
{}^{3}{}^{13} \\
743 \\
-427 \\
\hline
316
\end{array}
$$

1. Study each step.

$$
\begin{array}{r}
654 \\
-326 \\
\hline
\end{array}
\qquad
\begin{array}{r}
{}^{4}{}^{14} \\
6\,5\,4 \\
-3\,2\,6 \\
\hline
8
\end{array}
\qquad
\begin{array}{r}
{}^{4}{}^{14} \\
6\,5\,4 \\
-3\,2\,6 \\
\hline
2\,8
\end{array}
\qquad
\begin{array}{r}
{}^{4}{}^{14} \\
6\,5\,4 \\
-3\,2\,6 \\
\hline
3\,2\,8
\end{array}
$$

Subtract.

a.	**b.**	**c.**	**d.**
47	567	843	5,792
− 24	− 135	− 137	− 1,365

2. Sometimes we must regroup more than once.

$$
\begin{array}{r}
931 \\
-637 \\
\hline
\end{array}
\qquad
\begin{array}{r}
{}^{2}{}^{11} \\
9\,3\,1 \\
-6\,3\,7 \\
\hline
4
\end{array}
\qquad
\begin{array}{r}
{}^{12} \\
8\,{}^{2}\,11 \\
9\,3\,1 \\
-6\,3\,7 \\
\hline
9\,4
\end{array}
\qquad
\begin{array}{r}
{}^{12} \\
8\,{}^{2}\,11 \\
9\,3\,1 \\
-6\,3\,7 \\
\hline
2\,9\,4
\end{array}
$$

Subtract.

a.	**b.**	**c.**
947	983,517	737,248
− 378	− 120,289	− 411,892

Subtract.

1.	25 − 12	**2.**	39 − 18	**3.**	46 −21	**4.**	57 −24
5.	74 − 23	**6.**	92 − 30	**7.**	89 − 5	**8.**	56 − 6
9.	226 − 114	**10.**	345 − 124	**11.**	468 −216	**12.**	597 −214
13.	428 − 127	**14.**	567 −210	**15.**	473 − 301	**16.**	692 − 300
17.	2,468 − 1,111	**18.**	3,692 −2,232	**19.**	4,793 −2,191	**20.**	5,937 − 1,937
21.	827 − 314	**22.**	9,826 −2,405	**23.**	26,495 − 2,345	**24.**	78,676 −23,451
25.	86 − 19	**26.**	73 − 38	**27.**	492 − 135	**28.**	435 − 192
29.	715 − 358	**30.**	5,692 − 3,218	**31.**	5,429 − 1,278	**32.**	4,718 − 1,903
33.	6,633 −2,918	**34.**	764,861 − 122,136	**35.**	587,314 − 373,529	**36.**	966,633 − 409,912

Solve these problems.

37. Mary counted the money in her supermarket cash register. She had three $100-bills, eight $10-bills, and twenty-three $1-bills. How much money did she have?

38. Father wanted to keep his daily calorie count down to 1,500 calories. Before evening dinner, he counted his intake to be 950 calories. How many calories could his dinner have?

36

ZERO IN SUBTRACTION

Here is a way to subtract when 0 occurs.

$$
\begin{array}{r}
400 \\
-127 \\
\end{array}
\longrightarrow
\begin{array}{r}
\overset{39}{4\!\!\!/0} \text{ tens} + \overset{10}{\cancel{0}} \\
1\,2 \text{ tens} + 7 \\
\hline
2\,7 \text{ tens} + 3 \\
\end{array}
\qquad
\begin{array}{r}
\overset{3\ 9\ 10}{4\!\!\!/\,\cancel{0}\,0} \\
-1\,2\,7 \\
\hline
2\,7\,3 \\
\end{array}
$$

1. Practice regrouping. Complete.

   a. 302 = 30 tens + 2
   = 29 tens + ____

   b. 9,004 = 900 tens + 4
   = 899 tens + ____

   c. 900 = 90 tens + 0
   = ____ tens + 10

   d. 3,070 = 30 hundreds + 70 tens
   = ____ hundreds + 170 tens

2. Subtract.

   a.   802
   − 415

   b.   6,003
   − 2,935

   c.   7,025
   − 2,781

   d.   4,000
   − 3,567

EXERCISES

Subtract.

1.   302
− 145

2.   803
− 395

3.   9,004
− 7,315

4.   8,003
− 1,497

5.   3,079
− 1,285

6.   4,060
− 1,381

7.   74,006
− 23,928

8.   80,706
− 24,917

9.   7,004
−   234

10.   9,903
−   375

11.   7,040
−   96

12.   70,305
−   527

Solve this problem.

13. The Boeing 727 jet mainliner is smaller and faster than the Boeing 720. The wingspan of the 720 is 1,570 inches, where the 727 is only 1,303 inches. Find the difference.

X-RAY TECHNICIANS

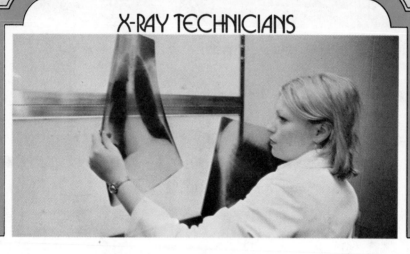

1. A patient needed 2 minutes of radiation therapy. The technician started the X-ray machine just as the digital clock showed 9:45. When should she shut off the machine?

2. The technician reported to the X-ray room at 8:49 am. When she left, the clock read 1:38 pm. How long did she work in the X-ray room?

3. A patient needed X-ray treatment each Monday for seven Mondays in a row. He had his third treatment on May 8. What are the dates for all seven treatments?

4. Susan is paid $700 a month as an X-ray technician in a hospital. How much does she earn in a year?

5. Last year Susan earned $8,100. She had to pay $380 for special clothing to prevent radiation burns. How much of her pay was left?

6. There were about 66,000 X-ray technicians in 1977. The number is expected to double by 1987. How many will there be in 1987?

7. Tom completed his two-year X-ray technician training program in 1978. In what year did he enter the program?

Add.

1. $1.20
  + 3.50

2. $2.34
  + 5.21

3. $7.29
  + 1.53

4. $29.34
  + 9.85

5. $15.47
  + 31.86

6. $86.42
  + 24.97

7. $1.29
   3.41
  + 5.71

8. $16.21
   18.35
  + 10.70

9. $452.70
   671.80
  + 765.50

Subtract.

10. $4.70
  − 2.10

11. $15.78
  − 9.61

12. $9.82
  − 5.33

13. $46.13
  − 23.81

14. $4.70
  − 1.29

15. $29.05
  − 10.70

16. $89.42
  − 67.48

17. $402.73
  − 134.21

ACTIVITY

Find someone who has a job that interests you. Ask that person the following questions about the job. Report the answers to the rest of the class.

1. a. Where do you work? Are there jobs like yours in other places? Where?

   b. How do you get to work? If by car, do you have a car pool?

   c. How far is it from your home to work? How long does it take you?

2. a. How many years of schooling do I need for this job?

   b. Which subjects will be most helpful to prepare me for the job?

39

REPLACEMENTS AND SOLUTIONS

Consider the equation.

$$n + 4 = 9$$

There are no solutions here.

a variable

if the replacements are   the solution is

1, 2, 3, . . ., 9, 10 ⟶ 5

1, 3, 5, 7, 9 ⟶ 5

2, 4, 6, 8, 10 ⟶ no solution

1. A sentence with this sign $=$ is an equation. Consider this equation.

   $x - 8 = 11$ Replacements: 17, 18, 19, 20

   a. Replace x by 17. $17 - 8 = 11$. Is the equation true?

   b. Replace x by 18. $18 - 8 = 11$. Is the equation true?

   c. Replace x by 19. $19 - 8 = 11$. Is the equation true?

   d. Replace x by 20. $20 - 8 = 11$. Is the equation true?

2. In Item 1, the only replacement that made the equation true was 19. We say 19 is the solution.

   Solve. Use these replacements: 1, 2, 3, 4, 5.

   a. $r + 17 = 21$ b. $5 - p = 1$ c. $18 + x = 20$

3. Consider the replacements 1, 2, 3, 4, 5 and the equation $x + 4 = 7$. The solution is 3. We draw its graph like this.

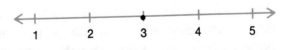

Graph the solutions. Replacements: $1, 2, 3, \ldots, 8$

   a. $x + 9 = 14$ b. $x - 3 = 5$ c. $7 - y = 3$

42

4. Consider the equation $p - 10 = 4$. Use these replacements: 11, 13, 15

Use replacements: $\left.\begin{array}{l}11 - 10 = 4 \\ 13 - 10 = 4 \\ 15 - 10 = 4\end{array}\right\}$ all false, so there is no solution for these replacements.

Solve. Use these replacements: 11, 13, 15

a. $y + 3 = 15$ **b.** $x - 7 = 14$ **c.** $n - 5 = 8$

EXERCISES

Solve. Use these replacements: 1, 2, 3, . . ., 19, 20

1. $x + 9 = 15$ **2.** $n + 9 = 19$ **3.** $y + 9 = 25$

4. $7 - 3 = c$ **5.** $15 - 3 = z$ **6.** $21 - 20 = p$

7. $b + 15 = 26$ **8.** $s + 5 = 16$ **9.** $r + 17 = 22$

10. $t - 7 = 3$ **11.** $s - 8 = 10$ **12.** $x - 9 = 20$

13. $y + 32 = 49$ **14.** $z + 12 = 13$ **15.** $j + 200 = 300$

16. $r + 38 = 40$ **17.** $19 - m = 15$ **18.** $s - 29 = 30$

Graph each solution. Use these replacements: 1, 2, 3, . . ., 14, 15

19. $x - 3 = 7$ **20.** $5 + y = 20$ **21.** $a + 4 = 15$

22. $b - 6 = 2$ **23.** $m + 9 = 16$ **24.** $10 + c = 14$

25. $8 + d = 19$ **26.** $7 + 18 = p$ **27.** $x - 7 = 8$

★ Solve. Use these replacements: 1, 19, 20, 21, 31

28. $25 - a = 20$ **29.** $33 - b = 18$ **30.** $40 - x = 10$

31. $n + 29 = 48$ **32.** $112 + y = 133$ **33.** $z - 431 = 20$

34. $x + 54 = 74$ **35.** $87 - 56 = p$ **36.** $725 - 724 = n$

USING A VARIABLE TWICE

Sometimes we use a variable more than once in an equation.

Replacements: 0, 1, 2, 3, . . .

Equation	$x + x = 10$	$a + a = 9$
Words	The sum of a number and itself is 10.	The sum of a number and itself is 9.
True Equation	$5 + 5 = 10$	none
Solution	5	no solution

Use these replacements: 0, 1, 2, 3, . . . for Items 1-4.

1. Consider this equation: $y + y = 6$

   a. Is one of the equations at the right true?

   b. What is the solution?

   $1 + 1 = 6$
   $2 + 2 = 6$
   $3 + 3 = 6$
   $4 + 4 = 6$

2. Consider this equation: $n + n = 5$

   a. Is one of these equations at the right true?

   b. What is the solution?

   $1 + 1 = 5$
   $2 + 2 = 5$
   $3 + 3 = 5$

3. Sometimes we have equations like this

   $$3 + b = b + 3$$

   a. Are these equations true?

   $3 + 0 = 0 + 3$ $3 + 1 = 1 + 3$ $3 + 2 = 2 + 3$

   b. The solutions are 0, 1, 2, 3, . . . Which property tells us that this is true: commutative or associative?

4. Consider this equation: $3 + b = b$.

    a. Is one of these sentences at the right true?

$$3 + 0 = 0$$
$$3 + 1 = 1$$
$$3 + 2 = 2$$

    b. Why is there no solution?

Solve. Use these replacements: 0, 1, 2, 3, . . .

1. $x + x = 18$ **2.** $y + y = 12$ **3.** $a + a = 13$

4. $b + b = 16$ **5.** $x + x = 20$ **6.** $n + n = 21$

7. $y + y = 26$ **8.** $y + y = 25$ **9.** $p + p = 30$

10. $b + b = 32$ **11.** $x + x = 48$ **12.** $4 + b = b + 4$

13. $5 + x = x + 5$ **14.** $5 + y = y$ **15.** $23 + s = s$

⋆ **16.** Which equations have the same solution?

     $c + c = 18$ $c + 2 = 18$ $2 \times c = 18$ $3 \times c = 18$

⋆ Solve. Use these replacements: 0, 1, 2, . . ., 20

17. $a + a + a = 15$ **18.** $c + c + c + c = 20$

Round to the nearest ten.

1. 74   **2.** 127   **3.** 6,192

Round to the nearest ten; hundred; thousand; ten thousand.

4. 26,351   **5.** 73,529   **6.** 80,969

7. 345,670   **8.** 78,528   **9.** 975,316

Keeping Fit

Round to the nearest ten thousand; hundred thousand; million.

10. 2,581,470   **11.** 14,715,050   **12.** 25,051,565

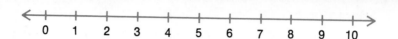

2 is to the left of 5, so 2 < 5.
6 is to the right of 5, so 6 > 5.

True Sentences	False Sentences
100,000 is greater than 999	3 is greater than 4
100,000 > 999	3 > 4
174 is less than 9,285	35 is less than 3
174 < 9,285	35 < 3

1. Make true sentences. Use >, =, or <.

   Example $7 \equiv 4$ $7 > 4$

   a. $8 \equiv 15$ **b.** $10 \equiv 17$ **c.** $12 \equiv 4$

   d. $4 + 3 \equiv 7$ **e.** $8 + 7 \equiv 14$ **f.** $12 - 3 \equiv 8$

2. True or false?

   a. $49 > 48$ **b.** $34 < 33$ **c.** $18 > 22$

   d. $49 > 48 + 2$ **e.** $34 < 33 + 1$ **f.** $17 > 18 - 3$

3. Consider $x + 6 < 10$. Use replacements: 1, 2, 3, . . . 6

   a. Which sentences are true?

$1 + 6 < 10$	$3 + 6 < 10$	$5 + 6 < 10$
$2 + 6 < 10$	$4 + 6 < 10$	$6 + 6 < 10$

   b. The solution set is $\{1, 2, 3\}$. We graph it this way.

   The replacement 0 would make the sentence $x + 6 < 10$ true. Why isn't 0 in the solution set?

4. Consider $x + 3 > 8$. Replacements: 1, 2, 3, 4, . . . 8

    a. Which sentences are true?

        $1 + 3 > 8$ $3 + 3 > 8$ $5 + 3 > 8$ $7 + 3 > 8$

        $2 + 3 > 8$ $4 + 3 > 8$ $6 + 3 > 8$ $8 + 3 > 8$

    b. What is the solution set?

    c. Graph it.

5. Graph solution sets. Replacements: 1, 2, 3, . . . 8

    a. $y + 5 > 7$ **b.** $p - 3 > 2$ **c.** $m + 4 > 7$

EXERCISES

Make true sentences. Use $>$, $=$, or $<$.

1. $17 \equiv 21$ **2.** $13 \equiv 10$ **3.** $27 \equiv 14$

4. $17 \equiv 16 + 1$ **5.** $35 + 5 \equiv 37$ **6.** $48 - 1 \equiv 47$

7. $35 \equiv 45 - 43$ **8.** $17 \equiv 45 - 25$ **9.** $29 \equiv 14 + 15$

True or false?

10. $7 < 6$ **11.** $14 > 5$ **12.** $9 > 17$

13. $7 - 2 < 1$ **14.** $6 - 5 > 0$ **15.** $8 - 3 > 4$

16. $3 + 25 < 98$ **17.** $20 + 33 < 51$ **18.** $25 + 50 > 100$

Find solution sets. Replacements: 1, 2, 3, . . . 9, 10

19. $x + 4 < 9$ **20.** $y + 7 > 13$ **21.** $b - 3 > 5$

22. $z - 5 > 2$ **23.** $n + 17 < 20$ **24.** $x + 4 < 13$

Graph solution sets. Replacements: 3, 6, 9, 12

25. $y + 4 < 12$ **26.** $x - 3 < 9$ **27.** $a + 4 > 20$

28. $10 + p > 20$ **29.** $r - 9 = 0$ **30.** $15 + s > 20$

CHAPTER REVIEW

True or false? If true, identify the property. [26, 28]

1. $10,350 + 3,967 = 3,967 + 10,350$

2. $7,824 + 0 = 0$

3. $(60 + 30) + 7 = 60 + (30 + 7)$

4. $0 + 777 = 777$

Add. [30, 39]

5. $\begin{array}{r} 39 \\ +27 \\ \hline \end{array}$

6. $\begin{array}{r} 82 \\ +73 \\ \hline \end{array}$

7. $\begin{array}{r} 89 \\ +65 \\ \hline \end{array}$

8. $\begin{array}{r} 739 \\ +227 \\ \hline \end{array}$

9. $\begin{array}{r} 395 \\ +217 \\ \hline \end{array}$

10. $\begin{array}{r} 12,394 \\ +71,862 \\ \hline \end{array}$

11. $\begin{array}{r} 21 \\ 38 \\ 47 \\ +65 \\ \hline \end{array}$

12. $\begin{array}{r} 123 \\ 435 \\ 268 \\ +709 \\ \hline \end{array}$

13. $\begin{array}{r} \$32.41 \\ +43.92 \\ \hline \end{array}$

14. $\begin{array}{r} \$70.07 \\ +51.96 \\ \hline \end{array}$

Subtract.

15. [35] $\begin{array}{r} 426 \\ -219 \\ \hline \end{array}$

16. [35] $\begin{array}{r} 5,839 \\ -4,261 \\ \hline \end{array}$

17. [35] $\begin{array}{r} 84,891 \\ -25,263 \\ \hline \end{array}$

18. [39] $\begin{array}{r} \$1,723.94 \\ -\ \ 914.78 \\ \hline \end{array}$

19. [37] $\begin{array}{r} 703 \\ -276 \\ \hline \end{array}$

20. [37] $\begin{array}{r} 4,007 \\ -1,629 \\ \hline \end{array}$

21. [39] $\begin{array}{r} \$507.02 \\ -249.86 \\ \hline \end{array}$

22. [39] $\begin{array}{r} \$3,001.45 \\ -\ \ 984.26 \\ \hline \end{array}$

Which sentence is open? true? false? [40]

23. $34 + 47 = 71$

24. $x + 47 = 48$

25. $72 - 29 = 43$

Find and graph the solutions.

Replacements: 1, 2, 3, 4, . . . 19, 20

26. $17 - 9 = x$
[42]

27. $y + 25 = 42$
[42]

28. $n + n = 18$
[44]

29. $x + 5 < 11$
[46]

30. $m + 6 > 20$
[46]

31. $x + 4 = x$
[44]

Solve this problem. [38]

32. Celia earned $9,200 as an X-ray technician last year. After paying for special clothing, $8,795 was left. How much did the clothing cost?

CHAPTER TEST

Add or subtract.

1. 234 + 405	**2.** 459 + 239	**3.** 1,237 + 4,956	**4.** 41,298 + 29,067
5. 5,642 − 2,937	**6.** 28,462 − 929	**7.** 74,008 − 34,209	**8.** 70,206 − 587
9. 14 − 8	**10.** 49 − 26	**11.** 83 − 46	**12.** 506 − 129
13. $2.43 + 6.99	**14.** $342.80 + 635.85	**15.** $16.95 − 9.94	**16.** $406.75 − 405.76

Without adding, find the missing numbers.

17. $97 + n = 97$

18. $(30 + 7) + 6 = 30 + (x + 6)$

19. $29 + 35 = y + 29$

20. $0 + m = 58$

Find and graph the solutions.

Replacements: 1, 2, 3, . . . 9, 10

21. $m + 9 = 12$

22. $x + 7 < 11$

23. $z + z = 12$

Which sentence is open? true? false?

24. $28 + 46 = 46$

25. $54 - 39 = 15$

26. $m + 8 = 11$

Solve this problem.

27. Ben earned $9,150 as an X-ray technician last year. After paying for a special course at the junior college, his earnings were $8,945. How much did he pay for the course?

3 MULTIPLICATION

MEANING OF MULTIPLICATION

We can think of multiplication in three ways.

$$3 \times 4 = 12$$

factors   product

Repeated Addition
$$4 + 4 + 4 = 12$$

Sets

Array

. . . . .
. . . . .
. . . . .

---

1. Solve this repeated addition problem.
   Lynn has three $5-bills. How much money is this?

   $$\$5 + \$5 + \$5 = x \qquad \text{so} \qquad 3 \times \$5 = x$$

2. Solve this problem thinking of sets.
   Martin has 2 bags of jumping beans. Each bag has 3 beans.
   How many beans does he have?

   so $2 \times 3 = n$

3. Solve this problem using an array.
   There are 3 rows of desks, and 4 desks in each row. How many desks are there in all?

   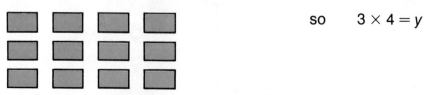
   so $3 \times 4 = y$

50

What multiplication is shown?

1. $2 + 2 + 2$

2.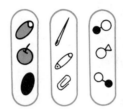

3.

4.

5.

6. $8 + 8 + 8 + 8 + 8$

Show each as a repeated addition, an array, and as sets.

7. $2 \times 4 = 8$

8. $4 \times 2 = 8$

9. $3 \times 1 = 3$

Write equations. Solve.

10.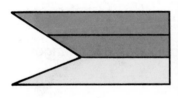

11.

12.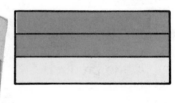

Race Time

See how fast you can multiply. No errors please!

1. 9×8	**2.** 5×8	**3.** 4×8	**4.** 3×1
5. 8×3	**6.** 7×0	**7.** 5×4	**8.** 2×5
9. 7×2	**10.** 6×8	**11.** 4×2	**12.** 7×6
13. 6×2	**14.** 8×8	**15.** 3×3	**16.** 2×8
17. 5×2	**18.** 5×3	**19.** 2×7	**20.** 4×6
21. 7×7	**22.** 6×3	**23.** 8×9	**24.** 0×2
25. 8×0	**26.** 3×5	**27.** 7×8	**28.** 5×5
29. 6×9	**30.** 9×0	**31.** 6×4	**32.** 3×6

Ralph sees 3 rows of 4 chairs.

$$3 \times 4 = 12$$

Mary sees 4 rows of 3 chairs.

$$4 \times 3 = 12$$

true sentence: $3 \times 4 = 4 \times 3$

Each of 2 boxes has 4 pencils. Each pencil costs 5¢.

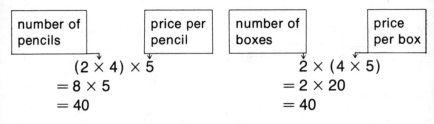

number of pencils	price per pencil	number of boxes	price per box

$$(2 \times 4) \times 5$$
$$= 8 \times 5$$
$$= 40$$

$$2 \times (4 \times 5)$$
$$= 2 \times 20$$
$$= 40$$

true sentence: $(2 \times 4) \times 5 = 2 \times (4 \times 5)$

1. Solve without multiplying.

    a. $26 \times 83 = n \times 26$ **b.** $47 \times 5 = 5 \times n$

Commutative Property of Multiplication

For each pair of whole numbers, the order does not change the product.

$$a \times b = b \times a$$

2. Which multiplications are easier?

    a. $(9 \times 2) \times 5$ or $9 \times (2 \times 5)$

    b. $(5 \times 2) \times 7$ or $5 \times (2 \times 7)$

Associative Property of Multiplication

For all whole numbers, the grouping does not change the product.

$$(a \times b) \times c = a \times (b \times c)$$

3. Multiply.

    a. 7×0 **b.** 17×1 **c.** 39×1 **d.** 485×0

Properties of Zero and One

For each counting number n, $n \times 0 = 0$, and $n \times 1 = n$.

4. Solve.

    a. $9 \times n = 9$ **b.** $8 \times n = 0$ **c.** $n \times 1 = 48$

Solve without multiplying.

  1. $31 \times 13 = n \times 31$ **2.** $40 \times 3 = 3 \times n$

  3. $29 \times 35 = x \times 29$ **4.** $59 \times n = 12 \times 59$

  5. $495 \times 17 = 17 \times y$ **6.** $4{,}128 \times 67 = 67 \times p$

  7. $(25 \times 17) \times y = 25 \times (9 \times 17)$

  8. $(8 \times 46) \times 10 = 8 \times (10 \times x)$

Which multiplications are easier?

  9. $(8 \times 2) \times 5$ or $8 \times (2 \times 5)$

10. $(2 \times 5) \times 9$ or $2 \times (5 \times 9)$

11. $(5 \times 2) \times 12$ or $5 \times (2 \times 12)$

12. $(13 \times 5) \times 2$ or $13 \times (5 \times 2)$

13. $(6 \times 4) \times 25$ or $6 \times (4 \times 25)$

14. $(4 \times 25) \times 11$ or $4 \times (25 \times 11)$

Solve.

15. $18 \times n = 18$ **16.** $n \times 95 = 0$ **17.** $n \times 107 = 107$

BUILDING CUSTODIANS

Ms. Bjornson is a building custodian for a 32-unit apartment complex. The water meter for Apartment 1 read 2,947 liters on August 31 and 3,037 liters on September 30.

1. How many liters were used in September?

2. Ms. Bjornson knows the charge for water is 2¢ per liter. How much will the tenant in Apartment 1 pay for the use of water in September?

3. Ms. Bjornson keeps track of the apartments according to the number of bedrooms. The table below shows the different kinds of apartments. The owner asked her to order paint for all the bedrooms to be repainted in 1978. How many rooms were repainted?

Number of bedrooms	Number of apartments
4	7
3	8
2	9
1	8

4. Mr. Aminov is the building custodian at a shopping center. The Tea House asked him to build a concrete patio. Concrete costs $30 per cubic meter. How much will it cost for 4 cubic meters?

THE DISTRIBUTIVE PROPERTY

We can group a 2-by-9 array in two ways.

Think of 2 rows with 6 + 3 in each row.

Or, think of a 2 by 6 array and a 2 by 3 array.

6 + 3

6 + 3

2× (6 + 3)

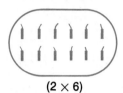 +

(2 × 6)   +   (2 × 3)

The Distributive Property

For all whole numbers *a*, *b*, and *c*,

$$a \times (b + c) = (a \times b) + (a \times c)$$

1. Complete.

   a. $2 \times (8 + n) = (2 \times 8) + (2 \times 5)$

   b. $2 \times (x + 6) = (2 \times 7) + (2 \times y)$

2. Here is one way to find a product.

$$2 \times 43 = 2 \times (40 + 3)$$
$$= (2 \times 40) + (2 \times 3)$$
$$= 86$$

Find the products.

   a. $2 \times (30 + 4)$ **b.** $3 \times (30 + 2)$ **c.** $4 \times (10 + 2)$

EXERCISES

Find the products. Use the distributive property.

1. $3 \times (10 + 2)$ **2.** $3 \times (20 + 2)$ **3.** $4 \times (20 + 2)$

4. $5 \times (10 + 1)$ **5.** $2 \times (40 + 2)$ **6.** $4 \times (20 + 1)$

7. $7 \times (20 + 1)$ **8.** $3 \times (30 + 3)$ **9.** $8 \times (40 + 1)$

A speed in kilometers per hour times 4 hours is 240 kilometers.

Suppose: y means speed in kilometers per hour.
Then: $4 \cdot y$ means the product of 4 hours and the speed.
Number Sentence: $4 \cdot y = 240$.

1. *Suppose:* z means the price of a can of soup.

   a. What could $5 \cdot z$ mean?

   b. Write a number sentence for this: The cost of 5 cans of soup is 95¢.

2. *Suppose:* c means a number of cupcakes.

   a. What could $c + 5$ mean?

   b. Write a number sentence for this: The sum of a number of cupcakes and 5 cupcakes is 17.

3. Write a number sentence for this: I have some cards and give away 3 of them. The difference is 18. Use n for some cards.

EXERCISES

Write number sentences.

1. The number of touchdowns times 6 points per touchdown is 30 points.

2. The number of liters of gas used times 12 kilometers per liter is 72 kilometers.

3. The number of sandwiches Dot ate plus the 2 Ed ate is 5.

4. The money Lisa had minus the 6¢ she spent is 28¢.

5. The number of candy bars times 10¢ per candy bar is 90¢.

56

6. 9 baskets times the number of points per basket is 18 points.

7. The number of hours driving times 30 miles per hour is 120 miles.

8. The number of cupcakes Tracy ate plus the 10 the rest of the family ate is 12.

9. The 25¢ Ralph had minus what he spent is 10¢.

10. The number of packages of gum times 6¢ a package is 30¢.

11. Six tropical fish times the price per fish is $3.00.

12. The six balls owned by the team times the price per ball is $7.50.

Round to the nearest ten.

1. 22   **2.** 92   **3.** 29

4. 38   **5.** 65   **6.** 45

7. 47   **8.** 74   **9.** 63

10. 736   **11.** 7,654   **12.** 23,986

Add.

13. 40 + 7   **14.** 50 + 18   **15.** 240 + 30 + 8

16. 600 + 80 + 14   **17.** 1,500 + 60 + 21   **18.** 2,400 + 280 + 12

Subtract.

19. 79
     − 26

20. 62
     − 35

21. 345
     − 226

22. 507
     − 279

23. 6,039
     − 2,394

24. 5,042
     − 1,869

REGROUPING

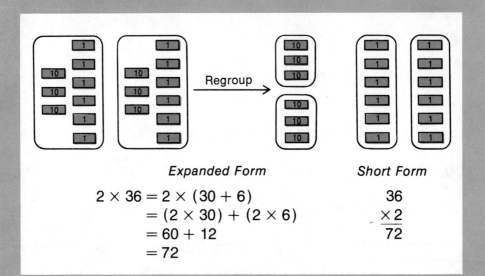

Expanded Form	Short Form
$2 \times 36 = 2 \times (30 + 6)$	36
$\qquad = (2 \times 30) + (2 \times 6)$	$\times 2$
$\qquad = 60 + 12$	72
$\qquad = 72$	

1. Complete.

Expanded Form *Short Form*

$3 \times 243 = 3 \times (200 + 40 + 3)$ 243

$\qquad = (\underline{\quad} \times 200) + (3 \times \underline{\quad}) + (3 \times 3)$ $\times 3$

$\qquad = 600 + 120 + \underline{\quad}$ 729

$\qquad = \underline{\quad}$

2. Multiply. Use the short form.

    a. 643   **b.** 417   **c.** 153   **d.** 3,258

       $\times 2$ $\times 3$ $\times 4$ $\times 3$

3. To estimate 4×29, round 29 to the nearest ten.

Think: $4 \times 30 = 120$

The product 4×29 should be about 120. Multiply: 4×29.
Is it about 120?

4. Round and estimate.

    a. 3×59 **b.** 5×61 **c.** 7×38

Multiply.

1. 32
   × 5

2. 91
   × 7

3. 46
   × 8

4. 83
   × 5

5. 213
   × 4

6. 316
   × 8

7. 420
   × 9

8. 856
   × 3

9. 1,061
   × 5

10. 2,846
    × 6

11. 12,301
    × 7

12. 16,322
    × 2

13. 82,234
    × 7

14. 90,004
    × 3

15. 92,734
    × 8

16. 510,121
    × 9

17. 6 × 341,082

18. 4 × 27,009

19. 8 × 271,143

Round and estimate.

20. 2 × 39

21. 4 × 32

22. 6 × 58

23. 8 × 41

24. 7 × 62

25. 9 × 35

26. 5 × 72

27. 3 × 88

28. 2 × 93

Solve these problems.

29. The Sandy Hill Marching Ant Corps marches with 6 ants in a row. There are 287 rows. How many ants are in the marching corps?

30. Marg bought 3 cans of peaches. Each cost 29¢. Estimate the total cost. What was the actual cost?

31. Zelda bought 4 pens at 39¢ each. Estimate the cost. What was the actual cost?

MULTIPLES OF 10, 100, AND 1,000

Study these multiplications. Look for a pattern.

432	432	432	432
×2	×20	×200	×2,000
864	8,640	86,400	864,000

1. Complete.

$$\begin{array}{r} 327 \\ \times 3 \\ \hline 981 \end{array} \qquad \begin{array}{r} 327 \\ \times 30 \\ \hline \end{array} \qquad \begin{array}{r} 327 \\ \times 300 \\ \hline \end{array}$$

2. Given: $4 \times 234 = 936$. Record these products as quickly as you can on your paper.

   a. 40×234 **b.** 400×234 **c.** $4,000 \times 234$

3. Given: $6 \times 4,213 = 25,278$. Record these products as quickly as you can on your paper.

   a. $60 \times 4,213$ **b.** $600 \times 4,213$ **c.** $6,000 \times 4,213$

4.

To Find	*Think*	*Write*
47	47	47
×20	×2	×20
	94	940

Multiply.

  a.   51   **b.**   513   **c.** 1,234   **d.**   2,401

      ×30   ×700   ×200   ×3,000

You can use these products to help solve Exercises 1–9.

$$2 \times 43 = 86$$
$$4 \times 32 = 128$$
$$3 \times 24 = 72$$

Record these products as quickly as you can on your paper.

1. 20×43 **2.** 30×24 **3.** 200×43

4. 300×24 **5.** 40×32 **6.** $2,000 \times 43$

7. 400×32 **8.** $3,000 \times 24$ **9.** $4,000 \times 32$

Multiply.

10. $\begin{array}{r} 35 \\ \times\,30 \\ \hline \end{array}$
11. $\begin{array}{r} 21 \\ \times\,40 \\ \hline \end{array}$
12. $\begin{array}{r} 54 \\ \times\,70 \\ \hline \end{array}$
13. $\begin{array}{r} 62 \\ \times\,30 \\ \hline \end{array}$

14. $\begin{array}{r} 213 \\ \times\,50 \\ \hline \end{array}$
15. $\begin{array}{r} 3,124 \\ \times\,20 \\ \hline \end{array}$
16. $\begin{array}{r} 213 \\ \times\,300 \\ \hline \end{array}$
17. $\begin{array}{r} 694 \\ \times\,800 \\ \hline \end{array}$

18. $\begin{array}{r} 487 \\ \times\,300 \\ \hline \end{array}$
19. $\begin{array}{r} 925 \\ \times\,600 \\ \hline \end{array}$
20. $\begin{array}{r} 842 \\ \times\,400 \\ \hline \end{array}$
21. $\begin{array}{r} 1,273 \\ \times\,500 \\ \hline \end{array}$

22. $\begin{array}{r} 63 \\ \times\,600 \\ \hline \end{array}$
23. $\begin{array}{r} 47 \\ \times\,800 \\ \hline \end{array}$
24. $\begin{array}{r} 1,213 \\ \times\,6,000 \\ \hline \end{array}$
25. $\begin{array}{r} 5,234 \\ \times\,2,000 \\ \hline \end{array}$

26. $\begin{array}{r} 53,478 \\ \times\,90 \\ \hline \end{array}$
27. $\begin{array}{r} 23 \\ \times\,6,000 \\ \hline \end{array}$
28. $\begin{array}{r} 452 \\ \times\,7,000 \\ \hline \end{array}$
29. $\begin{array}{r} 927 \\ \times\,9,000 \\ \hline \end{array}$

30. $\begin{array}{r} 200 \\ \times\,20 \\ \hline \end{array}$
31. $\begin{array}{r} 800 \\ \times\,30 \\ \hline \end{array}$
32. $\begin{array}{r} 300 \\ \times\,200 \\ \hline \end{array}$
33. $\begin{array}{r} 600 \\ \times\,400 \\ \hline \end{array}$

Solve these mini-problems.

34. 20 rows of chairs.
17 chairs in each row.
Total number of chairs?

35. Camping equipment store.
Canteens 98¢ each.
Cost of 50?

Mrs. Dill packages pickles. She has 23 packages of 24 pickles each. How many pickles does she have?

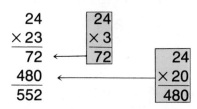

$$\begin{array}{r} 24 \\ \times\, 23 \\ \hline 72 \\ 480 \\ \hline 552 \end{array}$$

$$\begin{array}{r} 24 \\ \times\, 3 \\ \hline 72 \end{array}$$

$$\begin{array}{r} 24 \\ \times\, 20 \\ \hline 480 \end{array}$$

1. Consider the multiplication 16×43.

$$\begin{array}{r} 43 \\ \times\, 16 \\ \hline \end{array} \qquad \begin{array}{r} 43 \\ \times\, 16 \\ \hline 258 \end{array} \qquad \begin{array}{r} 43 \\ \times\, 16 \\ \hline 258 \\ 430 \end{array} \qquad \begin{array}{r} 43 \\ \times\, 16 \\ \hline 258 \\ 430 \\ \hline 688 \end{array}$$

Multiply.

a. $\begin{array}{r} 42 \\ \times\, 36 \\ \hline \end{array}$
  b. $\begin{array}{r} 27 \\ \times\, 19 \\ \hline \end{array}$
  c. $\begin{array}{r} 184 \\ \times\, 132 \\ \hline \end{array}$
  d. $\begin{array}{r} 204 \\ \times\, 623 \\ \hline \end{array}$

2. Laura saved time by not writing zeros. Compare Arthur's and Laura's work.

	Arthur's	Laura's

$$\text{Arthur's} \qquad \begin{array}{r} 472 \\ \times\, 203 \\ \hline 1\,416 \\ 0\,000 \\ 94\,400 \end{array} \qquad\qquad \text{Laura's} \qquad \begin{array}{r} 472 \\ \times\, 203 \\ \hline 1\,416 \\ 94\,400 \end{array}$$

a. Complete this work.

b. How do their products compare?

3. Multiply using Laura's method.

a. $\begin{array}{r} 379 \\ \times\, 504 \\ \hline \end{array}$
  b. $\begin{array}{r} 583 \\ \times\, 206 \\ \hline \end{array}$
  c. $\begin{array}{r} 457 \\ \times\, 602 \\ \hline \end{array}$

4. We don't need to write all the zeros. Complete this multiplication.

$$
\begin{array}{r}
246 \\
\times\,842 \\
\hline
492 \\
984 \\
1968 \\
\hline
\end{array}
$$

DAH...NO ZEROS

Multiply.

1. $\begin{array}{r} 21 \\ \times\,14 \\ \hline \end{array}$ **2.** $\begin{array}{r} 43 \\ \times\,26 \\ \hline \end{array}$ **3.** $\begin{array}{r} 27 \\ \times\,24 \\ \hline \end{array}$ **4.** $\begin{array}{r} 23 \\ \times\,93 \\ \hline \end{array}$ **5.** $\begin{array}{r} 14 \\ \times\,71 \\ \hline \end{array}$

6. $\begin{array}{r} 43 \\ \times\,43 \\ \hline \end{array}$ **7.** $\begin{array}{r} 52 \\ \times\,73 \\ \hline \end{array}$ **8.** $\begin{array}{r} 89 \\ \times\,47 \\ \hline \end{array}$ **9.** $\begin{array}{r} 27 \\ \times\,36 \\ \hline \end{array}$ **10.** $\begin{array}{r} 76 \\ \times\,82 \\ \hline \end{array}$

11. $\begin{array}{r} 237 \\ \times\,519 \\ \hline \end{array}$ **12.** $\begin{array}{r} 834 \\ \times\,156 \\ \hline \end{array}$ **13.** $\begin{array}{r} 927 \\ \times\,563 \\ \hline \end{array}$ **14.** $\begin{array}{r} 362 \\ \times\,807 \\ \hline \end{array}$ **15.** $\begin{array}{r} 427 \\ \times\,206 \\ \hline \end{array}$

16. $\begin{array}{r} 608 \\ \times\,487 \\ \hline \end{array}$ **17.** $\begin{array}{r} 754 \\ \times\,305 \\ \hline \end{array}$ **18.** $\begin{array}{r} 927 \\ \times\,101 \\ \hline \end{array}$ **19.** $\begin{array}{r} 407 \\ \times\,232 \\ \hline \end{array}$ **20.** $\begin{array}{r} 428 \\ \times\,283 \\ \hline \end{array}$

21. $\begin{array}{r} \$.32 \\ \times\,23 \\ \hline \end{array}$ **22.** $\begin{array}{r} \$5.53 \\ \times\,27 \\ \hline \end{array}$ **23.** $\begin{array}{r} \$8.29 \\ \times\,31 \\ \hline \end{array}$ **24.** $\begin{array}{r} \$9.34 \\ \times\,724 \\ \hline \end{array}$ **25.** $\begin{array}{r} \$2.56 \\ \times\,28 \\ \hline \end{array}$

Solve these problems.

26. Mario bought 25 packages of donuts for a party. Each package had 12 donuts. How many donuts did he have in all?

27. The Jones' took a family trip. They drove for 14 days and averaged 257 kilometers per day. How far did they drive?

28. Janet picked 17 daisies for each of her classmates as a Valentine's Day present. She has 38 classmates. How many daisies did she pick in all?

FLOW CHARTS

A flow chart is a way of describing an activity. Each shape represents a simple step. This flow chart shows one way to leave a house.

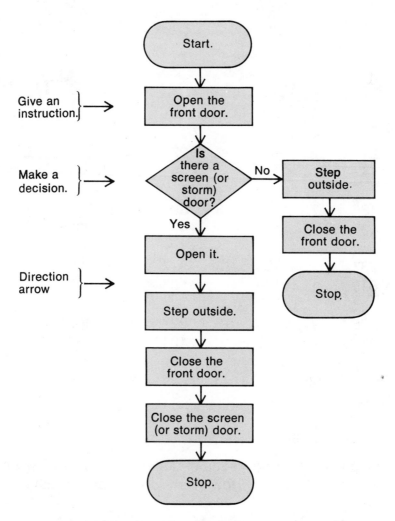

1. Use the flow chart above to answer these questions.

   a. Suppose there is a screen (or storm) door. What is the next step?

   b. Why are there two "stops"?

★ **2.** Make a flow chart for entering a house.

No matter how large the numbers, we use the same pattern.

$$
\begin{array}{r}
8,713 \\
\times\,425 \\
\hline
43565 \\
17426 \\
34852 \\
\hline
3703025
\end{array}
$$

or 3,703,025

1. Eliminating the zeros can save a great deal of time!

   Compare.

Long Way	Short Way

   $$
   \begin{array}{r}
   8,234 \\
   \times\,4,008 \\
   \hline
   65\,872 \\
   00\,000 \\
   00\,000 \\
   32936\,000 \\
   \hline
   \end{array}
   $$

   $$
   \begin{array}{r}
   8,234 \\
   \times\,4,008 \\
   \hline
   65\,872 \\
   32936 \\
   \hline
   \end{array}
   $$

   a. Complete each.

   b. How do their products compare?

2. Multiply.

   a. $\begin{array}{r} 4,862 \\ \times\,1,006 \\ \hline \end{array}$ **b.** $\begin{array}{r} 5,289 \\ \times\,2,013 \\ \hline \end{array}$ **c.** $\begin{array}{r} 6,024 \\ \times\,4,009 \\ \hline \end{array}$

EXERCISES

Multiply.

1. $\begin{array}{r} 6,124 \\ \times\,341 \\ \hline \end{array}$ **2.** $\begin{array}{r} 9,741 \\ \times\,568 \\ \hline \end{array}$ **3.** $\begin{array}{r} 1,364 \\ \times\,222 \\ \hline \end{array}$

4. 6,666	**5.** 2,465	**6.** 93,782
× 374	× 333	× 777

7. 5,814	**8.** 3,784	**9.** 9,876
× 3,692	× 406	× 505

10. 1,623	**11.** 2,953	**12.** 30,462
× 4,218	× 7,134	× 6,803

13. 97,832	**14.** 86,031	**15.** 46,236
× 4,016	× 6,004	× 4,009

16. 14,792	**17.** 58,146	**18.** 93,716
× 2,111	× 7,303	× 4,040

Solve these problems.

19. On one space flight, the spaceship traveled at an average speed of 3,509 miles per hour for 7,821 hours. How far had the spaceship gone in this time?

20. Your heart beats about 4,324 times an hour. How many times does it beat in a week? (Hint: A week is 168 hours.)

Brainteaser

Somewhere in the square below there are three boxes which touch at a point, and whose numbers have the product 100. Find them.

2	3	5	7	4	1
4	6	8	3	9	6
10	4	1	6	2	5
3	8	5	7	10	3
1	3	12	4	9	2
10	9	7	8	6	0

POWERS AND SQUARE ROOTS

Exponents help us write products more easily.

$$2 \times 2 \times 2 = 2^3$$
$$\text{so } 2^3 = 8$$

Study this chart.

Exponential Form	Read	Factored Form	Product
2^2	2 to the second power	2×2	4
5^2	5 to the second power	5×5	25
5^3	5 to the third power	$5 \times 5 \times 5$	125

1. Write the factored form. Find the products.

   a. 6^2 **b.** 7^2 **c.** 8^2 **d.** 4^3

2. The square root of 9 is 3 because $3^2 = 9$.

   $$\sqrt{9} = 3$$
   └ read: the square root of 9

   Find these square roots.

   a. $\sqrt{16}$ **b.** $\sqrt{49}$ **c.** $\sqrt{25}$ **d.** $\sqrt{4}$

EXERCISES

Find products.

1. 3^2	**2.** 4^2	**3.** 6^2	**4.** 7^2	**5.** 8^2
6. 11^2	**7.** 13^2	**8.** 4^3	**9.** 6^3	**10.** 7^3
11. 8^3	**12.** 10^3	**13.** 3^3	**14.** 9^2	**15.** 9^3

Find these square roots.

16. $\sqrt{16}$	**17.** $\sqrt{36}$	**18.** $\sqrt{64}$	**19.** $\sqrt{100}$	**20.** $\sqrt{81}$
21. $\sqrt{1}$	**22.** $\sqrt{121}$	**23.** $\sqrt{144}$	**24.** $\sqrt{9}$	**25.** $\sqrt{169}$

CANS AND THE U.S.A.

1. It has been estimated that each person in the U.S. used 150 cans in 1970. There were about 200,000,000 people in the U.S. that year. How many cans were used in all?

2. Suppose cans are used at the same rate in 1980. It has been estimated that there will be 230,000,000 Americans in that year. How many more cans will be used in 1980 than in 1970?

3. Suppose that in 1980 each person in the U.S. uses about 180 cans. Use the population estimate of 230,000,000 to find the number of cans Americans will use in 1980.

4. In one month, 6,547,217 metric tons of garbage were collected in Greenville City. Only 5,988,305 metric tons of this would burn. How many metric tons of garbage (mostly bottles and cans) were left unburned?

5. The city of Greenville held a big drive to recycle aluminum cans. In one month they collected 2,000 kilograms of cans. They got 10¢ for each kilogram. How much money did they make?

6. New City estimated that the total cost of disposing of each can is about 25¢. The city collects about 40,000 cans a month. What is the cost of disposing of the cans each month?

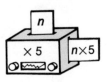

Input: n	1	2	3	4
Output: n × 5	5	10	15	20

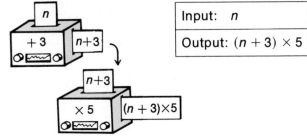

Input: n	1	2	3	4
Output: (n + 3) × 5	20	25	30	35

To compute (1 + 3) × 5, do the work in the parentheses first.

$$(1 + 3) \times 5 = 4 \times 5$$
$$= 20$$

1. Find the missing outputs.

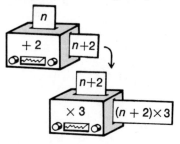

n	0	1	2	9	10
(n + 2) × 3					

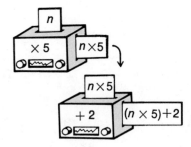

n	1	3	4	7	12
(n × 5) + 2					

69

2. Find the missing inputs.

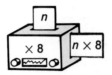

n		2			
n × 8	8	16	24	48	88

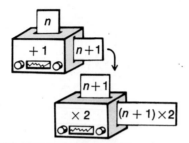

n			3		
(n + 1) × 2	4	6	8	10	20

Find the missing numbers.

1.

n	1	2	3	7	9	21
n × 9						

2.

n	0	1	2	6	9	24
n × 12						

3.

n		1	5	7	12	24
(n + 3) × 4						

4.

n		0	5	8	9	13
(n × 3) + 4						

5.

n					
n × 6	6	12	18	30	54

6.

n					
n × 11	0	11	22	77	99

7.

n		1	6		
n × 7	0			63	77

8.

n			1	2		7
(n + 4) × 2					16	28

9.

n		0			14	29
(n × 8) + 6			38	62		

10.

n			3		11	
(n + 7) × 3	24			39		66

Multiply.

1. 21
×2

2. 32
×4

3. 63
×3

4. 18
×7

5. 35
×6

6. 87
×4

7. 300
×6

8. 600
×5

9. 312
×3

10. 23
×12

11. 31
×24

12. 43
×32

13. 53
×14

14. 38
×56

15. 67
×48

16. 635
×62

17. 723
×45

18. 562
×97

19. 702
×68

20. 506
×46

21. 604
×73

22. 375
×401

23. 739
×205

24. 412
×607

ACTIVITY

Make a menu for a nutritious lunch you think your class would like to have. Decide how much to buy to feed the whole class. The school lunchroom manager might be able to help. Then, go to a supermarket and find out how much each item costs. Find the total cost of serving this lunch to your class.

71

CHAPTER REVIEW

Solve without multiplying.

1. $29 \times 38 = 38 \times n$ **2.** $6 \times (30 + 2) = (6 \times n) + (6 \times 2)$
[53]   [55]

3. $7 \times n = 0$ **4.** $39 \times n = 39$ **5.** $1 \times n = 57$
[52]   [52]   [52]

Multiply. [60]

6. 7×30 **7.** 2×700 **8.** 50×70

Multiply.

9. $\begin{array}{r} 36 \\ \times 4 \\ \hline \end{array}$ [58]   **10.** $\begin{array}{r} \$294 \\ \times 6 \\ \hline \end{array}$ [58]   **11.** $\begin{array}{r} 43 \\ \times 72 \\ \hline \end{array}$ [62]   **12.** $\begin{array}{r} \$207 \\ \times 38 \\ \hline \end{array}$ [62]   **13.** $\begin{array}{r} 954 \\ \times 90 \\ \hline \end{array}$ [60]

14. $\begin{array}{r} 2{,}931 \\ \times 56 \\ \hline \end{array}$ [62]   **15.** $\begin{array}{r} 938 \\ \times 231 \\ \hline \end{array}$ [62]   **16.** $\begin{array}{r} 739 \\ \times 308 \\ \hline \end{array}$ [62]   **17.** $\begin{array}{r} 4{,}506 \\ \times 342 \\ \hline \end{array}$ [65]   **18.** $\begin{array}{r} 81{,}634 \\ \times 286 \\ \hline \end{array}$ [65]

Find products. [67]

19. 7^2 **20.** 4^3 **21.** 5^2 **22.** 14^2 **23.** 12^3

Find square roots. [67]

24. $\sqrt{49}$ **25.** $\sqrt{9}$ **26.** $\sqrt{25}$ **27.** $\sqrt{100}$ **28.** $\sqrt{81}$

Find the missing numbers in these function tables. [69]

29.

n	2	3		7
$n \times 9$	18		45	

30.

n		2	1	0	9
$(n \times 3) + 5$	11				

Solve these problems. [56]

31. Ms. Casey is a building custodian in a hotel. She bought 340 light bulbs for the ballroom. Each cost 50¢. What was the total cost of these light bulbs?

32. There are 6 floors in the hotel. It takes 20 minutes to vacuum the hallway on each floor. How long does it take to do all 6 hallways?

CHAPTER TEST

Solve without multiplying.

1. $37 \times 45 = 45 \times n$ **2.** $3 \times (40 + 1) = (3 \times n) + (3 \times 1)$

3. $23 \times n = 23$ **4.** $8 \times n = 0$ **5.** $1 \times n = 34$

Multiply.

6. 4×20 **7.** 5×700 **8.** 60×80 **9.** 300×12

Multiply.

10. 34
    $\times 7$

11. 4,823
    $\times 6$

12. $2,074
    $\times 8$

13. 92
    $\times 58$

14. 342
    $\times 40$

15. $741
    $\times 23$

16. 608
    $\times 24$

17. 6,724
    $\times 304$

18. 82,372
    $\times 793$

Find products.

19. 6^2 **20.** 12^2 **21.** 2^3

22. Find the square root: $\sqrt{36}$.

Solve this problem.

23. Mr. Benjamin is a custodian for an office building. He wants to clean the tile floors in 23 offices. He has to use 16 grams of cleanser for each bucket of solution. A new bucket is needed for each office. How many grams of the cleaner will he need in all?

4 DIVISION

MULTIPLICATION AND DIVISION

Multiplication and division are **opposite** operations. One operation undoes the other.

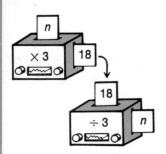

$n \times 3 = 18$

$18 \div 3 = n$

related sentences

Related sentences have the same solution.

1. Find the solution of each pair of related sentences.

    a. $27 \div 3 = y$
    $y \times 3 = 27$

    b. $n \times 6 = 48$
    $48 \div 6 = n$

    c. $m \div 6 = 7$
    $6 \times 7 = m$

2. Write related sentences. Solve.

    a. $m \div 5 = 7$

    b. $y \div 8 = 9$

    c. $n \div 5 = 7$

    d. $n \times 4 = 36$

    e. $y \times 7 = 28$

    f. $x \times 7 = 56$

EXERCISES

Write related division sentences. Solve.

1. $n \times 3 = 21$

2. $x \times 6 = 24$

3. $4 \times y = 28$

4. $6 \times y = 30$

5. $y \times 4 = 36$

6. $p \times 8 = 40$

7. $6 \times t = 42$

8. $z \times 9 = 45$

9. $z \times 7 = 56$

10. $n \times 9 = 81$ **11.** $n \times 1 = 7$ **12.** $x \times 7 = 0$

13. $r \times 8 = 32$ **14.** $6 \times p = 48$ **15.** $4 \times n = 40$

16. $x \times 7 = 63$ **17.** $4 \times s = 0$ **18.** $a \times 8 = 56$

19. $c \times 8 = 72$ **20.** $p \times 4 = 32$ **21.** $3 \times x = 27$

Write related multiplication sentences. Solve.

22. $x \div 8 = 6$ **23.** $y \div 6 = 9$ **24.** $a \div 7 = 8$

25. $p \div 8 = 8$ **26.** $x \div 9 = 8$ **27.** $m \div 5 = 7$

28. $y \div 5 = 8$ **29.** $s \div 6 = 3$ **30.** $y \div 4 = 5$

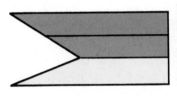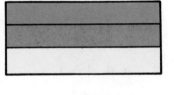

Race Time

See how fast you can divide. No errors please!

1. $36 \div 9$	**2.** $10 \div 2$	**3.** $16 \div 2$	**4.** $45 \div 5$
5. $56 \div 8$	**6.** $48 \div 6$	**7.** $0 \div 6$	**8.** $54 \div 6$
9. $18 \div 1$	**10.** $30 \div 5$	**11.** $42 \div 7$	**12.** $20 \div 4$
13. $21 \div 3$	**14.** $36 \div 4$	**15.** $9 \div 3$	**16.** $15 \div 3$
17. $0 \div 5$	**18.** $63 \div 9$	**19.** $8 \div 8$	**20.** $21 \div 7$
21. $45 \div 9$	**22.** $40 \div 5$	**23.** $63 \div 7$	**24.** $12 \div 2$
25. $0 \div 7$	**26.** $28 \div 4$	**27.** $42 \div 6$	**28.** $18 \div 9$
29. $18 \div 2$	**30.** $0 \div 8$	**31.** $12 \div 4$	**32.** $24 \div 3$
33. $28 \div 7$	**34.** $40 \div 8$	**35.** $16 \div 8$	**36.** $60 \div 6$
37. $56 \div 7$	**38.** $18 \div 3$	**39.** $15 \div 5$	**40.** $14 \div 2$
41. $54 \div 9$	**42.** $24 \div 8$	**43.** $36 \div 6$	**44.** $24 \div 6$
45. $12 \div 3$	**46.** $8 \div 2$	**47.** $18 \div 6$	**48.** $11 \div 1$
49. $27 \div 9$	**50.** $72 \div 8$	**51.** $0 \div 3$	**52.** $0 \div 8$
53. $20 \div 5$	**54.** $25 \div 5$	**55.** $49 \div 7$	**56.** $72 \div 9$
57. $64 \div 8$	**58.** $24 \div 4$	**59.** $27 \div 3$	**60.** $48 \div 8$

75

1 AND 0 IN DIVISION

Study these divisions. Find patterns.

$2 \div 1 = 2$
$3 \div 1 = 3$
$12 \div 1 = 12$

When we divide a number by 1, the quotient is that number.

$0 \div 2 = 0$
$0 \div 3 = 0$
$0 \div 12 = 0$

When we divide 0 by any counting number, the quotient is 0.

$2 \div 2 = 1$
$3 \div 3 = 1$
$12 \div 12 = 1$

When we divide a counting number by itself, the quotient is 1.

1. Divide.

   a. $4 \div 1$ **b.** $15 \div 1$ **c.** $0 \div 6$ **d.** $8 \div 8$

   e. $30 \div 1$ **f.** $0 \div 18$ **g.** $0 \div 40$ **h.** $14 \div 14$

2. Solve.

   a. $9 \div n = 9$ **b.** $8 \div n = 8$ **c.** $8 \div n = 1$

   d. $12 \div n = 1$ **e.** $n \div 9 = 0$ **f.** $n \div 12 = 0$

EXERCISES

Divide.

1. $5 \div 1$ **2.** $6 \div 1$ **3.** $10 \div 1$ **4.** $0 \div 10$

5. $0 \div 8$ **6.** $0 \div 18$ **7.** $9 \div 9$ **8.** $10 \div 10$

9. $15 \div 15$ **10.** $7 \div 1$ **11.** $11 \div 1$ **12.** $0 \div 6$

13. $598 \div 1$ **14.** $0 \div 372$ **15.** $981 \div 981$ **16.** $427 \div 1$

WHAT ABOUT DIVISION BY ZERO?

$$n \times 0 = 2 \qquad\qquad\qquad 2 \div 0 = n$$

related sentences

$$n \times 0 = 2 \text{ has no solution}$$
so
$$2 \div 0 = n \text{ has no solution}$$

Division by 0 is meaningless.

1. Consider $8 \div 0 = n$.

   a. A related multiplication sentence is $n \times 0 = 8$. Try to replace n with a number which makes a true sentence.

   b. Does the sentence $n \times 0 = 8$ have a solution?

   c. Then does the related sentence $8 \div 0 = n$ have a solution?

2. Consider $0 \div 0 = n$.

   a. A related multiplication sentence is $n \times 0 = 0$. Find a replacement for n which makes the sentence true.

   b. Is there any replacement for n which makes the sentence false?

Every number is a solution of $n \times 0 = 0$. Therefore, $0 \div 0$ is also meaningless. We never divide by zero.

EXERCISES

Find quotients, if any.

1. $2 \div 0$	**2.** $3 \div 0$	**3.** $4 \div 0$	**4.** $8 \div 0$
5. $18 \div 0$	**6.** $0 \div 5$	**7.** $15 \div 1$	**8.** $12 \div 0$
9. $16 \div 16$	**10.** $16 \div 0$	**11.** $0 \div 12$	**12.** $29 \div 0$

Here's a pattern.

$6 \div 2 = 3$	because	$3 \times 2 = 6$
$60 \div 2 = 30$	because	$30 \times 2 = 60$
$600 \div 2 = 300$	because	$300 \times 2 = 600$
$6000 \div 2 = 3000$	because	$3000 \times 2 = 6000$

Seeing patterns saves work.

$$\begin{array}{c} 6 \\ 4\overline{)24} \end{array} \quad \text{so} \quad \begin{array}{c} 60 \\ 4\overline{)240} \end{array} \quad \text{and} \quad \begin{array}{c} 600 \\ 4\overline{)2,400} \end{array}$$

1. Divide.

a.	$9\overline{)72}$	$9\overline{)720}$	$9\overline{)7,200}$	$9\overline{)72,000}$
b.	$3\overline{)12}$	$3\overline{)120}$	$3\overline{)1,200}$	$3\overline{)12,000}$
c.	$6\overline{)18}$	$6\overline{)180}$	$6\overline{)1,800}$	$6\overline{)18,000}$
d.	$5\overline{)35}$	$5\overline{)350}$	$5\overline{)3,500}$	$5\overline{)35,000}$

2. Here's an easy way to think of division.

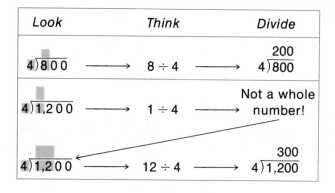

Divide.

a.	$3\overline{)60}$	**b.**	$3\overline{)150}$	**c.**	$5\overline{)3,500}$
d.	$8\overline{)400}$	**e.**	$6\overline{)2,400}$	**f.**	$5\overline{)4,000}$
g.	$7\overline{)\$420}$	**h.**	$5\overline{)\$2,500}$	**i.**	$\$4\overline{)\$1,600}$

Here are some division facts.

$$
6\overline{)48}^{\,8} \qquad 8\overline{)48}^{\,6} \qquad 8\overline{)24}^{\,3} \qquad 6\overline{)24}^{\,4}
$$

Use these facts to get the answers to the following.

1. $8\overline{)240}$ **2.** $8\overline{)4,800}$ **3.** $6\overline{)4,800}$

4. $6\overline{)480}$ **5.** $8\overline{)2,400}$ **6.** $8\overline{)480}$

7. $6\overline{)240}$ **8.** $6\overline{)24,000}$ **9.** $8\overline{)24,000}$

Divide.

10. $3\overline{)240}$ **11.** $2\overline{)180}$ **12.** $4\overline{)8,000}$

13. $5\overline{)150}$ **14.** $5\overline{)100}$ **15.** $5\overline{)3,000}$

16. $4\overline{)36,000}$ **17.** $7\overline{)5,600}$ **18.** $9\overline{)630}$

19. $4\overline{)240}$ **20.** $4\overline{)3,600}$ **21.** $6\overline{)42,000}$

22. $7\overline{)280}$ **23.** $9\overline{)4,500}$ **24.** $9\overline{)720}$

25. $9\overline{)\$2,700}$ **26.** $8\overline{)\$32,000}$ **27.** $7\overline{)\$5,600}$

28. $\$2\overline{)\$80}$ **29.** $\$7\overline{)\$4,900}$ **30.** $\$8\overline{)\$8,000}$

★ **31.** $72 \div 24 = 3.$ Solve: $7,200 \div 24 = n$

Solve these problems.

32. Mrs. Lee spent $60 on 3 Christmas presents. Each present cost the same. How much did each cost?

33. Yule City Mall has $600 to spend for decorative lights. Each one costs $3. How many can be bought?

79

Olga has 27 cents to share equally among 4 friends. What is the most she can give to each?

```
    6  ←—— 6¢ to each friend
4)27
   24
    3  ←—— 3¢ left over
```

Check:
```
      6
    × 4
   24 + 3 = 27
```

1. Divide.

Example
```
   7 r 1
3)22
```

a. $5)\overline{38}$ b. $4)\overline{26}$ c. $6)\overline{57}$ d. $8)\overline{63}$

2. Divide.

a. $7)\overline{37}$ b. $4)\overline{19}$ c. $5)\overline{29}$ d. $9)\overline{74}$

EXERCISES

Divide.

1. $3)\overline{22}$ 2. $5)\overline{43}$ 3. $6)\overline{20}$ 4. $3)\overline{13}$

5. $9)\overline{35}$ 6. $7)\overline{30}$ 7. $7)\overline{57}$ 8. $8)\overline{26}$

9. $7)\overline{44}$ 10. $8)\overline{36}$ 11. $7)\overline{22}$ 12. $6)\overline{25}$

13. $9)\overline{\$75}$ 14. $9)\overline{\$84}$ 15. $7)\overline{\$43}$ 16. $8)\overline{\$68}$

Solve.

17. $3 per record. How many records can $17 buy? How many dollars left?

18. 17 sandwiches. 7 people. How many whole sandwiches for each?

WASTE WATER TREATERS

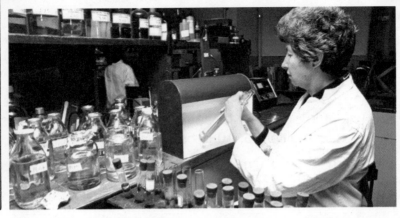

1. Yesterday, 12,736 liters of wastewater were treated. This was 3,211 more than today. How many liters were treated today?

2. Mr. Jacob added 25,472 kilograms of chemical to the wastewater this week. This is 6,422 kilograms more than he added last week. How much did he add last week?

3. He wanted to guess how much chemical to buy for the next three weeks. He used these amounts in the same period last year: 32,652 kg, 28,564 kg, and 22,396 kg. What is a good guess for the next three weeks?

4. Mr. Jacob knows it costs $2 to test a sample in the lab. Last year, 13,809 samples were tested. How much did the tests cost in all?

5. Ms. Magdala is in charge of wastewater treatment in a factory. She knows that 5,960 liters were treated last weekend. 10,907 liters were treated on each day this Saturday and Sunday. How much more was treated this weekend than last?

6. The business office told her it costs $2 a kilogram to remove sludge. Last year, it cost $32,652 to take out the sludge. How many kilograms were taken out?

In the division $161 \div 7$, we first estimate.

Think:

$$
\begin{array}{r}
1 \\
7\overline{)161} \\
7
\end{array}
\qquad
\begin{array}{r}
10 \\
7\overline{)161} \\
70
\end{array}
\qquad
\begin{array}{r}
100 \\
7\overline{)161} \\
700
\end{array}
$$

The quotient is between 10 and 100. Now we find which multiple of 10 is best.

$$
\begin{array}{r}
10 \\
7\overline{)161} \\
70
\end{array}
\qquad
\begin{array}{r}
20 \\
7\overline{)161} \\
140
\end{array}
\qquad
\begin{array}{r}
30 \\
7\overline{)161} \\
210
\end{array}
$$

$\nearrow$ too small   too large $\nwarrow$

The best estimate is 20.

Now we finish the division.

$$
\begin{array}{r}
23 \\
3 \\
20 \\
7\overline{)161} \\
140 \\
\hline
21 \\
21 \\
\hline
0
\end{array}
$$

1. Consider the division $2\overline{)1,854}$.

   a. Which estimate is best?

$$
\begin{array}{r}
10 \\
2\overline{)1,854} \\
20
\end{array}
\qquad
\begin{array}{r}
100 \\
2\overline{)1,854} \\
200
\end{array}
\qquad
\begin{array}{r}
1,000 \\
2\overline{)1,854} \\
2,000
\end{array}
$$

   b. The quotient is between 100 and 1,000. Which multiple of 100 is best?

$$
\begin{array}{r}
700 \\
2\overline{)1,854} \\
1,400
\end{array}
\qquad
\begin{array}{r}
800 \\
2\overline{)1,854} \\
1,600
\end{array}
\qquad
\begin{array}{r}
900 \\
2\overline{)1,854} \\
1,800
\end{array}
$$

   c. Now we divide our remainder 54 by 2. What is the next part of the quotient?

   d. Finish the division.

   e. Check.

$$
\begin{array}{r}
20 \\
900 \\
2\overline{)1,854} \\
1,800 \\
\hline
54 \\
40 \\
\hline
14
\end{array}
$$

2. Divide

    a. $3\overline{)258}$ **b.** $7\overline{)2,296}$ **c.** $5\overline{)4,332}$

Determine if the quotients are between 10 and 100, or 100 and 1,000.

1. $7\overline{)248}$ **2.** $7\overline{)2,296}$ **3.** $5\overline{)4,330}$

4. $5\overline{)1,645}$ **5.** $9\overline{)802}$ **6.** $8\overline{)4,721}$

7. $6\overline{)375}$ **8.** $4\overline{)144}$ **9.** $3\overline{)2,356}$

Divide.

10. $4\overline{)180}$ **11.** $4\overline{)1,806}$ **12.** $3\overline{)2,353}$

13. $5\overline{)438}$ **14.** $2\overline{)1,944}$ **15.** $6\overline{)299}$

16. $8\overline{)4,975}$ **17.** $7\overline{)6,104}$ **18.** $9\overline{)691}$

19. $5\overline{)940}$ **20.** $7\overline{)3,649}$ **21.** $9\overline{)2,223}$

22. $7\overline{)439}$ **23.** $3\overline{)291}$ **24.** $9\overline{)765}$

25. $6\overline{)3,078}$ **26.** $7\overline{)2,471}$ **27.** $4\overline{)7,250}$

28. $8\overline{)\$4,653}$ **29.** $5\overline{)\$625}$ **30.** $7\overline{)\$2,086}$

Solve these problems.

31. At the Thanksgiving Dance the tickets cost $3 each. The total receipts were $2,625. Richard said between 10 and 100 bought tickets. Melba said between 100 and 1,000. Without dividing, tell who's right?

32. Tickets to the park concert cost $2. The total receipts were $6,526. How many people bought tickets?

83

Compare these ways of dividing.

Long Form		Short Form

Long Form:

```
   30
8)275
  240
   35
```

```
   34
    4
   30
8)275
  240
   35
   32
    3
```

Short Form:

```
   3
8)275
  24
   3
```
Think:
$27 \div 8 \doteq 3$
$3 \times 8 = 24$
$27 - 24 = 3$

```
   34
8)275
  24↓
   35
```

```
   34
8)275
  24
  35
  32
   3
```
Think:
$35 \div 8 \doteq 4$
$4 \times 8 = 32$
$35 - 32 = 3$

---

1. Let's find the quotient $443 \div 7$ using the short form.

a. What is your first estimate?

```
     ▪
7)443
```

b. What is your second estimate?

```
    6▪
7)443
  42↓
  23
```

c. What is the quotient?
   Remainder?

```
   63
7)443
  42
  23
  21
   2
```

d. Complete the check.

```
  63
  ×7
 441 + 2 = ____
```

84

2. Study this short form for the division $2\overline{)1,953}$.

$$
\begin{array}{r}
9 \\
2\overline{)1,953} \\
18\downarrow \\
\hline
15
\end{array}
\qquad
\begin{array}{r}
97 \\
2\overline{)1,953} \\
18\downarrow \\
\hline
15 \\
14 \\
\hline
13
\end{array}
\qquad
\begin{array}{r}
976 \\
2\overline{)1,953} \\
18 \\
\hline
15 \\
14 \\
\hline
13 \\
12 \\
\hline
1
\end{array}
$$

   a. What is the quotient? Remainder?

   b. Check.

3. Divide.

   a. $4\overline{)231}$ **b.** $6\overline{)526}$ **c.** $3\overline{)790}$ **d.** $7\overline{)2,318}$

EXERCISES

Divide.

  1. $3\overline{)137}$ **2.** $4\overline{)275}$ **3.** $5\overline{)157}$

  4. $6\overline{)445}$ **5.** $9\overline{)769}$ **6.** $2\overline{)327}$

  7. $7\overline{)567}$ **8.** $8\overline{)499}$ **9.** $3\overline{)674}$

10. $7\overline{)4,146}$ **11.** $8\overline{)5,228}$ **12.** $6\overline{)2,741}$

13. $4\overline{)1,833}$ **14.** $4\overline{)9,325}$ **15.** $7\overline{)6,827}$

16. $5\overline{)8,126}$ **17.** $6\overline{)2,706}$ **18.** $9\overline{)5,512}$

19. $5\overline{)229,183}$ **20.** $4\overline{)85,391}$ **21.** $7\overline{)682,594}$

★**22.** $5\overline{)2,441,078}$ ★**23.** $8\overline{)4,790,497}$ ★**24.** $4\overline{)2,308,891}$

Solve this problem.

25. Very Sharp Pencil Sharpener Company packs their sharpeners in boxes of 6. One stationery store ordered 114 pencil sharpeners. How many boxes should they receive?

85

ZEROS IN THE QUOTIENT

Study the steps in this division.

$$
\begin{array}{r}
6 \\
3\overline{)1{,}8\,1\,6} \\
\underline{1\,8} \\
0
\end{array}
$$

$18 \div 3 = 6$
$6 \times 3 = 18$
$18 - 18 = 0$

$$
\begin{array}{r}
6\,0 \\
3\overline{)1{,}8\,1\,6} \\
\underline{1\,8\downarrow} \\
0\,1
\end{array}
$$

$1 \div 3 = ?$
Try 0.

$$
\begin{array}{r}
6\,0\,5 \\
3\overline{)1{,}8\,1\,6} \\
\underline{1\,8}\downarrow \\
0\,1\,6 \\
\underline{1\,5} \\
1
\end{array}
$$
605 r 1

$16 \div 3 \doteq 5$
$5 \times 3 = 15$
$16 - 15 = 1$

Don't forget zeros at the end of the quotient!

$$
\begin{array}{r}
6 \\
3\overline{)1{,}9\,5\,2} \\
\underline{1\,8} \\
1
\end{array}
$$

$$
\begin{array}{r}
6\,5 \\
3\overline{)1{,}9\,5\,2} \\
\underline{1\,8\downarrow} \\
1\,5 \\
\underline{1\,5} \\
0
\end{array}
$$

$$
\begin{array}{r}
6\,5\,0 \\
3\overline{)1{,}9\,5\,2} \\
\underline{1\,8}\downarrow \\
1\,5 \\
\underline{1\,5} \\
0\,2
\end{array}
$$
650 r 2

1. Copy and complete.

a.
$$
\begin{array}{r}
3\,0 \\
7\overline{)2{,}164} \\
\underline{2\,1}\downarrow\downarrow \\
6\,4
\end{array}
$$

b.
$$
\begin{array}{r}
4 \\
8\overline{)3{,}257} \\
\underline{3\,2}\downarrow \\
5
\end{array}
$$

c.
$$
\begin{array}{r}
9 \\
4\overline{)3{,}615} \\
\underline{3\,6}
\end{array}
$$

d.
$$
\begin{array}{r}
2\,3 \\
5\overline{)1{,}153} \\
\underline{1\,0}\downarrow \\
1\,5 \\
\underline{1\,5} \\
0\,3
\end{array}
$$

e.
$$
\begin{array}{r}
4\,5 \\
6\overline{)2{,}704} \\
\underline{2\,4}\downarrow \\
3\,0 \\
\underline{3\,0}
\end{array}
$$

f.
$$
\begin{array}{r}
7 \\
9\overline{)6{,}487} \\
\underline{6\,3}\downarrow \\
1\,8
\end{array}
$$

2. Divide.

a. $4\overline{)1{,}624}$

b. $7\overline{)4{,}318}$

c. $8\overline{)3{,}256}$

Divide.

1. 2)617

2. 3)2,521

3. 7)3,529

4. 7)3,432

5. 5)1,541

6. 6)3,062

7. 4)2,837

8. 3)2,107

ZERO IS A TROUBLE MAKER.

9. 6)3,627

10. 5)3,104

11. 9)957

12. 8)1,658

13. 9)2,432

14. 8)3,040

15. 2)1,901

16. 4)2,256

17. 6)4,805

18. 7)5,763

19. 9)3,605

20. 4)2,006

21. 5)2,702

22. 7)4,206

23. 5)10,151

24. 8)48,059

25. 9)65,701

26. 6)42,058

Solve these problems.

27. Lincoln School has 1,224 students. The same number of students eat during each of the 4 lunch periods. How many eat in each lunch period?

28. There is a 5th, a 6th, and a 7th grade in Lincoln School. There is the same number of students in each grade. With an enrollment of 1,224 students, how many students are in each grade?

29. Nine classes in the school gave a total of $1,080 to the Book Fund. Each class gave the same amount. How much did each give?

30. There are 912 portable chairs in the school. They will be set up for an outdoors assembly. Each of the 3 grades agrees to share the job of setting up the chairs. How many chairs will each grade set up?

Compare these function machines. They show a pattern.

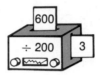

We can often use this pattern to help us find quotients.

$$\frac{2}{8)16} \quad \text{so} \quad \frac{2}{80)160} \quad \text{and} \quad \frac{2}{800)1,600}$$

1. Find the common solution for each pair.

a. $3)\overline{12}$ and $30)\overline{120}$

b. $4)\overline{24}$ and $400)\overline{2,400}$

c. $2)\overline{8}$ and $200)\overline{800}$

d. $6)\overline{18}$ and $600)\overline{1,800}$

2. Here's an easy way to think of division.

Look	Think	Divide
$20)\overline{80}$	$8 \div 2$	$\dfrac{4}{20)\overline{80}}$
$20)\overline{120}$	$1 \div 2$	Not a whole number!
$20)\overline{120}$	$12 \div 2$	$\dfrac{6}{20)\overline{120}}$

Divide.

a. $30)\overline{60}$ **b.** $30)\overline{150}$ **c.** $50)\overline{350}$

d. $50)\overline{400}$ **e.** $600)\overline{2,400}$ **f.** $800)\overline{5,600}$

g. $60)\overline{180}$ **h.** $40)\overline{80}$ **i.** $700)\overline{4,200}$

Here are some division facts.

$$\begin{array}{r} 6 \\ 4\overline{)24} \end{array} \qquad \begin{array}{r} 8 \\ 3\overline{)24} \end{array} \qquad \begin{array}{r} 8 \\ 4\overline{)32} \end{array}$$

Use these facts to find answers to the following.

1. $40\overline{)240}$ **2.** $30\overline{)240}$ **3.** $300\overline{)2,400}$

4. $30\overline{)240}$ **5.** $400\overline{)2400}$ **6.** $400\overline{)3,200}$

Divide.

7. $20\overline{)180}$ **8.** $70\overline{)490}$ **9.** $60\overline{)240}$

10. $40\overline{)80}$ **11.** $60\overline{)300}$ **12.** $70\overline{)210}$

13. $80\overline{)400}$ **14.** $50\overline{)400}$ **15.** $90\overline{)450}$

16. $60\overline{)420}$ **17.** $80\overline{)480}$ **18.** $30\overline{)270}$

19. $40\overline{)280}$ **20.** $20\overline{)180}$ **21.** $20\overline{)60}$

22. $300\overline{)900}$ **23.** $400\overline{)2,400}$ **24.** $500\overline{)4,500}$

25. $400\overline{)1,200}$ **26.** $500\overline{)3,000}$ **27.** $300\overline{)2,100}$

28. $900\overline{)2,700}$ **29.** $800\overline{)2,400}$ **30.** $700\overline{)2,800}$

Add.

Keeping Fit

1. $\begin{array}{r} 23 \\ +\ 46 \\ \hline \end{array}$ **2.** $\begin{array}{r} 304 \\ +485 \\ \hline \end{array}$ **3.** $\begin{array}{r} 279 \\ +516 \\ \hline \end{array}$

4. $\begin{array}{r} 654 \\ +186 \\ \hline \end{array}$ **5.** $\begin{array}{r} 278 \\ +954 \\ \hline \end{array}$ **6.** $\begin{array}{r} \$29.95 \\ +31.49 \\ \hline \end{array}$

Subtract.

7. $\begin{array}{r} 737 \\ -198 \\ \hline \end{array}$ **8.** $\begin{array}{r} 504 \\ -326 \\ \hline \end{array}$ **9.** $\begin{array}{r} 8,001 \\ -2,654 \\ \hline \end{array}$ **10.** $\begin{array}{r} \$29.95 \\ -15.39 \\ \hline \end{array}$

Keeping Fit

Add.

1.	26	2.	447	3.	$9.95
	39		382		4.98
	+ 45		+ 590		+ 7.91

4.	18	5.	298	6.	$39.51
	49		734		76.25
	36		623		82.85
	+ 82		+ 887		+ 63.39

Subtract.

7.	46	8.	83	9.	729	10.	811
	− 18		− 67		− 566		− 458

11.	7,426	12.	1,622	13.	6,441	14.	7,051
	− 845		− 918		− 83		− 277

15.	67,235	16.	579,134	17.	692,581	18.	715,937
	− 19,007		− 123,015		− 231,290		− 512,688

Multiply.

19.	30	20.	400	21.	50	22.	72
	× 7		× 6		× 90		× 40

23.	507	24.	609	25.	$7.25	26.	$9.95
	× 9		× 27		× 3		× 2

27.	598	28.	3,749	29.	$15.90	30.	$29.89
	× 38		× 25		× 63		× 20

Divide.

31. 4)‾80‾ 32. 6)‾180‾ 33. 4)‾200‾

34. 7)‾3,500‾ 35. 8)‾5,606‾ 36. 5)‾335‾

37. 6)‾1,746‾ 38. 8)‾2,472‾ 39. 7)‾3,641‾

40. 4)‾1,650‾ 41. 9)‾4,605‾ 42. 8)‾2,746‾

90

SAVING WATER

Ecologists say to save water.

1. The city of Stantonville's water system claims that an average drip wastes 35 liters of water in 24 hours. How much water would be wasted in a week? in the month of June?

2. Sandy's leaky kitchen faucet wastes 16 liters of water a day. How many days would it take to waste a 96 liter tank of water?

3. About 30,000 liters of water are used each hour in Newport. The average person uses about 6 liters of water each hour. How many people live in Newport?

4. The population of Savetown is 3,000. The average person there uses about 120 liters of water a day. How much water does Savetown use each day?

5. One liter of water weighs about 1 kilogram. The average person uses about 150 liters of water a day. Suppose you had to carry that water from a well. How much would your water weigh?

91

Compare the long form with the short form.

Long Form	Short Form	

$$
\begin{array}{r}
30 \\
20\overline{)747} \\
600 \\
\hline
147
\end{array}
$$

$$
\begin{array}{r}
3 \\
20\overline{)747} \\
60 \\
\hline
14
\end{array}
$$

Think:

$7 \div 2 \doteq 3$

$3 \times 20 = 60$

$74 - 60 = 14$

$$
\begin{array}{r}
3 \\
20\overline{)747} \\
60\downarrow \\
\hline
147
\end{array}
$$

$$
\begin{array}{r}
37 \\
\hline
7 \\
30 \\
20\overline{)747} \\
600 \\
\hline
147 \\
140 \\
\hline
7
\end{array}
$$

$$
\begin{array}{r}
37 \\
20\overline{)747} \\
60 \\
\hline
147 \\
140 \\
\hline
7
\end{array}
$$

Think:

$14 \div 2 = 7$

$7 \times 20 = 140$

$147 - 140 = 7$

1. Consider the division $1{,}357 \div 20$.

a. What is your first estimate?
Hint: Think of $13 \div 2$.

$$20\overline{)1{,}357}$$

b. What is your second estimate?
Hint: Think of $15 \div 2$.

$$
\begin{array}{r}
6 \\
20\overline{)1{,}357} \\
120\downarrow \\
\hline
157
\end{array}
$$

c. What is the quotient?
Remainder?

d. Complete the check.

$$
\begin{array}{r}
67 \\
\times 20 \\
\hline
1{,}340 + 17 = \underline{}
\end{array}
$$

$$
\begin{array}{r}
67 \\
20\overline{)1{,}357} \\
120 \\
\hline
157 \\
140 \\
\hline
17
\end{array}
$$

2. An extra step is needed when the quotient is over 100.

$$
\begin{array}{r}
4 \\
40\overline{)19{,}385} \\
160\downarrow \\
\hline
338
\end{array}
\qquad
\begin{array}{r}
48 \\
40\overline{)19{,}385} \\
160\downarrow \\
\hline
338 \\
320 \\
\hline
185
\end{array}
\qquad
\begin{array}{r}
484 \\
40\overline{)19{,}385} \\
160 \\
\hline
338 \\
320 \\
\hline
185 \\
160 \\
\hline
25
\end{array}
$$

a. What is the quotient?   Remainder?

b. Check.

3. Divide.

a. $50\overline{)4{,}297}$ **b.** $90\overline{)7{,}054}$ **c.** $80\overline{)13{,}490}$

d. $30\overline{)2{,}163}$ **e.** $70\overline{)65{,}481}$ **f.** $90\overline{)71{,}962}$

EXERCISES

Divide.

1. $20\overline{)998}$ **2.** $80\overline{)1{,}697}$ **3.** $40\overline{)3{,}098}$

4. $40\overline{)5{,}098}$ **5.** $70\overline{)222}$ **6.** $50\overline{)4{,}001}$

7. $60\overline{)316}$ **8.** $20\overline{)1{,}998}$ **9.** $80\overline{)8{,}923}$

10. $20\overline{)6{,}069}$ **11.** $90\overline{)998}$ **12.** $50\overline{)2{,}846}$

13. $60\overline{)4{,}865}$ **14.** $80\overline{)2{,}404}$ **15.** $80\overline{)9{,}277}$

16. $40\overline{)5{,}277}$ **17.** $60\overline{)4{,}799}$ **18.** $70\overline{)1{,}727}$

19. $20\overline{)4{,}509}$ **20.** $70\overline{)8{,}405}$ **21.** $30\overline{)31{,}518}$

22. $70\overline{)29{,}872}$ **23.** $40\overline{)25{,}093}$ **24.** $20\overline{)16{,}569}$

25. $60\overline{)57{,}904}$ **26.** $50\overline{)40{,}812}$ **27.** $40\overline{)26{,}900}$

Dividing by numbers between multiples of 10 is similar to our division in the last lesson.

Long Form	Short Form	
$$\begin{array}{r} 30 \\ 23\overline{)747} \\ 690 \\ \hline 57 \end{array}$$	$$\begin{array}{r} 3 \\ 2\,3\overline{)7\,4\,7} \\ 6\,9 \\ \hline 5 \end{array}$$	Think: $7 \div 2 \doteq 3$ $3 \times 23 = 69$ $74 - 69 = 5$
	$$\begin{array}{r} 3 \\ 2\,3\overline{)7\,4\,7} \\ 6\,9\downarrow \\ \hline 5\,7 \end{array}$$	
$$\begin{array}{r} 32 \\ \overline{2} \\ 30 \\ 23\overline{)747} \\ 690 \\ \hline 57 \\ 46 \\ \hline 11 \end{array}$$	$$\begin{array}{r} 3\,2 \\ 2\,3\overline{)7\,4\,7} \\ 6\,9\downarrow \\ \hline 5\,7 \\ 4\,6 \\ \hline 1\,1 \end{array}$$	Think: $5 \div 2 \doteq 2$ $2 \times 23 = 46$ $57 - 46 = 11$

1. Let's divide: $1,357 \div 21$.

   a. What is your first estimate?
   Hint: Think of $13 \div 2$.

   $$2\,1\overline{)1{,}3\,5\,7}$$

   b. What is your second estimate?
   Hint: Think of $9 \div 2$.

   $$\begin{array}{r} 6 \\ 2\,1\overline{)1{,}3\,5\,7} \\ 1\,2\,6\downarrow \\ \hline 9\,7 \end{array}$$

   c. What is the quotient?
   Remainder?

   $$\begin{array}{r} 6\,4 \\ 2\,1\overline{)1{,}3\,5\,7} \\ 1\,2\,6 \\ \hline 9\,7 \\ 8\,4 \\ \hline 1\,3 \end{array}$$

   d. Complete the check.
   $$\begin{array}{r} 64 \\ \times 21 \\ \hline 1{,}344 + 13 = \underline{} \end{array}$$

2. Divide.

    a. $62\overline{)4{,}452}$ **b.** $83\overline{)3{,}537}$ **c.** $91\overline{)4{,}643}$

3. This division requires one more step.

```
        5                    5 6                  5 6 2
32)17,987            32)17,987            32)17,987
   160↓                  160  ↓               160
   198                   198                  198
                         192                  192
                          67                   67
                                               64
                                                3
```

Divide.

    a. $42\overline{)30{,}506}$ **b.** $33\overline{)25{,}629}$ **c.** $21\overline{)19{,}995}$

EXERCISES

Divide.

  1. $73\overline{)222}$ **2.** $61\overline{)316}$ **3.** $31\overline{)1{,}697}$

  4. $42\overline{)3{,}098}$ **5.** $23\overline{)9{,}924}$ **6.** $64\overline{)1{,}729}$

  7. $45\overline{)5{,}098}$ **8.** $51\overline{)4{,}301}$ **9.** $24\overline{)998}$

10. $21\overline{)1{,}998}$ **11.** $81\overline{)8{,}999}$ **12.** $31\overline{)6{,}708}$

13. $93\overline{)1{,}184}$ **14.** $33\overline{)4{,}721}$ **15.** $21\overline{)1{,}789}$

16. $52\overline{)3{,}725}$ **17.** $42\overline{)1{,}959}$ **18.** $61\overline{)4{,}941}$

19. $73\overline{)9{,}709}$ **20.** $32\overline{)29{,}348}$ **21.** $72\overline{)29{,}882}$

22. $36\overline{)11{,}925}$ **23.** $42\overline{)25{,}893}$ **24.** $21\overline{)15{,}329}$

25. $32\overline{)7{,}400}$ **26.** $73\overline{)83{,}071}$ **27.** $51\overline{)66{,}881}$

★ **28.** Make a flow chart to show how you check division.

ZEROS IN THE QUOTIENT

Study the steps in this division.

$$
\begin{array}{r}
7 \\
32\overline{)22{,}568} \\
224 \\
\hline
1
\end{array}
\qquad
\begin{array}{r}
70 \\
32\overline{)22{,}568} \\
224\downarrow \\
\hline
16
\end{array}
\qquad
\begin{array}{r}
705 \\
32\overline{)22{,}568} \\
224\ \ \downarrow \\
\hline
168 \\
160 \\
\hline
8
\end{array}
$$

$22 \div 3 = 7$ $1 \div 3 = ?$ $16 \div 3 = 5$

$7 \times 32 = 224$ Try 0. $5 \times 32 = 160$

$225 - 224 = 1$ $168 - 160 = 8$

---

1. Let's divide: $1{,}278 \div 21$.

  a. What is your first estimate?
  Hint: Think of $12 \div 2$.
  $$21\overline{)1{,}278}$$

  b. What is your second estimate?
  Hint: Think of $18 \div 21$. Try 0.
  $$
  \begin{array}{r}
  6 \\
  21\overline{)1{,}278} \\
  126 \\
  \hline
  18
  \end{array}
  $$

  c. The quotient is 60.
  What is the remainder?

2. Divide.

  a. $2{,}517 \div 62$ **b.** $10{,}677 \div 52$

EXERCISES

Divide.

1. $72\overline{)3{,}660}$ **2.** $84\overline{)2{,}566}$ **3.** $34\overline{)6{,}823}$

4. $84\overline{)8{,}576}$ **5.** $31\overline{)21{,}876}$ **6.** $62\overline{)25{,}331}$

7. $33\overline{)26{,}466}$ **8.** $72\overline{)64{,}929}$ **9.** $91\overline{)45{,}926}$

10. $81\overline{)24{,}917}$ **11.** $23\overline{)13{,}880}$ **12.** $73\overline{)80{,}347}$

DIVISION WITH MONEY

Let's think of this division: 23) $97.75
Think of $97.75 as 9,775 cents.

425 cents		$4.25
23) 9,775 cents	so	23) $97.75
9 2		92
57		57
46		46
115		115
115		115
0		0

1. Three boys shared the job of cutting Mrs. Smith's lawn. She gave them $8.40. How much did each earn?

2. Jane and Beth shared the cost of buying gas for the car. The gas cost $6.38. How much did each pay?

3. The bus cost $26.25 to take the 21 boys on the team. They shared the cost. How much did each pay?

4. The 62 pupils in Grade 6 shared the cost of a museum visit. Bus Company A rents a bus for $37.20. Bus Company B rents a bus for $34.10. How much would each pupil save by renting the bus from Bus Company B?

5. The class party cost $.55 per person. The total collected was $17.60. How many went to the class party?

6. Food for the class picnic cost $41.60. Transportation cost $24. The 32 pupils shared the costs. How much did each pay?

Sometimes a quotient estimate is too large.

STEP 1

$$73)\overline{2917}$$ quotient 4
$$292$$

Think: $29 \div 7 \doteq 4$
$4 \times 73 = 292$
Can't subtract!

STEP 2

$$73)\overline{2{,}917}$$ quotient 3
$$219\downarrow$$
$$727$$

Change estimate to 3.
$3 \times 73 = 219$
$291 - 219 = 72$

STEP 3

$$73)\overline{2{,}917}$$ quotient 39
$$219\downarrow$$
$$727$$

Think: $72 \div 7 = ?$ Try 9, because 10 is always too large.

STEP 4

$$73)\overline{2{,}917}$$ quotient 39
$$2{,}19\downarrow$$
$$727$$
$$657$$
$$70$$

Answer: 39 r 70

---

1. Let's divide: $1{,}992 \div 28$.

$$28)\overline{1{,}992}$$ quotient 9
$$252$$

Think:
$19 \div 2 \doteq 9$
9 is too large.

$$28)\overline{1{,}992}$$ quotient 8
$$224$$

Try 8.
8 is too large.

$$28)\overline{1{,}992}$$ quotient 7
$$196$$

Try 7.

Copy and complete the division.

2. Divide.

   a. $37)\overline{2{,}294}$ **b.** $27)\overline{8{,}615}$ **c.** $48)\overline{18{,}289}$

Divide.

1. $76\overline{)222}$

2. $47\overline{)3,402}$

3. $55\overline{)4,821}$

4. $63\overline{)3,149}$

5. $67\overline{)316}$

6. $36\overline{)3,470}$

7. $57\overline{)1,650}$

8. $38\overline{)1,998}$

9. $28\overline{)4,271}$

10. $19\overline{)266}$

11. $37\overline{)1,697}$

12. $48\overline{)3,457}$

13. $56\overline{)4,301}$

14. $39\overline{)8,083}$

15. $28\overline{)1,981}$

16. $27\overline{)2,650}$

17. $48\overline{)3,359}$

18. $39\overline{)43,518}$

19. $36\overline{)22,800}$

20. $78\overline{)29,872}$

21. $49\overline{)23,693}$

22. $87\overline{)72,807}$

23. $66\overline{)24,823}$

24. $68\overline{)31,904}$

25. $29\overline{)16,569}$

26. $26\overline{)82,701}$

27. $97\overline{)25,006}$

Solve these problems.

28. The price of a season ticket to the games is $37. One ticket office collected $11,322 on season tickets. How many did it sell?

29. One section of the stadium has 3,450 seats. There are 46 seats in each row. How many rows are in the section?

30. David Cohen carried the ball 18 times in the game. He ran for a total of 108 yards. About how many yards did he run the ball per carry?

31. The team bought 38 new uniforms. The total cost was $4,066. How much did each uniform cost?

99

DIVIDING BY MULTIPLES OF 100

Compare the long and short forms.

Long Form	Short Form	

```
      40              4          Think:
300)13,753      300)13,753      13 ÷ 3 ≐ 4
    12 000          1200        4 × 300 = 1,200
     1 753           175        1,375 − 1,200 = 175
```

```
                     4
                300)13,753
      45            1200↓
       5            1753
```

```
      40             45         Think:
300)13,753      300)13,753      17 ÷ 3 ≐ 5
    12 000          1200        5 × 300 = 1,500
     1 753          1753        1,753 − 1,500 = 253
     1 500          1500
       253           253
```

1. Let's divide: $290{,}537 \div 400$.

a. What is your first estimate?
Hint: Think of $29 \div 4$.

```
        
400)290,537
```

b. What is your second estimate?
Hint: Think of $10 \div 4$.

```
        7
400)290,537
    2800↓
    1053
```

c. What is your third estimate?
Hint: Think of $25 \div 4$.

```
         72
400)290,537
    2800  ↓
    1053
```

d. Copy and complete the division.

e. Check.

```
     800
    2537
```

2. Divide.

a. 600)18,839   **b.** 700)48,793   **c.** 500)13,098

100

Divide.

1. $200\overline{)11{,}739}$

2. $300\overline{)23{,}798}$

3. $500\overline{)37{,}190}$

4. $400\overline{)33{,}485}$

5. $600\overline{)47{,}846}$

6. $400\overline{)24{,}929}$

7. $400\overline{)12{,}846}$

8. $700\overline{)57{,}900}$

9. $700\overline{)79{,}485}$

10. $200\overline{)83{,}420}$

11. $900\overline{)84{,}727}$

12. $200\overline{)92{,}418}$

13. $700\overline{)69{,}485}$

14. $500\overline{)99{,}842}$

15. $500\overline{)288{,}238}$

16. $600\overline{)120{,}619}$

17. $400\overline{)246{,}116}$

18. $800\overline{)123{,}456}$

19. $600\overline{)193{,}896}$

20. $800\overline{)360{,}000}$

21. $500\overline{)135{,}000}$

22. $900\overline{)491{,}500}$

23. $300\overline{)421{,}509}$

24. $800\overline{)721{,}955}$

Solve this problem.

25. In one school year 300 pupils spent $27,900 in the school cafeteria. Suppose each student spent the same amount. How much did each spend?

Brainteaser

Each letter stands for a digit. The O stands for zero. Break the codes for each. Find the digit which goes with each letter.

1.
```
          9MJ
  P)H,8ML
    H J
    ‾‾‾‾
     14
     LH
     ‾‾
     H1
     HL
     ‾‾
      O
```

2.
```
          R88
  S)2,TRR
    C O
    ‾‾‾
     3R
     TC
     ‾‾
     TR
     TC
     ‾‾
      T
```

101

Study each step of the short form division.

```
        4
314)13,752
    1256
     119
```

```
        4
314)13,752
    1256↓
    1192
```

```
       43
314)13,752
    1256
    1192
     942
     250
```

Think:
13 ÷ 3 ≐ 4
4 × 314 = 1256
1,375 − 1,256 = 119

Think:
11 ÷ 3 ≐ 3
3 × 314 = 942
1,192 − 942 = 250

1. Let's divide: 231,189 ÷ 712.

   a. What is your first estimate?
      Hint: Think of 23 ÷ 7.

   ```
   712)231,189
   ```

   b. What is your second estimate?
      Hint: Think of 17 ÷ 7.

   ```
         3
   712)231,189
       2136↓
       1758
   ```

   c. What is your third estimate?
      Hint: Think of 33 ÷ 7.

   ```
        32
   712)231,189
       2136 ↓
       1758
   ```

   d. Copy and complete the division.

   e. Check.

   ```
       1424
       3349
   ```

102

2. Sometimes estimates are too large.

$$\begin{array}{r} 4 \\ 231\overline{)9{,}097} \\ 924 \end{array}$$

$$\begin{array}{r} 3 \\ 231\overline{)9{,}097} \\ 693 \\ \hline 216 \end{array}$$

$$\begin{array}{r} 39 \\ 231\overline{)8{,}097} \\ 693\downarrow \\ \hline 2167 \\ 2079 \\ \hline 88 \end{array}$$

Think:
9 ÷ 2 ≐ 4
4 × 231 = 924
4 is too large.

Try 3.
3 × 231 = 693
909 − 693 = 216

Think:
21 ÷ 2 = ? Try 9.
9 × 231 = 2,079
2,167 − 2,079 = 88

Divide.

a. 485$\overline{)33{,}485}$ **b.** 294$\overline{)47{,}896}$ **c.** 673$\overline{)193{,}896}$

EXERCISES

Divide.

1. 312$\overline{)22{,}799}$ **2.** 231$\overline{)7{,}175}$ **3.** 614$\overline{)28{,}869}$

4. 523$\overline{)33{,}472}$ **5.** 421$\overline{)34{,}573}$ **6.** 326$\overline{)42{,}893}$

7. 624$\overline{)87{,}900}$ **8.** 809$\overline{)29{,}407}$ **9.** 732$\overline{)46{,}243}$

10. 824$\overline{)61{,}896}$ **11.** 478$\overline{)15{,}693}$ **12.** 395$\overline{)38{,}852}$

13. 395$\overline{)39{,}899}$ **14.** 386$\overline{)17{,}642}$ **15.** 273$\overline{)11{,}739}$

16. 211$\overline{)92{,}418}$ **17.** 491$\overline{)52{,}800}$ **18.** 523$\overline{)278{,}236}$

19. 406$\overline{)249{,}299}$ **20.** 983$\overline{)491{,}500}$ **21.** 725$\overline{)295{,}075}$

22. 781$\overline{)14{,}599}$ **23.** 287$\overline{)42{,}866}$ **24.** 116$\overline{)25{,}693}$

25. 869$\overline{)608{,}732}$ **26.** 598$\overline{)482{,}699}$ **27.** 879$\overline{)420{,}314}$

28. 797$\overline{)647{,}813}$ **29.** 634$\overline{)360{,}402}$ **30.** 982$\overline{)579{,}591}$

★**31.** 2,213$\overline{)721{,}431}$ ★**32.** 4,307$\overline{)286{,}911}$ ★**33.** 3,926$\overline{)842{,}455}$

AVERAGES

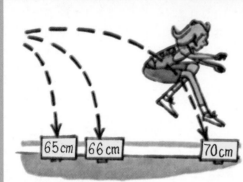

Jane figured the average of her three jumps.

Sum: $65 + 66 + 70 = 201$

Average: $201 \div 3 = 67$

65 cm **66 cm** **70 cm**

1. Complete.

   a. 10, 12, 14, 16

   Sum: $10 + \underline{\quad} + 14 + \underline{\quad}$

   $= \underline{\quad}$

   Average: $52 \div 4 = \underline{\quad}$

   b. $99, $105

   Sum: $99 + 105 = \underline{\quad}$

   Average:

   $204 \div \underline{\quad} = \underline{\quad}$

2. Find the averages.

   a. 5 test scores: 90, 92, 93, 95, 95

   b. 15 pay checks: $25, $25, $27, $21, $31, $32, $20, $26, $30, $22, $16, $26, $29, $23, $22,

---

EXERCISES

Find the averages.

1. 4 kg, 62 kg

2. 10 sec, 12 sec, 9 sec, 13 sec

3. 7 cm, 8 cm, 12 cm

4. 21¢, 9¢, 5¢, 8¢, 19¢, 10¢

5. $10, $12, $9, $17

6. 6, 6, 6, 6

7. 1, 2, 3, 4, 5, 6, 7, 8, 9, 10, 11, 12, 13, 14, 15

8. 70, 74, 66, 75, 62, 82, 96

Divide.

1. $7\overline{)50}$ 2. $8\overline{)71}$ 3. $6\overline{)49}$

4. $3\overline{)261}$ 5. $7\overline{)2,222}$ 6. $8\overline{)2,539}$

7. $8\overline{)5,623}$ 8. $3\overline{)1,950}$ 9. $7\overline{)22,402}$

10. $23\overline{)7,245}$ 11. $41\overline{)6,827}$ 12. $39\overline{)185}$

13. $58\overline{)1,147}$ 14. $42\overline{)12,902}$ 15. $34\overline{)3,454}$ 16. $214\overline{)11,342}$

ACTIVITY

Class Weights
Joe 27 kg
Sally 32 kg
Melba
Jimmy
Teresa

Do you know how much you weigh in kilograms? Take a guess. Guess the average weight of all the students in the class. Write it down.

Let us see who has the best guess. Get a metric scale. Weigh each person in turn. After the first two students have been weighed, find their average weight. After the third student has been weighed, find the average weight of these three. Keep this up until everyone has been weighed. Whose guess was best? What happened to the average weights as more and more students were weighed?

Suppose you wanted to make a good guess of another class in your school. How many students would you like to weigh before you guess the average weight?

105

CHAPTER REVIEW

Write related division sentences. [74]

1. $n \times 7 = 28$ **2.** $y \times 9 = 72$ **3.** $4 \times n = 20$

Write related multiplication sentences. [74]

4. $y \div 3 = 21$ **5.** $30 \div 6 = x$ **6.** $n \div 9 = 8$

Find the averages. [104]

7. 21 kg, 47 kg **8.** 10 sec, 16 sec, 11 sec, 15 sec

Divide.

9. $6\overline{)54}$ **10.** $5\overline{)35}$ **11.** $7\overline{)42}$ **12.** $8\overline{)32}$
[78]   [78]   [78]   [78]

13. $2\overline{)18}$ **14.** $9\overline{)36}$ **15.** $3\overline{)29}$ [80] **16.** $4\overline{)21}$
[78]   [78]   [80]

17. $4\overline{)320}$ **18.** $9\overline{)4,500}$ **19.** $5\overline{)3,000}$
[78]   [78]   [78]

20. $30\overline{)210}$ **21.** $400\overline{)2,000}$ **22.** $5\overline{)435}$
[88]   [88]   [84]

23. $6\overline{)208}$ **24.** $9\overline{)4,621}$ **25.** $8\overline{)2,461}$
[84]   [84]   [86]

26. $3\overline{)\$5.16}$ **27.** $7\overline{)\$38.15}$ **28.** $7\overline{)60,374}$
[97]   [97]   [84]

29. $4\overline{)1,283}$ **30.** $3\overline{)18,122}$ **31.** $50\overline{)312}$
[86]   [86]   [92]

32. $41\overline{)2,190}$ **33.** $71\overline{)4,973}$ **34.** $62\overline{)18,662}$
[94]   [96]   [96]

35. $87\overline{)3,311}$ **36.** $58\overline{)64,194}$ **37.** $345\overline{)216,515}$
[98]   [98]   [102]

Solve these problems. [81]

38. Mrs. Richard drove 312 miles in 6 hours. About how many miles per hour is this?

39. Mr. McLeod is in charge of taking the waste out of water. He knows it costs $31 a ton on the average. Last week it cost $224.75. How many tons of waste were taken out?

CHAPTER TEST

Write related division sentences.

1. $n \times 4 = 32$ **2.** $z \times 6 = 42$ **3.** $5 \times n = 30$

Write related multiplication sentences.

4. $y \div 2 = 18$ **5.** $x \div 7 = 5$

Find the averages.

6. 22 meters, 26 meters   **7.** 15 min, 16 min, 18 min, 19 min

Divide.

8. $6\overline{)360}$ **9.** $7\overline{)3,500}$ **10.** $40\overline{)320}$

11. $300\overline{)2,400}$ **12.** $8\overline{)349}$ **13.** $7\overline{)4,301}$

14. $8\overline{)3,251}$ **15.** $8\overline{)\$53.04}$ **16.** $4\overline{)12,243}$

17. $32\overline{)256}$ **18.** $51\overline{)3,180}$ **19.** $63\overline{)5,045}$

20. $74\overline{)29,674}$ **21.** $78\overline{)3,691}$ **22.** $237\overline{)101,778}$

Solve these problems.

23. Three kilograms of chemical were added to the waste water. The total cost was $10.65. How much did it cost for a kilogram?

24. At the table tennis match $456 was collected. The tickets cost $3 each. How many people attended the match?

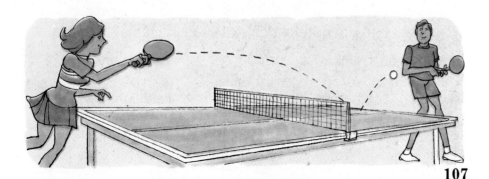

5 GEOMETRY

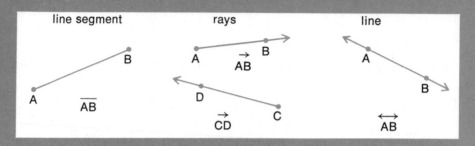

1. You cannot measure a line. Why?

2. Mark two points X and Y on a piece of paper. Draw a line $\overleftrightarrow{XY}$. Can you draw a line through points X and Y that is different from $\overleftrightarrow{XY}$?

   Through two points there is only one line.

3. In this figure, $\overleftrightarrow{XY}$ and $\overleftrightarrow{XW}$ are two different lines through X. Can you draw a third line through X? A fourth line? How many lines?

   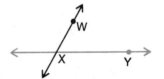

   Through one point there is an infinite number of lines.

EXERCISES

Which of these are good models of line segments? rays?

1. edge of a stick
2. clothes line
3. line of scrimmage in football
4. flashlight beam
5. edge of a piece of paper
6. ray of light

Draw a segment.

7. Name the endpoints C and D.

8. Mark a point X which is not between C and D and not on $\overrightarrow{CD}$.

9. Mark a point Y which is not between C and D but is on $\overrightarrow{CD}$.

10. Mark a point Z which is on $\overline{CD}$.

11. Which is longest, $\overline{CZ}$, $\overline{CY}$, or $\overline{CD}$?

Copy the figure at the right.

12. Draw as many segments as you can using D, E, and F as endpoints.

• D

• F

13. How many different segments could you draw?

• E

Copy the figures below. Draw $\overleftrightarrow{AB}$.

14. Is A on $\overleftrightarrow{AB}$?

• B

15. Is B on $\overleftrightarrow{AB}$?

C•

16. Is C on $\overleftrightarrow{AB}$?

• A

17. Are there any points on $\overleftrightarrow{AB}$ that are between A and B? How many?

18. What do we call all the points between A and B, together with A and B?

Answer the questions.

19. How many lines are there which contain the tip of your pencil and a corner of the room?

20. How many lines are there through any point on your desk?

21. How many lines are there through any point?

109

A sailor looked through his telescope in two directions. His two lines of sight make a model of an angle. We call the angle shown ∠*STL*, or ∠*T*, or ∠*LTS*.

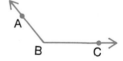

vertex: point *T*
sides: $\overrightarrow{TS}$ and $\overrightarrow{TL}$

1. Draw an angle.

   a. Label the vertex *F*.

   b. Label a point on one side *X*.

   c. Label a point on the other side *Y*.

   d. Give three names for this angle.

   e. Name the two sides.

2. Angle *XYZ* is called a **right angle.**

 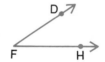

   a. Is ∠*DFH* smaller than or larger than a right angle?

   b. Is ∠*ABC* smaller than or larger than a right angle?

   An angle smaller than a right angle is an **acute angle.**
   An angle larger than a right angle is an **obtuse angle.**

3. Tell which angle is right, acute, or obtuse.

   a.   **b.**   **c.**

1. Name the angle, its vertex, and its sides.

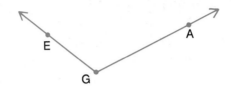

Draw an angle *DEF.*

2. What is the vertex?　　　**3.** What are the sides?

Draw a picture of these angles.

4. acute angle　　　**5.** obtuse angle　　　**6.** right angle

Tell which angles are right, acute, or obtuse.

7. 　　　**8.**

9. 　　**10.** 　　**11.** 　**12.**

13. 　　**14.** 　**15.** 　**16.**

1. 91$\overline{)29,612}$　　**2.** 29$\overline{)13,552}$

3. 48$\overline{)24,144}$　　**4.** 3$\overline{)\$5.22}$

5. 6$\overline{)\$34.02}$　　**6.** 22$\overline{)\$66.22}$

7. 63$\overline{)12,662}$　　**8.** 75$\overline{)41,646}$

9. 86$\overline{)61,200}$　　**10.** 92$\overline{)39,600}$

11. 77$\overline{)50,389}$　　**12.** 18$\overline{)9,499}$

Keeping Fit

MEASURING ANGLES

This is a picture of a compass. The tree is 40° north of East. We call ∠ABC a **central angle** of the circle. The measure of ∠ABC is 40°.

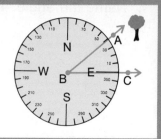

1. One way to measure an angle is to divide a circle into 360 equal lengths. The measure of each central angle is called a **degree.** Tell the measure of each angle.

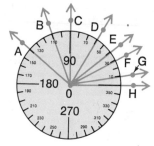

   a. ∠GOH   **b.** ∠COF

   c. ∠FOH   **d.** ∠HOA

   e. ∠COH   **f.** ∠GOA

2. A section $\frac{1}{4}$ of a circle is formed by a 90° central angle.

   $$\frac{1}{4} \times 360 = 90$$

   Which angle in the figure above measures 90°?

3. We can make a model like this to help us measure angles.

   a. Take a piece of paper. Draw a circle which measures about 3 inches across.

   b. Cut out your circle.

   c. Fold your circle twice in half so that the folds look like this. What is the measure of each central angle formed? Mark these measures.

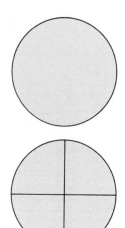

112

d. Now mark off each section into parts, and label them like this.

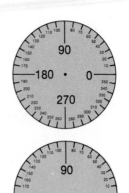

e. To use this model to measure angles, you need only half of your circle. Cut it so that it looks like this. This is called a **protractor.**

Find the measure of each angle using the protractor.

1. ∠BOA   **2.** ∠AOC

3. ∠EOA   **4.** ∠COA

5. ∠FOG   **6.** ∠AOD

7. ∠FOE   **8.** ∠FOD

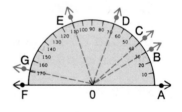

Use your protractor to measure these angles.

Example

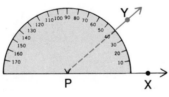

The measure of ∠XPY is 40°. We write m∠XPY = 40°.

9.   **10.**

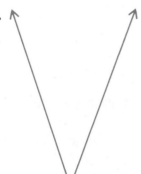
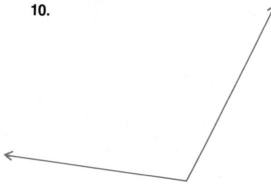

113

USING A PROTRACTOR

Most protractors have two scales. You can read one scale in a clockwise direction, and the other scale in a counterclockwise direction.

clockwise   counterclockwise

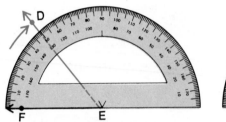   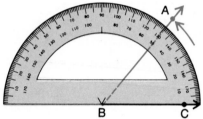

Because ∠ABC and ∠DEF have the same measure, we say they are **congruent.**

---

1. Consider the right angle XOY below.

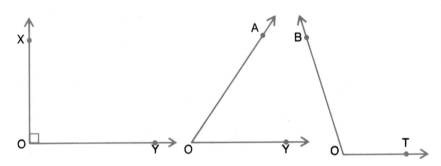

a. What is the measure of ∠XOY?

b. ∠AOY is an acute angle. What is its measure?

c. ∠BOT is an obtuse angle. What is its measure?

The measure of any right angle is 90°.
An acute angle measures less than 90°.
An obtuse angle measures more than 90°.

114

2. Before measuring, try to decide whether the angle is acute, right, or obtuse. Then you can make sure you use the right scale.

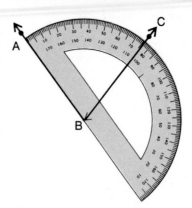

a. Does ∠ABC look acute, or obtuse?

b. What is its measure?

3. Here's how to draw a 30° angle.

a. Draw a picture of a ray $\overrightarrow{AB}$.

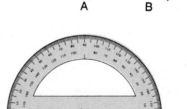

b. Place your protractor with its center mark on A, and the 0° mark along $\overrightarrow{AB}$.

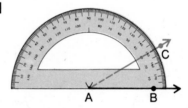

c. Mark C at the 30° mark, and draw a ray $\overrightarrow{AC}$.

EXERCISES

What are the measures?

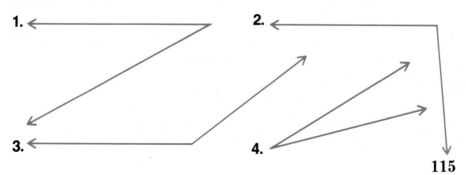

1.

2.

3.

4.

115

Find the measures.

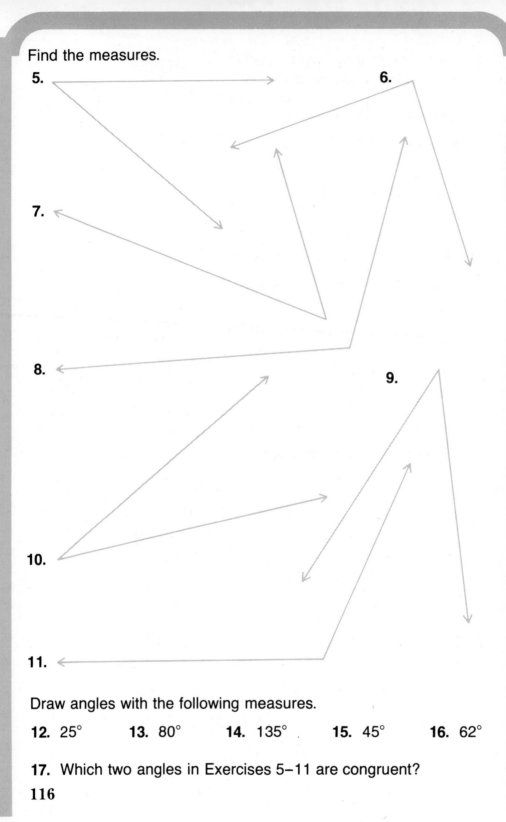

Draw angles with the following measures.

12. 25°   **13.** 80°   **14.** 135°   **15.** 45°   **16.** 62°

17. Which two angles in Exercises 5–11 are congruent?

116

MAKING GOOD ESTIMATES

Making a common sense estimate can help you solve a problem. In each problem, pick the best estimate.

1. The first known zoo was built in Ancient Egypt in 1490 BC. The first public zoo was built in Paris in 1793 AD. How many years are there from 1490 BC to 1793 AD?

   3 years   30 years   300 years   3,000 years

2. The San Diego Zoo has 255 kinds of mammals, 1,003 kinds of birds, and 291 kinds of reptiles. How many different kinds of animals does it have?

   15 kinds   150 kinds   1,500 kinds   15,000 kinds

3. The New York Zoological Society claims that of the 307 birds species about to die off, 47 could be raised successfully in a zoo. If this is done, then how many bird species will die off?

   26 species   260 species   360 species

4. Through good conservation practices, the population of trumpeter swans increased from 69 in 1932 to 5,000 in 1969. How many times had they increased?

   7 times   70 times   700 times   7,000 times

5. It is claimed that the London Zoo is the oldest in the world. It was started by William the Conqueror in 1070. About how many years ago was that?

   1900 years   1000 years   900 years   90 years

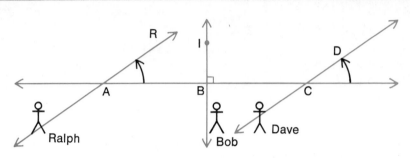

Ralph and Dave are headed in the same direction. We say that $\overleftrightarrow{AR}$ is **parallel** to $\overleftrightarrow{CD}$.

$$\overleftrightarrow{AR} \parallel \overleftrightarrow{CD}$$

Ralph's path and Bob's path cross. We say that $\overleftrightarrow{AR}$ and $\overleftrightarrow{BI}$ **intersect.**

$\angle IBC$ is a right angle. We say $\overleftrightarrow{BI}$ is **perpendicular** to $\overleftrightarrow{BC}$.

$$\overleftrightarrow{BI} \perp \overleftrightarrow{BC}$$

1. a. $\overleftrightarrow{AB}$ will intersect $\overleftrightarrow{CD}$ how many times?

   b. $\overleftrightarrow{CD}$ will intersect $\overleftrightarrow{EG}$ how many times?

   c. Will $\overleftrightarrow{AB}$ and $\overleftrightarrow{EG}$ intersect? How many times?

> Two lines intersect in at most one point.

2. a. Edges $\overline{CD}$ and $\overline{AB}$ are both part of the front of the desk. We say they are in the same plane. Are $\overline{AC}$ and $\overline{BD}$ in the same plane? Are $\overline{ED}$ and $\overline{BF}$?

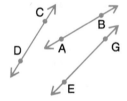

   b. $\overleftrightarrow{CD}$ and $\overleftrightarrow{AB}$ are parallel. Name two more parallel lines.

> Two lines in the same plane which do not intersect are called **parallel lines.**

3. A plumb bob helps you find a vertical line. A carpenter's level helps find a horizontal line. $\overleftrightarrow{PO} \perp \overleftrightarrow{LO}$. What are the measures of the four angles formed?

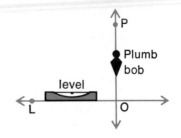

4. Look around your classroom. Find a model of each.

   a. horizontal lines

   b. perpendicular lines

   c. intersecting lines

   d. parallel lines

   e. vertical lines

EXERCISES

Tell if the following lines are parallel, or perpendicular. If neither of these, write "neither."

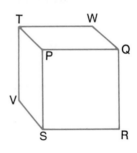

1. $\overleftrightarrow{TP}$ and $\overleftrightarrow{VS}$

2. $\overleftrightarrow{PQ}$ and $\overleftrightarrow{PS}$

3. $\overleftrightarrow{WT}$ and $\overleftrightarrow{PQ}$

4. $\overleftrightarrow{SR}$ and $\overleftrightarrow{TP}$

5. $\overleftrightarrow{TV}$ and $\overleftrightarrow{VS}$

6. $\overleftrightarrow{QR}$ and $\overleftrightarrow{PS}$

7. $\overleftrightarrow{TV}$ and $\overleftrightarrow{QR}$

8. $\overleftrightarrow{WQ}$ and $\overleftrightarrow{VS}$

Copy the figure at the right.

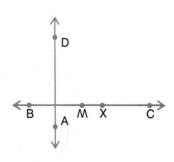

9. Draw a line which makes a 30° angle with $\overleftrightarrow{BC}$ at *M*. Will it intersect $\overleftrightarrow{DA}$?

10. Draw a line perpendicular to $\overleftrightarrow{BC}$ at *X*. Will it intersect $\overleftrightarrow{DA}$? Is it parallel to $\overleftrightarrow{DA}$?

119

ANGLE MEASURES OF A TRIANGLE

This is a picture of a baseball field. For each triangle in the infield, you can see that the sum of the measures of the angles is 180°.

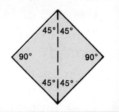

Here are two experiments to check that the sum of the angle measures of a triangle is 180°.

1. Draw a triangle which has the following measures.

$\overline{AB}$ measures 5 centimeters.

∠ CAB measures 60°.

∠ CBA measures 40°.

a. Measure ∠ ACB. Complete: $m\angle ACB =$ ___.

b. What is the sum of the angle measures of triangle *ABC*?

The sum of the measures of the angles of a triangle is 180°.

2. Here's the second experiment.

a. On a piece of paper, draw a triangle. Cut it out.

b. Tear the figure at two of the vertices, as shown.

c. Put the pieces together, as shown in the third drawing. They should fit together in a straight line.

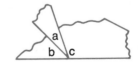

d. How does this show that the sum of the angle measures is 180°?

120

3. Given the measures of two angles of a triangle, we can find the measure of the third angle.

$$m \angle BAC: \quad 40°$$
$$m \angle ACB: \quad \underline{30°}$$
$$ 70°$$

$$ 180°$$
$$\underline{- 70°}$$
$$ 110°$$

Therefore, $m \angle ABC = 110°$

Find the measure of the third angle.

a.

b.

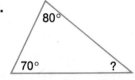

c.

Find the measure of the third angle.

1.

2.

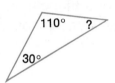

3.

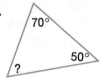

Find the missing angle measures.

	$\angle CAB$	$\angle ABC$	$\angle BCA$
4.	120°	10°	
5.	36°		49°
6.	right angle	45°	
7.	27°	56°	
8.		84°	51°
9.	95°		20°
10.	40°	50°	
11.	31°		27°

121

Find the missing angle measures.

	∠ CAB	∠ ABC	∠ BCA
12.	22°	right angle	
13.	95°		46°
14.		81°	10°
15.	52°	18°	
16.		129°	13°

Solve these problems.

17. Is it possible to have a triangle whose angles measure 90°, 90°, and 10°? Try to draw a picture of such a triangle.

★ **18.** Suppose one angle of a triangle is a right angle. The second angle is twice the third in measure. What are the measures of the three angles?

★ **19.** Suppose one angle of a triangle measures 80° and the other two angles have the same measure. What is the measure of each?

Keeping Fit

Subtract.

1.	14 − 5	**2.**	17 − 8	**3.**	75 −43
4.	368 − 142	**5.**	9,549 −7,513	**6.**	87 −59
7.	423 − 172	**8.**	38,464 − 19,059	**9.**	50 − 17

10.	607 − 318	**11.**	5,302 − 3,129	**12.**	$6.75 −$4.25	**13.**	$17.89 −$ 9.75

14.	$375.63 −$275.21	**15.**	$4.29 −$2.69	**16.**	$89.04 −$21.67	**17.**	$400.37 −$193.62

122

INDUSTRIAL DESIGNERS

1. Amy Kwong is designing a bubble gum package. One kind of package will weigh 9 grams, the other 12 grams. The cost of the materials is 1¢ per gram. How much more would one package cost than the other?

2. Juan Gomez is giving advice to a chocolate candy company. He tells them that 750,000 tons of cacao beans are grown in Ghana. The world uses about 1,000,000 tons a year. How many tons come from other countries?

3. Lulu Harris is designing a package for selling miniature sea shells. The longest shell is 2 centimeters long. She will put 17 shells in a package. If she lines them up, what will be the maximum length of the package?

4. Bob Nilak is building a package to hold toy soldiers. Its volume is 180 cubic centimeters. Each soldier needs 3 cubic centimeters of space. How many soldiers will fit in the package?

5. Josh Kaplan is making 250 models of a new package. The cost will be: $650 for paper, $1,200 for plastic, $200 for cellophane, and $1,700 for cardboard. What is the total cost for all 250 models? What is the average cost per model?

SIMPLE CLOSED CURVES AND POLYGONS

When you draw a **simple closed curve,** your pencil will
a) return to the starting point
b) never leave the paper
c) never cross a point twice.

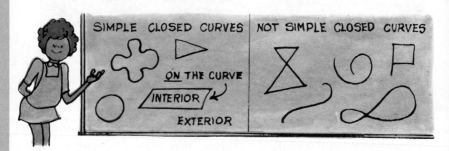

SIMPLE CLOSED CURVES | NOT SIMPLE CLOSED CURVES

ON THE CURVE
INTERIOR
EXTERIOR

Points can be **on** a simple closed curve, in the **interior,** or in the **exterior.**

A simple closed curve is called a **polygon** if it is made of line segments.

1. There are many kinds of polygons.

Number of sides	Name	Number of sides	Name
3	triangle	5	pentagon
4	quadrilateral	6	hexagon

Which of the figures is a triangle? quadrilateral? pentagon? hexagon?

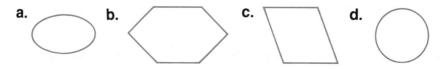

a. b. c. d.

There are several kinds of quadrilaterals.
A **trapezoid** is a quadrilateral with at least one pair of sides parallel.

A **parallelogram** is a quadrilateral with both pairs of opposite sides parallel.

A **rectangle** is a parallelogram whose angles are all right angles.

A **square** is a rectangle all of whose sides have the same measure.

A **rhombus** is a parallelogram all of whose sides have the same measure.

2. a. Figure *WZUT* is a parallelogram. Why?

   b. It is not a rectangle. Why?

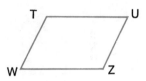

3. a. *QMLE* is a rectangle, a parallelogram and a trapezoid. Why?

   b. It is not a square. Why?

EXERCISES

Use these figures to answer Exercises 1–8.

1. Which of the figures are simple closed curves?

2. Which are polygons?

3. Which are rectangles?

4. Which are parallelograms?

5. Which are squares?

6. Which are trapezoids?

7. Which are pentagons?

8. Which are hexagons?

SLIDES, FLIPS, AND TURNS

There are three basic ways to move figures: **slide, flip,** or **turn.**

slide   *flip*   *turn*

1. In each pair, tell if the first figure will fit on the second figure with a slide.

   a. 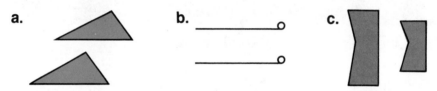 b.   c.

2. In each pair, tell if the first figure will fit on the second one with a flip.

   a. 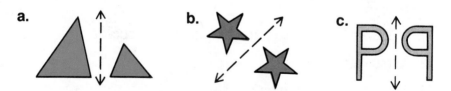 b.   c.

3. Will the first figure fit on the second one with a turn?

   a.  b.   c.

126

4. Make a figure like this one. Cut it out.

a. Trace around the figure on a piece of paper.

b. Turn the figure to a different position and trace it again.

c. Trace two more turns.

Determine whether the first figure will fit on the second one with a slide, a flip, or neither.

1.   **2.**   **3.**   **4.**

5.   **6.**   **7.**   **8.**

9.   **10.**   **11.**   **12.**

Determine whether the first figure will fit on the second one with a flip, a turn, or neither.

13.   **14.**   **15.**   **16.**

17.   **18.**   **19.**   **20.**

21.   **22.**   **23.**   **24.**

127

SYMMETRY

Symmetric figures are all around us.

  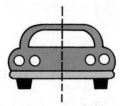

The dotted lines are called **lines of symmetry**. Symmetric figures can be folded on their lines of symmetry so that one part is a flip of the other.

1. Here are some symmetric figures. Where would you put a line of symmetry? Which has more than one line of symmetry?

a.  **b.**  **c.** **d.**

1. Which are symmetric?

a. **b.** **c.**  **d.**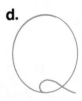

2. Trace each on a piece of paper. Draw as many lines of symmetry as you can.

a. **b.**  **c.** **d.**

128

If one figure can match another figure by a slide, a turn, or a flip, then the figures are **congruent.**

congruent   not congruent

1. Tell which pairs are congruent.

   a.  b.   c.   d.

2. Draw a figure congruent to this. Use tracing paper to help you, if you wish.

Tell which pairs are congruent.

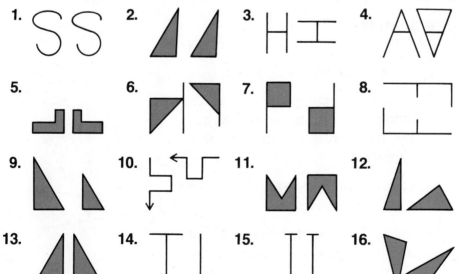

1.   2.   3.   4.

5.   6.   7.   8.

9.   10.   11.   12.

13.   14.   15.   16.

129

COPYING SEGMENTS AND ANGLES

We can copy figures using only a compass and a straightedge. The compass is used to draw circles or parts of circles, called arcs. The straightedge is used to draw line segments.

I LIKE TO USE A COMPASS AND STRAIGHTEDGE.

COPY CAT!

1. Let's copy this segment, $\overline{AB}$.

   a. First use a straightedge to draw a longer segment, $\overline{CD}$.

   b. Put your compass point on A. Spread the compass so that the pencil point is on B.

   c. With this opening, place the compass point on C and draw an arc. Label this point F. $\overline{CF}$ is a copy of $\overline{AB}$.

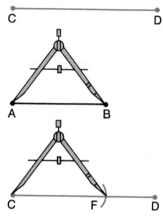

2. Now let's copy an angle.

   a. Draw an angle. Call it $\angle A$.

   b. Draw a ray with endpoint B.

   c. Open your compass to any distance. Draw an arc with A as center, then draw an arc with B as center.

   d. Open your compass to measure the distance shown.

   e. Transfer this distance to your second figure and draw an arc. Complete $\angle B$. $\angle B$ is a copy of $\angle A$.

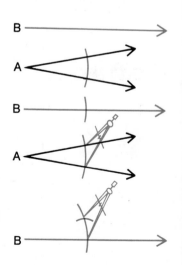

130

1. Copy this 2-inch segment. Check your work with a ruler.

---

2. Copy this 6-centimeter segment. Check your work with a ruler.

---

3. Copy these angles. Check your work with a protractor.

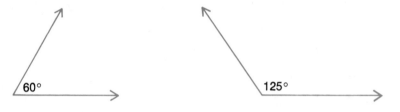

60°   125°

4. Copy the figure at the right.

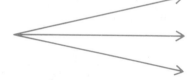

5. Construct a line segment which is twice the length of this segment.

---

6. Construct one segment as long as the sum of the measures of these two segments.

★ **7.** Copy this figure. (Hint: Copy the bottom segment first, then copy the angles at the ends of the segment.)

131

1. To **bisect** a segment or angle means to divide it into two parts of the same size. Here is a flow chart showing how to bisect a segment, $\overline{AB}$.

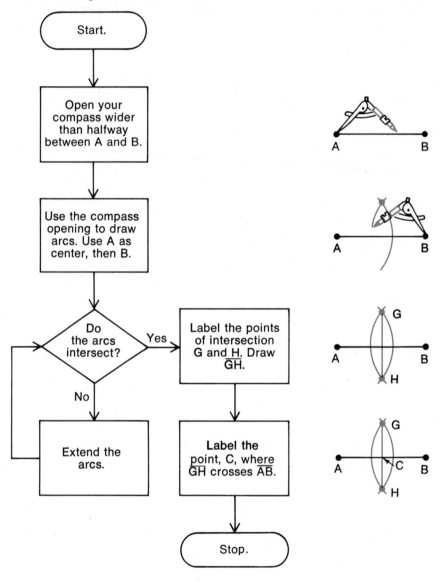

How would you check to make sure $\overline{AB}$ is bisected?

★ 2. Make a flow chart for copying a line segment.

3. Now we'll bisect an angle.

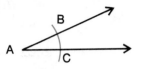

    a. Draw an angle, ∠A. Draw an arc with the center A.

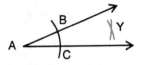

    b. Use B and C as centers to draw these new arcs which cross at Y. Be sure to keep your compass opening the same for making these new arcs.

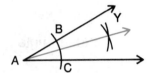

    c. Draw ray $\overrightarrow{AY}$. It bisects ∠BAC.

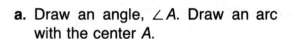

EXERCISES

Draw segments with these measures. Bisect each.

  1. 6 in.   **2.** 10 cm   **3.** 6 cm   **4.** 3 in.

Draw angles with these measures. Bisect each.

  5. 30°   **6.** 90°   **7.** 120°   **8.** 160°

Brainteaser

Copy this pattern of 5 rows of 5 dots each. Make a cross by connecting the dots. You must leave 5 dots remaining inside the cross and 8 dots outside. The cross looks like this.

133

CHAPTER REVIEW

Which are trapezoids? parallelograms? rhombuses? [124]

1. 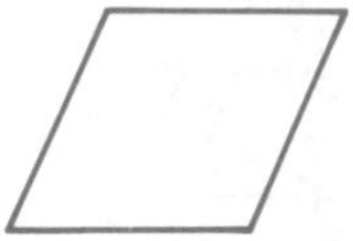 **2.** 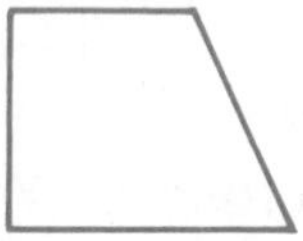 **3.** **4.**

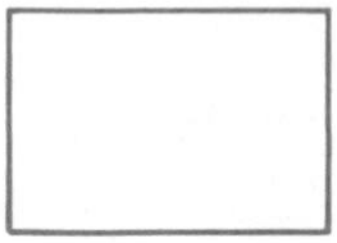

5. Which of the above figures are symmetric? [128]

Find one of each of these in figure *ABCDE*.

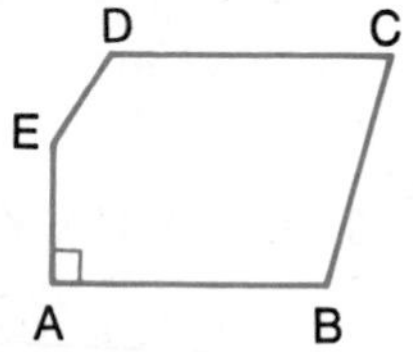

6. obtuse angle   **7.** acute angle

[110]   [110]

8. right angle   **9.** pair of parallel lines

[110]   [118]

10. pair of perpendicular lines

[118]

Use your compass and straightedge.

11. Copy $\overline{XY}$, then bisect it.   X ——————————— Y

[130, 132]

12. Copy ∠ *M*, then bisect it.

[130, 132]

13. With your protractor, measure ∠ *M*.

[114]

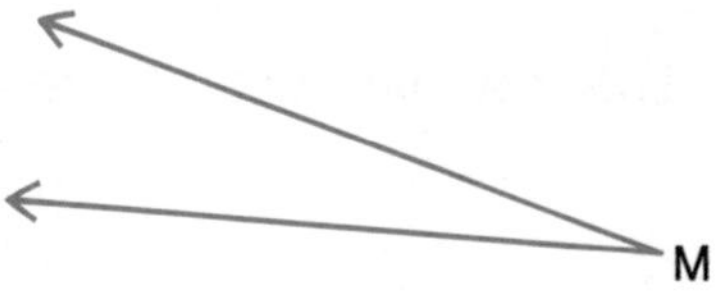

14. Draw an angle that measures 115°.

[114]

Find the measure of the third angle. [120]

15. 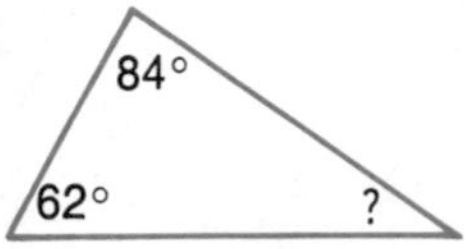   **16.** 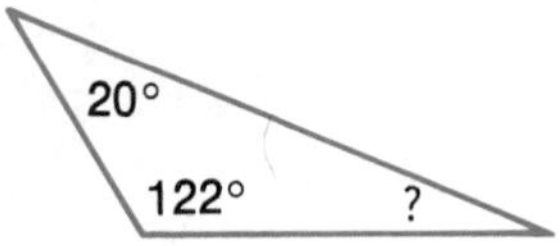   **17.**

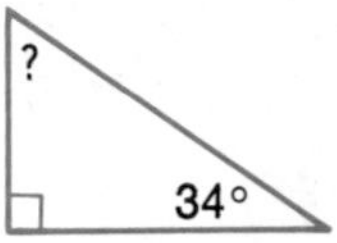

84°   20°

62°   ?   122°   ?   ?   34°

Solve this problem. [123]

18. Mr. Ito is designing a package for 12 pieces of bubble gum. Each piece of gum weighs 2 grams. The package weighs 4 grams. Total weight?

Which pairs are congruent? [129]

19. 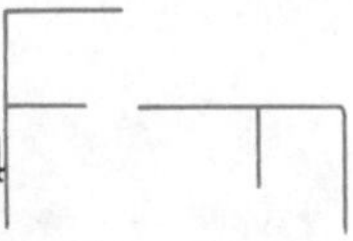   **20.** 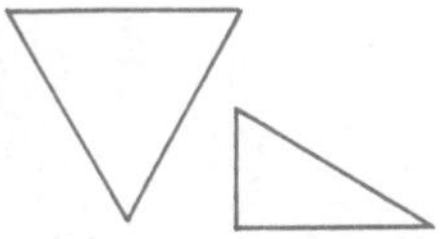   **21.**

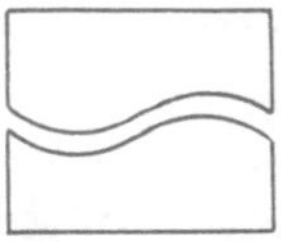

134

CHAPTER TEST

Which are trapezoids? rhombuses? pentagons?

1.   **2.** 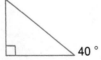   **3.**   **4.**

5. Which of the above figures are symmetric?

Find one of each of these in figure *ABCDE*.

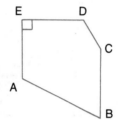

  6. obtuse angle   **7.** acute angle

  8. right angle   **9.** pair of parallel lines

10. pair of perpendicular lines

Use your compass and straightedge.

11. Copy $\overline{AB}$, then bisect it.

12. Copy ∠ *A*, then bisect it.

13. With your protractor, measure ∠ *A*.

14. Draw an angle that measures 120°.

Find the measure of the third angle.

  15.   **16.**

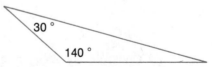

40 °   30 °   140 °

Solve this problem.

17. Mr. Byrne designed a 2-gram package. Each of the dozen balloons in it weighs 1 gram. What is the total weight?

Which pairs are congruent?

    18.    **19.**

135

6 NUMBER THEORY

$$
\begin{array}{r}
13 \\
4\overline{)52} \\
4 \\
\hline
12 \\
12 \\
\hline
0
\end{array}
$$
← remainder 0

$52 = 4 \times 13$

We say that 52 is divisible by 4.

$$
\begin{array}{r}
17 \\
3\overline{)52} \\
3 \\
\hline
22 \\
21 \\
\hline
1
\end{array}
$$
← non-zero remainder

$52 = 3 \times n$

There is no whole number solution. We say that 52 is not divisible by 3.

1. Study these divisions.

$$
\begin{array}{r}
37 \\
2\overline{)74} \\
6 \\
\hline
14 \\
14 \\
\hline
0
\end{array}
\qquad
\begin{array}{r}
14 \\
5\overline{)74} \\
5 \\
\hline
24 \\
20 \\
\hline
4
\end{array}
\qquad
\begin{array}{r}
67 \\
2\overline{)135} \\
12 \\
\hline
15 \\
14 \\
\hline
1
\end{array}
\qquad
\begin{array}{r}
27 \\
5\overline{)135} \\
10 \\
\hline
35 \\
35 \\
\hline
0
\end{array}
$$

a. Is 74 divisible by 2? by 5?

b. Is 135 divisible by 2? by 5?

2. Study these counting numbers.

evens: 2, 4, 6, 8, 10, 12, 14, 16, . . .
odds: 1, 3, 5, 7, 9, 11, 13, 15, . . .

a. Name 5 more even numbers.

136

b. Name 5 more odd numbers.

Counting numbers divisible by 2 are called **even.** Their last digit is a 0, 2, 4, 6, or 8. Counting numbers which are not divisible by 2 are called **odd.**

3. Consider divisibility by 5 and 10.

divisible by 5:   5, 10, 15, 20, 25, 30, . . .
divisible by 10:   10, 20, 30, 40, 50, 60, . . .

a. Name the next five numbers divisible by 5.

b. Name the next five numbers divisible by 10.

The last digit of a number divisible by 5 is a 0, or a 5.
The last digit of a number divisible by 10 is a 0.

EXERCISES

Tell which are divisible by 2, by 5, by 10. Do not divide.

1. 24	**2.** 30	**3.** 35	**4.** 63
5. 902	**6.** 1001	**7.** 400	**8.** 41
9. 805	**10.** 216	**11.** 2,225	**12.** 625
13. 13,578	**14.** 9,770	**15.** 5,559	**16.** 3,100
17. 4,605	**18.** 2,278	**19.** 84,504	**20.** 84,000

★**21.** You have learned that the sum of two whole numbers is a whole number. What about the sum of two even whole numbers? Is it always even? Always odd? Sometimes even and sometimes odd?

★**22.** What happens when both numbers are odd?

★**23.** What happens when one number is odd and the other even?

Number	15	20	36	37	48	339	999
Sum of Digits	6	2	9	10	12	15	27
Divisible by 3?	yes	no	yes	no	yes	yes	yes
Divisible by 9?	no	no	yes	no	no	no	yes

A counting number is divisible by 3 if the sum of the digits is divisible by 3.
A counting number is divisible by 9 if the sum of the digits is divisible by 9.

1. Tell which are divisible by 3.

Examples   431   5,322

$4 + 3 + 1 = 8$ $5 + 3 + 2 + 2 = 12$

not divisible by 3, so 431 is not divisible by 3.   divisible by 3, so 5,322 is divisible by 3.

     a. 329   **b.** 2,952   **c.** 48,201

2. Tell which are divisible by 9.

     a. 656   **b.** 9,297   **c.** 43,155

EXERCISES

Tell which are divisible by 3, and which by 9.

1. 303	**2.** 112	**3.** 450	**4.** 540
5. 405	**6.** 900	**7.** 738	**8.** 585
9. 9,486	**10.** 4,886	**11.** 5,556	**12.** 7,423
13. 56,322	**14.** 88,884	**15.** 17,259	**16.** 9,981
17. 7,851	**18.** 4,209	**19.** 106,523	**20.** 106,524

Mini-problems show all the information we need in a very brief way. Let's write mini-problems for long problems.

Sally wanted to visit her grandfather in Florida. She earned $87 in June, $91 in July, and only $39 in August because she got sick. What were her total earnings?

Mini-problem: Earned $87 in June.
　　　　　　　　Earned $91 in July.
　　　　　　　　Earned $39 in August.
　　　　　　　　Total earned?

Solve:　　87 + 91 + 39 = 217
Answer:　　$217

Write a mini-problem for each. Solve.

1. Sally took a plane to Atlanta, an air distance of 1,436 kilometers. In Atlanta she boarded a new plane to Tallahassee, a distance of 381 kilometers. What was the total distance Sally covered by plane?

2. Sally took her grandfather to dinner. Sally had a roast beef dinner for $5.95. Her grandfather had a turkey dinner for $5.45. How much change did Sally get from a $20 bill?

3. Sally bought 10 postcards. They cost 25 cents each. She also bought a 50-cent jumbo postcard. How much did the postcards cost?

4. Sally's mother gave her $100 to add to the $217 she earned. By being careful, she spent only $290. How much did she have left?

139

FACTORS

$$12 = 2 \times 6$$

We call 2 and 6 **factors** of 12.

Let's find all pairs of factors of 12. We start with 1.

1?	2?	3?	4?	5?	6?	7?	8?	9?	10?	11?	12?
yes	yes	yes	yes	no	yes	no	no	no	no	no	yes

All the factors of 12 are 1, 2, 3, 4, 6, and 12.

1. Find all the factors of 28.

1? 2? 3? 4? 5? 6? 7? 8? . . . 28?

2. Find all the factors of each.

a. 18 **b.** 19 **c.** 20 **d.** 24 **e.** 16

3. Some numbers have exactly two factors. Which have only two factors?

a. 1 **b.** 2 **c.** 3 **d.** 4 **e.** 9

A counting number which has exactly two factors is a **prime** number. Any counting number which has more than two factors is a **composite** number.

The number 1 is special. It is neither prime nor composite.

4. Prime or composite?

a. 14 **b.** 15 **c.** 7 **d.** 17 **e.** 16

140

Find all the factors.

1. 21   **2.** 23   **3.** 24   **4.** 25   **5.** 27

6. 29   **7.** 16   **8.** 10   **9.** 20   **10.** 26

11. 19   **12.** 13   **13.** 18   **14.** 28   **15.** 30

16. 40   **17.** 41   **18.** 81   **19.** 83   **20.** 90

21. 91   **22.** 97   **23.** 45   **24.** 36   **25.** 100

Solve.

26. Which numbers in Exercises 1–25 are prime? Which are composite?

27. List the prime numbers from 1–20.

Brainteaser

Here's a test for divisibility by 11. A number is divisible by 11 if the difference between the sums of the 1st, 3rd, 5th, etc. digits and the 2nd, 4th, 6th, etc., digits is divisible by 11.

3,278 — sum: 10
3,278 — sum: 10
$10 - 10 = 0$
3,278 divisible by 11

90,970 — sum: 18
90,970 — sum: 7
$18 - 7 = 11$
90,970 divisible by 11

4,876 — sum: 14
4,876 — sum: 11
$14 - 11 = 3$
4,876 not divisible by 11

Check for divisibility by 11.

1. 7,777   **2.** 912,395   **3.** 823,251

PRIME FACTORIZATIONS

There are many ways to factor a number.

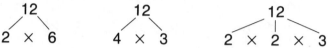

When every factor is prime, we have the **prime factorization.**
Prime factorization of 12: 2 × 2 × 3

1. Which is the prime factorization of 18?

   a. 2 × 9   **b.** 3 × 6   **c.** 2 × 3 × 3

2. Which is the prime factorization of 24?

   a. 2 × 12   **b.** 2 × 2 × 2 × 3   **c.** 2 × 2 × 6

3. Drawing a **factor tree** helps to find the prime factorization. No matter how you start to factor, you should always end up with the prime factorization.

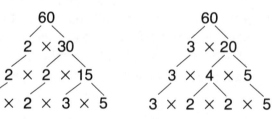

   Complete these factor trees.

   a.

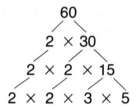

   b.

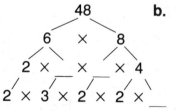

4. Draw factor trees to find prime factorizations.

   a. 36   **b.** 32   **c.** 40

142

Which are prime factorizations?

1. $3 \times 5 \times 5$ **2.** $2 \times 5 \times 7$ **3.** $3 \times 3 \times 4$

4. $2 \times 3 \times 6$ **5.** $3 \times 3 \times 7$ **6.** $2 \times 2 \times 9$

Find the missing factors.

7. $27 = 3 \times 3 \times n$ **8.** $44 = 2 \times 2 \times n$

9. $25 = 5 \times n$ **10.** $26 = 2 \times n$

11. $16 = 2 \times 2 \times 2 \times n$ **12.** $40 = n \times 2 \times 2 \times 2$

13. $21 = n \times 3$ **14.** $32 = 2 \times 2 \times 2 \times n \times 2$

15. $45 = n \times 3 \times 3$ **16.** $49 = 7 \times n$

17. $55 = n \times 5$ **18.** $54 = n \times 3 \times 3 \times 3$

Complete these factor trees.

19. 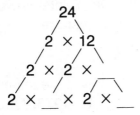   **20.**

21. 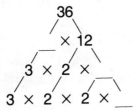   **22.**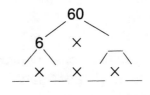

Draw factor trees to find prime factorizations.

23. 20   **24.** 66   **25.** 72   **26.** 96   **27.** 84

★ **28.** Make a flow chart to show how to make a factor tree.

143

SOCIAL WORKERS

Solve these problems.

1. Mercedes Díaz is a social worker. She is in charge of giving out a Social Security payment of $476 over 3 months. She knows a divisibility test that will tell her whether the payments can be the same each month. Can they? How does she know?

2. Ms. Díaz has 12 hours in which to hold 7 interviews. She knows that the interviews will take an average of 2 hours each. Does she have enough time?

3. Bob Plymouth had to find out whether two senior citizens were old enough to get special help in 1978. One was born in 1896, the other in 1897. How old were they in 1978?

4. If eligible, one senior citizen could get 11 bus tickets that cost 24¢ each. What is the total value of these tickets?

5. Sue O'Dwyer is in charge of collecting funds for a community activity. One day she received 2 checks for $10 each, 1 check for $15, and 3 checks for $5 each. What was the total amount of money collected?

COMMON FACTORS

Factors of 12: **1, 2, 3,** 4, **6,** 12
Factors of 18: **1, 2, 3, 6,** 9, 18
Common factors of 12 and 18: **1, 2, 3, 6**

1. Factors of 15: 1, 3, 5, 15
   Factors of 21: 1, 3, 7, 21

   Give the common factors of 15 and 21.

2. Let's find the common factors of 32 and 20.

   a. List all the factors of 32.

   b. List all the factors of 20.

   c. Give the common factors of 32 and 20.

EXERCISES

Consider these sets of factors.

10: 1, 2, 5, 10   24: 1, 2, 3, 4, 6, 8, 12, 24
 8: 1, 2, 4, 8   30: 1, 2, 3, 5, 6, 10, 15, 30

Find the common factors of each pair.

1. 10 and 8   2. 10 and 24   3. 10 and 30

4. 8 and 24   5. 8 and 30   6. 24 and 30

Find the common factors of each pair.

7. 12 and 20   8. 18 and 20   9. 6 and 16

10. 18 and 32   11. 12 and 15   12. 18 and 15

13. 45 and 6   14. 28 and 6   15. 45 and 16

16. 42 and 45   17. 28 and 42   18. 12 and 32

145

GREATEST COMMON FACTOR

Factors of 16:   1, 2, 4, 8, 16
Factors of 24:   1, 2, 3, 4, 6, 8, 12, 24
Common factors of 16 and 24:   1, 2, 4, 8
The **greatest common factor (GCF)** of
16 and 24 is 8.

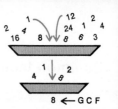

1. The common factors of 8 and 10 are 1 and 2. What is the greatest common factor?

2. Factors of 24:   1, 2, 3, 4, 6, 8, 12, 24
   Factors of 30:   1, 2, 3, 5, 6, 10, 15, 30

   a. What are their common factors?

   b. What is their GCF?

3. Here is a quick way to find the GCF of 8 and 28.

   a. List the factors of the smaller number, 8.

   b. What is its largest factor?

   c. Is 28 divisible by that factor?

   d. What is the second largest factor?

   e. Is 28 divisible by the second largest factor?
   Therefore, 4 is the GCF of 8 and 28.

EXERCISES

Study these sets of factors.

6:	1, 2, 3, 6	9:	1, 3, 9
8:	1, 2, 4, 8	12:	1, 2, 3, 4, 6, 12

Find the greatest common factor of each pair.

1. 6 and 9   **2.** 6 and 8   **3.** 6 and 12

4. 9 and 8   **5.** 9 and 12   **6.** 8 and 12

146

Find the greatest common factor of each pair.

7. 10 and 6   **8.** 6 and 12   **9.** 8 and 12

10. 8 and 24   **11.** 7 and 10   **12.** 2 and 8

13. 2 and 9   **14.** 3 and 9   **15.** 4 and 10

16. 2 and 12   **17.** 4 and 12   **18.** 18 and 30

19. 12 and 18   **20.** 15 and 25   **21.** 30 and 12

22. 21 and 30   **23.** 28 and 21   **24.** 16 and 28

25. 32 and 12   **26.** 18 and 24   **27.** 14 and 28

28. 9 and 24   **29.** 49 and 14   **30.** 40 and 10

31. 22 and 11   **32.** 36 and 8   **33.** 19 and 6

34. 48 and 12   **35.** 35 and 42   **36.** 42 and 14

★ When the greatest common factor of two numbers is 1, we say the numbers are **relatively prime.** Which are relatively prime?

37. 6 and 9   **38.** 5 and 9   **39.** 20 and 21

Write standard numerals.

1. three million, four hundred seventy-one thousand, two hundred fifty-six

2. forty billion, six hundred twenty-five million, eight hundred ninety-one thousand, forty-three

3. twenty-six million, four hundred seven thousand, six hundred eighty

Keeping Fit

Multiply.

| 1. | 7
× 3 | 2. | 6
× 4 | 3. | 7
× 8 |

| 4. | 9
× 5 | 5. | 6
× 7 | 6. | 8
× 6 |

| 7. | 7
× 9 | 8. | 9
× 8 | 9. | 9
× 6 |

| 10. | 40
× 3 | 11. | 500
× 9 | 12. | 6,000
× 8 |

| 13. | 73
× 4 | 14. | 806
× 7 | 15. | 9,852
× 6 |

| 16. | 47
× 30 | 17. | 346
× 60 | 18. | 524
× 20 |

| 19. | 58
× 26 | 20. | 746
× 37 | 21. | 6,703
× 78 |

| 22. | $8.25
× 3 | 23. | $17.98
× 2 | 24. | $21.34
× 86 |

Divide.

25. $24 \div 3$ 26. $36 \div 6$ 27. $36 \div 9$

28. $18 \div 3$ 29. $35 \div 5$ 30. $32 \div 4$

31. $49 \div 7$ 32. $18 \div 2$ 33. $20 \div 4$

34. $42 \div 6$ 35. $40 \div 5$ 36. $48 \div 8$

37. $2\overline{)174}$ 38. $3\overline{)2,361}$ 39. $4\overline{)35,754}$

40. $21\overline{)1,122}$ 41. $37\overline{)19,462}$ 42. $52\overline{)31,569}$

43. $6\overline{)\$7.32}$ 44. $9\overline{)\$23.85}$ 45. $41\overline{)\$192.70}$

148

COMMON MULTIPLES

$1 \times 4 = 4$ $2 \times 4 = 8$ $3 \times 4 = 12$

multiples of 4

All multiples of 4:   4, 8, 12, 16, 20, 24, 28, 32, 36, . . .
All multiples of 6:   6, 12, 18, 24, 30, 36, 42, . . .
Common multiples of 4 and 6:   12, 24, 36, . . .

1. Multiples of 2:   2, 4, 6, 8, 10, 12, 14, 16, 18, 20, . . .
   Multiples of 8:   8, 16, 24, 32, . . .
   Multiples of 10:   10, 20, 30, 40, 50, . . .

   Find the common multiples of each.

   a. 2 and 8   **b.** 2 and 10   **c.** 8 and 10

2. Find the common multiples of these.

   a. 2 and 7   **b.** 6 and 12   **c.** 4 and 10

EXERCISES

Find the first three common multiples of each pair.

1. 3 and 5   **2.** 3 and 6   **3.** 3 and 10

4. 5 and 6   **5.** 5 and 10   **6.** 6 and 10

7. 2 and 3   **8.** 2 and 5   **9.** 2 and 4

10. 2 and 6   **11.** 2 and 12   **12.** 3 and 4

13. 3 and 8   **14.** 3 and 9   **15.** 4 and 5

16. 4 and 8   **17.** 6 and 8   **18.** 6 and 9

★ **19.** Make a flow chart to show how to find the common multiples of two numbers.

LEAST COMMON MULTIPLES

Multiples of 6: 6, 12, 18, 24, 30, 36, 42, . . .
Multiples of 9: 9, 18, 27, 36, 45, . . .
Common multiples of 6 and 9: 18, 36, . . .
The **least common multiple (LCM)** of 6 and 9 is 18.

1. The common multiples of 2 and 5 are 10, 20, 30, 40, . . . What is the least common multiple?

2. The multiples of 4 are 4, 8, 12, 16, . . . The multiples of 6 are 6, 12, 18, 24, . . .
What is the LCM?

3. Here is a short cut to find the LCM of 4 and 6.

   (1) Start with the larger number, 6.
   (2) Think of its multiples: 6, 12, 18, 24, . . .
   (3) From these, find the smallest one which is a multiple of 4. Is it 6? (no) Is it 12? (yes) 12 is the LCM.

   Find the LCM of each pair.

   a. 5 and 7   **b.** 6 and 12   **c.** 3 and 9

   d. 3 and 4   **e.** 6 and 10   **f.** 8 and 12

EXERCISES

Consider these sets of multiples.

   3:   3, 6, 9, 12, 15, 18, . . .   5:   5, 10, 15, 20, 25, 30, . . .
   6:   6, 12, 18, 24, 30, . . .   10:   10, 20, 30, 40, 50, . . .

Find the least common multiple of each pair.

   1. 3 and 5   **2.** 3 and 6   **3.** 3 and 10

   4. 5 and 6   **5.** 5 and 10   **6.** 6 and 10

Find the least common multiple of each pair.

7. 3 and 8 **8.** 3 and 12 **9.** 4 and 5

10. 4 and 8 **11.** 4 and 9 **12.** 4 and 10

13. 5 and 8 **14.** 5 and 9 **15.** 6 and 8

16. 6 and 12 **17.** 6 and 7 **18.** 7 and 8

19. 7 and 9 **20.** 6 and 5 **21.** 7 and 5

22. 7 and 10 **23.** 4 and 6 **24.** 7 and 4

25. 7 and 3 **26.** 7 and 12 **27.** 8 and 9

28. 8 and 10 **29.** 8 and 12 **30.** 12 and 10

31. 12 and 9 **32.** 5 and 11 **33.** 12 and 18

Brainteaser

Here's a number trick you can play on your friends.

1. Ask a friend to put 24 paper clips (or any other object) in his hand.

2. Next have him put any number of the paper clips from 5 to 10 in his pocket.

3. Have him find the sum of the digits for the number of paper clips he has left. Whatever the sum is, have him put that many more clips in his pocket.

4. Now keep your eyes closed and have him hide any number of clips from the pile left in his hand.

5. Have him show you how many are left. You can just glance at the number he has left and tell him how many he hid.

Can you do the trick? Hint: Subtract the number left from 9; that will tell the number he hid.

151

CHAPTER REVIEW

Use the divisibility test to tell which of the following numbers are divisible by 2, by 3, by 5, by 9, by 10. [136, 138]

1. 78   **2.** 285   **3.** 459   **4.** 33,335   **5.** 95,956

Find all the factors of each number. [140]

6. 21   **7.** 24   **8.** 50   **9.** 73   **10.** 49

Which are prime numbers? Which are composite? [140]

11. 23   **12.** 25   **13.** 41   **14.** 83   **15.** 91

Find the prime factorizations of each number. [142]

16. 60   **17.** 210   **18.** 242

Find the common factors of each pair. [145]

19. 6 and 12   **20.** 6 and 21   **21.** 18 and 24

Find the greatest common factor of each pair. [146]

22. 9 and 18   **23.** 7 and 11   **24.** 9 and 12

25. 15 and 25   **26.** 30 and 12   **27.** 4 and 10

Find the first three common multiples of each pair. [149]

28. 8 and 12   **29.** 3 and 9   **30.** 6 and 10

Find the least common multiple of each pair. [150]

31. 6 and 8   **32.** 4 and 5   **33.** 8 and 14

34. 4 and 9   **35.** 5 and 11   **36.** 12 and 18

Solve this problem. [144]

37. Paul Peugout, a social worker, bought office supplies. He got 10 pencils for 15¢ each, stationery for $5.98, and a desk calendar for $9.95. What was the total cost?

CHAPTER TEST

Consider 24,630. Tell if it is divisible by each of the following numbers.

1. by 2   **2.** by 3   **3.** by 5   **4.** by 9   **5.** by 10

Find all the factors of each number.

6. 12   **7.** 23   **8.** 37   **9.** 42   **10.** 60

Which are prime numbers? Which are composite?

11. 5   **12.** 13   **13.** 24   **14.** 11   **15.** 7

Find the prime factorizations of each number.

16. 70   **17.** 90   **18.** 36

Find the common factors of each pair.

19. 8 and 12   **20.** 7 and 9

Find the greatest common factor of each pair.

21. 12 and 18   **22.** 14 and 28

Find the first three common multiples of each pair.

23. 3 and 5   **24.** 6 and 8

Find the least common multiple of each pair.

25. 8 and 12   **26.** 6 and 10

Solve this problem.

27. Joanne Volvo helped a family whose home burned down. She was able to get them money for a motel room and transportation. The motel cost $14 a night for 12 nights. The transportation cost $5. How much money did Miss Volvo get for the family?

7 FRACTIONS

MEANING OF FRACTIONS

Fractions can be used to measure lengths, areas, volume, and parts of sets.

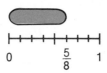

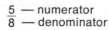

0     $\frac{5}{8}$ 1

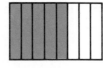

$\frac{5}{8}$ — numerator
$\frac{5}{8}$ — denominator

$\frac{5}{8}$ full

---

1. This box is $\frac{7}{10}$ of a meter long.
What is the numerator in $\frac{7}{10}$?
What is the denominator?

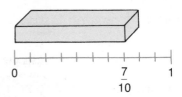

0        $\frac{7}{10}$ 1

2. What part is shaded?

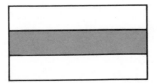

3. What part of the set is knocked down?

What part of the region is shaded?

1.   **2.**   **3.**   **4.**

What part of the set is shaded?

5.    **6.**    **7.**

154

EQUIVALENT FRACTIONAL NUMERALS

A school yard is divided into three congruent play areas.

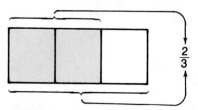 $\frac{2}{3}$

$\frac{2}{3}$ of the yard is painted.

Then it was divided into twice as many areas.

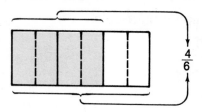 $\frac{4}{6}$

$\frac{4}{6}$ of the yard is painted.

$$\frac{2}{3} = \frac{2 \times 2}{3 \times 2} = \frac{4}{6}.$$

$\frac{2}{3}$ and $\frac{4}{6}$ are **equivalent fractional numerals.**

1. **a.** What fraction of this yard is painted?

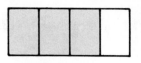

   b. The yard is now divided into twice as many parts. What fraction is painted?

   c. Complete: $\frac{3}{4} = \frac{\triangle}{8}$.

2. A fraction has many names. What is the next name for $\frac{3}{4}$?

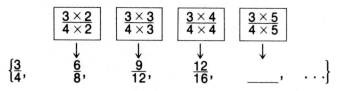

$$\left\{ \frac{3}{4}, \quad \boxed{\frac{3 \times 2}{4 \times 2}} \downarrow \frac{6}{8}, \quad \boxed{\frac{3 \times 3}{4 \times 3}} \downarrow \frac{9}{12}, \quad \boxed{\frac{3 \times 4}{4 \times 4}} \downarrow \frac{12}{16}, \quad \boxed{\frac{3 \times 5}{4 \times 5}} \downarrow \underline{\quad}, \quad \ldots \right\}$$

155

3. Let's find the name for $\frac{3}{4}$ with the denominator 24.

	Think:	Answer:
$\frac{3}{4} = \frac{\square}{24}$	$\begin{array}{l} 4 \times ? = 24 \\ 4 \times 6 = 24 \end{array}$ so $\frac{3}{4} = \frac{3 \times 6}{4 \times 6}$	$\frac{3}{4} = \frac{18}{24}$

Solve.

a. $\frac{2}{3} = \frac{\square}{15}$ 　　　　**b.** $\frac{2}{5} = \frac{\square}{15}$ 　　　　**c.** $\frac{3}{7} = \frac{6}{\square}$

EXERCISES

Give the next three equivalent fractional numerals.

1. $\frac{1}{3}, \frac{2}{6}, \frac{3}{9}, \cdots$ 　　　　**2.** $\frac{3}{8}, \frac{6}{16}, \cdots$ 　　　　**3.** $\frac{5}{6}, \frac{10}{12}, \cdots$

4. $\frac{4}{5}, \frac{8}{10}, \frac{12}{15}, \cdots$ 　　**5.** $\frac{2}{3}, \frac{4}{6}, \cdots$ 　　　**6.** $\frac{1}{4}, \frac{2}{8}, \cdots$

List the next four equivalent fractional numerals for each.

7. $\frac{1}{5}$ 　　**8.** $\frac{2}{7}$ 　　**9.** $\frac{5}{8}$ 　　**10.** $\frac{1}{6}$ 　　**11.** $\frac{4}{5}$

Solve.

12. $\frac{1}{2} = \frac{\square}{8}$ 　　**13.** $\frac{2}{5} = \frac{\square}{10}$ 　　**14.** $\frac{2}{9} = \frac{\square}{27}$ 　　**15.** $\frac{1}{4} = \frac{\square}{28}$

16. $\frac{5}{6} = \frac{\square}{24}$ 　　**17.** $\frac{1}{9} = \frac{\square}{81}$ 　　**18.** $\frac{7}{8} = \frac{\square}{32}$ 　　**19.** $\frac{4}{5} = \frac{\square}{40}$

20. $\frac{1}{5} = \frac{\square}{30}$ 　　**21.** $\frac{7}{8} = \frac{\square}{24}$ 　　**22.** $\frac{2}{3} = \frac{\square}{12}$ 　　**23.** $\frac{3}{4} = \frac{\square}{12}$

24. $\frac{4}{5} = \frac{\square}{25}$ 　　**25.** $\frac{3}{7} = \frac{\square}{28}$ 　　**26.** $\frac{8}{9} = \frac{\square}{36}$ 　　**27.** $\frac{5}{7} = \frac{\square}{14}$

28. $\frac{3}{5} = \frac{\square}{30}$ 　　**29.** $\frac{2}{5} = \frac{\square}{35}$ 　　**30.** $\frac{3}{8} = \frac{\square}{24}$ 　　**31.** $\frac{1}{10} = \frac{\square}{50}$

32. $\frac{1}{2} = \frac{4}{\square}$ 　　**33.** $\frac{2}{3} = \frac{12}{\square}$ 　　**34.** $\frac{1}{3} = \frac{9}{\square}$ 　　**35.** $\frac{4}{7} = \frac{28}{\square}$

Consider 2 pies cut into halves or into thirds.

$$2 = \frac{4}{2} = \frac{6}{3}$$

Think of 2 as $\frac{2}{1}$. Then the following is true.

$$2 = \frac{2 \times 2}{1 \times 2} \qquad\qquad 2 = \frac{2 \times 3}{1 \times 3}$$

$$= \frac{4}{2} \qquad\qquad\qquad = \frac{6}{3}$$

So we know $2 = \frac{4}{2} = \frac{6}{3} = \frac{8}{4} = \frac{10}{5} = \ldots$

1. Find the next four fractional numerals equivalent to 8.

$$8 = \frac{8}{1} = \frac{16}{2} = \underline{\qquad} = \underline{\qquad} = \underline{\qquad} = \underline{\qquad}$$

2. We can find fractional numerals equivalent to 1.

$$1 = \frac{1}{1} = \frac{2}{2} = \frac{3}{3} = \frac{4}{4} = \frac{5}{5} = \ldots$$

Find the next four fractional names for 1.

EXERCISES

Find the next four equivalent fractional numerals.

1. $5 = \frac{5}{1} = \frac{10}{2} = \ldots$ **2.** $9 = \frac{9}{1} = \ldots$ **3.** $10 = \frac{10}{1} = \ldots$

4. $12 = \frac{12}{1} = \ldots$ **5.** $4 = \frac{4}{1} = \ldots$ **6.** $7 = \frac{7}{1} = \ldots$

Find the fractional numeral equivalent to 6 with the following denominators.

7. 2   **8.** 3   **9.** 5   **10.** 7   **11.** 10

Compare these shaded regions.

We can see from the drawings that

$$\frac{2}{5} < \frac{3}{5}.$$

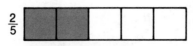

Let's compare two fractions whose denominators are not the same.

Compare	Write equivalent fractional numerals with common denominator.	Compare
$\frac{3}{5} \equiv \frac{2}{3}$	$\frac{3}{5} = \frac{9}{15}$ $\frac{2}{3} = \frac{10}{15}$	$\frac{9}{15} < \frac{10}{15}$ so $\frac{3}{5} < \frac{2}{3}$

1. Compare. Use > or <.

   a. $\frac{2}{5} \equiv \frac{7}{5}$

   b. $\frac{5}{9} \equiv \frac{2}{9}$

   c. $\frac{4}{5} \equiv \frac{3}{5}$

2. Let's compare $\frac{3}{5}$ and $\frac{4}{7}$.

   a. The LCM of the denominators 5 and 7 is 35. This is called the **least common denominator.**

   b. Now we find equivalent fractional numerals with the same denominator. Complete.

   $$\frac{3}{5} = \frac{\square}{35} \qquad \frac{4}{7} = \frac{\triangle}{35}$$

   c. Compare. Use > or <: $\frac{3}{5} \equiv \frac{4}{7}$.

3. Compare. Write > or <.

   a. $\frac{2}{6} \equiv \frac{2}{3}$

   b. $\frac{2}{9} \equiv \frac{2}{5}$

   c. $\frac{2}{3} \equiv \frac{1}{5}$

   d. $\frac{3}{7} \equiv \frac{5}{9}$

   e. $\frac{1}{4} \equiv \frac{1}{3}$

   f. $\frac{5}{6} \equiv \frac{7}{8}$

4. Let's consider pairs of fractions which have the same numerator, like $\frac{1}{4}$ and $\frac{1}{3}$.

a. Into how many equal pieces is the first bar divided?

b. Into how many equal pieces is the second bar divided?

c. Which piece is bigger, $\frac{1}{4}$ or $\frac{1}{3}$?

5. Compare. Draw pictures if you wish.

a. $\frac{1}{6} \equiv \frac{1}{4}$ b. $\frac{1}{5} \equiv \frac{1}{9}$ c. $\frac{2}{3} \equiv \frac{2}{5}$

Compare.

1. $\frac{2}{10} \equiv \frac{7}{10}$ 2. $\frac{11}{11} \equiv \frac{7}{11}$ 3. $\frac{1}{3} \equiv \frac{3}{5}$ 4. $\frac{4}{7} \equiv \frac{3}{7}$

5. $\frac{5}{8} \equiv \frac{3}{8}$ 6. $\frac{3}{5} \equiv \frac{7}{8}$ 7. $\frac{5}{10} \equiv \frac{3}{5}$ 8. $\frac{4}{8} \equiv \frac{2}{9}$

9. $\frac{4}{7} \equiv \frac{5}{8}$ 10. $\frac{2}{3} \equiv \frac{3}{4}$ 11. $\frac{3}{9} \equiv \frac{1}{5}$ 12. $\frac{7}{8} \equiv \frac{5}{9}$

13. $\frac{7}{8} \equiv \frac{3}{4}$ 14. $\frac{9}{10} \equiv \frac{3}{5}$ 15. $\frac{4}{9} \equiv \frac{2}{3}$ 16. $\frac{5}{7} \equiv \frac{4}{5}$

17. $\frac{3}{8} \equiv \frac{4}{9}$ 18. $\frac{2}{9} \equiv \frac{4}{5}$ 19. $\frac{1}{7} \equiv \frac{1}{8}$ 20. $\frac{1}{5} \equiv \frac{1}{10}$

Solve these problems.

21. Sue ate $\frac{3}{8}$ of a pie. Jenny ate $\frac{1}{4}$ of the same pie. Who ate more?

22. Jeff walked $\frac{3}{10}$ mile. Jane walked $\frac{1}{2}$ mile. Who walked farther?

159

CHECKING FOR EQUIVALENCE

We can check for equivalence by finding common denominators and comparing.

Compare: $\frac{2}{6}$ and $\frac{3}{9}$

$$\frac{2}{6} = \frac{18}{54} \qquad \frac{3}{9} = \frac{18}{54}$$

equivalent

Here's a quick way! We call it **cross multiplication.**

$$\frac{2}{6} \diagdown \frac{3}{9}$$

$3 \times 6 = 18 \qquad 2 \times 9 = 18$

checks!

so, $\frac{2}{6} = \frac{3}{9}$

---

1. Let's check to see if $\frac{2}{4}$ and $\frac{5}{10}$ are equivalent.

   a. Use cross multiplication.

   $4 \times 5 = $ _____ $\qquad 2 \times 10 = $ _____ $\qquad \frac{2}{4} \diagdown \frac{5}{10}$

   b. Are $\frac{2}{4}$ and $\frac{5}{10}$ equivalent?

2. When two numerals are not equivalent, we use a $\neq$ sign.

   $$\frac{1}{2} \neq \frac{1}{3}$$

   read: is not equal to

   Check for equivalence. Use $=$ or $\neq$.

   a. $\frac{2}{8} \equiv \frac{3}{12}$ $\qquad$ **b.** $\frac{4}{6} \equiv \frac{6}{9}$ $\qquad$ **c.** $\frac{6}{8} \equiv \frac{7}{10}$

EXERCISES

Check for equivalence. Use $=$ or $\neq$.

1. $\frac{3}{6} \equiv \frac{5}{10}$ $\qquad$ **2.** $\frac{3}{6} \equiv \frac{2}{8}$ $\qquad$ **3.** $\frac{3}{9} \equiv \frac{5}{20}$ $\qquad$ **4.** $\frac{2}{3} \equiv \frac{6}{8}$

5. $\frac{2}{4} \equiv \frac{3}{9}$ $\qquad$ **6.** $\frac{6}{9} \equiv \frac{8}{12}$ $\qquad$ **7.** $\frac{4}{8} \equiv \frac{3}{6}$ $\qquad$ **8.** $\frac{3}{9} \equiv \frac{4}{10}$

9. $\frac{2}{3} \equiv \frac{4}{8}$ $\qquad$ **10.** $\frac{1}{4} \equiv \frac{4}{16}$ $\qquad$ **11.** $\frac{6}{9} \equiv \frac{2}{6}$ $\qquad$ **12.** $\frac{4}{5} \equiv \frac{8}{10}$

160

JEWELRY

1. Purest gold is 24 carats. Peggy's ring is 18-carat gold. This means it has 18 parts pure gold, while the rest is other metals. What part of Peggy's ring is pure gold?

2. What part is gold in a 14-carat ring?

3. White gold is 12 carats gold and 12 carats silver. What part of white gold is gold?

4. Alice's ring is $\frac{2}{3}$ pure gold. Fran's ring is $\frac{5}{8}$ pure gold. Which ring has the purer gold?

5. Chris has earrings which are $\frac{19}{24}$ pure gold. How many carats is this?

6. Miguel's watch loses 1 minute every 3 hours. What fraction of a minute would it lose in 1 hour?

7. Susan's watch loses $\frac{2}{3}$ minute in 1 hour. Lynda's watch loses $\frac{3}{4}$ minute in 1 hour. Whose watch is losing more time in each hour?

8. Bob's watch gains $\frac{1}{2}$ minute each hour. Tamu's watch loses $\frac{1}{3}$ minute each hour. If both watches are correct at 12 noon, which watch will be farthest from correct later in the afternoon?

This flow chart shows one way to simplify a fractional numeral.

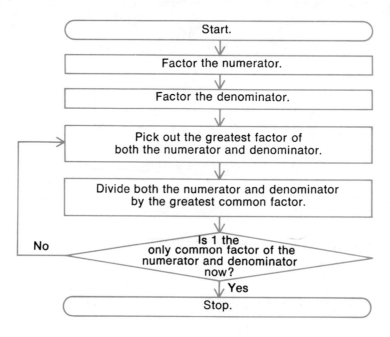

A fractional numeral is in **simplest form** if the greatest common factor of the numerator and denominator is 1.

1. Use the flow chart above to help you simplify $\frac{12}{16}$.

   a. What are the factors of the numerator?

   b. What are the factors of the denominator?

   c. What is the greatest common factor of both the numerator and denominator?

   d. Divide both the numerator and denominator by the GCF. What are the quotients?

   e. Is the fraction in simplest form now? Why?

2. Simplify the fractional numeral $\frac{20}{24}$.

Simplify.

1. $\frac{4}{8}$ 2. $\frac{6}{10}$ 3. $\frac{4}{12}$ 4. $\frac{8}{12}$ 5. $\frac{6}{8}$

6. $\frac{10}{12}$ 7. $\frac{10}{15}$ 8. $\frac{12}{15}$ 9. $\frac{10}{18}$ 10. $\frac{6}{15}$

11. $\frac{12}{14}$ 12. $\frac{16}{18}$ 13. $\frac{16}{20}$ 14. $\frac{12}{32}$ 15. $\frac{24}{36}$

16. $\frac{16}{24}$ 17. $\frac{18}{27}$ 18. $\frac{15}{45}$ 19. $\frac{27}{36}$ 20. $\frac{18}{21}$

21. $\frac{30}{50}$ 22. $\frac{42}{56}$ 23. $\frac{45}{55}$ 24. $\frac{40}{64}$ 25. $\frac{49}{56}$

26. $\frac{25}{40}$ 27. $\frac{36}{42}$ 28. $\frac{64}{72}$ 29. $\frac{44}{55}$ 30. $\frac{63}{84}$

31. $\frac{45}{81}$ 32. $\frac{48}{60}$ 33. $\frac{13}{26}$ 34. $\frac{22}{46}$ 35. $\frac{15}{60}$

Simplify the fractional numerals, if possible.

36. On a hockey team, $\frac{2}{6}$ of the players are guards.

37. On a basketball team, $\frac{2}{5}$ of the players are guards.

38. Madelyn ate $\frac{2}{4}$ of the pie.

ACTIVITY

Many people in ancient times used their fingers and palms to measure the lengths of objects. Measure your desk, a book, the height of a chair, and the width of a doorway using your index finger. Now, measure these objects using your palm. Compare answers with other students. What would result if we all used our fingers and palms to measure with? List some good things and some bad things about this way of measuring.

163

A SHORT CUT

Here's a short cut for finding simplest fractional numerals.

Long Way	Short Cut
$\frac{18}{24} = \frac{18 \div 2}{24 \div 2} = \frac{9}{12}$	$\overset{3}{\underset{4}{\cancel{\cancel{\frac{\cancel{18}}{\cancel{24}}}}}} = \frac{3}{4}$
$\frac{9}{12} = \frac{9 \div 3}{12 \div 3} = \frac{3}{4}$	

1. Let's use the short cut to simplify $\frac{12}{16}$.

   Divide numerator and denominator by 2. $\quad\overset{6}{\underset{8}{\cancel{\frac{12}{16}}}}$

   Now divide numerator and denominator by 2 again. $\quad\overset{3}{\underset{4}{\cancel{\overset{6}{\cancel{\frac{12}{16}}}}}}$

   Simplify.

   a. $\frac{10}{12}$ **b.** $\frac{9}{12}$ **c.** $\frac{4}{8}$ **d.** $\frac{12}{18}$

2. If you know the greatest common factor, you can do all your work in one step. $\quad\overset{2}{\underset{3}{\cancel{\frac{18}{27}}}}$

   Find the greatest common factors to simplify.

   a. $\frac{12}{16}$ **b.** $\frac{16}{20}$ **c.** $\frac{24}{30}$ **d.** $\frac{18}{27}$

EXERCISES

Simplify. Use the short cut.

1. $\frac{18}{48}$ **2.** $\frac{24}{36}$ **3.** $\frac{12}{32}$ **4.** $\frac{27}{36}$ **5.** $\frac{16}{24}$

6. $\frac{42}{56}$ **7.** $\frac{40}{50}$ **8.** $\frac{18}{21}$ **9.** $\frac{45}{54}$ **10.** $\frac{74}{96}$

Add.

1. 43
   + 36

2. 732
   + 246

3. 43,207
   + 51,430

4. 39
   + 57

5. 463
   + 382

6. 56,789
   + 17,421

7. 71
   63
   48
   + 93

8. 985
   469
   874
   + 358

9. $21.75
   $34.69
   $58.72
   + $83.98

Subtract.

10. 79
   − 23

11. 643
   − 215

12. 805
   − 329

13. 867
   − 298

14. 2,721
   −   136

15. 7,003
   − 1,428

16. $39.59
   − $12.69

17. $42.00
   −   3.29

Multiply.

18. 37
   × 3

19. 802
   × 7

20. 21,347
   × 9

21. 70,509
   × 8

22. 37
   × 20

23. 802
   × 40

24. 593
   × 800

25. 211
   × 400

26. 37
   × 23

27. 802
   × 47

28. 983
   × 651

29. 366
   × 423

30. 795
   × 804

31. 27,832
   × 46

32. 5,632
   × 730

33. 7,042
   × 136

Divide.

34. 3)84

35. 6)347

36. 9)42,906

37. 20)806

38. 40)3,721

39. 60)14,072

40. 31)247

41. 46)8,321

42. 92)46,411

165

ADDING FRACTIONS: SAME DENOMINATOR

Ribbon for dress.

$\frac{2}{10}$ meter for sleeves.

$\frac{4}{10}$ meter for waist.

How much in all?

$\frac{2}{10} + \frac{4}{10} = \frac{6}{10}$ $\frac{6}{10}$ meter

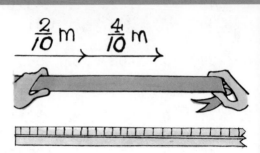

To add two fractions when the denominators are the same, add the numerators and keep the denominator.

$$\frac{a}{c} + \frac{b}{c} = \frac{a+b}{c}$$

1. This drawing shows $\frac{3}{8} + \frac{2}{8}$.
   What is the sum?

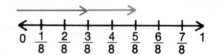

2. Add.

   a. $\frac{2}{5} + \frac{2}{5}$

   b. $\frac{5}{12} + \frac{6}{12}$

   c. $\frac{1}{8} + \frac{5}{8}$

3. Sometimes we can simplify the sum.

   $$\frac{3}{10} + \frac{2}{10} = \frac{5}{10}$$
   $$= \frac{1}{2}$$

   Add. Simplify the sum.

   a. $\frac{3}{8} + \frac{1}{8}$

   b. $\frac{1}{9} + \frac{5}{9}$

   c. $\frac{3}{10} + \frac{5}{10}$

4. We can add more than two fractions.

   $$\frac{1}{9} + \frac{3}{9} + \frac{2}{9} = \frac{6}{9}$$
   $$= \frac{2}{3}$$

   Add. Simplify the sum, if possible.

   a. $\frac{1}{12} + \frac{5}{12} + \frac{3}{12}$

   b. $\frac{3}{10} + \frac{3}{10} + \frac{1}{10}$

166

Add.

1. $\frac{2}{7} + \frac{3}{7}$ 2. $\frac{1}{4} + \frac{2}{4}$ 3. $\frac{1}{9} + \frac{4}{9}$ 4. $\frac{3}{8} + \frac{4}{8}$

5. $\frac{4}{9} + \frac{3}{9}$ 6. $\frac{3}{5} + \frac{1}{5}$ 7. $\frac{5}{7} + \frac{1}{7}$ 8. $\frac{8}{12} + \frac{3}{12}$

9. $\frac{2}{5} + \frac{2}{5}$ 10. $\frac{5}{8} + \frac{2}{8}$ 11. $\frac{9}{16} + \frac{4}{16}$ 12. $\frac{5}{12} + \frac{6}{12}$

13. $\frac{3}{14} + \frac{8}{14}$ 14. $\frac{4}{17} + \frac{5}{17}$ 15. $\frac{14}{19} + \frac{3}{19}$ 16. $\frac{3}{16} + \frac{4}{16}$

17. $\begin{array}{r} \frac{3}{7} \\ + \frac{1}{7} \\ \hline \end{array}$ 18. $\begin{array}{r} \frac{5}{9} \\ + \frac{2}{9} \\ \hline \end{array}$ 19. $\begin{array}{r} \frac{3}{16} \\ \frac{5}{16} \\ + \frac{1}{16} \\ \hline \end{array}$ 20. $\begin{array}{r} \frac{1}{9} \\ \frac{5}{9} \\ + \frac{2}{9} \\ \hline \end{array}$

Add and simplify.

21. $\frac{5}{18} + \frac{4}{18}$ 22. $\frac{7}{10} + \frac{1}{10}$ 23. $\frac{4}{12} + \frac{2}{12}$ 24. $\frac{1}{8} + \frac{3}{8}$

25. $\frac{7}{16} + \frac{5}{16}$ 26. $\frac{5}{12} + \frac{4}{12}$ 27. $\frac{8}{15} + \frac{1}{15}$ 28. $\frac{6}{14} + \frac{6}{14}$

29. $\frac{7}{20} + \frac{8}{20}$ 30. $\frac{7}{18} + \frac{8}{18}$ 31. $\frac{3}{25} + \frac{2}{25}$ 32. $\frac{9}{12} + \frac{1}{12}$

33. $\frac{4}{21} + \frac{10}{21}$ 34. $\frac{7}{12} + \frac{5}{12}$ 35. $\frac{14}{25} + \frac{1}{25}$ 36. $\frac{13}{30} + \frac{2}{30}$

Solve these problems.

37. Susan walked $\frac{3}{10}$ mile from home to the grocery store, then $\frac{2}{10}$ mile to school. How far did she walk in all?

38. John ate $\frac{1}{6}$ of the batch of cookies. Richard ate $\frac{2}{6}$ of them. What part of the batch of cookies did they eat in all?

167

ADDING FRACTIONS: DIFFERENT DENOMINATORS

Suppose the denominators are different.

$$\frac{1}{4} + \frac{1}{6}$$

Find the equivalent fractional numerals.

$$\frac{1}{4}: \left\{\frac{1}{4}, \frac{2}{8}, \frac{3}{12}, \frac{4}{16}, \cdots\right\} \qquad \frac{1}{6}: \left\{\frac{1}{6}, \frac{2}{12}, \frac{3}{18}, \frac{4}{24}, \cdots\right\}$$

$$\frac{3}{12} + \frac{2}{12} = \frac{5}{12}$$

To add when denominators are different, first find equivalent fractional numerals with the same denominator. Then add.

---

1. Let's add $\frac{2}{3}$ and $\frac{1}{4}$.

   a. What is the least common multiple of the denominators?

   b. Complete.

   $$\frac{2}{3} = \frac{\triangle}{12}$$
   $$+\frac{1}{4} = \frac{\square}{12}$$

   c. Now, we can add. Complete.

   $$\frac{2}{3} = \frac{8}{12}$$
   $$+\frac{1}{4} = \frac{3}{12}$$
   $$\frac{\triangledown}{12}$$

2. Here's a quick way to add $\frac{3}{8}$ and $\frac{1}{6}$.

   a. Look at the larger denominator, 8. Think of the multiples of 8: $\{8, 16, 24, 32, 40, \ldots\}$.

   b. Which is also a multiple of 6?

   $$\{8, 16, 24, 32, 40, \ldots\}$$
   $$\text{no} \quad \text{no} \quad \text{yes}$$

   c. 24 is the **least common denominator.** Copy and complete the addition.

   $$\frac{3}{8} = \frac{\triangle}{24}$$
   $$+\frac{1}{6} = \frac{\square}{24}$$
   $$\frac{\triangledown}{24}$$

3. Add.

a. $\frac{1}{2}$
$+\frac{2}{5}$

b. $\frac{2}{3}$
$+\frac{1}{5}$

c. $\frac{2}{5}$
$+\frac{3}{10}$

d. $\frac{5}{6}$
$+\frac{1}{12}$

Add.

1. $\frac{1}{4}$
$+\frac{1}{2}$

2. $\frac{2}{3}$
$+\frac{1}{6}$

3. $\frac{1}{5}$
$+\frac{2}{3}$

4. $\frac{3}{4}$
$+\frac{1}{8}$

5. $\frac{6}{7}$
$+\frac{2}{21}$

6. $\frac{1}{4}$
$+\frac{3}{16}$

7. $\frac{3}{8}$
$+\frac{5}{16}$

8. $\frac{1}{6}$
$+\frac{2}{3}$

9. $\frac{3}{5}$
$+\frac{1}{10}$

10. $\frac{1}{3}$
$+\frac{2}{5}$

11. $\frac{7}{10}$
$+\frac{2}{5}$

12. $\frac{1}{8}$
$+\frac{1}{10}$

13. $\frac{5}{9}$
$+\frac{1}{4}$

14. $\frac{6}{7}$
$+\frac{3}{14}$

15. $\frac{1}{4}$
$+\frac{3}{5}$

16. $\frac{5}{12}$
$+\frac{1}{8}$

17. $\frac{1}{6}$
$+\frac{1}{4}$

18. $\frac{5}{8}$
$+\frac{1}{3}$

19. $\frac{6}{7}$
$+\frac{1}{8}$

20. $\frac{2}{11}$
$+\frac{1}{3}$

Add. Then simplify.

21. $\frac{1}{5}$
$+\frac{2}{6}$

22. $\frac{3}{8}$
$+\frac{4}{16}$

23. $\frac{2}{8}$
$+\frac{3}{10}$

24. $\frac{1}{3}$
$+\frac{1}{6}$

25. $\frac{3}{9}$
$+\frac{1}{4}$

26. $\frac{2}{8}$
$+\frac{1}{3}$

27. $\frac{1}{6}$
$+\frac{9}{30}$

28. $\frac{2}{4}$
$+\frac{1}{6}$

29. $\frac{2}{8}$
$+\frac{3}{12}$

30. $\frac{3}{7}$
$+\frac{2}{6}$

Solve these mini-problems.

31. $\frac{1}{2}$ cup regular sugar.

$\frac{1}{3}$ cup brown sugar.

How much sugar in all?

32. $\frac{3}{4}$ cup milk.

$\frac{1}{6}$ cup water.

How much liquid?

SUBTRACTING FRACTIONS

Bicycle race $\frac{7}{10}$ kilometer.

Jeff has gone $\frac{4}{10}$.

How much farther?

$$\frac{7}{10} - \frac{4}{10} = \frac{3}{10}$$

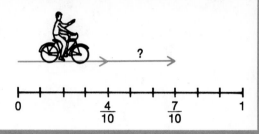

1. Subtract.

   a. $\frac{7}{9} - \frac{5}{9}$
   b. $\frac{9}{10} - \frac{8}{10}$
   c. $\frac{12}{17} - \frac{6}{17}$

2. Let's subtract when the denominators are different.
   Subtract: $\frac{3}{8} - \frac{1}{6}$.

   a. The least common denominator is 24.

   b. Complete.

   $$\frac{3}{8} = \frac{\square}{24}$$
   $$-\frac{1}{6} = \frac{\triangle}{24}$$

   c. Now, subtract. Complete.

   $$\frac{3}{8} = \frac{9}{24}$$
   $$-\frac{1}{6} = \frac{4}{24}$$
   $$\frac{\triangledown}{24}$$

3. Subtract.

   a. $\frac{1}{2}$
   $-\frac{1}{3}$

   b. $\frac{5}{6}$
   $-\frac{1}{4}$

   c. $\frac{4}{5}$
   $-\frac{1}{3}$

   d. $\frac{7}{8}$
   $-\frac{3}{4}$

EXERCISES

Subtract.

1. $\frac{6}{7} - \frac{4}{7}$
2. $\frac{4}{5} - \frac{3}{5}$
3. $\frac{3}{5} - \frac{1}{5}$
4. $\frac{5}{7} - \frac{2}{7}$

5. $\frac{9}{10} - \frac{2}{10}$
6. $\frac{7}{13} - \frac{3}{13}$
7. $\frac{5}{9} - \frac{3}{9}$
8. $\frac{8}{19} - \frac{2}{19}$

9. $\frac{18}{25} - \frac{16}{25}$ **10.** $\frac{6}{11} - \frac{2}{11}$ **11.** $\frac{16}{21} - \frac{5}{21}$ **12.** $\frac{8}{15} - \frac{4}{15}$

13. $\frac{22}{25} - \frac{19}{25}$ **14.** $\frac{14}{29} - \frac{6}{29}$ **15.** $\frac{15}{23} - \frac{5}{23}$ **16.** $\frac{11}{19} - \frac{5}{19}$

17. $\frac{3}{4} - \frac{5}{8}$ **18.** $\frac{7}{8} - \frac{5}{6}$ **19.** $\frac{5}{6} - \frac{1}{4}$ **20.** $\frac{3}{5} - \frac{3}{10}$

21. $\frac{7}{16} - \frac{1}{4}$ **22.** $\frac{5}{6} - \frac{3}{4}$ **23.** $\frac{9}{10} - \frac{1}{5}$ **24.** $\frac{13}{16} - \frac{1}{8}$

25. $\frac{2}{3} - \frac{1}{2}$ **26.** $\frac{4}{5} - \frac{3}{4}$ **27.** $\frac{1}{2} - \frac{4}{9}$ **28.** $\frac{2}{3} - \frac{1}{5}$

Subtract. Then simplify.

29. $\frac{7}{10} - \frac{3}{10}$ **30.** $\frac{5}{8} - \frac{1}{8}$ **31.** $\frac{7}{16} - \frac{3}{16}$ **32.** $\frac{8}{9} - \frac{2}{9}$

33. $\frac{9}{16} - \frac{5}{16}$ **34.** $\frac{13}{18} - \frac{4}{18}$ **35.** $\frac{19}{22} - \frac{8}{22}$ **36.** $\frac{9}{10} - \frac{1}{6}$

37. $\frac{18}{20} - \frac{4}{5}$ **38.** $\frac{9}{10} - \frac{2}{5}$ **39.** $\frac{7}{9} - \frac{2}{6}$ **40.** $\frac{8}{9} - \frac{1}{12}$

41. $\frac{10}{12} - \frac{3}{5}$ **42.** $\frac{11}{12} - \frac{2}{8}$ **43.** $\frac{20}{21} - \frac{2}{7}$ **44.** $\frac{5}{6} - \frac{1}{12}$

Solve these mini-problems.

45. $\frac{5}{6}$ of a pie. Ate $\frac{1}{5}$.
How much left?

46. Amy's earring $\frac{5}{7}$ in. long.
Jan's earring $\frac{2}{3}$ in. long.
Difference?

47. Hamburger meat.
Large hamburger, $\frac{1}{10}$ kg.
Small, $\frac{1}{12}$ kg.
Difference?

171

CENTRAL EQUIPMENT INSTALLERS

Solve these problems.

1. Installers in a training program were tested to see what part of a connection they could make in 1 minute. Lulu Robinson did $\frac{3}{4}$ of a connection in 1 minute. Sam Jones did $\frac{2}{3}$ of a connection in 1 minute. Who did more? How much more?

2. Half of a job was done by welding. One third was done by splicing. It took 1 hour to do the welding. It took 1 hour to do the splicing. What part of the job was done in those two hours? What part of the job was left to be done?

3. Agnes Byrne installed two switchboards. She used $\frac{3}{10}$ meter of wire on one switchboard. She used $\frac{1}{2}$ meter on the other. Which switchboard used more wire? How much wire did Agnes use all together?

4. Sonny Budzinski can put together $\frac{1}{10}$ of a switchboard in one hour. He started at 3 pm and stopped at 5 pm. What part of the switchboard did he get done?

Properties of addition hold for fractions.

Commutative Property of Addition

No matter in which order you add two fractions, the sum is the same.

$$\tfrac{3}{8} + \tfrac{5}{16} = \tfrac{5}{16} + \tfrac{3}{8}$$

Associative Property of Addition

No matter which pair of fractions you add first, the sum is the same.

$$\left(\tfrac{1}{10} + \tfrac{3}{5}\right) + \tfrac{5}{6} = \tfrac{1}{10} + \left(\tfrac{3}{5} + \tfrac{5}{6}\right)$$

1. Consider these additions.

$$\tfrac{1}{2} + \tfrac{1}{3} = \tfrac{5}{6} \qquad \tfrac{1}{3} + \tfrac{1}{4} = \tfrac{7}{12} \qquad \tfrac{1}{2} + \tfrac{1}{4} = \tfrac{3}{4}$$

Solve without computing.

a. $\tfrac{1}{4} + \tfrac{1}{2} = n$ **b.** $\tfrac{1}{4} + \tfrac{1}{3} = r$ **c.** $\tfrac{1}{3} + \tfrac{1}{2} = p$

2. Solve without computing.

a. $\tfrac{1}{7} + n = \tfrac{3}{7} + \tfrac{1}{7}$ **b.** $\tfrac{2}{3} + \left(\tfrac{1}{5} + \tfrac{1}{12}\right) = \left(n + \tfrac{1}{5}\right) + \tfrac{1}{12}$

EXERCISES

Solve without computing.

1. $\tfrac{1}{2} + \tfrac{1}{3} = \tfrac{1}{3} + n$

2. $\left(\tfrac{1}{2} + \tfrac{1}{3}\right) + \tfrac{1}{5} = \tfrac{1}{2} + \left(\tfrac{1}{3} + n\right)$

3. $\tfrac{1}{2} + \tfrac{3}{4} = n + \tfrac{1}{2}$

4. $\left(\tfrac{3}{4} + \tfrac{7}{8}\right) + \tfrac{2}{3} = \tfrac{3}{4} + \left(n + \tfrac{2}{3}\right)$

5. $\tfrac{3}{8} + n = \tfrac{1}{3} + \tfrac{3}{8}$

6. $\tfrac{1}{5} + \left(\tfrac{3}{5} + \tfrac{2}{5}\right) = \tfrac{1}{5} + \left(n + \tfrac{3}{5}\right)$

173

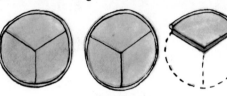

$2\frac{1}{3}$ means $2 + \frac{1}{3}$.

$2\frac{1}{3} = \frac{7}{3}$ because $2\frac{1}{3} = 2 + \frac{1}{3}$

$\qquad\qquad\qquad\quad = \frac{6}{3} + \frac{1}{3}$

$\qquad\qquad\qquad\quad = \frac{7}{3}$

1. Rewrite as mixed numerals.

    a. $4 + \frac{2}{3}$ **b.** $5 + \frac{3}{4}$ **c.** $7 + \frac{2}{3}$

2. Rewrite as sums.

    Example $6\frac{7}{8} = 6 + \frac{7}{8}$

    a. $4\frac{2}{3}$ **b.** $5\frac{3}{8}$ **c.** $8\frac{5}{6}$

3. We can write fractional numerals for mixed numerals by renaming the whole number first.

    Example $2\frac{4}{5} = 2 + \frac{4}{5}$

$\qquad\qquad\qquad\quad = \frac{10}{5} + \frac{4}{5}$

$\qquad\qquad\qquad\quad = \frac{14}{5}$

Complete.

    a. $6\frac{1}{3} = 6 + \frac{1}{3}$ **b.** $4\frac{1}{5} = 4 + \frac{1}{5}$ **c.** $5\frac{3}{5} = 5 + \frac{3}{5}$

$\qquad\quad = \frac{18}{3} + \frac{1}{3}$ $= \frac{\triangle}{5} + \frac{1}{5}$ $= \underline{\quad} + \frac{3}{5}$

$\qquad\quad = \underline{\quad}$ $= \underline{\quad}$ $= \underline{\quad}$

174

4. Write fractional numerals.

    a. $4\frac{2}{3}$ **b.** $5\frac{3}{8}$ **c.** $8\frac{5}{6}$

Rewrite as mixed numerals.

1. $3+\frac{3}{8}$ **2.** $8+\frac{2}{3}$ **3.** $12+\frac{3}{4}$ **4.** $9+\frac{5}{6}$

5. $8+\frac{5}{6}$ **6.** $9+\frac{3}{7}$ **7.** $3+\frac{2}{3}$ **8.** $5+\frac{2}{3}$

Rewrite as sums.

Example $6\frac{7}{8} = 6+\frac{7}{8}$

9. $6\frac{1}{8}$ **10.** $4\frac{5}{6}$ **11.** $8\frac{2}{3}$ **12.** $9\frac{4}{5}$

13. $7\frac{1}{8}$ **14.** $10\frac{2}{7}$ **15.** $5\frac{1}{5}$ **16.** $12\frac{4}{9}$

Write fractional numerals.

17. $1\frac{5}{8}$ **18.** $1\frac{1}{5}$ **19.** $1\frac{3}{8}$ **20.** $4\frac{1}{6}$

21. $7\frac{1}{4}$ **22.** $3\frac{2}{3}$ **23.** $3\frac{1}{4}$ **24.** $4\frac{2}{5}$

25. $2\frac{9}{10}$ **26.** $7\frac{2}{3}$ **27.** $4\frac{1}{9}$ **28.** $5\frac{4}{5}$

29. $3\frac{2}{5}$ **30.** $7\frac{4}{9}$ **31.** $5\frac{8}{10}$ **32.** $9\frac{3}{4}$

33. $7\frac{3}{10}$ **34.** $7\frac{3}{11}$ **35.** $5\frac{3}{8}$ **36.** $6\frac{3}{4}$

37. $6\frac{4}{10}$ **38.** $5\frac{8}{9}$ **39.** $2\frac{7}{8}$ **40.** $7\frac{7}{9}$

41. $4\frac{9}{11}$ **42.** $6\frac{2}{5}$ **43.** $8\frac{3}{11}$ **44.** $10\frac{4}{5}$

DIVISION AND MIXED NUMERALS

Three boys shared 5 cupcakes.

Each boy got $\frac{5}{3}$, or $1\frac{2}{3}$ cupcakes. $5 \div 3 = 1\frac{2}{3}$

1. Rewrite as divisions.

   Example $\frac{6}{5} = 6 \div 5$

   a. $\frac{7}{3}$ **b.** $\frac{8}{5}$ **c.** $\frac{9}{4}$ **d.** $\frac{10}{7}$

2. 10 cupcakes. 4 girls.

$$
\begin{array}{r}
2 \text{ r } 2, \text{ or } 2\frac{2}{4} \\
4\overline{)10} \\
8 \\
\hline
2
\end{array}
$$

   First, each girl gets 2 whole cupcakes. Then they share the remaining 2 cupcakes, so they each get $\frac{2}{4}$ of a cupcake more.

   So, $10 \div 4 = 2\frac{2}{4}$, or $2\frac{1}{2}$

Write mixed numerals. Simplify.

   a. $\frac{12}{5}$ **b.** $\frac{22}{3}$ **c.** $\frac{37}{4}$ **d.** $29 \div 5$

EXERCISES

Write mixed numerals. Simplify.

1. $\frac{17}{3}$ **2.** $17 \div 6$ **3.** $\frac{16}{6}$ **4.** $\frac{48}{5}$ **5.** $\frac{92}{5}$

6. $\frac{60}{8}$ **7.** $\frac{75}{10}$ **8.** $42 \div 9$ **9.** $\frac{58}{7}$ **10.** $134 \div 4$

The commutative and associative properties help us add.

$$1\tfrac{1}{5} + 2\tfrac{3}{5} = \left(1 + \tfrac{1}{5}\right) + \left(2 + \tfrac{3}{5}\right)$$
$$= (1 + 2) + \left(\tfrac{1}{5} + \tfrac{3}{5}\right)$$
$$= 3\tfrac{4}{5}$$

$$\begin{array}{r} 1\tfrac{1}{5} \\ + 2\tfrac{3}{5} \\ \hline 3\tfrac{4}{5} \end{array}$$

1. Copy and complete.

Long form

$$2\tfrac{1}{3} + 1\tfrac{1}{3} = \left(2 + \tfrac{1}{3}\right) + \left(1 + \tfrac{1}{3}\right)$$
$$= (2 + \underline{}) + \left(\underline{} + \tfrac{1}{3}\right)$$
$$= \underline{}$$

Short form

$$\begin{array}{r} 2\tfrac{1}{3} \\ + 1\tfrac{1}{3} \\ \hline \underline{} \end{array}$$

2. Sometimes we must find equivalent fractional numerals to add. Add $4\tfrac{2}{3}$ and $2\tfrac{1}{4}$.

a. The least common denominator for $\tfrac{2}{3}$ and $\tfrac{1}{4}$ is 12. Copy and complete.

$$4\tfrac{2}{3} = 4\tfrac{\triangle}{12}$$
$$2\tfrac{1}{4} = 2\tfrac{\triangle}{12}$$

b. Now add.

$$\begin{array}{r} 4\tfrac{2}{3} = 4\tfrac{8}{12} \\ + 2\tfrac{1}{4} = 2\tfrac{3}{12} \\ \hline \underline{} \end{array}$$

3. Sometimes the sum of fractional parts is greater than 1. Complete.

$$\begin{array}{r} 9\tfrac{5}{6} \\ + 5\tfrac{5}{6} \\ \hline 14\tfrac{10}{6} = 14 + 1\tfrac{4}{6} \\ = 15 + \tfrac{4}{6} \\ = \underline{} \end{array}$$

$$\boxed{\tfrac{4}{6} = \tfrac{2}{3}}$$

Add.

1. $1\frac{1}{9}$
    $+2\frac{7}{9}$

2. $3\frac{3}{10}$
    $+2\frac{4}{10}$

3. $7\frac{1}{8}$
    $+4\frac{6}{8}$

4. $8\frac{7}{12}$
    $+9\frac{4}{12}$

5. $3\frac{1}{3}$
    $+2\frac{1}{3}$

6. $7\frac{5}{8}$
    $+31\frac{2}{8}$

7. $42\frac{4}{7}$
    $+35\frac{1}{7}$

8. $7\frac{1}{3}$
    $+2\frac{1}{2}$

9. $4\frac{1}{6}$
    $+3\frac{2}{3}$

10. $8\frac{2}{5}$
    $+2\frac{1}{2}$

11. $6\frac{3}{7}$
    $+14\frac{2}{5}$

12. $9\frac{1}{2}$
    $+7$

13. $14\frac{2}{3}$
    $+\ 8$

14. $8\frac{4}{9}$
    $+7\frac{3}{6}$

15. $8\frac{1}{10}$
    $+4\ \frac{3}{7}$

16. $6\frac{5}{8}$
    $+3\frac{1}{5}$

Add and simplify.

17. $3\frac{1}{4}$
    $+6\frac{1}{4}$

18. $5\frac{2}{5}$
    $+2\frac{4}{6}$

19. $7\frac{5}{12}$
    $+5\ \frac{1}{3}$

20. $6\frac{2}{3}$
    $+12\frac{1}{3}$

21. $7\frac{7}{10}$
    $+5\ \frac{3}{5}$

22. $10\frac{3}{9}$
    $+\ 3\frac{4}{6}$

23. $4\frac{5}{6}$
    $+10\frac{3}{4}$

24. $16\frac{2}{3}$
    $+\ 4\frac{5}{9}$

25. $15\frac{3}{8}$
    $+13\frac{2}{3}$

26. $14\frac{9}{15}$
    $+43\frac{4}{10}$

27. $24\frac{3}{5}$
    $+36\frac{7}{8}$

28. $97\frac{7}{11}$
    $+43\frac{4}{5}$

29. $14\frac{5}{12}+6\frac{7}{8}+1\frac{1}{3}$

30. $22\frac{6}{7}+9\frac{2}{3}+2\frac{3}{7}$

Solve this problem.

31. John pushed two desks together. The width of one desk was $1\frac{2}{3}$ meters. The width of the other was $1\frac{1}{2}$ meters. What was the total width?

Mr. Taggart had $3\frac{3}{4}$ pizza pies. He put mushrooms on $1\frac{1}{2}$ of them. How many did not have mushrooms?

$$3\frac{3}{4} = \quad 3\frac{3}{4}$$
$$-1\frac{1}{2} = \quad 1\frac{2}{4}$$
$$\overline{\qquad 2\frac{1}{4}}$$

1. Subtract. Simplify if possible.

a. $4\frac{5}{12}$ **b.** $2\frac{1}{2}$ **c.** $7\frac{6}{7}$ **d.** $5\frac{1}{8}$
$\quad -2\frac{1}{12}$ $-1\frac{1}{3}$ $-3\frac{2}{3}$ -2

2. Sometimes regrouping is necessary.

STEP 1.

$$3\frac{1}{4} = \quad 3\frac{1}{4}$$
$$-1\frac{1}{2} = \quad 1\frac{2}{4}$$

↳We can't subtract $\frac{2}{4}$ from $\frac{1}{4}$.

STEP 2. RENAME $3\frac{1}{4}$.

$$3\frac{1}{4} = \left(2 + \frac{4}{4}\right) + \frac{1}{4}$$
$$= 2 + \left(\frac{4}{4} + \frac{1}{4}\right)$$
$$= 2 + \frac{5}{4}$$
$$= 2\frac{5}{4}$$

STEP 3. SUBTRACT.

$$3\frac{1}{4} = \quad 3\frac{1}{4} = \quad 2\frac{5}{4}$$
$$-1\frac{1}{2} = \quad 1\frac{2}{4} = \quad 1\frac{2}{4}$$
$$\overline{\qquad\qquad 1\frac{3}{4}}$$

Subtract. Simplify if possible.

a. $6\frac{2}{5}$ **b.** $18\frac{1}{8}$ **c.** $4\frac{1}{2}$ **d.** $5\frac{1}{8}$
$\quad -1\frac{4}{5}$ $-2\frac{7}{8}$ $-1\frac{7}{12}$ $-1\frac{5}{6}$

179

Subtract. Simplify if possible.

1. $3\frac{3}{5}$
   $-1\frac{2}{5}$

2. $8\frac{5}{6}$
   $-2\frac{3}{6}$

3. $4\frac{5}{8}$
   $-3\frac{1}{8}$

4. $12\frac{4}{5}$
   $-\ 8\frac{3}{4}$

5. $10\frac{3}{5}$
   $-\ 4\frac{1}{8}$

6. $12\frac{11}{12}$
   $-\ 3\frac{3}{4}$

7. $17\frac{6}{7}$
   $-14\frac{2}{3}$

8. $7\frac{8}{9}$
   $-4\frac{1}{4}$

9. $12\frac{5}{6}$
   $-\ 2\frac{1}{4}$

10. $9\frac{1}{12}$
    $-2\frac{8}{12}$

11. $10\frac{1}{3}$
    $-\ 4$

12. $28\frac{7}{10}$
    -14

13. $8\frac{7}{12}$
    $-4\frac{9}{12}$

14. $6\frac{1}{3}$
    $-5\frac{1}{2}$

15. $23\frac{2}{3}$
    $-15\frac{3}{4}$

16. $6\frac{3}{8}$
    $-1\frac{4}{5}$

17. $14\frac{1}{8}$
    $-\ 6\frac{3}{4}$

18. $4\frac{1}{5}$
    -3

19. $35\frac{1}{3}$
    $-16\frac{3}{4}$

20. $40\frac{2}{9}$
    $-23\frac{5}{6}$

21. $7\frac{3}{10}$
    $-6\frac{5}{8}$

22. $9\frac{2}{3}$
    -6

23. 17
    $-\ 6\frac{1}{3}$

24. 12
    $-\ 8\frac{3}{4}$

25. 21
    $-10\frac{2}{3}$

26. 27
    $-14\frac{1}{8}$

27. 41
    $-31\frac{3}{5}$

28. 32
    $-\ 1\frac{5}{9}$

Solve these mini-problems.

29. John's fishing line, $7\frac{2}{3}$ m.
    Caralee's line, $3\frac{3}{4}$.
    Difference?

30. Spent 1 hr playing.
    $2\frac{1}{2}$ hr doing homework.
    Difference?

180

TWO-STEP PROBLEMS

Mrs. Sams is a dressmaker. She has 5 meters of blue material. She uses $2\frac{1}{2}$ meters for one dress, and $2\frac{1}{4}$ meters for a second dress. How much does she have left?

STEP 1 Add $2\frac{1}{2}$ and $2\frac{1}{4}$. $2\frac{1}{2} + 2\frac{1}{4} = 4\frac{3}{4}$

STEP 2   Subtract the sum from 5. $5 - 4\frac{3}{4} = \frac{1}{4}$

Answer: $\frac{1}{4}$ meter

Solve these problems.

1. Harold painted $\frac{3}{10}$ of a house. Martin painted $\frac{2}{5}$ of it. Jan painted the rest. What part did Jan paint?

2. Paul rode his bike $1\frac{3}{4}$ kilometers to school. Then he walked $\frac{5}{8}$ of a kilometer to football practice. How many kilometers less than 4 kilometers did he cover altogether?

3. Chou needed $1\frac{1}{2}$ kilograms of butter for a recipe. He had $\frac{3}{4}$ kilogram. Barbara lent him $1\frac{1}{8}$ kilograms. How much could he return to Barbara?

4. Ms. Keil drove $5\frac{3}{10}$ kilometers to her office. She went $3\frac{9}{10}$ kilometers to the library. Then she drove home. Her total distance was $11\frac{1}{2}$ kilometers. How far was it from the library to her home?

5. Ralph earns $2 an hour. He worked $35\frac{1}{4}$ hours one week and $41\frac{3}{4}$ hours the next. How much did he earn in those two weeks?

181

CHAPTER REVIEW

1. What part of these sets are shaded? [154]

   a. 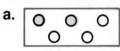   b.

Solve. [155, 157]

2. $\frac{3}{10} = \frac{\square}{40}$

3. $\frac{2}{9} = \frac{\square}{54}$

4. $4 = \frac{\square}{6}$

5. $1 = \frac{\square}{2}$

Compare. Use < or >. [158]

6. $\frac{2}{6} \equiv \frac{5}{6}$

7. $\frac{2}{5} \equiv \frac{1}{4}$

8. $\frac{11}{13} \equiv \frac{8}{13}$

9. $\frac{5}{6} \equiv \frac{8}{9}$

Check for equivalence. Use = or ≠. [160]

10. $\frac{1}{3} \equiv \frac{3}{10}$

11. $\frac{4}{6} \equiv \frac{3}{4}$

12. $\frac{5}{8} \equiv \frac{15}{24}$

13. $\frac{9}{12} \equiv \frac{3}{4}$

Simplify. [162, 164]

14. $\frac{6}{10}$

15. $\frac{8}{16}$

16. $\frac{9}{12}$

17. $\frac{12}{30}$

Add or subtract. Simplify the answer, if possible.

18. $\frac{2}{9} + \frac{6}{9}$
[166]

19. $\frac{3}{8} + \frac{5}{8}$
[166]

20. $\frac{4}{5} + \frac{2}{3}$
[168]

21. $\frac{1}{7} + \frac{4}{7} + \frac{5}{7}$
[166]

22. $8\frac{2}{3} + 6\frac{2}{3}$
[177]

23. $2\frac{4}{7} + 4\frac{5}{7}$
[177]

24. $5\frac{1}{2} + 2\frac{2}{5}$
[177]

25. $8\frac{2}{3} + 4\frac{5}{6}$
[177]

26. $\frac{7}{8} - \frac{4}{8}$
[170]

27. $\frac{5}{6} - \frac{3}{8}$
[170]

28. $4\frac{1}{6} - 2\frac{2}{9}$
[179]

29. $5\frac{1}{2} - 2\frac{2}{3}$
[179]

Write fractional numerals. [174]

30. $9\frac{3}{7}$

31. $8\frac{2}{3}$

32. $3\frac{3}{8}$

33. $12\frac{2}{5}$

Write mixed numerals. [176]

34. $\frac{18}{4}$

35. $\frac{47}{7}$

36. $\frac{39}{6}$

37. $82 \div 10$

Solve this problem.

38. Fri: worked $2\frac{1}{2}$ hr. Sat: $3\frac{7}{8}$ hr. How many hours in all?

CHAPTER TEST

1. What part of the region is shaded?

Solve.

2. $\frac{5}{7} = \frac{\square}{35}$ 3. $\frac{4}{9} = \frac{\square}{63}$ 4. $3 = \frac{\square}{3}$ 5. $1 = \frac{\square}{8}$

Compare. Use $<$ or $>$.

6. $\frac{11}{12} \equiv \frac{7}{12}$ 7. $\frac{3}{4} \equiv \frac{5}{8}$ 8. $\frac{3}{10} \equiv \frac{4}{10}$ 9. $\frac{5}{6} \equiv \frac{3}{8}$

Check for equivalence. Use $=$ or $\neq$.

10. $\frac{5}{9} \equiv \frac{4}{7}$ 11. $\frac{3}{8} \equiv \frac{6}{16}$ 12. $\frac{3}{9} \equiv \frac{4}{12}$ 13. $\frac{2}{3} \equiv \frac{5}{7}$

Simplify.

14. $\frac{8}{12}$ 15. $\frac{5}{10}$ 16. $\frac{18}{30}$ 17. $\frac{40}{56}$

Add or subtract. Simplify the answer, if possible.

18. $\frac{2}{7} + \frac{4}{7}$ 19. $\frac{5}{6} + \frac{3}{8}$ 20. $\frac{3}{16} + \frac{7}{16} + \frac{9}{16}$

21. $7\frac{3}{8} + 5\frac{1}{8}$ 22. $5\frac{1}{4} + 2\frac{4}{8}$ 23. $3\frac{2}{3} + 9\frac{5}{6}$

24. $\frac{7}{16} - \frac{3}{16}$ 25. $\frac{11}{12} - \frac{1}{4}$ 26. $7\frac{1}{3} - 2\frac{5}{6}$

Write fractional numerals.

27. $8\frac{2}{5}$ 28. $11\frac{3}{4}$ 29. $6\frac{7}{9}$

Write mixed numerals.

30. $\frac{14}{3}$ 31. $\frac{22}{8}$ 32. $57 \div 9$

Solve this problem.

33. Need $1\frac{3}{4}$ liters. Have $1\frac{5}{8}$ liters. How much more to get?

8 FRACTIONS, RATIO, PROBABILITY

MULTIPLICATION OF FRACTIONS

We can find $\frac{2}{3}$ of $\frac{4}{5}$ this way.

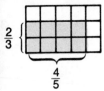

shaded region:	total region:
2 rows of 4 little regions	3 rows of 5 little regions
8 little regions	15 little regions

The blue region is $\frac{8}{15}$ of the total. $\frac{2}{3} \times \frac{4}{5} = \frac{8}{15}$

To multiply two fractions, multiply their numerators and denominators.

$$\frac{a}{b} \times \frac{c}{d} = \frac{a \times c}{b \times d}$$

1. Multiply. Simplify if possible.

   Example $\frac{5}{6} \times \frac{3}{4} = \frac{15}{24} = \frac{5}{8}$

   a. $\frac{1}{2} \times \frac{2}{3}$
   b. $\frac{1}{4} \times \frac{3}{4}$
   c. $\frac{2}{5} \times \frac{3}{4}$

2. To multiply with mixed numerals, change to fractional form.

   Examples $1\frac{2}{3} \times \frac{2}{7} = \frac{5}{3} \times \frac{2}{7}$ $1\frac{2}{3} \times 2\frac{1}{2} = \frac{5}{3} \times \frac{5}{2}$
   $$= \frac{10}{21}$$
   $$= \frac{25}{6}$$
   $$= 4\frac{1}{6}$$

   Multiply. Simplify if possible.

   a. $6\frac{1}{2} \times \frac{4}{7}$
   b. $1\frac{3}{4} \times 1\frac{1}{5}$
   c. $1\frac{1}{3} \times 2\frac{1}{2}$

184

3. To multiply a whole number and a fraction, think of the whole number as a fraction.

$$3 \times \tfrac{2}{7} = \tfrac{3}{1} \times \tfrac{2}{7} = \tfrac{6}{7}$$

Multiply. Simplify if possible.

a. $4 \times \tfrac{1}{7}$ **b.** $3 \times \tfrac{2}{5}$ **c.** $\tfrac{2}{3} \times 9$

Multiply.

1. $\tfrac{1}{2} \times \tfrac{3}{4}$ **2.** $\tfrac{1}{3} \times \tfrac{1}{2}$ **3.** $\tfrac{3}{4} \times \tfrac{5}{7}$ **4.** $\tfrac{1}{3} \times \tfrac{5}{8}$

5. $\tfrac{9}{11} \times \tfrac{6}{7}$ **6.** $\tfrac{7}{8} \times \tfrac{3}{5}$ **7.** $\tfrac{2}{5} \times \tfrac{1}{7}$ **8.** $\tfrac{2}{3} \times \tfrac{2}{5}$

9. $\tfrac{4}{9} \times 2\tfrac{1}{5}$ **10.** $5\tfrac{4}{7} \times \tfrac{4}{9}$ **11.** $1\tfrac{1}{3} \times \tfrac{7}{9}$ **12.** $2\tfrac{2}{3} \times \tfrac{2}{5}$

13. $4 \times \tfrac{1}{11}$ **14.** $3 \times \tfrac{2}{5}$ **15.** $\tfrac{1}{9} \times 7$ **16.** $\tfrac{7}{8} \times 5$

17. $2\tfrac{3}{8} \times \tfrac{3}{5}$ **18.** $10 \times \tfrac{4}{7}$ **19.** $2\tfrac{3}{8} \times 5\tfrac{1}{4}$ **20.** $6\tfrac{3}{8} \times 4\tfrac{3}{5}$

Multiply. Simplify the product.

21. $\tfrac{3}{4} \times \tfrac{4}{7}$ **22.** $\tfrac{2}{3} \times \tfrac{5}{8}$ **23.** $6 \times \tfrac{1}{12}$ **24.** $\tfrac{7}{9} \times \tfrac{3}{5}$

25. $5 \times \tfrac{1}{10}$ **26.** $2 \times \tfrac{7}{16}$ **27.** $2\tfrac{1}{8} \times \tfrac{4}{5}$ **28.** $8\tfrac{2}{3} \times \tfrac{3}{12}$

29. $10 \times \tfrac{3}{5}$ **30.** $14 \times 1\tfrac{1}{7}$ **31.** $5 \times 3\tfrac{4}{5}$ **32.** $2\tfrac{2}{3} \times 5\tfrac{1}{4}$

Solve this mini-problem.

33. $\tfrac{1}{2}$ of a pie left.

Bob eats $\tfrac{1}{3}$ of it.

Bob ate what part of the whole pie?

185

A SHORT CUT

Here's a short cut whenever there is a common factor.

Long Form	Short Cut
$\frac{6}{7} \times \frac{5}{6} = \frac{6 \times 5}{7 \times 6}$	
$\qquad = \frac{30}{42}$	$\frac{\overset{1}{\cancel{6}}}{7} \times \frac{5}{\underset{1}{\cancel{6}}} = \frac{5}{7}$
$\qquad = \frac{5}{7}$	

1. Practice the short cut.

Example $\quad \frac{5}{8} \times \frac{8}{9} \qquad \frac{5}{\underset{1}{\cancel{8}}} \times \frac{\overset{1}{\cancel{8}}}{9} = \frac{5}{9}$

a. $\frac{5}{9} \times \frac{4}{5}$ **b.** $\frac{8}{29} \times \frac{29}{31}$ **c.** $4 \times \frac{3}{4}$

2. Sometimes there are several common factors.

STEP 1
$$\frac{\overset{3}{\cancel{6}}}{10} \times \frac{5}{\underset{4}{\cancel{8}}}$$

STEP 2
$$\frac{\overset{3}{\cancel{6}}}{\underset{2}{\cancel{10}}} \times \frac{\overset{1}{\cancel{5}}}{\underset{4}{\cancel{8}}}$$

STEP 3
$$\frac{\overset{3}{\cancel{6}}}{\underset{2}{\cancel{10}}} \times \frac{\overset{1}{\cancel{5}}}{\underset{4}{\cancel{8}}} = \frac{3}{8}$$

Multiply. Use the short cut.

a. $\frac{3}{7} \times \frac{14}{15}$ **b.** $\frac{8}{15} \times \frac{5}{12}$ **c.** $\frac{25}{32} \times \frac{12}{50}$

EXERCISES

Multiply. Use the short cut.

1. $\frac{3}{8} \times \frac{5}{6}$ **2.** $\frac{2}{3} \times \frac{3}{5}$ **3.** $\frac{5}{8} \times \frac{8}{11}$ **4.** $\frac{5}{9} \times \frac{9}{5}$

5. $\frac{4}{5} \times \frac{1}{6}$ **6.** $\frac{8}{13} \times \frac{5}{16}$ **7.** $\frac{3}{4} \times \frac{4}{9}$ **8.** $\frac{16}{13} \times \frac{13}{16}$

9. $\frac{12}{25} \times \frac{15}{26}$ **10.** $\frac{5}{9} \times \frac{21}{25}$ **11.** $4 \times \frac{3}{16}$ **12.** $\frac{16}{24} \times 12$

13. $\frac{7}{10} \times \frac{12}{21}$ **14.** $\frac{5}{9} \times \frac{6}{15}$ **15.** $\frac{2}{3} \times \frac{3}{5}$ **16.** $\frac{2}{3} \times 36$

186

17. $\frac{8}{9} \times \frac{12}{24}$ **18.** $8 \times \frac{5}{24}$ **19.** $\frac{10}{17} \times 34$ **20.** $\frac{11}{13} \times \frac{1}{22}$

21. $\frac{24}{30} \times \frac{8}{12}$ **22.** $\frac{14}{20} \times \frac{25}{21}$ **23.** $1\frac{1}{3} \times \frac{3}{4}$ **24.** $2\frac{3}{4} \times 1\frac{3}{5}$

25. $7\frac{1}{3} \times 1\frac{1}{11}$ **26.** $5\frac{2}{3} \times 4\frac{1}{8}$ **27.** $6\frac{2}{5} \times 3\frac{1}{8}$ **28.** $1\frac{1}{9} \times 3\frac{3}{8}$

★ Multiply. Use the short cut.

29. $\frac{2}{5} \times \frac{5}{8} \times \frac{2}{6}$ **30.** $\frac{4}{9} \times \frac{7}{14} \times \frac{3}{10}$ **31.** $\frac{6}{7} \times \frac{21}{24} \times \frac{3}{6}$

32. $\frac{2}{3} \times 12 \times \frac{1}{2}$ **33.** $\frac{5}{8} \times 1\frac{1}{5} \times \frac{1}{6}$ **34.** $1\frac{3}{5} \times 25 \times \frac{1}{4}$

Solve these problems.

35. The school let the boys play on $\frac{1}{2}$ of the playground. They used $\frac{2}{3}$ of their half for soccer. What part of the whole playground was used for boys' soccer?

36. Miriam had $\frac{4}{5}$ glass of milk. Then she drank $\frac{5}{6}$ of it. What part of a glassful of milk did she drink?

ACTIVITY

How about you and your friends making these guesses?

1. Each of you stand at a point you believe to be 10 meters from a tree. (A flagpole or a corner of a building will do also.) Then measure each distance. Who made the best guess? Do the same for a distance of 100 meters.

2. Try guessing a time interval of 10 seconds. Check your guesses with a stop watch. Who made the best estimate? Now see who can come closest to guessing when 1 minute has passed.

3. Walk 20 meters to the north. Check guesses with a compass and a meter stick. Who came closest?

4. Walk 100 meters in 40 seconds. Check results with a meter stick and a stop watch. Whose estimate was best?

GLAZIERS

1. A large department store had 24 plate glass windows broken in a wind storm. Mary Washington is a glazier. She charged $864 for labor and materials to fix the windows. What was her average charge per window?

2. Jim Jones is the glazier for the Lincoln School District. The district schools have a total of 7,000,000 windowpanes. About $\frac{1}{5}$ of them need to be replaced every four years. About how many will Mr. Jones have to replace in the next four years?

3. Mr. Jones spends about $\frac{3}{4}$ of his time cutting the glass and fitting it in place. The rest of the time he works with putty. About how many hours in an 8-hour day does he work with putty?

4. Sara Mazzoni will be the chief glazier for a huge new high-rise building. There are 10,000 windows in the building. 2,500 of them are tinted. What fraction of them are tinted?

5. Ms. Mazzoni places an order for 100 windows. She knows that $\frac{3}{5}$ of them should be untinted. How many windows should be untinted? How many windows should be tinted?

The commutative and associative properties of multiplication hold for fractions too.

Property	Example
Commutative property	$\frac{4}{5} \times \frac{2}{3} = \frac{2}{3} \times \frac{4}{5}$
Associative property	$\left(\frac{3}{4} \times \frac{2}{3}\right) \times \frac{1}{2} = \frac{3}{4} \times \left(\frac{2}{3} \times \frac{1}{2}\right)$

The property of 1 for multiplication holds too.

$$\frac{4}{5} \times 1 = \frac{4}{5}$$

1. Solve. Do not compute.

   a. $\frac{3}{4} \times n = \frac{1}{7} \times \frac{3}{4}$ b. $\left(\frac{1}{5} \times \frac{3}{5}\right) \times \frac{2}{3} = \frac{1}{5} \times \left(n \times \frac{2}{3}\right)$

   c. $\frac{2}{3} \times \frac{4}{5} = \frac{4}{5} \times n$ d. $\left(\frac{4}{9} \times \frac{5}{8}\right) \times \frac{1}{10} = \frac{4}{9} \times \left(n \times \frac{5}{8}\right)$

2. Multiply and simplify. Is each product the same?

   a. $\frac{1}{1} \times \frac{17}{19}$ b. $\frac{2}{2} \times \frac{17}{19}$ c. $\frac{6}{6} \times \frac{17}{19}$ d. $1 \times \frac{17}{19}$

No matter what name for 1 we use, when we multiply a fraction by 1, the product is the fraction itself.

Solve without computing.

1. $n \times \frac{1}{2} = \frac{1}{2} \times \frac{3}{5}$ 2. $\left(\frac{8}{9} \times \frac{9}{8}\right) \times \frac{7}{17} = \frac{8}{9} \times \left(\frac{7}{17} \times n\right)$

3. $n \times \frac{1}{2} = \frac{1}{2}$ 4. $\frac{1}{3} \times n = \frac{4}{7} \times \frac{1}{3}$

5. $\frac{3}{3} \times n = \frac{1}{2}$ 6. $\frac{3}{5} \times \left(\frac{5}{6} \times \frac{5}{7}\right) = \left(\frac{5}{6} \times n\right) \times \frac{5}{7}$

189

The distributive property sometimes helps make multiplication with mixed numerals easier.

$$3 \times 2\tfrac{1}{2} = 3 \times \left(2 + \tfrac{1}{2}\right)$$
$$= (3 \times 2) + \left(3 \times \tfrac{1}{2}\right)$$
$$= 6 + 1\tfrac{1}{2}$$
$$= 7\tfrac{1}{2}$$

$$
\begin{array}{r}
2\tfrac{1}{2} \\
\times 3 \\
\hline
1\tfrac{1}{2} \quad \leftarrow 3 \times \tfrac{1}{2} \\
6 \quad \leftarrow 3 \times 2 \\
\hline
7\tfrac{1}{2}
\end{array}
$$

1. Let's multiply $4\tfrac{5}{6} \times 2$. Complete.

$$
\begin{array}{r}
4\tfrac{5}{6} \\
\times 2 \\
\hline
\end{array}
\qquad
\begin{array}{r}
4\tfrac{5}{6} \\
\times 2 \\
\hline
1\tfrac{2}{3}
\end{array}
\qquad
\begin{array}{r}
4\tfrac{5}{6} \\
\times 2 \\
\hline
1\tfrac{2}{3} \\
8 \\
\hline
\end{array}
$$

$$2 \times \tfrac{\overset{1}{5}}{\underset{3}{6}} = \tfrac{5}{3}$$
$$= 1\tfrac{2}{3}$$

2. Multiply.

a. $\begin{array}{r} 3\tfrac{1}{5} \\ \times 2 \\ \hline \end{array}$

b. $\begin{array}{r} 4\tfrac{2}{7} \\ \times 3 \\ \hline \end{array}$

c. $\begin{array}{r} 6\tfrac{4}{7} \\ \times 5 \\ \hline \end{array}$

Multiply.

1. $\begin{array}{r} 5\tfrac{2}{3} \\ \times 4 \\ \hline \end{array}$

2. $\begin{array}{r} 4\tfrac{5}{8} \\ \times 2 \\ \hline \end{array}$

3. $\begin{array}{r} 2\tfrac{5}{12} \\ \times 3 \\ \hline \end{array}$

4. $\begin{array}{r} 2\tfrac{3}{4} \\ \times 3 \\ \hline \end{array}$

5. $\begin{array}{r} 2\tfrac{3}{16} \\ \times 3 \\ \hline \end{array}$

6. $\begin{array}{r} 4\tfrac{1}{2} \\ \times 3 \\ \hline \end{array}$

7. $\begin{array}{r} 2\tfrac{1}{3} \\ \times 4 \\ \hline \end{array}$

8. $\begin{array}{r} 9 \\ \times 6\tfrac{1}{2} \\ \hline \end{array}$

RECIPROCALS

The number line shows that the product of 5 and $\frac{1}{5}$ is 1.

$5 \times \frac{1}{5} = 1$

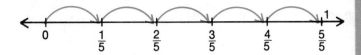

When the product of two numbers is 1, we call each number the **reciprocal** of the other.

$\frac{3}{4}$ is the reciprocal of $\frac{4}{3}$, and $\frac{4}{3}$ is the reciprocal of $\frac{3}{4}$.

$\frac{1}{7}$ is the reciprocal of 7, and 7 is the reciprocal of $\frac{1}{7}$.

1. Solve.

   a. $3 \times \frac{1}{3} = n$ **b.** $\frac{1}{27} \times 27 = n$ **c.** $6 \times n = 1$

2. The reciprocal of $\frac{2}{5}$ is $\frac{5}{2}$.

   Check: $\frac{2}{5} \times \frac{5}{2} = \frac{10}{10} = 1$

   Find the reciprocals.

   a. $\frac{3}{8}$ **b.** $\frac{5}{7}$ **c.** $\frac{1}{4}$ **d.** 3

EXERCISES

Find the reciprocals.

   1. $\frac{5}{7}$ **2.** $\frac{9}{5}$ **3.** $\frac{2}{10}$ **4.** $\frac{7}{8}$

   5. $\frac{1}{8}$ **6.** $\frac{4}{11}$ **7.** $\frac{3}{8}$ **8.** $\frac{3}{14}$

   9. $\frac{1}{6}$ **10.** 5   **11.** 8   **12.** $\frac{83}{35}$

191

DIVIDING BY A FRACTION

How many $\frac{1}{3}$'s are in 2? Count jumps on the number line.

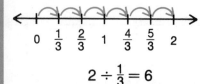

$$2 \div \frac{1}{3} = 6$$

1. Check these sentences with the number line.

$$3 \div \frac{1}{4} = 12 \qquad 6 \div \frac{3}{4} = 8$$

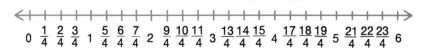

Divide. Use the number line.

a. $2 \div \frac{1}{4}$ **b.** $3 \div \frac{3}{4}$ **c.** $5 \div \frac{1}{4}$

2. Check these sentences with the number line.

$$\frac{7}{3} \div \frac{1}{3} = 7 \qquad \frac{10}{3} \div \frac{2}{3} = 5$$

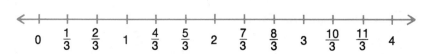

Divide. Use the number line.

a. $\frac{2}{3} \div \frac{1}{3}$ **b.** $\frac{5}{3} \div \frac{1}{3}$ **c.** $\frac{8}{3} \div \frac{2}{3}$

3. Dividing by 4 is the same as multiplying by $\frac{1}{4}$.

$$8 \div 4 = 2 \qquad 8 \times \frac{1}{4} = 2$$

Complete these function tables.

Input: n	24	16	4
Output: $n \div 4$			

Input: n	24	16	4
Output: $n \times \frac{1}{4}$			

4. Compare to find a pattern. Use number lines to divide.

a. $8 \div \frac{1}{2}$ and 8×2 **b.** $8 \div \frac{2}{3}$ and $8 \times \frac{3}{2}$

c. $9 \div \frac{3}{4}$ and $9 \times \frac{4}{3}$ **d.** $\frac{8}{3} \div \frac{2}{3}$ and $\frac{8}{3} \times \frac{3}{2}$

Dividing by a fraction and multiplying by its reciprocal give the same answer.

$$\frac{a}{b} \div \frac{c}{d} = \frac{a}{b} \times \frac{d}{c}$$

5. Divide.

Examples $\frac{1}{5} \div \frac{6}{7} = \frac{1}{5} \times \frac{7}{6}$ $7 \div \frac{1}{6} = \frac{7}{1} \times \frac{6}{1}$

$= \frac{7}{30}$ $= 42$

a. $\frac{3}{5} \div \frac{5}{6}$ **b.** $6 \div \frac{1}{3}$ **c.** $\frac{12}{7} \div \frac{5}{2}$

EXERCISES

Divide.

1. $5 \div \frac{1}{4}$ **2.** $\frac{9}{4} \div 4$ **3.** $5 \div \frac{1}{3}$ **4.** $\frac{1}{3} \div \frac{2}{5}$

5. $\frac{1}{8} \div \frac{1}{5}$ **6.** $\frac{3}{7} \div \frac{2}{3}$ **7.** $\frac{4}{9} \div \frac{3}{5}$ **8.** $\frac{7}{8} \div \frac{5}{3}$

9. $\frac{6}{5} \div \frac{5}{3}$ **10.** $\frac{6}{5} \div \frac{7}{3}$ **11.** $\frac{13}{3} \div 7$ **12.** $\frac{3}{7} \div \frac{4}{11}$

13. $\frac{7}{8} \div \frac{5}{3}$ **14.** $\frac{10}{11} \div \frac{9}{5}$ **15.** $\frac{3}{7} \div \frac{7}{8}$ **16.** $\frac{4}{5} \div 5$

17. $\frac{3}{8} \div 4$ **18.** $\frac{12}{13} \div 5$ **19.** $12 \div \frac{1}{2}$ **20.** $16 \div \frac{1}{4}$

Solve this problem.

21. Grade 6 is making Pep Club ribbons for the football game. Each ribbon is to be $\frac{1}{4}$ meter long. How many ribbons can they make from a roll 25 meters long?

193

SIMPLIFYING IN DIVISION

Often we can use the short-cut method of simplifying.

STEP 1

STEP 2

$$\frac{4}{21} \div \frac{16}{3}$$

$$\frac{4}{21} \div \frac{16}{3} = \frac{4}{21} \times \frac{3}{16}$$

$$\frac{4}{21} \div \frac{16}{3} = \frac{\cancel{4}}{\cancel{21}_{7}} \times \frac{\cancel{3}^{1}}{\cancel{16}_{4}}$$

$$= \frac{1}{28}$$

1. Divide and simplify.

 a. $\frac{2}{3} \div \frac{8}{3}$ **b.** $\frac{5}{9} \div \frac{5}{3}$ **c.** $\frac{12}{18} \div \frac{8}{9}$

2. Divide. Write a mixed numeral for your answer.

Example

$$\frac{6}{5} \div \frac{4}{15} = \frac{\cancel{6}^{3}}{\cancel{5}_{1}} \times \frac{\cancel{15}^{3}}{\cancel{4}_{2}}$$

$$= \frac{9}{2}, \text{ or } 4\frac{1}{2}$$

 a. $\frac{5}{6} \div \frac{4}{9}$ **b.** $\frac{9}{10} \div \frac{3}{4}$ **c.** $\frac{12}{15} \div \frac{8}{12}$

EXERCISES

Divide and simplify. Write mixed numerals if possible.

 1. $\frac{7}{8} \div \frac{3}{2}$ **2.** $\frac{10}{9} \div \frac{2}{3}$ **3.** $\frac{4}{5} \div \frac{6}{7}$ **4.** $\frac{3}{7} \div \frac{3}{8}$

 5. $\frac{7}{5} \div \frac{14}{9}$ **6.** $\frac{5}{3} \div \frac{7}{12}$ **7.** $\frac{3}{5} \div \frac{7}{10}$ **8.** $\frac{5}{6} \div \frac{5}{7}$

 9. $\frac{7}{10} \div \frac{3}{4}$ **10.** $\frac{6}{7} \div \frac{3}{14}$ **11.** $\frac{2}{5} \div \frac{6}{25}$ **12.** $\frac{9}{10} \div \frac{3}{4}$

 13. $\frac{3}{8} \div \frac{7}{8}$ **14.** $12 \div \frac{3}{5}$ **15.** $\frac{4}{9} \div 12$ **16.** $\frac{11}{15} \div \frac{4}{5}$

★ **17.** Make a flow chart to show how to divide and simplify two fractions.

194

If a fraction is named as a mixed numeral, change to fraction form before dividing.

$$2\frac{2}{5} \div 1\frac{1}{2}$$
$$= \frac{12}{5} \div \frac{3}{2}$$
$$= \frac{\overset{4}{\cancel{12}}}{5} \times \frac{2}{\underset{1}{\cancel{3}}}$$
$$= \frac{8}{5}, \text{or } 1\frac{3}{5}$$

1. Divide. Simplify where possible.

   a. $3\frac{1}{2} \div 4\frac{2}{3}$ **b.** $5\frac{1}{2} \div 1\frac{1}{8}$ **c.** $1\frac{1}{6} \div 1\frac{2}{5}$

2. Don't let whole numbers bother you!

$$6 \div 1\frac{4}{5} = 6 \div \frac{9}{5} \qquad\qquad 2\frac{2}{3} \div 4 = \frac{8}{3} \div \frac{4}{1}$$
$$= \frac{\overset{2}{\cancel{6}}}{1} \times \frac{5}{\underset{3}{\cancel{9}}} \qquad\qquad = \frac{\overset{2}{\cancel{8}}}{3} \times \frac{1}{\underset{1}{\cancel{4}}}$$
$$= \frac{10}{3}, \text{ or } 3\frac{1}{3} \qquad\qquad = \frac{2}{3}$$

   Divide. Simplify where possible.

   a. $5 \div 1\frac{3}{7}$ **b.** $2\frac{2}{5} \div 4$ **c.** $6 \div 2\frac{2}{3}$

EXERCISES

Divide. Simplify where possible.

1. $3\frac{5}{8} \div \frac{3}{4}$ 2. $7\frac{2}{3} \div \frac{5}{6}$ 3. $6\frac{2}{3} \div \frac{5}{9}$ 4. $1\frac{3}{4} \div 4\frac{2}{3}$

5. $2\frac{5}{8} \div 1\frac{1}{6}$ 6. $4\frac{1}{2} \div 4\frac{1}{2}$ 7. $6 \div 1\frac{2}{3}$ 8. $7 \div 2\frac{1}{3}$

9. $1\frac{7}{10} \div 3\frac{1}{5}$ 10. $5\frac{1}{3} \div 8$ 11. $4\frac{2}{5} \div 11$ 12. $10 \div 1\frac{3}{7}$

FRACTIONS AT WORK

Madelyn had $\frac{4}{5}$ meter of crepe paper. She cut it into 3 equal pieces. How long was each piece?

$$\frac{4}{5} \div 3 = \frac{4}{5} \times \frac{1}{3}$$
$$= \frac{4}{15}$$

Answer: $\frac{4}{15}$ meter

Solve these problems.

1. Susan has a piece of drapery material $\frac{3}{4}$ meter long. How many pieces, each $\frac{1}{8}$ meter long, can she cut from it?

2. A box $1\frac{2}{3}$ feet long is divided into 2 compartments of equal length. How long is each compartment?

3. Farmer Jones took 35 pounds of cantaloupes to market. Each cantaloupe weighed about $1\frac{2}{5}$ pounds. How many cantaloupes did he take to market?

4. A piece of board is $6\frac{1}{2}$ meters long. Cari cut it into pieces $\frac{1}{2}$ meter long. How many pieces did she get?

5. A Scout Troop went on a 26-kilometer hike. They planned to hike $6\frac{1}{2}$ kilometers each day. How many days did it take them?

6. How long would it take to get 20 liters of water out of a tank if it is taken out at the rate of $\frac{1}{3}$ liter per minute?

7. Mrs. Keil baked 3 pies. She cut each pie in sixths. How many pieces did she get?

Solve.

1. $\frac{1}{2} = \frac{\square}{12}$

2. $\frac{3}{4} = \frac{\square}{24}$

3. $\frac{1}{5} = \frac{\square}{25}$

4. $\frac{6}{7} = \frac{\square}{42}$

5. $\frac{2}{3} = \frac{\square}{12}$

6. $\frac{1}{4} = \frac{\square}{12}$

7. $\frac{7}{8} = \frac{\square}{24}$

8. $\frac{5}{9} = \frac{\square}{27}$

9. $\frac{6}{9} = \frac{\square}{36}$

10. $\frac{3}{7} = \frac{\square}{21}$

11. $\frac{5}{8} = \frac{\square}{48}$

12. $\frac{2}{7} = \frac{\square}{35}$

13. $\frac{8}{11} = \frac{\square}{22}$

14. $\frac{3}{10} = \frac{\square}{50}$

15. $\frac{2}{15} = \frac{\square}{45}$

16. $\frac{5}{12} = \frac{\square}{48}$

17. $\frac{4}{9} = \frac{\square}{81}$

18. $\frac{11}{12} = \frac{\square}{60}$

19. $\frac{4}{5} = \frac{\square}{80}$

20. $\frac{9}{10} = \frac{\square}{100}$

21. $\frac{4}{7} = \frac{\square}{63}$

22. $\frac{3}{13} = \frac{\square}{26}$

23. $\frac{8}{9} = \frac{\square}{72}$

24. $\frac{5}{6} = \frac{\square}{54}$

25. $\frac{6}{25} = \frac{\square}{100}$

26. $\frac{7}{15} = \frac{\square}{60}$

For each exercise below, think of a triangle ABC. Find the missing angle measure.

	$m\angle A$	$m\angle B$	$m\angle C$
27.	40°	25°	
28.	90°		62°
29.	37°		26°
30.		84°	35°
31.	50°	21°	
32.	40°	40°	
33.		42°	53°
34.	39°		67°
35.	83°	47°	

197

COMPARING BY RATIO

Joe saves 3¢ a day. Sue saves 5¢ a day.

SAVINGS IN ONE WEEK

	Sun	Mon	Tues	Wed	Thurs	Fri	Sat
Joe	3¢	6¢	9¢	12¢	15¢	18¢	21¢
Sue	5¢	10¢	15¢	20¢	25¢	30¢	35¢

We say their savings are in the **ratio** 3 to 5.
We write $\frac{3}{5}$. Joe's savings are always $\frac{3}{5}$ of Sue's.

$$\frac{3}{5} = \frac{6}{10} = \frac{9}{15} = \frac{12}{20} = \frac{15}{25} = \frac{18}{30} = \frac{21}{35}$$

1. The ratio 4 to 5 is equal to the ratio 12 to 15.
$$\frac{4}{5} = \frac{12}{15}$$
Solve. 7 is to 10 as ☐ is to 40.
$$\frac{7}{10} = \frac{\square}{40}$$

2. Solve.

   a. 10 is to 6 as ☐ is to 24.

   b. 5 is to 12 as ☐ is to 24.

   c. 4 is to 15 as 12 is to ☐.

3. We can compare 4 and 5 in two ways.

4 to 5	5 to 4
$\frac{4}{5}$	$\frac{5}{4}$

   Which are equal to the ratio 4 to 5?

   a. 20 to 25   **b.** 8 to 10   **c.** 15 to 12

   Which are equal to the ratio 5 to 4?

   d. 15 to 12   **e.** 20 to 16   **f.** 25 to 15

Which are equal to the ratio 2 to 3?

1. 4 to 6   **2.** 9 to 6   **3.** 10 to 15   **4.** 12 to 8

Which are equal to the ratio 5 to 4?

5. 4 to 5   **6.** 20 to 16   **7.** 15 to 4   **8.** 30 to 24

Which show the ratio 3 to 8?

9. $\frac{8}{3}$ **10.** $\frac{6}{16}$ **11.** $\frac{15}{40}$ **12.** $\frac{6}{11}$

Solve.

13. $\frac{5}{2} = \frac{\square}{4}$ **14.** $\frac{2}{5} = \frac{\square}{30}$ **15.** $\frac{7}{8} = \frac{\square}{40}$ **16.** $\frac{1}{2} = \frac{\square}{14}$

17. $\frac{2}{3} = \frac{4}{\square}$ **18.** $\frac{5}{8} = \frac{15}{\square}$ **19.** $\frac{8}{9} = \frac{16}{\square}$ **20.** $\frac{4}{9} = \frac{12}{\square}$

21. 2 is to 5 as $\square$ is to 10.

22. 6 is to 10 as $\square$ is to 60.

23. 4 is to 7 as $\square$ is to 21.

24. 9 is to 27 as $\square$ is to 3.

25. 16 is to 32 as $\square$ is to 2.

26. 12 is to 18 as $\square$ is to 36.

27. 15 is to 25 as $\square$ is to 75.

28. 32 is to 36 as $\square$ is to 9.

Solve this problem.

29. Marty saves 6¢ and Steve saves 5¢ each day. What is the ratio of Marty's savings to Steve's?

199

Ralph knows a store that sells 2 candy bars for 25¢.

Ratios help us find out the cost of 4 candy bars.

$$\frac{2}{25} = \frac{4}{\square}$$

$$\frac{2}{25} = \frac{4}{50}$$

Then 4 candy bars cost 50¢.

Write equations using ratios. Solve.

1. Chewing gum costs 7 sticks for 10¢. How much would 21 sticks cost?   28 sticks?

2. Chewing gum costs 7 sticks for 10¢. How many sticks for 20¢? for $1.00?

3. Every 2 weeks Lisa puts $3 into her savings account. How much money will she have saved in 16 weeks?

4. Tomatoes cost $3 for 2 kilograms. How much for 10 kilograms?

5. At a sale, records cost 4 for $5. How much would 16 records cost?

6. Barbara had 45¢. The price of candy bars is 2 for 15¢. How many could she buy?

7. A recipe for punch calls for 2 parts ginger ale to 3 parts of fruit juice. How much ginger ale should Scott use if he uses 6 liters of fruit juice?

8. The dance decoration committee found they would need 4 boxes of sparkle for 7 ornaments. How many boxes would they need for 28 ornaments?

9. Tracy will earn $25 every 4 weeks. How many weeks will it take her to earn $75?

COMPARING RATIOS

Which is cheaper, 10¢ for 3 or 9¢ for 2?

10¢ for 3   9¢ for 2

$\frac{10}{3} = 3\frac{1}{3}$ $\frac{9}{2} = 4\frac{1}{2}$

$3\frac{1}{3}$¢ for 1 $4\frac{1}{2}$¢ for 1

1. Show that 15¢ for 2 is cheaper than 25¢ for 3.

2. Here's another way to compare the ratios 10¢ for 3 and 9¢ for 2.

   We compare: $\frac{10}{3} \equiv \frac{9}{2}$.

   $\frac{10}{3} = \frac{20}{6}$ $\frac{9}{2} = \frac{27}{6}$

   $\frac{20}{6} < \frac{27}{6}$, so $\frac{10}{3} < \frac{9}{2}$

   Compare 15¢ for 2 and 25¢ for 3.

EXERCISES

Which is cheaper?

1. 15¢ for 2 or 49¢ for 6

2. 36¢ for 6 or 59¢ for 9

3. 3 for 19¢ or 4 for 25¢

4. 2 for 29¢ or 3 for 59¢

5. 15¢ for 2 or 41¢ for 6

6. 2 for 19¢ or 3 for 25¢

7. 4 for 27¢ or 3 for 20¢

8. 17¢ for 2 or 50¢ for 6

9. 60¢ for 9 or 37¢ for 6

10. 35¢ for 6 or 59¢ for 9

PROBABILITY

Here are 4 cards with names on them.
We can turn them over and mix them up.

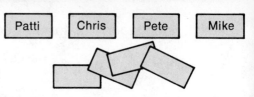

Patti   Chris   Pete   Mike

The probability of choosing Patti's name is 1 out of 4 cards, or $\frac{1}{4}$.

1. Here's another set of cards.

   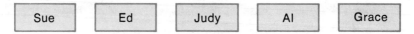

   Sue   Ed   Judy   Al   Grace

   a. How many cards have Ed's name?

   b. How many cards are there in all?

   c. The probability of choosing Ed is 1 out of 5. Write a fractional numeral for this ratio.

2. Look at the cards in Item 1 again.

   a. How many have a girl's name on them?

   b. How many cards are there?

   c. The probability of choosing a girl's name is 3 out of 5. Write a fractional numeral for this.

3. Lucille has a block. Two sides are red, three sides are white, and one side is blue. She tosses the block in the air.

   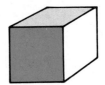

   a. How many sides are red?

   b. How many sides are there in all?

   c. What is the probability that the block will land with a red side up?

   d. What is the probability that the block will land with a white side up?   the blue side up?

4. Consider this tin with blue marbles in it.

a. Is it possible to choose a green marble from it?

We say the probability of the event which is certain not to happen is $\frac{0}{6}$, or 0.

b. What is the probability of choosing a blue marble?

We say the probability of the event which is certain to happen is $\frac{6}{6}$, or 1.

1. A coin can land with either heads up or tails up. What is the probability of it landing heads up?

Heads   Tails

2. What is the probability of the spinner pointing to an even number? an odd number?

Think of a baby's block with the letters A, B, C, D, E, and F, one on each side. What is the probability of each event?

3. Block landing A-face up

4. Block landing F-face up

5. Block landing with a vowel up
(*Hint:* the vowels are A and E.)

Count the number of boys and girls in your class. If all the names were written on slips of paper and mixed up in a box, find the probability of each of these events.

6. Your name being selected

7. A girl's name being selected

8. A card with the name Donald Duck being selected

Bob and Lulu played a game with both a red and a blue spinner.

They recorded all possible outcomes this way.

(1, 6)	(2, 6)	(3, 6)
(1, 5)	(2, 5)	(3, 5)
(1, 4)	(2, 4)	(3, 4)

(1, 4) means a 1 on the red spinner and a 4 on the blue spinner.

1. What is the meaning of each outcome?

   a. (1, 5)   **b.** (2, 5)   **c.** (3, 4)

2. **a.** How many possible outcomes are there in the game with the two spinners?

   b. What is the probability of the outcome (2, 5)? of the outcome (3, 4)?

3. We can set up a probability table like this. Complete.

Event	Favorable Outcomes	Probability of Event
Sum of 1st and 2nd number is 6.	(1, 5) (2, 4)	$\frac{2}{9}$
1st number is odd.	(1, 4) (1, 5) (1, 6) (3, 4) (3, 5) (3, 6)	$\frac{6}{9}$, or $\frac{2}{3}$
Sum of 1st and 2nd number is 7.		$\frac{3}{9}$, or $\frac{1}{3}$
Sum of 1st and 2nd number is 8.	(2, 6) (3, 5)	
1st number is even.		
1st and 2nd numbers are even.		
	(1, 5) (3, 5)	$\frac{2}{9}$
2nd number is a 5.		

Consider two spinners like this.

1. Copy and complete the list of possible outcomes.

(1, 7)	(2, 7)	(3, 7)	(____ , ____)
(1, 6)	(2, ____)	(3, ____)	(4, 6)
(1, 5)	(____ , ____)	(____ , ____)	(____ , ____)

Complete the table.

	Event	Favorable Outcomes	Probability
2.	Sum of 1ˢᵗ and 2ⁿᵈ number is 8.	(1, 7) (2, 6) (3, 5)	
3.	Sum of 1ˢᵗ and 2ⁿᵈ number is?	(2, 7) (3, 6) (4, 5)	
4.	1ˢᵗ number is even.		
5.	2ⁿᵈ number is 5.		
6.	Both numbers are even.		
7.		(1, 5) (1, 7) (3, 5) (3, 7)	$\frac{4}{12}$, or $\frac{1}{3}$

Suppose we toss a nickel and a penny. Here are the possible outcomes.

(H, H)	(T, H)
(H, T)	(T, T)

8. What is the probability of getting two heads?

9. What is the probability of getting two tails?

10. What is the probability of getting a head on the nickel and a tail on the penny?

11. Try the experiment yourself. Flip the coins 40 times each. Complete this chart. Record a tally mark each time you have an outcome.

Outcome	Number of Occurrences
(H, H)	
(H, T)	
(T, H)	
(T, T)	

12. Make five cards like these.

JIM	JOE	ART	AL	ANDY

Without looking, pick either Jim's card or Joe's card first. Then pick either Art's, Al's or Andy's. Here are all possible outcomes.

(Jim, Art) (Jim, Al) (Jim, Andy)
(Joe, Art) (Joe, Al) (Joe, Andy)

Now try this experiment. Pick a pair of cards 30 times. (Make sure you shuffle them and don't peek each time!) Complete this chart.

Outcome	Probability	Number of Occurrences
(Jim, Art)		
(Jim, Al)		
(Jim, Andy)		
(Joe, Art)		
(Joe, Al)		
(Joe, Andy)		

Some problems have extra information. Others have not enough. Some have just the right amount.

A fabric that is 90 cm wide sells for $1.35 per meter of length. How much will you pay for a piece $2\frac{1}{3}$ meters long?

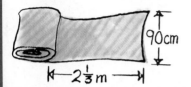

90cm

$2\frac{1}{3}$ m

The fabric width is not needed.

$$2\frac{1}{3} \times 1.35 = 3.15$$

Answer: $3.15

Which problems have extra information? Which have not enough information? Solve, if possible. If not, tell what information is needed to solve the problem.

1. A 2-meter length of shelving costs $2.50. How much will Richard pay to build shelves for his stereo?

2. Mary's bike cost $65. She averages $5\frac{1}{2}$ kilometers per hour going to college. If it takes 15 minutes, how far is it to college?

3. Sandie does part-time work at the hospital. She is paid $2.50 per hour. How much does she earn per week?

4. Baby Joshua drinks 30 milliliters of milk every 3 hours. How much does he drink in a day?

5. Buffy eats 2 cans of dog food a day. How much does it cost to feed Buffy each day?

6. Mom is paid time-and-a-half for each overtime hour. She gets $4 an hour for regular time. What does she get for each overtime hour?

7. Susan likes to eat a 10-cent candy bar every school day. How much did she spend this past school year?

CHAPTER REVIEW

Multiply. Simplify if possible. [184, 186]

1. $\frac{1}{3} \times \frac{2}{5}$ **2.** $\frac{7}{8} \times \frac{1}{2}$ **3.** $\frac{3}{10} \times \frac{5}{6}$ **4.** $\frac{5}{6} \times \frac{4}{7}$

5. $6 \times \frac{3}{8}$ **6.** $2\frac{1}{3} \times \frac{4}{7}$ **7.** $3\frac{3}{5} \times 2\frac{2}{9}$ **8.** $5\frac{1}{2} \times 7\frac{2}{3}$

9. $\frac{5}{6} \times \frac{3}{8} \times \frac{4}{10}$ **10.** $\frac{2}{7} \times 14 \times \frac{1}{8}$ **11.** $1\frac{5}{9} \times 27 \times \frac{3}{7}$

Find the reciprocals. [191]

12. $\frac{1}{7}$ **13.** 2 **14.** $\frac{3}{5}$ **15.** $\frac{19}{27}$

Divide. Simplify if possible.

16. $6 \div \frac{1}{2}$ **17.** $\frac{1}{5} \div \frac{2}{3}$ **18.** $\frac{8}{9} \div \frac{2}{9}$ **19.** $9 \div \frac{3}{5}$
[192] [192] [194] [194]

20. $\frac{2}{5} \div \frac{3}{10}$ **21.** $\frac{6}{7} \div \frac{8}{21}$ **22.** $\frac{5}{6} \div 5$ **23.** $5 \div 1\frac{2}{3}$
[194] [194] [194] [195]

24. $4\frac{4}{5} \div 8$ **25.** $7\frac{1}{2} \div 4\frac{2}{3}$ **26.** $3\frac{5}{6} \div 5\frac{1}{4}$ **27.** $7\frac{1}{3} \div 7\frac{1}{3}$
[195] [195] [195] [195]

Solve. [198, 200]

28. $\frac{6}{5} = \frac{\square}{10}$ **29.** 2 is to 3 as $\square$ is to 15 **30.** $\frac{3}{10} = \frac{12}{\square}$

31. Apples: 3 for 29¢. Jane wants 15 apples. How much?

Which is cheaper? [201]

32. 43¢ for 6 or 65¢ for 9. **33.** 2 for 21¢ or 3 for 29¢

Consider Cards A. What is the probability of choosing the following?

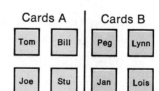

34. Bill's name **35.** Andy's name
[202] [202]

Consider Cards A and B. [204]

36. What is the probability of choosing (Stu, Lynn)?

208

CHAPTER TEST

Multiply. Simplify if possible.

1. $\frac{4}{5} \times \frac{2}{3}$ **2.** $\frac{2}{5} \times \frac{3}{8}$ **3.** $\frac{9}{10} \times \frac{5}{6}$

4. $8 \times \frac{5}{12}$ **5.** $3\frac{3}{4} \times 1\frac{1}{5}$ **6.** $1\frac{1}{3} \times 1\frac{1}{5}$

7. $2\frac{2}{3} \times 15 \times \frac{5}{16}$

Find the reciprocals.

8. $\frac{1}{3}$ **9.** 6 **10.** $\frac{4}{9}$

Divide. Simplify if possible.

11. $\frac{1}{7} \div \frac{2}{9}$ **12.** $\frac{4}{3} \div 5$ **13.** $\frac{9}{10} \div \frac{3}{10}$

14. $\frac{5}{6} \div \frac{10}{15}$ **15.** $6 \div \frac{2}{3}$ **16.** $7 \div 2\frac{1}{3}$

17. $1\frac{1}{5} \div 6$ **18.** $3\frac{1}{2} \div 2\frac{3}{4}$

Solve.

19. $\frac{2}{3} = \frac{\square}{15}$ **20.** 3 is to 8 as $\square$ is to 24

21. Tickets: 2 for $15. El wants 8 tickets. How much?

Which is cheaper?

22. 23¢ for 3 or 33¢ for 4

Consider Spinner A. What is the probability of each of these outcomes?

23. 5   **24.** An odd number

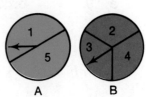

Consider the two spinners.

25. What is the probability of the outcome (1, 3)?

9 DECIMALS

DECIMALS

Fractions can be named in fractional or decimal form.

	Use	Read	Decimal Form	Fractional Form
car odometer	☐☐☐☐☐☐**2**	two tenths	.2	$\frac{2}{10}$
	☐☐☐☐☐**1 2**	one and two tenths	1.2	$1\frac{2}{10}$
weighing meat in supermarket	wt. Price Price Per lb. .57 $.60 $1.0	fifty-seven hundredths	.57	$\frac{57}{100}$
	wt. price price per lb. 2.53 $1.90 $.75	two and fifty-three hundredths	2.53	$2\frac{53}{100}$

1. Read these decimals.

Examples .4 four tenths
.03 three hundredths
.26 twenty-six hundredths

a. .3 **b.** .7 **c.** .06 **d.** .05 **e.** .93

f. 2.7 **g.** .42 **h.** 5.8 **i.** 7.21 **j.** 3.09

2. Write in fractional form.

Examples $.7 = \frac{7}{10}$ $3.7 = 3\frac{7}{10}$ $.49 = \frac{49}{100}$

a. .9 **b.** .09 **c.** .48 **d.** .08 **e.** 5.7

3. Write in decimal form.

Examples $\frac{3}{10} = .3$ $8\frac{7}{10} = 8.7$ $\frac{83}{100} = .83$

a. $\frac{4}{10}$ **b.** $\frac{4}{100}$ **c.** $3\frac{1}{10}$ **d.** $\frac{31}{100}$ **e.** $5\frac{37}{100}$

Write decimals.

1. Four and nine tenths

2. Six tenths

3. Twenty-six hundredths

4. Five and three tenths

5. Eighty-four hundredths

6. Seven hundredths

7. Three and sixty-five hundredths

8. Nine and four hundredths

WOW! FOUR AND THIRTY-TWO HUNDREDTHS METERS.

Write in fractional form.

9. .1	10. .01	11. .70	12. .11
13. 3.6	14. 4.01	15. 20.6	16. .35
17. .05	18. .03	19. .87	20. 4.6
21. .90	22. 3.62	23. 5.8	24. .99

Write in decimal form.

25. $\frac{6}{10}$	26. $\frac{4}{100}$	27. $6\frac{8}{10}$	28. $\frac{68}{100}$
29. $\frac{9}{100}$	30. $3\frac{9}{100}$	31. $7\frac{1}{10}$	32. $\frac{5}{10}$
33. $2\frac{7}{10}$	34. $12\frac{9}{10}$	35. $4\frac{6}{100}$	36. $48\frac{13}{100}$
37. $4\frac{3}{10}$	38. $2\frac{36}{100}$	39. $4\frac{53}{100}$	40. $6\frac{21}{100}$

211

Each place in a decimal has its own value.

tenths   hundredths   thousandths   ten thousandths

$.4536$

$$.4536 = \frac{4}{10} + \frac{5}{100} + \frac{3}{1,000} + \frac{6}{10,000}$$
$$= \frac{4,536}{10,000}$$

Word Name

four thousand five hundred thirty-six ten thousandths

1. Read these decimals.

   Examples   .923   nine hundred twenty-three thousandths

   .7864   seven thousand eight hundred sixty-four ten thousandths

   a. .498   **b.** .5207   **c.** 3.455   **d.** 8.6042

   e. .007   **f.** .9006   **g.** 4.730   **h.** .0001

   i. .078   **j.** .4956   **k.** 8.026   **l.** 4.4040

   m. .203   **n.** .1032   **o.** 6.901   **p.** 1.0101

2. Write in fractional form.

   Examples $.685 = \frac{685}{1,000}$ $.3685 = \frac{3,685}{10,000}$

   a. .635   **b.** .071   **c.** .4256   **d.** .0037

3. Write in decimal form.

   Examples $\frac{73}{1,000} = .073$ $\frac{4,027}{10,000} = .4027$

   a. $\frac{2}{1,000}$ **b.** $\frac{523}{1,000}$ **c.** $\frac{2,135}{10,000}$ **d.** $\frac{71}{10,000}$

212

Write in fractional form.

1. .308   **2.** .873   **3.** .013   **4.** .008

5. .030   **6.** .200   **7.** .2159   **8.** .2083

9. .0004   **10.** .0017   **11.** .0326   **12.** .8700

13. .2456   **14.** .067   **15.** .001   **16.** .0003

Write in decimal form.

17. $\frac{503}{1,000}$ **18.** $\frac{129}{1,000}$ **19.** $\frac{17}{1,000}$ **20.** $\frac{3}{1,000}$

21. $\frac{421}{1,000}$ **22.** $\frac{73}{1,000}$ **23.** $\frac{4,238}{10,000}$ **24.** $\frac{321}{10,000}$

25. $\frac{2,496}{10,000}$ **26.** $\frac{8,007}{10,000}$ **27.** $\frac{57}{10,000}$ **28.** $\frac{5}{10,000}$

29. $\frac{7,401}{10,000}$ **30.** $\frac{1}{1,000}$ **31.** $\frac{1}{10,000}$ **32.** $\frac{12}{10,000}$

Find the missing numbers.

33. .001, .002, .003, . . . , .006, .007, . . . , .013

34. .097, .098, .099, .100, . . . , .110

35. .0001, .0002, .0003, ... , .0013

36. .0097, .0098, .0099, . . . , .0115

37. .0997, .0998, .0999, . . . , .1005

38. .1007, .1008, .1009, . . . , .1021

Solve this problem.

39. Did you know that .0001 kilometer is 10 centimeters long? Draw a segment which is .0002 kilometer long.

213

Place values to the right of the ones place are similar to those to the left.

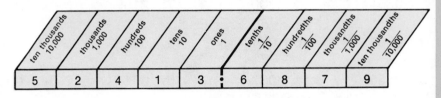

$$50,000 + 2,000 + 400 + 10 + 3 + \frac{6}{10} + \frac{8}{100} + \frac{7}{1,000} + \frac{9}{10,000}$$

$$52,413.6879$$

1. Complete.

a. $14.3 = 10 + 4 + \frac{\square}{10}$

b. $627.36 = \underline{\quad} + \underline{\quad} + 7 + \frac{\square}{10} + \frac{\triangle}{100}$

c. $63.824 = 60 + \underline{\quad} + \frac{8}{10} + \frac{\square}{100} + \frac{\triangle}{1,000}$

d. $24.9563 = \underline{\quad} + \underline{\quad} + \frac{\square}{10} + \frac{5}{100} + \frac{\triangle}{1,000} + \frac{\triangledown}{10,000}$

2. Write expanded numerals.

   a. 927.67   **b.** 439.926   **c.** 75.8924

3. Write in fractional form.

   Example $2.009 = 2\frac{9}{1,000}$, or $\frac{2009}{1,000}$

   a. 3.27   **b.** 14.038   **c.** 19.2075

4. Give the value of the underlined digit.

   Example   72.4<u>3</u>6   3 hundredths

   a. 19.7<u>6</u>54   **b.** 5.3<u>2</u>98   **c.** 348.743<u>9</u>

   d. 2.987<u>6</u>   **e.** .00<u>4</u>2   **f.** 17.91<u>3</u>2

5. Read these numerals.

Example   24.239   twenty-four and two hundred thirty-nine thousandths

a. 4,728.3561   **b.** 246.004   **c.** 3,561.4728

d. 18.0713   **e.** 4,860.1   **f.** 3,400.0073

g. 520.113   **h.** 436.326   **i.** 2,002.0006

EXERCISES

Write expanded numerals.

1. 2.73   **2.** 439.8   **3.** 35.426   **4.** 3.47

5. 5,544.96   **6.** 6.029   **7.** 73.9176   **8.** 881.3478

9. 9,876.305   **10.** 1.0004   **11.** 26.0040   **12.** 38.9372

Write in fractional form.

13. 3.24   **14.** 5.8   **15.** 4.73   **16.** 7.427

17. 34.7   **18.** 18.9   **19.** 48.63   **20.** 9.73

Give the value of the underlined digit.

21. 1.21   **22.** 37.415   **23.** 4.932   **24.** 7.301

25. 18.37   **26.** 58.4671   **27.** 8.2036   **28.** 5.1111

29. 6.07   **30.** 5.3621   **31.** 93.42   **32.** 87.336

33. 8.457   **34.** 300.59   **35.** 84.567   **36.** 3.2003

Solve.

★ **37.** Each decimal place has a value $\frac{1}{10}$ of the value of the place to the left. What is the value of the underlined digits in .23457 and .452367?

EQUIVALENT DECIMALS

This ruler shows that .30 = .3

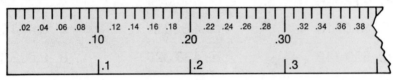

$$.30 = \frac{30}{100} \qquad\qquad .3 = \frac{3}{10}$$
$$= \frac{3}{10} \qquad\qquad\qquad = \frac{30}{100}$$
$$= .3 \qquad\qquad\qquad = .30$$

1. Copy and complete.

a. $.70 = \frac{\triangle}{100}$
$= \frac{\triangle}{10}$
$= .7$

b. $.6 = \frac{6}{\square}$
$= \frac{\triangle}{100}$
$= .60$

2. Write these decimals as tenths.

a. .60   **b.** .40   **c.** .90   **d.** 1.20

3. Write these decimals as hundredths.

a. .7   **b.** .2   **c.** .5   **d.** 2.3

4. We can think of .300 as .30 or as .3, and vice versa.

$$.300 = \frac{300}{1,000} \qquad\qquad .30 = \frac{30}{100}$$
$$= \frac{30}{100} \qquad\qquad\qquad = \frac{3}{10}$$
$$= .30 \qquad\qquad\qquad = .3$$

Change to hundredths; to tenths.

a. .600   **b.** .400   **c.** .500   **d.** .900

Change to thousandths.

e. .6   **f.** .7   **g.** .40   **h.** .02

216

We can rename any decimal by adding or taking away zeros from the right end of the numeral.

$$.4 = .40 = .400 = .4000, \text{etc.}$$
$$.32 = .320 = .3200, \text{etc.}$$

Write as tenths.

1. .40	**2.** .600	**3.** 1.50	**4.** .700
5. .800	**6.** .4000	**7.** .6000	**8.** .9000

Write as hundredths.

9. .050	**10.** .240	**11.** .6	**12.** .500
13. .230	**14.** .3000	**15.** .9	**16.** .3
17. .3500	**18.** .0600	**19.** .4	**20.** .400

Write as thousandths.

21. .2000	**22.** .0070	**23.** .5	**24.** .2500
25. .30	**26.** .04	**27.** .56	**28.** .3500

Write as ten thousandths.

29. .400	**30.** .470	**31.** .623	**32.** .2
33. .03	**34.** .37	**35.** .4	**36.** .013

Brainteaser

Twin Primes are primes which differ by 2. Here are the first twin primes.

3 and 5	5 and 7
11 and 13	17 and 19

Find the next three twin primes. How many twin primes are there less than 100?

217

COMPARING DECIMALS

Surveyors use very precise
measuring instruments.
Compare these rulers.

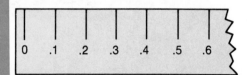

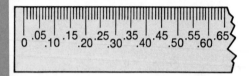

We can see that these sentences
are true.

.03 < .2   .47 < .5   .1 > .01

1. Let's compare .05 and .4.

STEP 1. RENAME

.4 = .40

STEP 2. COMPARE

.05 ≣ .40
.05 < .40
so, .05 < .4

Compare. Use <, >, or =.

a. .03 ≣ .3   **b.** .2 ≣ .045   **c.** .044 ≣ .44

2. Let's compare .1 with .001.

Compare .100 with .001 instead of .1 with .001.

.100 > .001
so, .1 > .001

Compare. Use <, >, or =.

a. .2 ≣ .013   **b.** .047 ≣ .7   **c.** .500 ≣ .5

218

Compare, Use $<$, $>$, or $=$.

1. .7 ☰ .89   2. .71 ☰ .8   3. .5 ☰ .43

4. .403 ☰ .0895   5. .1111 ☰ .22   6. .3 ☰ .1234

7. .0987 ☰ .1001   8. .0702 ☰ .207   9. .099 ☰ .1000

10. .78 ☰ .9003   11. .4 ☰ .5123   12. .45 ☰ .134

13. .3 ☰ .12   14. .35 ☰ .278   15. .832 ☰ .0999

16. .47 ☰ .5312   17. .4 ☰ .4000   18. .111 ☰ .0222

19. .405 ☰ .4050   20. .380 ☰ .38   21. .7 ☰ .803

22. .2 ☰ .451   23. .68 ☰ .139   24. .55 ☰ .055

25. .71 ☰ .7100   26. .437 ☰ .6   27. .94 ☰ .946

★ 28. Which is the smallest number?   the largest?

   .0089   .0009   .1000   .2   .0321

★ 29. Arrange from smallest to largest.

   .400   .111   .088   .30   .7

Solve.

1. $\frac{2}{3} = \frac{\square}{6}$ 2. $\frac{2}{3} = \frac{\square}{15}$ 3. $\frac{2}{3} = \frac{6}{\square}$

4. $\frac{3}{4} = \frac{12}{\square}$ 5. $\frac{1}{2} = \frac{\square}{12}$ 6. $\frac{3}{5} = \frac{\square}{45}$

7. $\frac{7}{10} = \frac{\square}{100}$ 8. $\frac{3}{10} = \frac{\square}{1,000}$ 9. $\frac{27}{100} = \frac{\square}{1,000}$

10. $\frac{9}{10} = \frac{90}{\square}$ 11. $\frac{43}{100} = \frac{430}{\square}$ 12. $\frac{1}{10} = \frac{100}{\square}$

Keeping Fit

We can write $\frac{1}{2}$ and $\frac{3}{4}$ in decimal form like this.

$$\frac{1}{2} = \frac{1 \times 5}{2 \times 5}$$
$$= \frac{5}{10}$$
$$= .5$$

$$\frac{3}{4} = \frac{3 \times 25}{4 \times 25}$$
$$= \frac{75}{100}$$
$$= .75$$

1. Let's write $\frac{3}{5}$ in decimal form.

$$\frac{3}{5} = \frac{3 \times 2}{5 \times 2}$$
$$= \frac{6}{10}$$
$$= .6$$

Write in decimal form.

a. $\frac{1}{5}$ **b.** $\frac{2}{5}$ **c.** $\frac{4}{5}$ **d.** $\frac{3}{2}$ **e.** $\frac{6}{5}$

2. Let's write $\frac{3}{25}$ in decimal form.

$$\frac{3}{25} = \frac{3 \times 4}{25 \times 4}$$
$$= \frac{12}{100}$$
$$= .12$$

Write in decimal form.

a. $\frac{6}{25}$ **b.** $\frac{11}{25}$ **c.** $\frac{1}{4}$ **d.** $\frac{3}{50}$ **e.** $\frac{5}{4}$

220

3. Now let's write $\frac{5}{8}$ in decimal form.

$$\frac{5}{8} = \frac{5 \times 125}{8 \times 125}$$
$$= \frac{625}{1,000}$$
$$= .625$$

Write in decimal form.

a. $\frac{1}{8}$ **b.** $\frac{3}{8}$ **c.** $\frac{3}{40}$ **d.** $\frac{7}{8}$ **e.** $\frac{7}{40}$

Solve.

1. $\frac{2}{4} = \frac{\square}{100}$ **2.** $\frac{6}{8} = \frac{\square}{1,000}$ **3.** $\frac{4}{25} = \frac{\square}{100}$

4. $\frac{11}{50} = \frac{\square}{100}$ **5.** $\frac{7}{4} = \frac{\square}{100}$ **6.** $\frac{3}{20} = \frac{\square}{100}$

7. $\frac{13}{40} = \frac{\square}{1,000}$ **8.** $\frac{7}{5} = \frac{\square}{10}$ **9.** $\frac{26}{25} = \frac{\square}{100}$

Write in decimal form.

10. $\frac{5}{8}$ **11.** $\frac{1}{25}$ **12.** $\frac{7}{25}$ **13.** $\frac{8}{25}$ **14.** $\frac{7}{50}$

15. $\frac{9}{50}$ **16.** $\frac{11}{25}$ **17.** $\frac{9}{40}$ **18.** $\frac{13}{20}$ **19.** $\frac{9}{8}$

20. $\frac{12}{25}$ **21.** $\frac{32}{50}$ **22.** $\frac{21}{40}$ **23.** $\frac{13}{500}$ **24.** $\frac{11}{40}$

Solve these problems.

25. Lucy found the length of a metal piece in an auto to be $\frac{1}{5}$ meter. She had to report this measurement in tenths, in hundredths, and in thousandths. Give these three decimals.

★**26.** Change $\frac{17}{80}$ to decimal form.

221

Keeping Fit

Add. Simplify if possible.

1. $\frac{1}{5}$
$+\frac{3}{5}$

2. $\frac{7}{10}$
$+\frac{1}{10}$

3. $\frac{11}{20}$
$+\frac{7}{20}$

4. $\frac{3}{4}$
$+\frac{3}{4}$

5. $\frac{1}{4}$
$+\frac{1}{5}$

6. $\frac{3}{5}$
$+\frac{3}{10}$

7. $\frac{3}{4}$
$+\frac{3}{5}$

8. $\frac{4}{5}$
$+\frac{7}{10}$

9. $\frac{3}{4}$
$+\frac{9}{10}$

10. $\frac{7}{10}$
$+\frac{19}{20}$

11. $1\frac{3}{5}$
$+4\frac{1}{5}$

12. $7\frac{3}{10}$
$+4\frac{1}{10}$

13. $3\frac{3}{5}$
$+4\frac{4}{5}$

14. $34\frac{1}{5}$
$27\frac{1}{10}$
$+16\frac{2}{5}$

15. $41\frac{1}{4}$
$25\frac{9}{10}$
$+23\frac{3}{10}$

16. $78\frac{17}{20}$
$21\frac{9}{10}$
$+19\frac{7}{10}$

Subtract. Simplify if possible.

17. $\frac{3}{5}$
$-\frac{2}{5}$

18. $\frac{7}{10}$
$-\frac{3}{10}$

19. $\frac{19}{20}$
$-\frac{7}{20}$

20. $\frac{7}{10}$
$-\frac{2}{5}$

21. $\frac{9}{10}$
$-\frac{2}{5}$

22. $\frac{3}{4}$
$-\frac{3}{10}$

23. $\frac{3}{4}$
$-\frac{3}{5}$

24. $\frac{19}{20}$
$-\frac{7}{10}$

25. $4\frac{7}{25}$
$-2\frac{3}{25}$

26. $32\frac{9}{10}$
$-17\frac{1}{10}$

27. $9\frac{12}{25}$
$-5\frac{7}{25}$

28. $42\frac{1}{5}$
$-23\frac{3}{5}$

29. $83\frac{3}{20}$
$-29\frac{7}{20}$

30. $73\frac{3}{4}$
$-22\frac{4}{5}$

ESTIMATING MONEY

1. Mrs. Outler rounds prices to the nearest dollar.

   Example $4.49 is rounded to $4.00
                     $4.50 is rounded to $5.00

   Round the cost of a piece of roast beef marked $3.71.

2. She adds her estimates so she can guess how much she is spending.

   a. Estimate the price of each of these items: $.87; $1.23; $2.09; $5.94; $.57.

   b. What is the difference between the estimated total of these items and the exact total price?

3. Mrs. Outler rounds prices to the nearest dime.

   Example $4.44 is rounded to $4.40
                     $4.45 is rounded to $4.50

   Round the cost of a piece of meat marked $3.71.

4. Matt has the following items in his shopping cart.

   milk 54¢   pickles 59¢   cleanser 39¢
   bread 35¢   coffee $1.29   chicken $2.18

   Estimate each item to the nearest dime and estimate the total.

5. Ground beef is priced at 89¢ a pound. Round this to the nearest dime, and tell how much Matt should expect to pay for 4 pounds of ground beef.

A car goes .3 kilometers, then goes .5 km more. Total distance?

Fraction Form	Decimal Form
$\frac{3}{10}$	.3
$+\frac{5}{10}$	$+.5$
$\frac{8}{10}$	.8

1. Compare these two ways of adding.

$$\frac{9}{10}$$
$$+\frac{3}{10}$$
$$\frac{12}{10}, \text{ or } 1\frac{2}{10}$$

$$.9$$
$$+.3$$
$$1.2$$

Add using decimals.

a. .2 + .6   **b.** .3 + .4   **c.** .7 + .8

2. We can add hundredths in a similar way.

$$\frac{43}{100}$$
$$+\frac{9}{100}$$
$$\frac{52}{100}$$

$$.43$$
$$+.09$$
$$.52$$

Add using decimals.

a. .72 + .06   **b.** .38 + .25   **c.** .57 + .13

3. Add thousandths.

Example
$$.136$$
$$+.427$$
$$.563$$

a. .003 + .004   **b.** .091 + .084   **c.** .462 + .087

Add.

1. .7
   +.2

2. .32
   +.56

3. .32
   +.59

4. .70
   +.21

5. .9
   +.8

6. .305
   +.002

7. .176
   +.913

8. .06
   +.28

9. .70
   +.73

10. .09
    +.08

11. .90
    +.80

12. .49
    +.87

13. .318
    +.847

14. .562
    +.093

15. .586
    +.079

16. .1234
    +.4321

17. .1717
    +.0029

18. .0035
    +.0008

19. .3500
    +.0800

20. .7168
    +.5234

21. .0735
    +.1523

22. .8198
    +.3477

23. .4168
    +.5234

24. .2198
    +.3477

25. .06
    .42
    +.01

26. .27
    .84
    +.91

27. .003
    .214
    +.306

28. .462
    .831
    +.046

Solve these problems.

29. An engineer has two pieces of wire. One measures .37 centimeter and the other measures .26 centimeter. What is their combined length?

30. Joe took a bike ride. He went .3 kilometer to the grocery store. Then he went .4 kilometer to the library. He rode .8 kilometer back home. How far did he ride?

31. Michael paid $.37 for a loaf of bread and $.65 for milk. How much did he spend altogether?

32. A scientist measured .17 units of a liquid. She added .35 units. What was the new total?

ADDING

The delivery men drove 1.2 kilometers and made their first delivery. Then they drove .6 kilometer to make their second delivery. Later, they drove 2.3 kilometers and made their third delivery. How many kilometers did they drive in all?

$$\begin{array}{r} 1.2 \\ .6 \\ + 2.3 \\ \hline 4.1 \end{array}$$

1. Add. Compare the fraction and decimal answer.

a. $2\frac{4}{10}$ 2.4   **b.** $3\frac{7}{10}$ 3.7

$+ \frac{5}{10}$ $+ .5$ $+ \frac{8}{10}$ $+ .8$

c. $5\frac{23}{100}$ 5.23   **d.** $8\frac{97}{100}$ 8.97

$+ \frac{64}{100}$ $+ .64$ $+ \frac{15}{100}$ $+ .15$

When adding decimals, add tenths to tenths, hundredths to hundredths, etc. To do this, line up the decimal points and add as with whole numbers.

2. Add.

Example   .4 + .23

$$\begin{array}{r} .4 \\ +.23 \\ \hline \uparrow \end{array}$$
line up decimal points.

$$\begin{array}{r} .4 \\ +.23 \\ \hline .63 \end{array}$$

a. .4 + .52   **b.** .3 + .09   **c.** .37 + .081

d. .2 + 6.71   **e.** .19 + 83.5   **f.** 36.007 + .424

226

Add.

1. .2 + 1.7

2. .2 + .17

3. .2 + .017

4. .2 + .0017

5. .5 + 3.9

6. .5 + .39

7. .6 + .042

8. .3 + .0021

9. .2 + 27.2

10. .2 + 2.74

11. .2 + .274

12. .3 + .0411

13. .4 + 378.1

14. 4.1 + 23.61

15. .8 + 6.043

16. .7 + .0068

17. 9.81 + 8.4

18. .43 + .06

19. .84 + .0006

20. .43 + .0007

21. 13.294 + 5.5

22. .374 + .07

23. .362 + .005

24. .026 + .0007

25. 7.27 + .04 + 5.356

26. 9.83 + 1.0046 + 14.0292

27. .671 + 2.9 + 46.3

28. .973 + 5.62 + .42

Solve these problems.

29. The odometer on the new car read .3. The mechanic test-drove it for 1.9 kilometers. What was the new reading?

30. Gale's times for each quarter of her record mile run were 59.2, 59.9, 60.3, and 60.1 seconds. What was her total time in seconds?

31. The radio announcer said at noon that the temperature was 23.8 degrees. At 1 pm she announced that the temperature had gone up .4 of a degree. What was the temperature at 1 pm?

32. Johnnie paid $2 for hamburger meat, and $.37 for bread. How much did he pay altogether?

SUBTRACTING

Ms. Roberts rented a new car. After a couple of minutes of driving, the odometer looked like this.

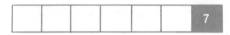

At the start it looked like this.

How far had she driven the car?

Fraction Form

$$\frac{7}{10}$$
$$-\frac{3}{10}$$
$$\frac{4}{10}$$

Decimal Form

.7
$$-.3$$
.4

To subtract decimals, we line up the decimal points. Then we subtract as with whole numbers.

1. Subtract.

Example   .74 − .51

```
  .74
 −.51
  ↑
Line up
decimal
points.
```

```
  .74
 −.51
  .23
```

a. .8 − .6   **b.** .59 − .25   **c.** .897 − .003

2. Regroup just as you would with whole numbers.

Example

```
   6 12
   7 2
 −2 8
   4 4
```

```
   6 12
  .7 2
  .2 8
  .4 4
```

a. .83 − .45   **b.** .536 − .364   **c.** .4775 − .0183

228

3. Sometimes it helps to write zeros in order to subtract.

$$
\begin{array}{r}
1.42 \\
- \ \ .1372 \\
\hline
\end{array}
\qquad
\begin{array}{r}
1.4200 \\
- \ \ .1372 \\
\hline
\end{array}
\qquad
\begin{array}{r}
{\scriptstyle 11\ 9} \\
{\scriptstyle 3\ \cancel{4}\ \cancel{10}\ 10} \\
1.4\,2\,0\,0 \\
- \ \ .1\,3\,7\,2 \\
\hline
\end{array}
$$

Subtract. Write zeros if you wish.

a. .6 − .584 **b.** .49 − .377 **c.** 4.62 − .0074

Subtract.

1. .9 − .3 **2.** .99 − .56 **3.** .91 − .49

4. .91 − .60 **5.** .407 − .003 **6.** 1.489 − .305

7. .594 − .176 **8.** .539 − .263 **9.** .666 − .4321

10. .2746 − .0039 **11.** .0053 − .0007 **12.** .7200 − .0400

13. .5986 − .3007 **14.** .8253 − .125 **15.** .7285 − .72

16. 3.9 − .2 **17.** .38 − .1 **18.** .397 − .2

19. .4564 − .3 **20.** 7.4 − .5 **21.** 6.8 − .92

22. 4.63 − .572 **23.** .5 − .214 **24.** .975 − .46133

25. 6.71 − .046 **26.** 10.2 − .73 **27.** 14 − .36

28. 52 − .76 **29.** 84.1 − .006 **30.** 305 − .02

Solve these problems.

31. Mr. Dickerson cut .67 cm from a piece of wire .92 cm long. How long was the piece of wire which was left?

32. Lu had a $5-bill. She spent $.37. How much was left?

33. Alice's fever dropped from 101.6° to 98.6°. How many degrees did it drop?

MULTIPLYING

Here's a pattern in multiplying decimals.

Factor	Factor	Product
	tenths ⟶	tenths
	hundredths ⟶	hundredths
whole number ⟶ ×	thousandths ⟶	thousandths
	ten thousandths ⟶	ten thousandths

To multiply decimals, first multiply as with whole numbers. Then mark the decimal point in the product.

$$
\begin{array}{r} .623 \\ \times\,4 \\ \hline \end{array}
\qquad
\begin{array}{r} .623 \\ \times\,4 \\ \hline 2.492 \end{array}
$$

1. Copy. Mark the decimal point in the product.

   a.
   $$\begin{array}{r} .23 \\ \times\,6 \\ \hline 138 \end{array}$$

   b.
   $$\begin{array}{r} .084 \\ \times\,17 \\ \hline 1428 \end{array}$$

   c.
   $$\begin{array}{r} .3567 \\ \times\,29 \\ \hline 103443 \end{array}$$

2. Multiply.

   a. $3 \times .2$ b. $7 \times .25$ c. $6 \times .4126$

3. The pattern works for a decimal greater than 1 also.

   $$\begin{array}{r} 1.3 \\ \times\,14 \\ \hline 52 \\ 13 \\ \hline 18.2 \end{array}$$

   Multiply.

   a. 4×3.7 b. 16×12.7 c. 23×7.34

Multiply.

1. .8
    × 9

2. .08
    × 9

3. .04
    × 7

4. .006
    × 5

5. .34
    × 8

6. .026
    × 6

7. .0031
    × 7

8. .0123
    × 8

9. .824
    × 7

10. .0431
    × 4

11. 1.824
    × 6

12. 3.248
    × 4

13. 1.4631
    × 3

14. 6.25
    × 5

15. 4.071
    × 6

16. .38
    × 12

17. .042
    × 12

18. .037
    × 13

19. .0061
    × 14

20. .036
    × 21

21. .0042
    × 22

22. 4.23
    × 27

23. .312
    × 17

24. 1.37
    × 13

25. .648
    × 82

26. .2765
    × 31

27. 5.4
    × 18

28. 2.48
    × 17

29. 13.5
    × 59

30. 11.7
    × 42

31. 10.6
    × 14

32. 104.72
    × 23

Solve these problems.

33. 5 frozen dinners.
    Cost $1.29 each.
    Total cost?

34. 6 pairs of socks.
    $1.29 a pair.
    Total cost?

35. 3 packs of cards.
    $1.45 a pack.
    Total cost?

MULTIPLYING ANY TWO DECIMALS

Here are three ways to show .3 × .4.

Area Picture	Fractional Form	Decimal Form

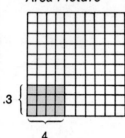

$$\frac{3}{10} \times \frac{4}{10} = \frac{12}{100}$$

$$\begin{array}{r} .4 \\ \times .3 \\ \hline .12 \end{array}$$

1. Multiply. Use the fractional form and then the decimal form.

a. .4 × .2   **b.** .4 × .4   **c.** .6 × .7   **d.** .3 × .5

2. Look at this multiplication.

$$\frac{4}{10} \times \frac{3}{100} = \frac{12}{1,000}$$

so
$$\begin{array}{r} .03 \\ \times .4 \\ \hline .012 \end{array}$$

The product is
a number of
thousandths.

Multiply. Use the fractional form and then the decimal form.

a. .4 × .02   **b.** .3 × .04   **c.** .6 × .07   **d.** .5 × .15

3. A decimal is said to have decimal places.

$$\left.\begin{array}{l} .0003 \\ .3920 \\ 13.2137 \end{array}\right\} \text{4 decimal places}$$

$$\left.\begin{array}{l} .005 \\ .290 \\ 8.312 \end{array}\right\} \text{3 decimal places}$$

$$\left.\begin{array}{l} .72 \\ .80 \\ 4.25 \end{array}\right\} \text{2 decimal places}$$

$$\left.\begin{array}{l} .2 \\ 1.8 \\ .4 \end{array}\right\} \text{1 decimal place}$$

$$\left.\begin{array}{l} 4 \\ 12 \\ 115 \end{array}\right\} \text{0 decimal places}$$

Complete this chart. Look for a pattern.

Number of Decimal Places			
Multiplication	1st Factor	2nd Factor	Product
6 × .7 = 4.2	0	1	1
12 × .21 = 2.52	0	2	
.6 × .7 = .42			2
.3 × .04 = .012		2	
.012 × .13 = .00156			5

The number of decimal places in the first factor plus the number of places in the second factor is equal to the number of places in the product.

4. Multiply.

    a. .7 × 1.3   **b.** .21 × 1.03   **c.** 3.2 × .073

EXERCISES

Multiply.

1. .8 × .7   **2.** .8 × .07   **3.** .4 × .6

4. .8 × .0007   **5.** .3 × .004   **6.** .2 × .0011

7. .9 × .32   **8.** .04 × .05   **9.** .6 × 1.1

10. .06 × .12   **11.** .03 × .0031   **12.** .05 × 6.2

13. .002 × 1.3   **14.** .04 × .025   **15.** .11 × 3.07

16. 4.3 × .81   **17.** .007 × 2.14   **18.** .5 × .3852

19. .5009 × 3.11   **20.** 4.008 × 2.2006   **21.** .009 × 4.36

22. .7001 × .53   **23.** 20.31 × .0071   **24.** 51.63 × 3.24

Study these multiplications by 10. Compare the decimal points in the first factor and in the products.

$2.7 \times 10 = 27.$ $.27 \times 10 = 2.7$

$.027 \times 10 = .27$ $.0027 \times 10 = .027$

When we multiply by 10, we can just "move" the decimal point one place to the right to quickly find the product.

1. Use the pattern to find these products quickly.

    a. 2.5×10 **b.** $.036 \times 10$ **c.** 1.34×10

2. Study these multiplications. Look for a pattern.

    $1.27 \times 100 = 127.$ $.127 \times 100 = 12.7$
    $1.27 \times 1,000 = 1,270.$ $.127 \times 1,000 = 127.$

When we multiply by 100, we "move" the decimal point two places to the right. When we multiply by 1,000 we "move" the decimal point three places to the right.

3. Multiply.

    a. $.25 \times 100$ **b.** $.36 \times 100$ **c.** $.0756 \times 1,000$

EXERCISES

Multiply.

1. $.6 \times 10$ **2.** $.03 \times 100$ **3.** $.03 \times 10$

4. 2.4×10 **5.** $.37 \times 100$ **6.** $.59 \times 10$

7. $.029 \times 100$ **8.** $.361 \times 1,000$ **9.** $.417 \times 1,000$

10. 1.29×10 **11.** $.4028 \times 100$ **12.** $.5166 \times 1,000$

MISSING FACTORS

Consider this open equation.

$$.2 \times n = .6$$

Is the solution 3? .3? .03?

The solution is 3, because this sentence is true.

$$.2 \times 3 = .6$$

HMMMM...

$$\begin{array}{r} .03 \\ \underline{\times\,2} \\ .006 \end{array} \qquad \begin{array}{r} .3 \\ \underline{\times\,2} \\ .06 \end{array} \qquad \begin{array}{r} 3 \\ \underline{\times\,2} \\ .6 \end{array}$$

THAT'S IT! SOLUTION IS 3!

---

1. Solve.

   a. $.3 \times n = 1.2$ **b.** $.3 \times n = 12$

   c. $.05 \times n = .25$ **d.** $.05 \times n = .025$

2. Use the patterns for multiplying by 10, 100, 1,000 to help solve these.

   a. $2.5 \times n = 25$ **b.** $13.4 \times n = 134$

   c. $.72 \times n = 72$ **d.** $1.86 \times n = 186$

EXERCISES

Solve.

1. $3 \times n = .6$ **2.** $3 \times n = .006$ **3.** $4 \times n = 1.2$

4. $4 \times n = .0012$ **5.** $.6 \times n = 6$ **6.** $.7 \times n = .21$

7. $.347 \times n = 347$ **8.** $.07 \times n = .021$ **9.** $.24 \times n = 24$

10. $1.1 \times n = .33$ **11.** $21.3 \times n = 213$ **12.** $.12 \times n = .36$

13. $1.75 \times n = 175$ **14.** $.16 \times n = 160$ **15.** $.4 \times n = 400$

16. $.324 \times n = 324$ **17.** $.8 \times n = 64$ **18.** $7.02 \times n = 702$

Study this division.

$$
\begin{array}{r}
1.87 \\
2\overline{)3.74} \\
\underline{2} \\
17 \\
\underline{16} \\
14 \\
\underline{14} \\
0
\end{array}
$$

Let's check.

$$
\begin{array}{r}
1.87 \\
\times 2 \\
\hline
3.74
\end{array}
$$

Thinking of money helps to check.

1. Because $2 \times .3 = .6$, then $.6 \div 2 = .3$.

$$
\begin{array}{r}
.3 \\
2\overline{).6}
\end{array}
$$

Use the multiplication sentence to find quotients.

a. $2 \times .6 = 1.2$

$$2\overline{)1.2}$$

b. $7 \times 3.6 = 25.2$

$$7\overline{)25.2}$$

c. $8 \times 4.32 = 34.56$

$$8\overline{)34.56}$$

d. $2 \times .009 = .018$

$$2\overline{).018}$$

2. Study these divisions.

$$
\begin{array}{r}
3.6 \\
7\overline{)25.2} \\
\underline{21} \\
42 \\
\underline{42} \\
0
\end{array}
\qquad
\begin{array}{r}
.36 \\
7\overline{)2.52} \\
\underline{21} \\
42 \\
\underline{42} \\
0
\end{array}
\qquad
\begin{array}{r}
.036 \\
7\overline{).252} \\
\underline{21} \\
42 \\
\underline{42} \\
0
\end{array}
$$

Compare the position of the decimal point in each division. Do you see a pattern?

When dividing a decimal by a whole number, divide as with whole numbers. Then place the decimal point in the quotient just above the decimal point in the dividend.

3. Copy. Place the decimal point in the right place in the quotient.

a. $\dfrac{7}{6\overline{)4.2}}$ **b.** $\dfrac{74}{8\overline{)5.92}}$ **c.** $\dfrac{2\,75}{5\overline{)13.75}}$

4. Divide.

Example
```
        6.21
  12)74.52
     72
      2 5
      2 4
        12
        12
         0
```

Check
```
    6.21
  × 12
  12 42
  62 1
  74.52
```

a. $8\overline{)19.04}$ **b.** $13\overline{)70.59}$ **c.** $21\overline{)49.266}$

Copy. Place the decimal point in the right place in the quotient.

1. $\dfrac{6}{4\overline{)2.4}}$ **2.** $\dfrac{3}{7\overline{).21}}$ **3.** $\dfrac{6}{8\overline{).048}}$

4. $\dfrac{4\,7}{3\overline{)14.1}}$ **5.** $\dfrac{46}{6\overline{)2.76}}$ **6.** $\dfrac{3\,214}{9\overline{)28.926}}$

Divide.

7. $2\overline{).46}$ **8.** $3\overline{).711}$ **9.** $4\overline{)1.324}$

10. $5\overline{).835}$ **11.** $5\overline{).035}$ **12.** $5\overline{).0835}$

13. $5\overline{).7835}$ **14.** $5\overline{)7.835}$ **15.** $6\overline{)37.2}$

16. $9\overline{)137.43}$ **17.** $2\overline{)3.952}$ **18.** $7\overline{)15.33}$

19. $12\overline{)28.8}$ **20.** $41\overline{)174.25}$ **21.** $13\overline{)30.108}$

DECIMALS AS DIVISORS

Let's divide: $.3\overline{)\,.12}$

First think of $.3\overline{)\,.12}$ as $\frac{.12}{.3}$. Think of an equivalent fractional numeral with the denominator a whole number.

$$\frac{.12}{.3} = \frac{.12 \times 10}{.3 \times 10}$$
$$= \frac{1.2}{3}$$

Now divide:
$$\begin{array}{r} .4 \\ 3\overline{)1.2} \end{array} \text{ so } \begin{array}{r} .4 \\ .3\overline{)\,.12} \end{array}$$

Check: $.4 \times .3 = .12$

---

1. To find the quotient $.21\overline{)\,.063}$, think of $\frac{.063}{.21}$.

a. By what do we multiply the denominator to make it a whole number? Think: $.21 \times n = 21$.

b. Find an equivalent fractional numeral.

$$\frac{.063}{.21} = \frac{.063 \times 100}{.21 \times 100}$$
$$= \frac{\triangle}{21}$$

c. Now divide: $21\overline{)6.3}$

d. Check.

2. Divide.

Example $.16\overline{)\,.384}$

Think

$$\frac{.384}{.16} = \frac{.384 \times 100}{.16 \times 100}$$
$$= \frac{38.4}{16}$$

Write

$$\begin{array}{r} 2.4 \\ 16\overline{)38.4} \\ \underline{32} \\ 6\,4 \\ \underline{6\,4} \\ 0 \end{array}$$

a. $.4\overline{)2.44}$ **b.** $.12\overline{)\,.084}$ **c.** $.023\overline{)\,.276}$

3. Instead of the thinking step, use a caret (∧) to "move" the decimal point.

$$2.5\overline{)13.25}$$

$$2.5\overline{)1\,3.2\,5}_{\wedge\quad\wedge}\quad.$$

$$\begin{array}{r} 5.3 \\ 2.5_{\wedge}\overline{)1\,3.2\,5}_{\wedge} \\ 125_{\wedge} \\ \hline 75 \\ 75 \\ \hline 0 \end{array}$$

Use a caret to "move" the decimal point. Place the decimal point in the quotient.

a. $.43\overline{)\,.258}^{\,6}$ **b.** $.7\overline{)\,.567}^{\,81}$ **c.** $5.6\overline{)19.04}^{\,34}$

d. $3.5\overline{)14.70}^{\,42}$ **e.** $.67\overline{)2.144}^{\,32}$ **f.** $.018\overline{)\,.01314}^{\,73}$

4. Sometimes we must write zeros in the dividend.

$$.125\overline{)2.5}$$

$$.1\,2\,5\overline{)2.5\,0\,0}_{\wedge\qquad\wedge}\quad.$$

$$\begin{array}{r} 2\,0. \\ .1\,2\,5_{\wedge}\overline{)2.5\,0\,0}_{\wedge} \\ 2\,5\,0 \\ \hline 0\,0 \end{array}$$

Use a caret to "move" the decimal point. Place the decimal point in the quotient.

a. $.25\overline{)12.5}^{\,50}$ **b.** $.026\overline{)8.19}^{\,315}$ **c.** $1.2\overline{)108}^{\,9}$

d. $.14\overline{)29.4}^{\,2\,10}$ **e.** $2.1\overline{)756}^{\,360}$ **f.** $.123\overline{)56.58}^{\,460}$

5. Divide.

a. $.7\overline{)3.64}$

b. $.41\overline{)7.38}$

c. $.026\overline{)\,.39}$

d. $5.3\overline{)1007}$

e. $.112\overline{)26.656}$

239

Use a caret to "move" the decimal point. Place the decimal point in the quotient.

1. $\dfrac{8}{.3\,)\overline{2.4}}$

2. $\dfrac{4}{.007\,)\overline{.028}}$

3. $\dfrac{524}{.031\,)\overline{.16244}}$

4. $\dfrac{9}{1.2\,)\overline{1.08}}$

5. $\dfrac{16}{.006\,)\overline{.0096}}$

6. $\dfrac{48\,1}{.04\,)\overline{1.924}}$

7. $\dfrac{40}{1.2\,)\overline{48}}$

8. $\dfrac{9}{\$.23\,)\overline{\$2.07}}$

9. $\dfrac{70}{.042\,)\overline{2.94}}$

10. $\dfrac{13}{1.7\,)\overline{2.21}}$

11. $\dfrac{11100}{.27\,)\overline{2997}}$

12. $\dfrac{42}{.186\,)\overline{7.812}}$

13. $\dfrac{61}{1.1\,)\overline{6.71}}$

14. $\dfrac{1700}{.33\,)\overline{561}}$

15. $\dfrac{114}{1.5\,)\overline{171}}$

Divide.

16. $\$.09\,)\overline{\$.81}$

17. $\$.12\,)\overline{\$1.44}$

18. $.6\,)\overline{7.44}$

19. $.04\,)\overline{1.924}$

20. $.8\,)\overline{9.6}$

21. $.07\,)\overline{.056}$

22. $.013\,)\overline{.091}$

23. $2.4\,)\overline{.504}$

24. $\$.13\,)\overline{\$19.50}$

25. $3.1\,)\overline{7.75}$

26. $.007\,)\overline{.1498}$

27. $.25\,)\overline{1}$

28. $.012\,)\overline{15.6}$

29. $.72\,)\overline{2.304}$

30. $.021\,)\overline{298.2}$

Solve these problems.

31. Ms. Lopez made 3.5 liters of solution. She wants to put them in jars that hold .25 liter each. How many jars will she need?

32. Luberta is thinking of a number. She says that .07 times the number is .91. What is the number?

240

METEOROLOGISTS

1. Rich Jackson talked about his science project with Mrs. Maria Prinz, the airport meteorologist. He learned that air cools 2° Celsius for each 1,000 meters when it rises up a mountain side. Mt. Kilmo is 7,000 meters high. How many degrees will the temperature drop in rising to the top of Mt. Kilmo?

2. Mrs. Prinz also told Rich that air temperature rises 2.5°C for each 1,000 meters when the air current goes down the mountain side. How many degrees does the temperature rise when it goes down the side of Mt. Kilmo, which is 7,000 meters high?

3. Amy Siegel talked with Mr. John Curci, another meteorologist. He told Amy that this January there was 20.4 centimeters of rain. Last January there was 16.7 centimeters of rain. How much more rain fell this January than last January?

4. Mr. Curci also told Amy that the temperature dropped from 25.2°C to 19.1°C yesterday afternoon. How many degrees did the temperature fall?

5. Mr. Curci explained that the average temperature for a day is found by taking the average of the day's high and low temperatures. Yesterday's high was 28.6°. The low was 18.8°. What was yesterday's average?

WRITING DECIMALS FOR FRACTIONS

Let's write a decimal for $\frac{1}{5}$.

THAT'S SIMPLE 'CAUSE $\frac{1}{5}$ MEANS 5⟌1 !

$\frac{1}{5}$ means $1 \div 5$ or $5\overline{)1}$

$5\overline{)1.0}^{.2}$ so, $\frac{1}{5} = .2$

1. Let's write a decimal for $\frac{1}{4}$.

$\frac{1}{4} \longrightarrow 4\overline{)1.00}^{.25}$ so, $\frac{1}{4} = .25$

Write decimals.

a. $\frac{1}{2}$ b. $\frac{3}{5}$ c. $\frac{4}{5}$ d. $\frac{2}{4}$

2. Add as many zeros as you wish after the decimal point. Complete.

$\frac{3}{8} \longrightarrow 8\overline{)3.000}^{.375}$ so, $\frac{3}{8} = $ _____

EXERCISES

Write decimals.

1. $\frac{5}{8}$ 2. $\frac{9}{20}$ 3. $\frac{3}{25}$ 4. $\frac{2}{5}$ 5. $\frac{3}{4}$

6. $\frac{5}{16}$ 7. $\frac{7}{20}$ 8. $\frac{7}{8}$ 9. $\frac{3}{16}$ 10. $\frac{1}{8}$

11. $\frac{1}{16}$ 12. $\frac{7}{16}$ 13. $\frac{9}{16}$ 14. $\frac{11}{16}$ 15. $\frac{13}{16}$

16. $\frac{1}{20}$ 17. $\frac{3}{20}$ 18. $\frac{11}{20}$ 19. $\frac{13}{20}$ 20. $\frac{17}{20}$

The decimal for $\frac{1}{9}$ never ends. It keeps repeating 1's.

$$\frac{1}{9} \longrightarrow 9\overline{)1.00}^{\quad.11}$$

$$\begin{array}{r} .11 \\ 9\overline{)1.00} \\ \underline{9} \\ 10 \\ \underline{9} \\ 1 \end{array}$$

so, $\frac{1}{9} = .11\ldots$

$\frac{1}{9} = .\overline{1}$

1. Consider this division.

   a. Continue the division. What is the thousandths digit in the quotient? What is the ten thousandths digit?

   $$\begin{array}{r} .16 \\ 6\overline{)1.0000} \\ \underline{6} \\ 40 \\ \underline{36} \\ 4 \end{array}$$

   b. Will the decimal for the quotient ever end?

2. Sometimes more than one digit repeats.

   $$\frac{3}{11} \longrightarrow 11\overline{)3.0000}^{\quad.2727\ldots} \longrightarrow .\overline{27}$$

Find the repeating decimals.

   a. $\frac{5}{11}$ b. $\frac{7}{9}$ c. $\frac{1}{7}$

EXERCISES

Find the repeating decimals.

1. $\frac{2}{9}$ 2. $\frac{2}{11}$ 3. $\frac{4}{9}$ 4. $\frac{4}{11}$

5. $\frac{5}{9}$ 6. $\frac{6}{11}$ 7. $\frac{5}{22}$ 8. $\frac{3}{7}$

243

CHAPTER REVIEW

Write decimals. [210]

1. Eight hundredths

2. Six and five thousandths

Write in fractional form. [210, 212]

3. .37   **4.** .024   **5.** 1.7   **6.** .8179

Write in decimal form.

7. $\frac{9}{10}$ [210]   **8.** $\frac{319}{1,000}$ [212]   **9.** $1\frac{3}{10}$ [210]   **10.** $\frac{73}{100}$ [210]

11. $\frac{3}{5}$ [242]   **12.** $\frac{3}{8}$ [242]   **13.** $\frac{1}{3}$ [243]   **14.** $\frac{5}{12}$ [243]

Compare. Use >, <, or =. [218]

15. .9 ≡ .27   **16.** .307 ≡ .0725   **17.** .5 ≡ .500

Add or subtract.

18. .5 + .3 [224]   **19.** .41 + .35 [224]   **20.** .5 + .38 [226]

21. 1.4 + .3 + .2 [226]   **22.** 4.6 + .155 + .29 [226]   **23.** .8 − .2 [228]

24. 8.4 − .7 [228]   **25.** .7396 − .7391 [228]   **26.** 4.7 − .361 [228]

Multiply or divide.

27. 8 × .9 [230]   **28.** 5 × .009 [230]   **29.** .8 × .6 [232]

30. .8 × .09 [232]   **31.** .08 × .13 [232]   **32.** 34.87 × 5.06 [232]

33. 1.8 ÷ 2 [236]   **34.** .36 ÷ .04 [238]   **35.** .063 ÷ .07 [238]

36. .0078 ÷ .006 [238]   **37.** 1.496 ÷ .04 [238]   **38.** 384.4 ÷ .31 [238]

Solve this problem. [223, 241]

39. The price of fryer chickens is $1.25 per kilogram. Emily wants 1.6 kilograms. How much will this cost?

CHAPTER TEST

1. Write the decimal seven and thirty-two hundredths.

Write in fractional form.

2. .9   **3.** 3.8   **4.** .21   **5.** .7259

Write in decimal form.

6. $\frac{7}{10}$ **7.** $\frac{35}{100}$ **8.** $3\frac{7}{10}$ **9.** $\frac{234}{1,000}$

10. $\frac{3}{4}$ **11.** $\frac{3}{5}$ **12.** $\frac{5}{6}$ **13.** $\frac{2}{3}$

Compare. Use $<$, $>$, or $=$.

14. .8 ≡ .49   **15.** .30 ≡ .3   **16.** .037 ≡ .02

Add or subtract.

17. .3 + .4   **18.** .3 + .58   **19.** 4.5 + .267 + .31

20. .7 − .3   **21.** 1.63 − .29   **22.** .9 − .213

Multiply or divide.

23. 7 × .3   **24.** .06 × .004   **25.** .023 × .4

26. 1.8 ÷ 3   **27.** 2.736 ÷ .4   **28.** 25.2 ÷ .21

Solve this problem.

29. On a test run in the early 1930's, a pilot flew his plane at 404.29 kilometers per hour. Several years later, this time was beaten by a plane which flew 422.82 kilometers per hour. How much faster was the second plane?

10 MEASUREMENT

MEASURING

Many years ago people used their hands, arms, fingers, and feet as units of measure.

1 CUBIT   1 PALM   1 NAIL   1 FOOT

1. The measure of $\overline{AB}$ is 8 centimeters. Complete.

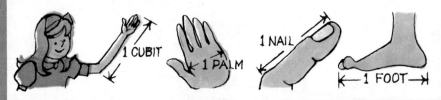

a. $CD =$ ____   **b.** $EF =$ ____   **c.** $GH =$ ____

2. The measure of $\overline{AB}$ and $\overline{GH}$ is the same. They are **congruent**.

$$\overline{AB} \cong \overline{GH}$$

Which segment is congruent to $\overline{CD}$?

EXERCISES

Measure these line segments. Name the congruent segments.

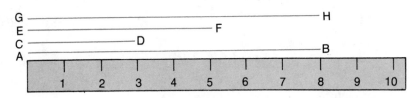

1. A ———— B   **2.** C ———— D

3. E ——— F   **4.** G ——— H

5. I ———— J   **6.**   K — L

7. M ———————— N

246

Measurements are always approximations. See how precise we are in measuring the eraser with these rulers.

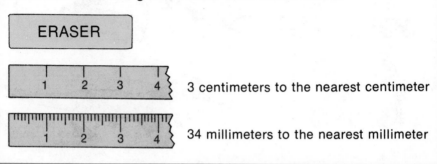

3 centimeters to the nearest centimeter

34 millimeters to the nearest millimeter

1. This ruler is marked in 1-centimeter intervals. The guppie and the worm are both 3 cm long, to the nearest centimeter. How long is the ant to the nearest centimeter?

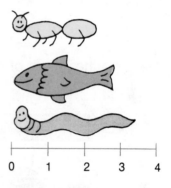

2. This ruler is marked in 1-millimeter intervals. 10 millimeters is the same as 1 centimeter. The guppie is 27 mm long to the nearest millimeter. The ant is 23 mm long to the nearest millimeter. How long is the worm to the nearest millimeter?

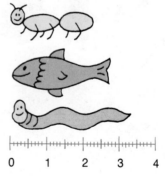

3. Find the length and width of your classroom to the nearest meter.

247

Measure the length of each to the nearest centimeter.

1.

2.

3.

4.

5.

Measure the length of each to the nearest millimeter.

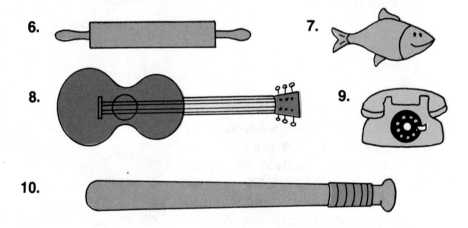

6.

7.

8.

9.

10.

DRAFTERS

1. Sue Memphis has to make a copy of the side of a generator. It has the dimensions shown in the picture. Use your protractor to find the angle at *B*.

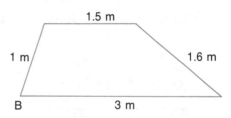

2. For each meter shown on this rectangle, Mrs. Memphis will draw a 2-centimeter length on her plans. Find the dimensions of her plans.

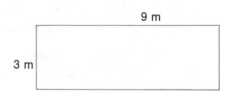

Les Lee made a drawing of a rectangle. The longer dimension is made up of two lengths. One is 7.4 cm long. The other is 2.7 cm long.

3. What is the total length of the longer dimension?
4. Will the drawing fit on a square piece of paper whose side measures 10 cm?
5. Mrs. Memphis was checking Mr. Lee's work. She rounded each segment length to the nearest centimeter. What did she get for the total length? Would Mrs. Memphis expect this rectangle to fit on a square piece of paper whose side measures 10 cm?

THE METRIC SYSTEM

Most countries use the metric system.

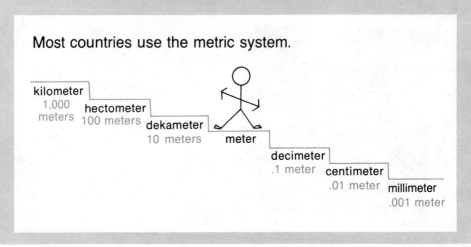

1. **a.** Use a meter stick to measure a strip of paper **1 meter (m)** long.

   b. Mark off the strip into 10 equal parts. Each part is 1 **decimeter (dm)** long.

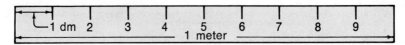

   c. Divide each decimeter into 10 parts of the same length. Each new part is **1 centimeter (cm)** long.

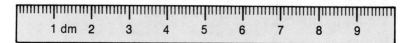

   Count how many centimeters there are in a decimeter. How many centimeters are in a meter?

   d. Divide each centimeter into 10 parts of the same length. Each new part is **1 millimeter (mm)** long.

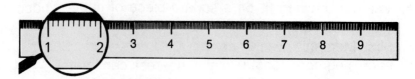

   Count how many millimeters there are in a centimeter. How many millimeters are in a meter?

2. Let's think about metric units larger than the meter.

   a. Imagine a wall 10 meters high. That is the length of 1 **dekameter (dam)**. Find something in the school yard which you think is 1 dekameter long. Check its length with a meter stick.

   b. Think about a football field. The distance from the goal posts at one end to the goal posts at the other end is about 100 meters. That is the length of **1 hectometer (hm).** Does any part of your school yard appear to be 1 hectometer long? Check your estimate.

   c. Do you know of a street that is 1,000 meters long? That is the length of 1 **kilometer (km)**. Find a street you think is 1 kilometer long. Can you find a bicycle or automobile odometer to check your estimate?

EXERCISES

Estimate and measure.

1. Find some objects you can measure in millimeters. (Examples: your fingernail or the eraser on your pencil) Estimate the lengths before you measure.

2. Find some things you can measure in centimeters. (Examples: the length of a desk or a windowpane) Estimate the lengths before you measure.

3. Find some objects you can measure with a meter stick. (Examples: the length of a room or a building) Estimate the lengths before you measure.

4. Find someone who has a bicycle or automobile odometer. Ride a distance of 1 kilometer. Describe that distance to the rest of the class.

251

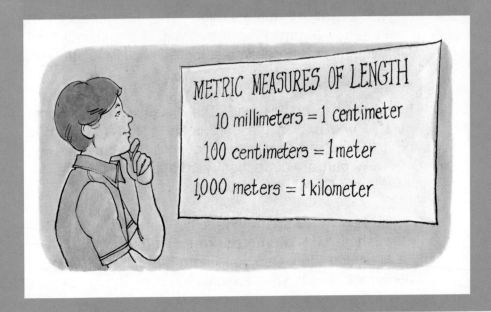

METRIC MEASURES OF LENGTH
10 millimeters = 1 centimeter
100 centimeters = 1 meter
1,000 meters = 1 kilometer

1. Copy and complete. Use the sign above or your meter stick if you need help.

   a. ____ cm = 1 m

   b. ____ mm = 1 cm

   c. ____ mm = 1 m

   d. 200 cm = ____ m

   e. 50 mm = ____ cm

   f. 4 cm = ____ mm

2. Here is another way to change measures.

   Example   7 m = ____ cm Think: 7 meters is the same as
   7 m = 7 × (1 m)   7 times 1 meter.
   = 7 × (100 cm)   1 m = 100 cm
   = 700 cm

Complete.

   a. 4 m = 4 × (1 m)
   = 4 × (100 cm)
   = ____ cm

   b. 6 cm = 6 × (1 cm)
   = 6 × (10 mm)
   = ____ mm

   c. 9 km = 9 × (1 km)
   = 9 × (____ m)
   = ____ m

   d. 12 cm = 12 × (1 cm)
   = 12 × (____ mm)
   = ____ mm

252

3. Sometimes we can use decimals.

Example   800 cm = 800 × (1 cm)
= 800 × (.01 m)
= 8 m

Complete.

a. 600 cm = 600 × (1 cm)   **b.** 70 mm = 70 × (1 mm)
= 600 × (.01 m)   = 70 × (.1 cm)
= ___ m   = ___ cm

c. 400 cm = 400 × (1 cm)   **d.** 50 m = 50 × (1 m)
= 400 × (___)   = 50 × (___ km)
= ___ m   = ___ km

EXERCISES

Change to centimeters.

1. 2 m   **2.** 8 m   **3.** 120 mm   **4.** 240 mm

5. 20 mm   **6.** 40 mm   **7.** 13 m   **8.** 27 m

Change to millimeters.

9. 2 cm   **10.** 5 m   **11.** 11 cm   **12.** 23 m

Change to meters.

13. 200 cm   **14.** 5 km   **15.** 700 cm   **16.** 1,200 mm

Solve these problems.

17. John measured his index finger. It was 6 centimeters long. How many millimeters is this?

18. Sandie told John to buy their dog Buffy a collar that was 13 centimeters long. However, the pet shop measured all its collars in millimeters. How many millimeters long should Buffy's collar be?

PRECISION

You cannot always tell the *exact* measure of an object. If you are careful, however, you can be precise to the nearest centimeter or to the nearest millimeter.

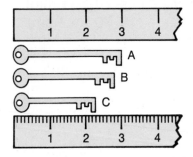

	Nearest Centimeter	Nearest Millimeter
Key A	3 cm	30 mm
Key B	3 cm	28 mm
Key C	2 cm	23 mm

1. Measure to the nearest centimeter, then to the nearest millimeter.

   a. _____
   b. _____
   c. _____
   d. _____
   e. _____
   f. _____

2. Measure these.

   a. Your classroom to the nearest meter

   b. The chalkboard to the nearest meter

   c. A classmate's height to the nearest meter, then to the nearest centimeter

3. Measurements are never exact. The greatest possible error in measuring with this ruler is one-fourth centimeter.

The greatest possible error of measurement is one half the smallest unit of measurement on your ruler.

Give the greatest possible error made in measuring with these rulers.

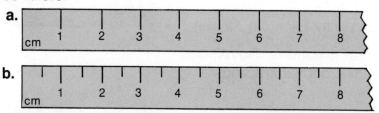

a.

b.

Measure to the nearest centimeter, then to the nearest millimeter.

1. A —————————— B

2. C ——————————————————— D

3. E ————————————————————— F

4. G ——————— H

5. J ———————————————— K

6. M ———————————— N

7. O ——————————— P

8. S ————————————————————— T

Measure these.

9. The length and width of a windowpane to the nearest centimeter

10. The width of a hallway or a path in your school to the nearest meter

What is the greatest possible error of measurements made with rulers whose smallest units of measure are given below?

11. 1 millimeter   **12.** 1 meter   ★**13.** .5 centimeter

ADDITION AND SUBTRACTION

The ruler shows that

7 cm 3 mm = 6 cm 13 mm

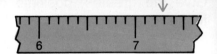

We can use this fact to regroup in adding and subtracting.

<table>
<tr><td>2 cm 6 mm</td></tr>
<tr><td>+4 cm 7 mm</td></tr>
<tr><td>6 cm 13 mm = 7 cm 3 mm</td></tr>
</table>

$$\begin{array}{r} \overset{6}{7} \text{ cm } \overset{13}{3} \text{ mm} \\ -3 \text{ cm } 5 \text{ mm} \\ \hline 3 \text{ cm } 8 \text{ mm} \end{array}$$

1. Complete these additions.

   a. 3 cm 8 mm
   +5 cm 9 mm
   ———————
   8 cm 17 mm =
          9 cm __ mm

   b. 3 m 93 cm
   +4 m 46 cm
   ———————
   7 m 139 cm =
          8 m __ cm

2. Complete these subtractions.

   a. $\overset{8}{9}$ cm $\overset{14}{4}$ mm
   −2 cm 8 mm
   ———————
   __ cm __ mm

   b. $\overset{4}{5}$ m $\overset{146}{46}$ cm
   −2 m 85 cm
   ———————
   __ m __ cm

EXERCISES

Add or subtract.

1. 2 cm 2 mm
   +5 cm 9 mm

2. 3 cm 5 mm
   +4 cm 8 mm

3. 4 cm 7 mm
   +2 cm 7 mm

4. 5 m 75 cm
   +1 m 63 cm

5. 7 cm 3 mm
   −2 cm 5 mm

6. 8 cm 2 mm
   −5 cm 7 mm

7. 9 cm 4 mm
   −1 cm 9 mm

8. 6 m 25 cm
   −1 m 31 cm

9. 9 m 49 cm
   −5 m 82 cm

We measure things like milk and gasoline in liters.

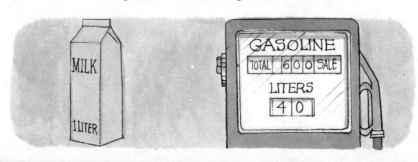

1. One **liter (L)** is 1,000 milliliters (mL), so 2 liters is 2,000 milliliters. Change to milliliters.

   a. 3 L   **b.** 5 L   **c.** 7 L

Change to liters.

   d. 6,000 mL   **e.** 4,000 mL   **f.** 10,000 mL

2. A small bottle of medicine might contain 50 milliliters. A gas tank in a car might contain 50 liters. Match these.

eyedropper	2 milliliters
glass of milk	20 liters
bucket of water	200 milliliters

3. Bob measured a liquid for a science experiment. First he poured in 1 liter 234 milliliters. Then he added 2 liters 307 milliliters. How much altogether? Complete.

   ```
     1 liter   234 milliliters
   + 2 liters  307 milliliters
   ─────────────────────────────
       liters  541 milliliters
   ```

4. Sometimes we need to regroup when adding.

   Example
   ```
     1 liter     234 milliliters
   + 2 liters    807 milliliters
   ──────────────────────────────
     3 liters  1,041 milliliters = 4 L 41 mL
   ```

257

Add.

a. 3 L 452 mL
  + 2 L 613 mL

b. 7 L 598 mL
  + 3 L 923 mL

5. We regroup the same way when we subtract. Complete.

Example   3 L 340 mL is the same as   2 L 1,340 mL
  − 1 L 500 mL   − 1 L   500 mL
  ─────────────   ────────────────
                                        1 L _____ mL

Suppose each of these is full. Which would you measure in milliliters? liters?

1. paper cup   **2.** gas tank   **3.** baby bottle

4. coffee cup   **5.** soda bottle   **6.** bathtub

Complete.

7. 4 L = _____ mL   **8.** 8,000 mL = _____ L

Add or subtract.

9.   2 L 882 mL   **10.**   4 L 882 mL
     + 3 L 113 mL   + 3 L 139 mL

11.   7 L 473 mL   **12.**   71 L 71 mL
     − 3 L 169 mL   − 29 L 79 mL

Solve these problems.

13. Ms. Madel bought 5 liters of milk on sale for 59¢ a liter. How much did she pay in all?

14. Mr. Boichik bought 6 liters of milk at 68¢ a liter. How much change did he get from a $10 bill?

METRIC WEIGHT

This book weighs a little less than 1 **kilogram (kg)**.

about 1 gram

1 kilogram = 1,000 grams. So, **1 gram (g)** of butter is a very small portion.

1 gram = 1,000 milligrams. It is very hard to see a **milligram (mg)** of butter.

1. Which would you measure in milligrams? in grams? in kilograms?

   a. a toothbrush   **b.** a person   **c.** a feather

2. Let's change kilograms and grams.

   $$1 \text{ kg} = 1,000 \text{ g}$$
   $$\text{so,} \quad 3 \text{ kg} = 3 \times 1,000 \text{ g}$$
   $$= 3,000 \text{ g}$$

   AND TO CHANGE GRAMS TO KILOGRAMS I JUST DIVIDE BY 1,000!

   Change grams to kilograms and kilograms to grams.

   a. 4 kg   **b.** 5.7 kg   **c.** 5,000 g   **d.** 6,825 g

3. We can change grams to milligrams also.

   $$1 \text{ g} = 1,000 \text{ mg}$$
   $$\text{so,} \quad 4 \text{ g} = 4 \times 1,000 \text{ mg}$$
   $$= 4,000 \text{ mg}$$

   AND TO CHANGE MILLIGRAMS TO GRAMS, JUST DIVIDE BY 1,000!

   Change grams to milligrams and milligrams to grams.

   a. 5 g   **b.** 6.48 g   **c.** 6,000 mg   **d.** 7,900 mg

Would you use milligrams, grams, or kilograms?

1. Hot dog
2. Bicycle
3. Penny
4. Drop of water
5. Hamburger
6. Dog

Change to grams.

7. 3 kg
8. 5 kg
9. 13 kg
10. 2.470 kg
11. 4,000 mg
12. 11,000 mg
13. 15,000 mg
14. 4,672 mg

Change to milligrams.

15. 6 g
16. 12 g
17. 17 g
18. 3.826 g

Change to kilograms.

19. 3,000 g
20. 7,000 g
21. 12,000 g
22. 8,205 g

Solve this problem.

23. Four vitamin tablets. All the same. Total 1 gram. How many milligrams each?

ACTIVITY

Do this activity with a friend. Get two scales. One scale should allow you to weigh in grams; the other scale should allow you to weigh in kilograms. Find objects like these: coins, a glass of water, an apple, a bottle of soda, a can of vegetables, a carrot. Estimate the weight of each item in grams. Use the scale to check your estimates.

Ask for several volunteers from the class. Estimate the weight of each in kilograms. Check your estimates by using the scale. Who had the best estimates?

WHAT'S THE TEMPERATURE?

1. Read the temperature.

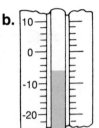 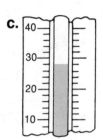

a. b. c.

2. To find the average temperature of the day, we average that day's highest and lowest temperatures.

Example   High: 30°C $\dfrac{30° + 18°}{2} = 24°C$
            Low: 18°C

Find the average temperature for days with these readings.

    a. High: 23°C   **b.** High: 11°C   **c.** High: 19°C
        Low: 17°C   Low: 5°C   Low: 3°C

EXERCISES

Read the temperature.

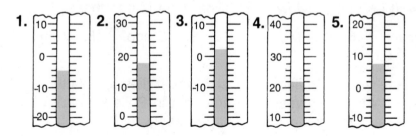

1. **2.** **3.** **4.** **5.**

Find the average temperature.

   6. High: 32°C **7.** High: 15°C   **8.** High: 16°C
      Low: 24°C   Low: 9°C   Low: 10°C

   9. High: 12°C **10.** High: 9°C   ★**11.** High: 2° below zero
      Low: 8°C   Low: 7°C   Low: 10° below zero

261

WHAT TIME IS IT?

Suppose it is 9 am in St. Louis. What time is it in these cities?

1. Atlanta   **2.** Las Vegas   **3.** Memphis   **4.** Phoenix

Suppose it is 2 pm in New York. What time is it in these cities?

5. Denver   **6.** Des Moines   **7.** San Diego   **8.** Miami

9. A plane leaves Philadelphia at 5 pm. It flies to Seattle in 4 hours. When it arrives, what time is it in Philadelphia? Why does the clock in the Seattle airport say 6 pm?

10. A plane can fly from Denver to Washington D.C. in 3 hours. Suppose it leaves Denver at 4 pm. What time will it be in Washington D.C. when the plane arrives?

11. At 9:30 am in New York City, Ms. Carbone decides to call the home office in Boise, Idaho. However, she knows that that office opens at 8:30 am. How many hours must she wait before she can call the Boise office?

262

Write decimals.

1. $\frac{3}{10}$ 2. $\frac{4}{100}$ 3. $\frac{34}{100}$

Keeping Fit

4. $\frac{6}{1,000}$ 5. $\frac{46}{1,000}$ 6. $\frac{346}{1,000}$

7. $\frac{52}{100}$ 8. $\frac{50}{100}$ 9. $\frac{527}{1,000}$

10. $\frac{520}{1,000}$ 11. $\frac{500}{1,000}$ 12. $\frac{5,671}{10,000}$ 13. $\frac{3}{10,000}$

14. $\frac{49}{10,000}$ 15. $\frac{506}{10,000}$ 16. $\frac{1}{2}$ 17. $\frac{3}{4}$

18. $\frac{3}{8}$ 19. $\frac{2}{3}$ 20. $\frac{2}{11}$ 21. $\frac{1}{7}$

Write in fractional form.

22. .3   23. .03   24. .23   25. .007

26. .237   27. .037   28. .39   29. .30

30. .395   31. .390   32. .300   33. .4189

34. .0008   35. .0053   36. .0708   37. .9000

Multiply.

38. $3 \times .2$ 39. $.3 \times .2$ 40. $.7 \times 5$

41. $.07 \times 4$ 42. $9 \times .23$ 43. $8 \times .124$

44. $\begin{array}{r} .49 \\ \times\,.4 \\ \hline \end{array}$ 45. $\begin{array}{r} 7.28 \\ \times\,.6 \\ \hline \end{array}$ 46. $\begin{array}{r} 9.47 \\ \times\,.08 \\ \hline \end{array}$

47. $\begin{array}{r} .59 \\ \times\,.73 \\ \hline \end{array}$ 48. $\begin{array}{r} .623 \\ \times\,9 \\ \hline \end{array}$ 49. $\begin{array}{r} .708 \\ \times\,12 \\ \hline \end{array}$

50. $\begin{array}{r} 1.23 \\ \times\,1.1 \\ \hline \end{array}$ 51. $\begin{array}{r} 2.40 \\ \times\,.36 \\ \hline \end{array}$ 52. $\begin{array}{r} 41.3 \\ \times\,4.7 \\ \hline \end{array}$

263

MEASURING IN THE CUSTOMARY SYSTEM

Measurements are always approximations.

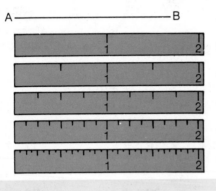

A————————————B   Precision

2 in. to the nearest in.

$1\frac{1}{2}$ in. to the nearest $\frac{1}{2}$ in.

$1\frac{3}{4}$ in. to the nearest $\frac{1}{4}$ in.

$1\frac{6}{8}$ in. to the nearest $\frac{1}{8}$ in.

$1\frac{11}{16}$ in. to the nearest $\frac{1}{16}$ in.

1. This ruler is marked only in $\frac{1}{2}$-inch intervals Each segment except $\overline{GH}$ measures $2\frac{1}{2}$ inches to the nearest $\frac{1}{2}$ inch. What is the length of $\overline{GH}$ to the nearest $\frac{1}{2}$ inch?

G ————— H
E ————————— F
C ————————— D
A ————— B

2. A ruler is marked in $\frac{1}{4}$-inch intervals. Each segment except $\overline{GH}$ measures $1\frac{2}{4}$ inches to the nearest $\frac{1}{4}$ inch. How long is $\overline{GH}$ to the nearest $\frac{1}{4}$ inch?

G ————— H
E ——— F
C ——— D
A ——— B

3. A ruler is divided into $\frac{1}{8}$ inch intervals. How long is $\overline{GH}$ to the nearest $\frac{1}{8}$ inch?

G ————— H

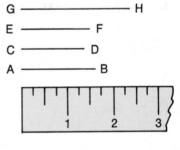

4. Measurements are never exact. The **greatest possible error** in measuring in Item 3 is $\frac{1}{16}$ inch. What about Item 2? Item 1?

264

The greatest possible error of measurement is one half the smallest unit of measurement on your ruler.

5. Give the greatest possible error made in measuring with these rulers.

a.
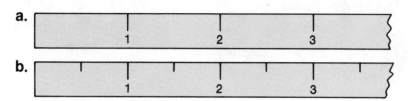

b.

6. Often rulers are marked in $\frac{1}{16}$-inch intervals. What is the measure of each segment to the nearest $\frac{1}{16}$ inch?

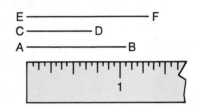

7. What is the greatest possible error in Item 6?

Measure these line segments to the nearest 1 inch; $\frac{1}{2}$ inch; $\frac{1}{4}$ inch; $\frac{1}{8}$ inch; $\frac{1}{16}$ inch.

1. A ——————— B
2. C ————————————————— D
3. E ——————————————————— F
4. G ——————H
5. J ————————————————— K
6. M ————————————— N
7. O ————————————— P
8. S ——————————————————— T

What is the greatest possible error of measurements made with rulers whose smallest units of measure are given below?

9. $\frac{1}{8}$ inch   10. 1 yard   11. $\frac{1}{4}$ inch

LENGTH IN THE CUSTOMARY SYSTEM

12 in. = 1 ft
3 ft = 1 yd
5,280 ft = 1 mi
1,760 yd = 1 mi

Here's a way to change from one unit to another.

24 in. = 24 × (1 in.)

$= 24 \times \left(\frac{1}{12} \text{ ft}\right)$

= 2 ft

1. Complete.

a. 6 in. = 6 × (1 in.)

$= \underline{\ } \times \left(\frac{1}{12} \text{ ft}\right)$

= __ ft

b. 2 ft = 2 × (1 ft)

= __ × (12 in.)

= __ in.

2. Change feet to inches and inches to feet.

a. 8 in.　　　**b.** 18 in.　　　**c.** 36 in.

d. 3 ft　　　**e.** 5 ft　　　**f.** 2 ft

3. Complete.

a. 6 yd = 6 × (1 yd)

= __ × (3 ft)

= __ ft

b. 6 ft = 6 × (1 ft)

$= \underline{\ } \times \left(\frac{1}{3} \text{ yd}\right)$

= __ yd

4. Change yards to feet and feet to yards.

a. 2 yd　　　**b.** 12 yd　　　**c.** 13 yd

d. 12 ft　　　**e.** 24 ft　　　**f.** 48 ft

5. Change to feet.

Example　　3 mi = 3 × (1 mi)

= 3 × (5,280 ft)

= 15,840 ft

a. 4 mi　　　**b.** 5 mi　　　**c.** 10 mi

6. Add. Regroup the sum if necessary.

Example
$$5 \text{ yd } 2 \text{ ft}$$
$$+3 \text{ yd } 2 \text{ ft}$$
$$8 \text{ yd } 4 \text{ ft} = 9 \text{ yd } 1 \text{ ft}$$

a. 5 ft 7 in.
    +3 ft 9 in.

b. 6 ft   4 in.
     +5 ft 10 in.

7. Subtract. Regroup if necessary.

Example
$$\overset{8}{\cancel{9}} \text{ ft } \overset{17}{\cancel{5}} \text{ in.}$$
$$-2 \text{ ft } 8 \text{ in.}$$
$$6 \text{ ft } 9 \text{ in.}$$

a. 6 ft 3 in.
    −2 ft 7 in.

b. 12 ft 4 in.
     − 9 ft 9 in.

EXERCISES

Change to feet.

1. 9 in. **2.** 48 in. **3.** 15 in. **4.** 3 yd

5. 4 yd **6.** $5\frac{1}{3}$ yd **7.** 6 mi **8.** $\frac{1}{2}$ mi

Change to inches.

9. 4 ft **10.** 6 ft **11.** 9 ft **12.** $\frac{1}{3}$ ft

Change to yards.

13. 9 ft **14.** 15 ft **15.** 21 ft **16.** 36 ft

Add or subtract.

17. 7 yd 1 ft
     +4 yd 2 ft

18. 17 yd 1 ft
      + 9 yd 2 ft

19. 3 ft 10 in.
      +4 ft   8 in.

20. 17 yd 1 ft
      − 9 yd 2 ft

21. 7 ft   7 in.
      −4 ft 10 in.

22. 35 ft 2 in.
      −12 ft 8 in.

CAPACITY IN THE CUSTOMARY SYSTEM

Here's a way to change liquid measures.

3 cups = 3 × (1 cup)
      = 3 × (8 fl oz)
      = 24 fl oz

8 qt = 8 × (1 qt)
    = 8 × ($\frac{1}{4}$ gal)
    = 2 gal

TABLE OF LIQUID MEASURE

1 fl oz	= 2 tbs
8 fl oz	= 1 cup
2 cups	= 1 pt
2 pt	= 1 qt
4 qt	= 1 gal

1. Complete.

a. 6 cups = 6 × (1 cup)
          = __ × ($\frac{1}{2}$ pt)
          = __ pt

b. 6 qt = __ × (1 qt)
        = 6 × (2 pt)
        = __ pt

2. Change to pints.

a. 4 cups   **b.** 8 cups   **c.** 5 qt

3. Complete.

a. 4 pt = 4 × (1 pt)
        = __ × ($\frac{1}{2}$ qt)
        = __ qt

b. 4 gal = __ × (1 gal)
         = 4 × (4 qt)
         = __ qt

4. Change to quarts.

a. 6 pt   **b.** 9 pt   **c.** 5 gal

5. Complete.

a. 4 fl oz = 4 × (1 fl oz)
          = 4 × (2 tbs)
          = __ tbs

b. 4 pt = __ × (1 pt)
        = 4 × (2 cups)
        = __ cups

6. Change to tablespoons.

a. 3 fl oz   **b.** 6 fl oz   **c.** 7 fl oz

Change to cups.

d. 3 pt   **e.** 6 pt   **f.** 7 pt

7. Add. Rename the sum if necessary.

a.   6 gal 1 qt   **b.**   1 pt 1 cup
   $+$ 3 gal 3 qt $+$ 3 pt 1 cup

8. Subtract. Rename if necessary.

Example   6 cups 5 fl oz $\overset{5}{\cancel{6}}$ cups $\overset{13}{\cancel{5}}$ fl oz
                  $-$ 2 cups 7 fl oz $-$ 2 cups 7 fl oz
                                              3 cups 6 fl oz

a.   4 cups 3 fl oz   **b.**   6 gal 1 qt
   $-$ 1 cup 6 fl oz $-$ 3 gal 3 qt

EXERCISES

Copy and complete.

1. 10 cups = __ pt   **2.** 8 qt = __ pt   **3.** 7 qt = __ pt

4. 8 pt = __ qt   **5.** 12 gal = __ qt   **6.** 3 gal = __ qt

7. 8 fl oz = __ tbs   **8.** 7 gal = __ qt   **9.** 12 qt = __ gal

10. 4 fl oz = __ tbs   **11.** 5 tbs = __ fl oz   **12.** 5 pt = __ qt

13. 2 cups = __ fl oz   **14.** 8 pt = __ cups   **15.** 7 qt = __ gal

Add or subtract.

16.   7 gal 3 qt   **17.**   12 gal 3 qt
   $+$ 9 gal 3 qt $+$ 3 gal 2 qt

18.   7 cups 1 fl oz   **19.**   9 gal 2 qt
   $-$ 3 cups 5 fl oz $-$ 4 gal 3 qt

WEIGHT IN THE CUSTOMARY SYSTEM

We can use a similar method to change measures of weight.

$$8 \text{ lb} = 8 \times (1 \text{ lb})$$
$$= 8 \times (16 \text{ oz})$$
$$= 128 \text{ oz}$$

TABLE OF WEIGHT MEASURES

| 16 oz = 1 lb |
| 2,000 lb = 1 ton |

1. Complete.

   a. $4 \text{ lb} = 4 \times (1 \text{ lb})$
   $= \underline{} \times (16 \text{ oz})$
   $= \underline{} \text{ oz}$

   b. $4 \text{ oz} = \underline{} \times (1 \text{ oz})$
   $= 4 \times \left(\frac{1}{16} \text{ lb}\right)$
   $= \underline{} \text{ lb}$

2. Change to ounces.

   a. 2 lb   **b.** 3 lb   **c.** 12 lb

   Change to pounds.

   d. 2 oz   **e.** 12 oz   **f.** 32 oz

3. Complete.

   a. $2 \text{ tons} = 2 \times (1 \text{ ton})$
   $= \underline{} \times (2,000 \text{ lb})$
   $= \underline{} \text{ lb}$

   b. $500 \text{ lb} = 500 \times (1 \text{ lb})$
   $= 500 \times \left(\frac{1}{2,000} \text{ ton}\right)$
   $= \frac{500}{2,000} \text{ ton}$
   $= \underline{} \text{ ton}$

4. Change to pounds.

   a. 4 tons   **b.** 8 tons   **c.** 10 tons

   Change to tons.

   d. 1,000 lb   **e.** 1,500 lb   **f.** 4,000 lb

5. Add. Complete.

a.   6 lb   8 oz
    + 2 lb 10 oz
    8 lb 18 oz =
          __ lb 2 oz

b.   8 lb 14 oz
    + 2 lb 15 oz
   10 lb __ oz =
          11 lb 13 oz

6. Subtract. Complete.

a.   ⁴ ²³
    $\cancel{5}$ lb $\cancel{7}$ oz
   − 2 lb 9 oz
    __ lb __ oz

b.   ¹³¹⁸
   $\cancel{14}$ lb $\cancel{2}$ oz
   − 6 lb 5 oz
    __ lb __ oz

Copy and complete.

1. 6 tons = ____ lb   **2.** 3 tons = ____ lb   **3.** 7 tons = ____ lb

4. 6 oz = ____ lb   **5.** 10 oz = ____ lb   **6.** 32 oz = ____ lb

7. 6 lb = ____ oz   **8.** 10 lb = ____ oz   **9.** 5 lb = ____ oz

10. 15 lb = ____ oz   **11.** 9 lb = ____ oz   **12.** 20 lb = ____ oz

13. 48 oz = ____ lb   **14.** 1,600 lb = ____ ton

★ **15.** 1 ton = ____ oz   ★ **16.** .4 ton = ____ lb

Add or subtract.

17.   3 lb 7 oz
   + 4 lb 5 oz

18.   12 lb 7 oz
   + 5 lb 10 oz

19.   23 lb 9 oz
   − 6 lb 11 oz

20.   7 lb 8 oz
   − 1 lb 3 oz

★ **21.** Make a flow chart to show how to add two measures, both in pounds and ounces.

CHAPTER REVIEW

Measure these segments to the nearest centimeter and the nearest millimeter. [247]

1. —————— **2.** —————— **3.** ——————

What is the greatest possible error of measurement made with rulers whose smallest units of measure are given below? [254]

4. 1 millimeter **5.** 2 centimeters **6.** 1 meter

Complete.

7. 2 m = ____ cm
[252]

8. 50 mm = ____ cm
[252]

9. 63 m = ____ cm
[252]

10. 400 cm = ____ m
[252]

11. 290 mm = ____ cm
[252]

12. 7 cm = ____ mm
[252]

13. 6 g = ____ mg
[259]

14. 4,000 g = ____ kg
[259]

15. 5,000 mL = ____ L
[257]

16. 20 L = ____ mL
[257]

17. 6,785 m = ____ km
[252]

18. .462 km = ____ m
[252]

Add or subtract. [256]

19. 3 cm 7 mm
  + 2 cm 9 mm
  ————————

20. 9 m 45 cm
  − 3 m 71 cm
  ————————

21. 1 L 456 mL
  + 2 L 902 mL
  ————————

Find the average temperature. [261]

22. High: 31°C
  Low: 27°C

23. High: 21°C
  Low: 15°C

24. It is 9:30 am in the Mountain Time Zone. What time is it in the Central Time Zone? [262]

Solve this problem. [249]

25. Amy jogged 300 meters in the morning and 450 meters in the afternoon. How many meters did she jog in all?

CHAPTER TEST

1. Measure this segment to the nearest centimeter.

   _____

2. Measure this segment to the nearest millimeter.

   _____

3. What is the greatest possible error of measurement made with a ruler whose smallest unit of measure is 5 millimeters?

Complete.

4. 70 mm = _____ cm

5. 68 m = _____ cm

6. 3 g = _____ mg

7. 700 cm = _____ m

8. 10 L = _____ mL

9. 5 kg = _____ g

10. 6 cm = _____ mm

11. .8 km = _____ m

Add or subtract.

12.　　4 cm　8 mm
　　+3 cm　5 mm
　　‾‾‾‾‾‾‾‾‾‾‾‾

13.　　5 m　19 cm
　　−2 m　39 cm
　　‾‾‾‾‾‾‾‾‾‾‾‾

Find the average temperature.

14. High: 12°C
    Low: 8°C

15. High: 23°C
    Low: 17°C

16. It is 10:00 pm in the Eastern Time Zone. What time is it in the Pacific Time Zone?

Solve this problem.

17. Josh weighed 38 kilograms last March. This March, he weighs 43 kilograms. How much weight did he gain during the year?

11 PERCENT

Here is Tom's test record.

Test	Correct Answers	No. of Questions	Fraction Correct	Denominator 100	Percent
1st	80	100	$\frac{80}{100}$	$\frac{80}{100}$	80%
2nd	15	20	$\frac{15}{20}$	$\frac{75}{100}$	75%
3rd	45	50	$\frac{45}{50}$	$\frac{90}{100}$	90%
4th	22	25	$\frac{22}{25}$	$\frac{88}{100}$	88%

Read 75% as "75 percent."

1. Are these four sentences true about the 4th test?

   a. Tom answered $\frac{22}{25}$ of the questions correctly.

   b. Tom answered $\frac{88}{100}$ of the questions correctly.

   c. Tom answered 22 out of 25 of the questions correctly.

   d. Tom answered 75% of the questions correctly.

Percent is a ratio in which the second number is 100.

80% means 80 out of 100, or $\frac{80}{100}$.

2. **a.** What does 90% mean?

   b. What does 42% mean?

   c. What does 17% mean?

3. Tom did the worst on the 2nd test. On which test did he do the best?

274

Complete the table showing Lucy's spelling test record.

	Test	Correct Answers	No. of Questions	Fraction Correct	Denominator 100	Percent
1.	A	16	20		$\frac{80}{100}$	80%
2.	B	21	25	$\frac{21}{25}$		84%
3.	C	9	10		$\frac{90}{100}$	
4.	D	5	5		$\frac{100}{100}$	

5. On which test did Lucy do best?

6. On which test did she do worst?

Write these using percent notation.

7. 40 out of 100

8. 23 out of 100

9. 62 out of 100

10. 84 out of 100

11. $\frac{36}{100}$

12. $\frac{57}{100}$

13. $\frac{56}{100}$

14. $\frac{25}{100}$

15. $\frac{37}{100}$

16. $\frac{42}{100}$

17. $\frac{67}{100}$

18. $\frac{21}{100}$

Brainteaser

Arrange 5 coins as shown below.

Move the coins so that the 3 like coins are together in a line next to the 2 unlike coins.

You are allowed only 3 moves. You must move 2 coins at a time, and the 2 coins must be next to each other. These 2 coins may be placed alongside or between the other coins.

FRACTIONS, DECIMALS, AND PERCENTS

Robert earned $100 and saved $50. Madelyn earned $20 and saved $15. We can compare their savings in several ways.

		Ratio	Fraction	Decimal	Percent
Robert	$50 out of $100	$\frac{50}{100}$	.50	50%
Madelyn	$15 out of $20	$\frac{15}{20}$	.75	75%

1. Write each fraction as a percent.

   Example $\frac{12}{25}$ $\frac{12}{25} = \frac{48}{100}$
   $$= 48\%$$

   a. $\frac{43}{100}$ **b.** $\frac{33}{50}$ **c.** $\frac{9}{25}$ **d.** $\frac{9}{10}$

2. Write each decimal as a percent.

   Example   .3 $.3 = .30$
   $$= \frac{30}{100}$$
   $$= 30\%$$

   a. .37   **b.** .2   **c.** .98   **d.** .5

3. Percents make comparing easier. Here's an example.

   In January, Jo saved $12 out of the $25 she earned. In February, she saved $11 out of $20.

   $$\frac{12}{25} = \frac{48}{100} \qquad \frac{11}{20} = \frac{55}{100}$$
   $$= 48\% \qquad\qquad = 55\%$$

   larger percent

   Compare.

   a. 14 out of 20 and 19 out of 25.

   b. 9 out of 10 and 4 out of 5

276

Write percents.

1. $\frac{39}{100}$ 2. $\frac{43}{100}$ 3. $\frac{12}{100}$ 4. $\frac{13}{50}$ 5. $\frac{3}{5}$

6. $\frac{1}{2}$ 7. $\frac{1}{4}$ 8. $\frac{1}{5}$ 9. $\frac{8}{10}$ 10. $\frac{2}{5}$

11. $\frac{8}{25}$ 12. $\frac{6}{100}$ 13. $\frac{6}{10}$ 14. $\frac{3}{10}$ 15. $\frac{3}{100}$

16. $\frac{4}{10}$ 17. $\frac{3}{4}$ 18. $\frac{16}{50}$ 19. $\frac{14}{25}$ 20. $\frac{18}{20}$

21. $\frac{12}{20}$ 22. $\frac{46}{50}$ 23. $\frac{4}{5}$ 24. $\frac{7}{10}$ 25. $\frac{20}{25}$

26. .71   27. .18   28. .10   29. .23   30. .63

31. .56   32. .96   33. .47   34. .80   35. .60

36. .88   37. .47   38. .39   39. .56   40. .19

41. .72   42. .66   43. .84   44. .27   45. .08

46. .06   47. .07   48. .31   49. .99   50. .01

This chart shows one car factory's daily goal of cars to be made compared with the number actually made.

	Mon	Tues	Wed	Thurs	Fri
Cars Made	40	20	15	15	9
Goal	50	25	25	20	10

51. Write in fractional form the ratio of cars made to the goal for each day.

52. Write percents for the fractions in Exercise 51.

53. On which day did the factory come closest to making its goal?

277

CHANGING TO PERCENT

YIKES! I CAN'T DO IT!

$\frac{21}{30} = \frac{}{100}$ Here's a method for changing all fractions to percents.

$$\frac{21}{30} \to 30\overline{)21.00}^{\ \ .70} \to 70\%$$

1. Sometimes we cannot easily change a fraction to a percent by finding an equivalent fractional numeral with a denominator 100.

$$\frac{6}{15} = \frac{\square}{100}$$

This method works all the time. Complete.

$$\frac{6}{15} \to 15\overline{)6.00}^{\ \ .40} \to \underline{\quad}\%$$

2. Write each fraction as a percent.

   a. $\frac{12}{30}$ b. $\frac{6}{12}$ c. $\frac{9}{12}$ d. $\frac{9}{15}$

EXERCISES

Write percents.

1. $\frac{17}{20}$ 2. $\frac{9}{30}$ 3. $\frac{3}{4}$ 4. $\frac{3}{6}$ 5. $\frac{6}{8}$

6. $\frac{6}{12}$ 7. $\frac{7}{14}$ 8. $\frac{3}{15}$ 9. $\frac{3}{5}$ 10. $\frac{1}{2}$

11. $\frac{14}{40}$ 12. $\frac{18}{50}$ 13. $\frac{18}{45}$ 14. $\frac{6}{10}$ 15. $\frac{14}{35}$

16. $\frac{14}{25}$ 17. $\frac{12}{16}$ 18. $\frac{9}{18}$ 19. $\frac{18}{24}$ 20. $\frac{21}{28}$

21. $\frac{34}{40}$ 22. $\frac{100}{125}$ 23. $\frac{80}{500}$ 24. $\frac{60}{300}$ 25. $\frac{72}{96}$

278

Sometimes we must express percents using fractions.

$$\frac{1}{3} \rightarrow 3\overline{)1.00}^{.33} \rightarrow .33\frac{1}{3} \rightarrow 33\frac{1}{3}\%$$

$$\begin{array}{r} .33 \\ 3\overline{)1.00} \\ \underline{9} \\ 10 \\ \underline{9} \\ 1 \end{array}$$

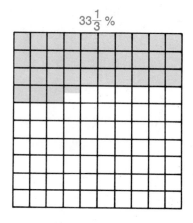

$33\frac{1}{3}\%$

Read $.33\frac{1}{3}$ as

"33 and $\frac{1}{3}$ hundredths."

Read $33\frac{1}{3}\%$ as

"33 and $\frac{1}{3}$ percent."

Here's a table of important percents. Copy and complete it.

	Fraction	Percent
	$\frac{1}{3}$	$33\frac{1}{3}\%$
1.	$\frac{1}{8}$	
2.	$\frac{3}{8}$	
3.	$\frac{5}{8}$	
4.	$\frac{1}{6}$	
5.	$\frac{1}{12}$	

IT WOULD BE VERY HANDY TO LEARN THESE BY HEART!

EXERCISES

Solve these problems.

1. Five of Bob's 30 classmates were absent Monday. What percent were absent?

2. Jeff lost $1 of the $3 he had in his wallet. What percent of his money did he lose?

279

RENAMING PERCENTS

Many states have a sales tax. In some states it is 5%.

Cindy thinks of 5% as a ratio.
5% means 5 out of 100

Roger thinks of 5% as a fraction.
$$5\% = \frac{5}{100}$$

Agnes thinks of 5% as a decimal.
5% = .05

1. Write ratios.

   Example　23%　23 out of 100

   a. 35%　　　　　**b.** 7%　　　　　**c.** 40%

2. Write fractions. Simplify if possible.

   Example　$20\% = \frac{20}{100} = \frac{1}{5}$

   a. 43%　　　　　**b.** 40%　　　　　**c.** 4%

3. Write decimals.

   Example　50% = .50

   a. 24%　　　　　**b.** 7%　　　　　**c.** 70%

EXERCISES

Write as a ratio, a simplified fraction, and a decimal.

1. 20%　　**2.** 22%　　**3.** 60%　　**4.** 66%　　**5.** 10%

6. 11%　　**7.** 30%　　**8.** 12%　　**9.** 25%　　**10.** 75%

11. 2%　　**12.** 6%　　**13.** 8%　　**14.** 1%　　**15.** 45%

1. 48% of Canadian land is forest land.

   a. What fraction of the land is this?

   b. Would you say that most of Canada is forest land?

   c. Do you think this is a lot of forest land for a country?

2. About 85% of an iceberg is hidden beneath the water.

   a. Is most of an iceberg hidden or visible?

   b. Sketch an above-and-below-the-water drawing of what you think an iceberg looks like.

3. About 55% of all families have three or fewer persons.

   a. Write a fraction for 55%.

   b. Is this more or less than half of all families?

4. About 70% of all known uranium oxide is in North America.

   a. Is most of the known uranium oxide in North America?

   b. 20% of the uranium oxide is in Africa. Is more in Africa than in North America?

5. Almost 20% of the U.S. population lives in cities between Boston and Washington, D.C.

   a. Do you think this is a lot of people, considering the size of the U.S.A.?

   b. Does more than $\frac{1}{4}$ of the population live there?

Jill loved dogs. She had 20 of them, no less! 25% of them beagles. How many was this?

Think: 25% of 20 dogs is n dogs

Equation: $.25 \times 20 = n$

$= 5$

$$\begin{array}{r} .25 \\ \times\, 20 \\ \hline 5.00 \end{array}$$

Answer: 5 dogs

1. Sarah got 80% of the 25 questions correct on a test. Let's find how many answers she got correct.

$$80\% \text{ of } 25 \text{ is } n$$
$$.80 \times 25 = n$$

Multiply to find the answer.

2. Jack saves 10% of his $40 earnings. Let's find out how much money he saves.

$$10\% \text{ of } 40 \text{ is } n$$

a. Write an equation for this problem.

b. How much money does Jack save?

EXERCISES

Here are percent scores on a math test with 50 questions. How many did each person get correct?

1. Sandie   90%   2. John   92%   3. Kevin   88%

4. Joanne   80%   5. Paul   96%   6. Anne   86%

7. Peg   94%   8. Carol   98%   9. Dave   100%

Compute.

10. 25% of 16   **11.** 14% of 200

12. 50% of 28   **13.** 72% of 25

14. 68% of 75   **15.** 75% of 44

16. 60% of 55   **17.** 40% of 30

18. 86% of 20   **19.** 92% of 300

Solve these problems.

20. Joy has read 20% of the 50-page first aid manual. How many pages has she read?

21. Ellen spends 40% of her $5 allowance on snacks. How much money is this?

22. Sandra read that 35% of the people who work in downtown Chicago ride to work in cars. If 430,000 work there, how many ride in cars?

Keeping Fit

Add or subtract.

1. .3 + .4   **2.** .37 + .41   **3.** .3 + .04

4. .98 − .35   **5.** .95 − .38   **6.** .7 − .02

Multiply.

7. 7 × .3   **8.** .9 × .4   **9.** 8 × .36

10. .4 × .26   **11.** .41 × .78   **12.** 8 × $2.95

Divide.

13. $2\overline{)3.98}$ **14.** $7\overline{)23.8}$ **15.** $.6\overline{)34.2}$

16. $.8\overline{)7.44}$ **17.** $.23\overline{)7.82}$ **18.** $.23\overline{)1,062.6}$

Bike.
Marked price: $80.
Discount: 15%.
Sale price?

15% of $80 is n dollars

$.15 \times 80 = n$
$\qquad = 12$

The discount is $12. We can figure the sale price like this.

$\$80 - \$12 = \$68$

1. Nilak's Discount Store gives a discount of 10%. Tell the dollar discount on these marked prices.

   a. $25   **b.** $30   **c.** $12.50

2. Town Dress Shop advertises a 25% discount sale. Let's find the sales price for a $30 item.

   25% of 30 is n dollars

   $.25 \times 30 = n$
   $\qquad = \$7.50$

   Now we subtract this discount from the marked price. Complete.

   $\$30 - \$7.50 =$

3. Find the sale price for each of these items at a "30% off" sale.

   a. $40   **b.** $50   **c.** $22.70

   d. $64.20   **e.** $17.90   **f.** $52

Harry's Store sells items at 5% discount. What would be the price at Harry's for items usually costing these prices?

1. $20   **2.** $24   **3.** $30   **4.** $40

5. $10   **6.** $120   **7.** $12.40   **8.** $1.20

Malinda's Boutique is offering a 30% discount sale off the marked price. Find the sales price on items with these marked prices.

9. $25   **10.** $20   **11.** $10   **12.** $45

13. $86.40   **14.** $32   **15.** $12.50   **16.** $15.20

Add.

| **1.** $\begin{array}{r}29\\+\,35\end{array}$ | **2.** $\begin{array}{r}394\\+\,582\end{array}$ | **3.** $\begin{array}{r}706\\+\,583\end{array}$ |

Keeping Fit

Subtract.

4. $\begin{array}{r}48\\-\,19\end{array}$ **5.** $\begin{array}{r}928\\-\,651\end{array}$ **6.** $\begin{array}{r}6{,}307\\-\,2{,}189\end{array}$

Multiply.

7. $\begin{array}{r}34\\\times\,2\end{array}$ **8.** $\begin{array}{r}729\\\times\,6\end{array}$ **9.** $\begin{array}{r}38\\\times\,42\end{array}$ **10.** $\begin{array}{r}405\\\times\,76\end{array}$ **11.** $\begin{array}{r}5{,}124\\\times\,835\end{array}$

Divide.

12. $38\overline{)19{,}269}$ **13.** $18\overline{)29{,}657}$ **14.** $145\overline{)250{,}123}$

Rename in simplest form.

15. $\frac{27}{36}$ **16.** $\frac{56}{63}$ **17.** $\frac{5}{40}$ **18.** $\frac{12}{27}$

Find the product. Name it in simplest form.

19. $\frac{3}{7}\times\frac{2}{3}$ **20.** $\frac{4}{5}\times\frac{7}{8}$ **21.** $\frac{3}{4}\times\frac{7}{16}$

BANK INTEREST

> GEE, I GET 5% INTEREST FROM THE BANK.

> I TOLD YOU SAVING MONEY COULD BE INTERESTING!

This bank pays 5% **interest** on savings accounts. This means each year the bank will pay a customer 5% of the amount of money left on deposit for a year.

1. Let's compute interest on $200 at an annual interest rate of 5%.

$$5\% \text{ of } \$200 \text{ is } n \text{ dollars}$$
$$.05 \times 200 = n$$
$$= 10$$

The interest is $10.

Find the yearly interest on these amounts. The annual interest rate is 5%.

  a. $300   **b.** $250   **c.** $2,400

2. Consider an annual interest rate of 6%. Find the interest on these amounts.

  a. $400   **b.** $260   **c.** $1,800

EXERCISES

Find the interest on each year's deposit if the annual interest rate is 4%.

1. $100   **2.** $50   **3.** $700   **4.** $750

5. $1,100   **6.** $2,400   **7.** $940   **8.** $7,825

Solve these problems.

9. Find the interest for one year for $300 at an annual interest rate of 5%.

10. Casey kept $2,400 in a bank paying 5% annual interest. Sue kept $2,000 in a bank paying 6%. Who got more interest for one year? How much more?

11. Mrs. Jones has $500 to put in the bank. Bank A pays 4% interest. Bank B pays 5%. How much more money would she get from Bank B at the end of a year?

12. Mr. Smith put $500 in the credit union, which paid 6% interest. What was the interest at the end of the year?

★13. Cecile had $400 in a bank that paid 5% interest. She left her $400 and its interest in the bank at the end of the first year. What interest did she get at the end of the second year?

Match the phrase at the left with a word at the right so that you make a mathematical pun.

1. Mildred Liter's nickname   polygon
2. Many people pulling together   centimeter
3. The bird who flew away   pi
4. A type of cracker   bisects
5. A penny that purrs like a cat   square root
6. A parking meter that takes a penny   milliliter
7. Numbers that count   multiple
8. Two insects   counting numbers
9. You can eat it for dessert   gram
10. Underground part of a quadrilateral tree   percent

287

INSURANCE AGENTS

1. Last year, Kim Bonk's auto insurance cost $380. Because she has a safe driving record, her insurance will cost only 90% as much this year. How much will it cost this year?

2. Kim's father told her that his house insurance costs $2 per $1,000 of its value. The value of the house is $30,000. How much does the insurance cost?

3. Mr. Ben Ryan sold health insurance to the Bonk family. The premium is $6.40 a month. How much does it cost per year?

4. Mr. Ryan spends a lot of time working on claims. Each claim takes him about 5 hours. This week he must work on 12 claims. How long will these probably take him?

5. Ms. Garcia is Mr. Chin's insurance agent. She told him that 90% of the accident claims in 1970 were settled by a judge in court. There were 25,000 claims in her city that year. How many were settled by a judge in court?

6. Ms. Garcia said that only 50% of the claims went to court in 1975. There were 32,000 claims that year. How many were settled in court?

We can make up a problem to fit this sentence.

$$.80 \times 30 = n$$

In Joe's class, 80% of the students are girls. There are 30 students in the class. How many are girls?

1. Here is an equation: $.75 \times 32 = n$.
   Use this equation to make up a problem for each of these ideas. Solve the problem.

   a. The number of boys in a class

   b. The number of U.S. stamps in a stamp collection

   c. The number of nickels in a coin collection

2. Here is a table which the principal of Garden City Intermediate School made. Make up two problems using this information. Solve them.

	Number Absent	Total Enrollment
Mon	10	50
Tues	5	50
Wed	12	50

3. Here's another table. It shows the percent of the 150 full school days that certain students were absent. Make up two problems using this table. Solve them.

	Percent of Days Absent
Barbara	2%
Ralph	10%
Lisa	6%

Make up a problem to fit each drawing.

4. 1 WAY / 2 MARK   12 mi

5. 50% DISCOUNT ON PURCHASES $50 OR MORE   TIRES $20 EACH

CHAPTER REVIEW

Write percents.

1. 23 out of 100
[274]

2. $\frac{6}{100}$
[274]

3. $\frac{7}{10}$
[276]

4. 34 out of 50
[276]

5. $\frac{3}{4}$
[276]

6. .08
[276]

7. 9 out of 20
[276]

8. .39
[276]

9. .40
[276]

10. 20 out of 30
[278]

11. $\frac{16}{40}$
[278]

12. $\frac{3}{6}$
[278]

Write ratios. [280]

13. 40%

14. 26%

15. 5%

Write fractions. Simplify if possible. [280]

16. 28%

17. 6%

18. 75%

Write decimals. [280]

19. 39%

20. 80%

21. 9%

Solve these problems. [282, 284]

22. A class has 30 students. 40% of them are girls. How many are girls?

23. Paula has 66 stamps. $33\frac{1}{3}$% of them are foreign. How many are foreign?

24. Sam spelled 25% of the 16 words on the test wrong. How many did he spell wrong?

25. How much money will a $58-savings account earn in one year in a bank which pays 5% interest annually?

26. The price of a plane ticket is usually $32, but Alice gets a 30% discount. How much will Alice have to pay for the ticket?

CHAPTER TEST

Write percents.

1. 46 out of 100

2. $\frac{9}{100}$

3. $\frac{1}{4}$

4. 14 out of 20

5. .23

6. .60

7. 10 out of 30

8. $\frac{2}{5}$

9. $\frac{3}{25}$

Write ratios.

10. 49%

11. 20%

12. 3%

Write fractions. Simplify if possible.

13. 23%

14. 7%

15. 80%

Write decimals.

16. 35%

17. 8%

18. 70%

Solve these problems.

19. At a class party 25% of the children were girls. There were 36 children at the party. How many were girls?

20. Arthur planted 50 plants and 34% of them died. How many died?

21. Jack got 75% of the test questions correct. There were 40 questions. How many questions did he get correct?

22. Country Girl Dress Shop was having a 25% discount on all items. Doris bought a dress originally priced at $28. What was the sale price?

12 GEOMETRY

PERIMETER

The **perimeter** of a simple closed curve is the distance around it. Here are three ways to find the perimeter of a rectangle.

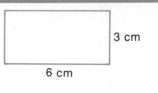
3 cm
6 cm

A	B	C
$l + w + l + w$	$(2 \cdot l) + (2 \cdot w)$	$2 \cdot (l + w)$
$6 + 3 + 6 + 3$	$(2 \cdot 6) + (2 \cdot 3)$	$2 \cdot (3 + 6)$
18	18	18

1. Find the perimeter of this quadrilateral.

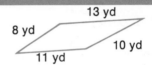
13 yd
8 yd
11 yd
10 yd

2. The perimeter of a square is 4 times the length of one side. Find the perimeters.

a. 3 mm

b. 6 cm

c. 4 in.

Find perimeters.

1.
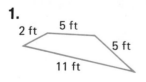
2 ft
5 ft
5 ft
11 ft

2.

2 m
7 m

3.
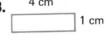
4 cm
1 cm

AREA

A **region** is a simple closed curve and its interior. Its area is the number of square units that cover it. We multiply to find the area of any rectangle.

length: 11

width: 5

Area $= 5 \times 11$
Area $= 55$ square units

To find the area of a rectangle, multiply its length and its width.

$$A = l \times w$$

1. Find the areas of rectangles with these dimensions.

　a. length: 9 cm, width: 6 cm　　**b.** length: 10 m, width: 7 m

2. If a rectangle is a square, its length and width are equal.

5 m

5 m

Area $=$ side $\times$ side
$A = s \times s$
$\quad = 5 \times 5$
$\quad = 25$ square meters, or 25 m²

Find the area of a square that measures 7 centimeters on each side.

Find the areas of rectangles with these dimensions.

1. l: 7 m　　w: 5 m　　　　　　**2.** l: 15 cm　　w: 7 cm

3. l: $2\frac{1}{2}$ m　　w: $3\frac{3}{4}$ m　　　　**4.** l: 7.1 m　　w: 5.9 m

Find the areas of squares whose sides have these measures.

5. s: 23 mm　　　　　　　　**6.** s: 4.7 cm

Look at these figures.

Area of square
16 cm²
Area of the shaded triangle
$\frac{1}{2} \times 16$, or 8 cm²

4 cm

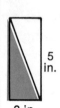

5 in.

2 in.

Area of rectangle
10 in.²
Area of shaded triangle
$\frac{1}{2} \times 10$, or 5 in.²

The area of a right triangle is given by this formula.
$$A = \frac{1}{2} \times l \times w$$

1. Let's find the area of triangle *ABC*. Complete.

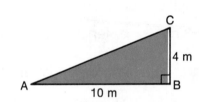

C

4 m

A

B

10 m

$A = \frac{1}{2} \times l \times w$

$= \frac{1}{2} \times 10 \times 4$

$= \underline{\quad}$

Area: _____ m²

2. Find the areas.

a.

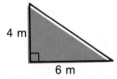

4 m

6 m

b.

3 cm

2 cm

c.

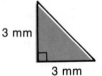

3 mm

3 mm

Find the areas of triangles with these dimensions.

1. *l*: 9 in.   *w*: 16 in.

2. *l*: 10 mm   *w*: 10 mm

3. *l*: 18 cm   *w*: 13 cm

4. *l*: 46 m   *w*: 38 m

5. *l*: $9\frac{1}{2}$ m   *w*: 4 m

6. *l*: 2.4 cm   *w*: 8.6 cm

OCEANOGRAPHERS

1. Oceanographer Ben Jacob discovered that a certain kind of fish is usually found 1,900 meters below sea level. This distance is closest to which of the following?

   1 kilometer   2 kilometers   19 kilometers

2. Peg Sung watched a school of fish. First, they swam in one direction for 4 minutes. Then they splashed in one place for 11 minutes. Then they started the whole cycle all over again. How many times in one hour should Ms. Sung expect to see them swim and splash?

3. Madelyn Gomez uses a seismograph to record earthquakes on the ocean bottom. She knows that earthquake vibrations will reach her seismograph at a speed of 8 kilometers per second. In how many seconds will she learn of an earthquake that takes place 160 kilometers away?

4. One story of a building is about 3 meters tall. Bob Lakin measured a water spout that was 120 meters tall. About how many stories tall was the water spout?

5. Sound travels 1,450 meters per second in water. It took 4 seconds for sound to go from Mr. Lakin's ship to the ocean bottom and back. Mr. Lakin guessed that the depth of the ocean was 2,900 meters where he was. Was he right?

AREA OF A PARALLELOGRAM

Compare the parallelogram with the rectangle. Let's call the width of the parallelogram its **height**. Also, let's call the length of the parallelogram its **base**.

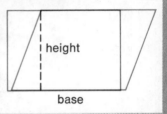

Let's find a formula for the area of a parallelogram.

1. a. Draw a parallelogram like this. Graph paper helps.

b. Cut out your parallelogram.

c. Draw a segment like this, and cut along it.

d. Move this little piece to the other end of your parallelogram. Now what kind of quadrilateral do you have?

e. Are the areas of your parallelogram and rectangle equal?

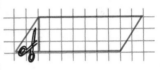

The area of a parallelogram is the base times the height.

$$A = b \times h$$

2. Find the areas.

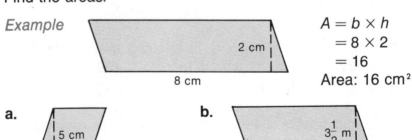

Example

8 cm
2 cm

$A = b \times h$
$= 8 \times 2$
$= 16$
Area: 16 cm²

a.
5 cm
5 cm

b.
$3\frac{1}{2}$ m
8 m

296

Find the areas.

1.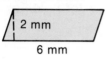
2 mm
6 mm

2.
3 cm
4 cm

3.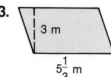
3 m
$5\frac{1}{3}$ m

4.
9 mm
15 mm

5.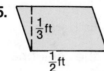
$\frac{1}{3}$ ft
$\frac{1}{2}$ ft

6.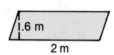
.6 m
2 m

Find the areas of parallelograms with these dimensions.

7. b: 9 cm h: 4 cm   **8.** b: 12 mm h: 3 mm

9. b: 7 m h: $3\frac{1}{2}$ m   **10.** b: 24 cm h: 33 cm

11. b: 3.4 m h: 3 m   **12.** b: 6.7 cm h: 2.2 cm

Solve.

13. Find both the area and perimeter of this parallelogram.

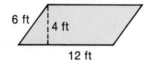
6 ft   4 ft
12 ft

14. Andrea's backyard has this shape.

   a. How many meters of fence does she need to go around the yard?

   b. What is the area of the yard?

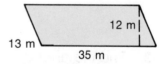
12 m
13 m
35 m

Brainteaser

n: 1   2   3   4   5

n^2:   1   4   9   16   25

differences: 3   5   7   9

1. Observe that 4^2 is 9 less than 5^2. Then, 5^2 must be 11 less than 6^2. Is it?

2. 6^2 must be how much less than 7^2?

AREA OF ANY TRIANGLE

Not all triangles are right triangles. We need a formula for the area of any triangle.

1. a. Draw any parallelogram.

   b. Draw a diagonal like this.

   c. Cut out your parallelogram.

   d. Now cut along the diagonal and see if the two pieces of the parallelogram match.

   e. Each triangle is what part of your parallelogram?

   f. The area of each triangle is what part of the area of the parallelogram?

2. Consider the parallelogram *ABCD*.

   a. What is the area of the parallelogram?

   b. What is the area of the shaded triangle?

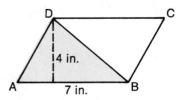

The area of any triangle is one half the base times the height.

$$A = \tfrac{1}{2} \times b \times h$$

3. Find the areas.

Example

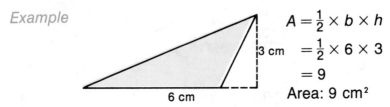

$$A = \tfrac{1}{2} \times b \times h$$
$$ = \tfrac{1}{2} \times 6 \times 3$$
$$ = 9$$

Area: 9 cm²

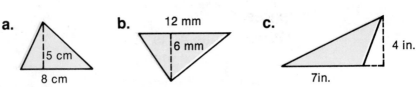

a. 5 cm / 8 cm

b. 12 mm / 6 mm

c. 4 in. / 7 in.

298

Find the areas.

1.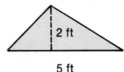

2 ft

5 ft

2.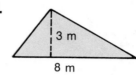

3 m

8 m

3.

9 cm

12 cm

4.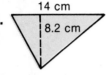

14 cm

8.2 cm

5.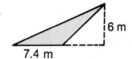

6 m

7.4 m

6.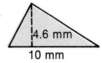

4.6 mm

10 mm

Find the areas of triangles with these dimensions.

7. *b*: 7 cm   *h*: 4 cm   **8.** *b*: 10 m   *h*: 5 m

9. *b*: $2\frac{1}{2}$ m   *h*: 8 m   **10.** *b*: 2.5 cm   *h*: 4 cm

11. *b*: 3.3 m   *h*: 6 m   **12.** *b*: 9 m   *h*: 10.2 m

ACTIVITY

Do you believe it possible to make a piece of paper have only one side? Get a strip of paper like this. Mark its ends as shown.

1   3

2   4

Twist the paper once so that the 1 is on the 4, and the 2 is on the 3. Tape the ends. Start drawing a line down the center of the strip. Keep drawing until you end up where you started. Does your line appear on both "sides" of the strip?

If you cut along your line, will you end up with one loop, or with two loops? Check your guess.

Now cut your new loop along the center a second time. Do you think you will have one loop or two?

Keeping Fit

Identify and name each figure.

1.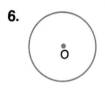

2.

3.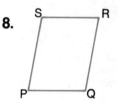

4.

5.

6.

7.

8.

Use your protractor to measure each angle.

9.

10.

11.

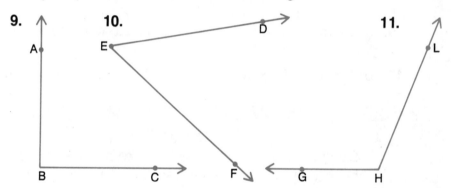

Which angles in Exercises 9–11, if any, are the following?

12. acute

13. right

14. obtuse

Find the measure of the 3rd angle of the triangle.

15. 1st : 40°   2nd : 50°

16. 1st : 100°   2nd : 25°

Which pairs are congruent?

17.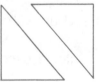

18.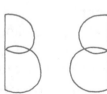

19.

300

CIRCLES

Circles are an important part of our everyday lives. The wheel is part of a machine which can make work easier.

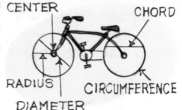

CENTER   CHORD
RADIUS   CIRCUMFERENCE
DIAMETER

A **circle** is all points in a plane that are the same distance from a given point, the **center**.

---

1. Bob's club uses this emblem.

    a. Which stripe is a chord, but not a diameter?

    b. Which stripe is a diameter?

2. Draw a circle. Draw a radius and a diameter. Measure both. How do their measures compare?

EXERCISES

Study this figure. *O* is the center.

1. Name two diameters.

2. Name four radii.

3. Name two chords which are not diameters.

Draw $\overline{HK}$ 2 cm long. Draw a circle with $\overline{HK}$ as a radius.

4. How long should each diameter of this circle be? Draw a diameter and measure it.

5. Draw a chord. What is the measure of the longest chord?

CIRCUMFERENCE

The length around any circle is called its **circumference**. Study this experiment to find the circumference of these circles. Each circle has been rolled once.

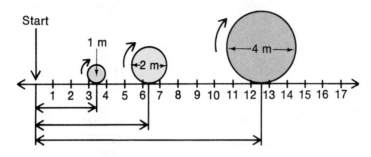

Length of Diameter (d)	Circumference (c) to nearest hundredth of a meter	Ratio $\dfrac{c}{d}$
1 m	3.14	$\dfrac{3.14}{1}$, or 3.14
2 m	6.28	$\dfrac{6.28}{2}$, or 3.14
4 m	12.56	$\dfrac{12.56}{4}$, or 3.14

The ratio $\dfrac{c}{d}$ is the number π (pi). The circumference of any circle is about 3.14 times the length of any of its diameters.

$$c = 3.14 \times d$$
$$\text{or, } c = \pi \times d$$

1. Repeat the experiment. Use coins or other circular objects. Make a chart like this. Be as accurate as you can!

Object	Length of Diameter	Circumference	$\dfrac{c}{d}$

2. Now let's use the formula to find the circumference. (We can use either $\frac{22}{7}$ or 3.14 for π.) Complete.

4 cm

$$c = \pi \times d$$
$$= 3.14 \times 4$$
$$= \underline{\hspace{1cm}}$$
Circumference: _____ cm

3. Because a diameter is twice as long as a radius, we can use the formula $c = 2 \times \pi \times r$ also. Complete.

6 cm

$$c = 2 \times \pi \times r$$
$$= 2 \times 3.14 \times 6$$
$$= \underline{\hspace{1cm}}$$
Circumference: _____

EXERCISES

Find the circumference. Use 3.14 for π.

1. $d = 2$ mm

2. $d = 3$ cm

3. $d = 6$ yd

4. $d = 5$ cm

5. $d = 9$ mm

6. $d = 10$ in.

7. $d = 12$ cm

8. $d = 23$ m

9. $d = 2.1$ cm

10. $r = 2$ cm

11. $r = 3$ in.

12. $r = 6$ cm

Find the circumference. Use $\frac{22}{7}$ for π.

13. $d = 7$ m

14. $d = 14$ m

15. $d = 4\frac{2}{10}$ cm

16. $d = 3\frac{1}{2}$ m

17. $r = 7$ m

18. $r = 1\frac{3}{4}$ m

19. The diameter of Diane's bike wheel is 26 inches What is the circumference of the bike wheel? Use 3.14 for π.

20. The diameter of Stan's bike wheel measures 28 inches. What is the circumference? Use $\frac{22}{7}$ for π.

Let's experiment to find a formula for the area of a circle.

1. a. Take a circle with an 8-centimeter radius. Imagine that we divide the region into 16 pieces the same size.

b. Now cut the region apart and rearrange the slices.

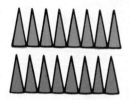

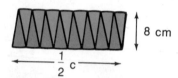

8 cm

$\frac{1}{2}$ c

We get a figure which looks like a parallelogram.

c. Let's find its area. Complete.

$h = 8$ cm

$b = \frac{1}{2} c$

$A = b \times h$

$\quad = 8 \times \frac{1}{2} c$

$\quad = 8 \times \frac{1}{2} \times (2 \times \pi \times r)$

$\quad = 8 \times \frac{1}{2} \times (2 \times 3.14 \times 8)$

$\quad = \underline{\quad}$

Area: _____ cm²

2. Let's find a formula now.

r

a. What is the height of this parallelogram? $h = $ _____

b. What is the base? $b = $ _____ $\frac{1}{2} \times (2 \times \pi \times r)$, or $\pi \times r$

c. Now we find the area by using our formula for the area of a parallelogram.

$A = b \times h$

$A = (\pi \times r) \times$ _____

$A = \pi \times$ _____ $\times$ _____

The area of a circle is π times a radius squared.

$$A = \pi \times r^2$$

3. Find the areas.

Example

4 m

$A = \pi \times r^2$
  $= 3.14 \times 4 \times 4$
  $= 50.24$
Area: 50.24 m²

a. $r = 5$ in.

b. $r = 1.2$ cm

EXERCISES

Find the areas. Use 3.14 for π.

1. $r = 2$ mm

2. $r = 6$ ft

3. $r = 1$ m

4. $r = 7$ cm

5. $r = 10$ m

6. $r = .5$ cm

7. $r = 9$ m

8. $r = 4$ m

9. $r = 1.6$ cm

Solve these problems.

10. A pie has a radius of 4 inches. What is the area of its top crust? Use 3.14 for π.

★**11.** The area of Rose's circular rug is 12.56 square feet. What is the length of a radius? a diameter?

★**12.** Before Terry knew the formula for finding the area of a circle, she drew a square inside a circle, as shown below. She measured b. It was 8 centimeters. Then she guessed the area of the circle by knowing the area of the square.

a. What is the area of the square?

b. Is the area of the circle greater than or less than that of the square?

b
5.7 cm
b   b
b

c. Find the area of the circle using the formula.

Geometric Figures	A Model	We Measure Its
─────────── segment		length
rectangular region		boundary: perimeter region: area
rectangular prism	SOUP	surface: area interior: volume

Find a model of a rectangular prism. Any box with a cover will do. Each side of the box is called a **face** of the prism. Each corner is called a **vertex** of the prism. Each edge of the box is called an **edge** of the prism.

1. A prism has 6 faces. Use the box to check this.
2. How many vertices does a prism have? How many edges?

3. Which of these are models of rectangular prisms?

cereal box   can of pears   piece of string
balloon   ice cream cone   desk drawer

4. A can like this is a model of a **cylinder**.   A balloon is a model of a **sphere**.   An ice cream cone is a model of a **cone**.

a. Give another model of a cylinder.

b. Give another model of a sphere.

c. Give another model of a cone.

5. There is a difference between a prism and its interior.

model of prism: cereal box
model of its interior: space occupied by the cereal

What is in the interior of a party balloon?

Which are models of rectangular prisms? cylinders? spheres? cones?

1. Sipping straw   **2.** Tin can   **3.** Baseball

4. Ice cream sandwich   **5.** Dunce cap   **6.** Globe

7. Rubber ball   **8.** Funnel   **9.** Megaphone

10. Wastebasket   **11.** Classroom   **12.** Shoe box

Tell the difference between the surface and interior of these objects.

13. Wastebasket   **14.** Banana   **15.** Box

Which action is being done to the surface? Which is being done to the interior?

16. Painting the wall of a room

17. Putting a picture on a wall

18. Filling a bathtub with water

19. Putting a gift in a package

20. Wrapping a package

Name three objects shaped like these.

21. Rectangular prism   **22.** Cylinder

23. Sphere   **24.** Cone

CORRECTING MISTAKES

Susan's fish tank measures 60 centimeters by 20 centimeters by 45 centimeters. She found the volume. Her answer was 125 cubic centimeters. Is her answer reasonable?

No! We know that Volume $= l \times w \times h$. Also, we know $60 \times 20 \times 45$ must be greater than 125.

Correct answer: 54,000 cubic centimeters

Correct the unreasonable answers. Write "reasonable" for those which are reasonable.

1. Hiroko's backyard is rectangular. Its length is 16 meters and its width is 14 meters. How much fencing is needed to go around the yard?

   Answer: 224 meters   Is this reasonble?

2. The Traveler's Motor Inn has a circular pool. The diameter of the pool is 10 meters. What is the distance around the pool?

   Answer: 3,140 meters   Is this reasonable?

3. Joanie has only $2\frac{2}{4}$ cups of uncooked instant rice left in the package. She figures she needs about $\frac{1}{4}$ cup of uncooked rice for each serving. How many people can Joanie serve?

   Answer: 10 people   Is this reasonable?

4. The fleece of sheep is cut with clipping machines. The average weight of the fleece of one sheep is 7.9 pounds. What is the weight of the fleece of 2,000 sheep?

   Answer: 158,000 pounds   Is this reasonable?

VOLUME

Sometimes it's hard to tell which container has the greater volume just by looking at them. Patti tried two tests.

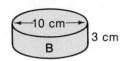

Test 1: Wrap paper around each can. *A* needed about 126 cm². *B* needed about 94 cm².

Test 2: Fill *B* with water. Pour into *A*. After *A* was full, there was water left in *B*!

Patti decided *B* had the greater volume.

1. Which can had the greater surface area, according to test 1?

2. What does test 2 tell us about their volumes?

3. Is Patti right?

EXERCISES

1. Try Patti's test 2 on a few cans. See which can has the greatest volume.

Find cereal boxes with about the same size at the bottom but with different heights.

2. Which do you think has the greater volume?

3. Use Patti's test 2 to check.

Find two cereal boxes with the same height but different sizes at the bottom.

4. Which do you think has the larger volume?

5. Use Patti's test 2 to check.

VOLUME OF A RECTANGULAR PRISM

To measure volume we use a cube that measures 1 unit on a side. Very often we use the cubic centimeter.

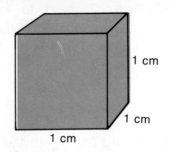

1 cm

1 cm

1 cm

1. One cubic meter (m^3) is the volume of a cube measuring 1 meter on each edge. What is a cubic centimeter (cm^3)? a cubic inch?

2. Study this prism.

   a. How many cubes cover the bottom layer?

   b. How many layers are there?

   c. How many cubic units are in this prism? So what is its volume?

3. Look at this prism.

   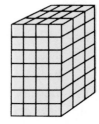

   a. The length of the base is 4 cm. What is the width? the height?

   b. What is the product of the length, the width, and the height?

   c. Count the cubes to find the volume. (Don't forget the hidden ones!)

   d. Is this the same as the product of the length, width, and height?

The volume of a rectangular prism is the product of the length, width, and height.

$$V = l \times w \times h$$

4. Find the volumes.

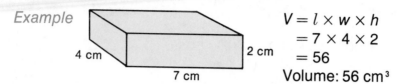

Example

4 cm

7 cm

2 cm

$V = l \times w \times h$
$= 7 \times 4 \times 2$
$= 56$
Volume: 56 cm³

a.

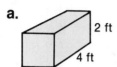

2 ft

4 ft

2 ft

b.

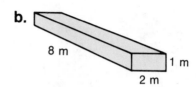

8 m

2 m

1 m

EXERCISES

Find the volumes.

1.

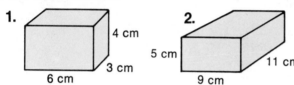

4 cm

6 cm

3 cm

2.

5 cm

9 cm

11 cm

3.

7 m

7 m

7 m

Find the volumes of prisms with these dimensions.

4. l: 4 in. w: 9 in. h: 3 in.

5. l: 3 cm w: 6 cm h: 5 cm

6. l: 2 yd w: 3 yd h: 5 yd

7. l: 8 cm w: 6 cm h: 2.1 cm

8. l: $2\frac{1}{2}$ m w: 4 m h: 2 m

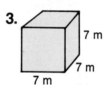

★ Find the volumes.

9.

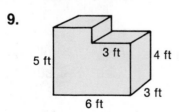

5 ft

3 ft

4 ft

3 ft

6 ft

10.

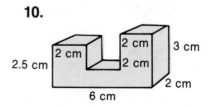

2.5 cm

2 cm

2 cm

2 cm

2 cm

3 cm

2 cm

6 cm

311

Take a look at this potato chip box.

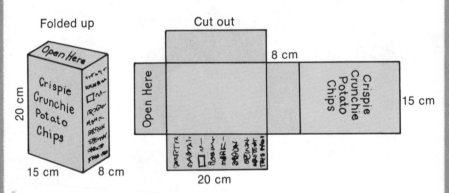

Folded up   Cut out

Here's how we can find the surface area.

Back and front: $2 \times (15 \times 20)$
Bottom and top: $2 \times (8 \times 15)$
Two sides: $2 \times (8 \times 20)$

Total $= 2 \times (15 \times 20) + 2 \times (8 \times 15) + 2 \times (8 \times 20)$
$= 1,160$

Total surface area: $1,160 \text{ cm}^2$

1. Look at this cookie box. Complete.

   a. Area of back and front
      $2 \times (\underline{} \times \underline{})$

   b. Area of bottom and top
      $2 \times (\underline{} \times \underline{})$

   c. Area of two sides
      $2 \times (\underline{} \times \underline{})$

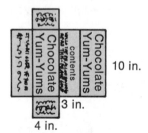

   d. What is the total surface area?

2. Find an empty box which you can take apart. Carefully cut it along the folds to open it out flat. Find the total surface area.

312

3. Now find another box, but don't take it apart. Try to find the total surface area. Don't forget to include all 6 sides in your total!

Find the surface areas.

1.
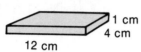
1 cm
4 cm
12 cm

2.

6 cm
2 cm
2 cm

3.
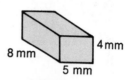
8 mm
4 mm
5 mm

4.
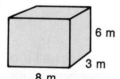
6 m
3 m
8 m

5.
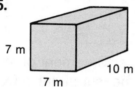
7 m
7 m
10 m

6.
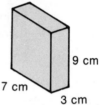
9 cm
7 cm
3 cm

★ Find the surface areas.

7.
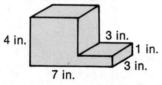
4 in.
3 in.
1 in.
3 in.
7 in.

8.

1 cm
5 cm

Keeping Fit

1. Which ratios are equivalent to the ratio 3 to 2?
    a. 6 to 4   **b.** 2 to 3   **c.** 15 to 5   **d.** 21 to 14

Solve.

2. $\dfrac{5}{4} = \dfrac{\square}{8}$
    3. $\dfrac{7}{3} = \dfrac{\square}{9}$
    4. $\dfrac{6}{11} = \dfrac{30}{\square}$

5. $\dfrac{4}{9} = \dfrac{\square}{36}$
    6. $\dfrac{8}{11} = \dfrac{48}{\square}$
    7. $\dfrac{3}{14} = \dfrac{\square}{28}$

8. 2 is to 3 as $\square$ is to 12
    9. 6 is to 9 as 18 is to $\square$

Don enlarged a photo of Kim to twice the original size.

	Original	Blow-up
Kim's height	1.5 cm	3 cm
sign height	1 cm	2 cm
sign base	1.5 cm	3 cm

When one picture is an enlargement of the other, we call the pictures **similar**. Every measurement in Don's second picture is twice that of the original.

1. Here is a pair of similar triangles.

Look at $\overline{AB}$ and $\overline{DE}$. We call them **corresponding sides**. What side in triangle *DEF* corresponds to $\overline{BC}$? to $\overline{AC}$?

2. Now look at this pair of similar triangles.

  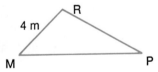

a. Name the pairs of corresponding sides. Complete.

$\overline{GL}$ corresponds to

$\overline{GH}$ corresponds to

$\overline{HL}$ corresponds to

b. Each side of triangle *MPR* is twice the length of the corresponding side of triangle *GHL*. Complete.

$$GL = 2 \text{ m, so } MR = 4 \text{ m}$$
$$GH = 4 \text{ m, so } MP = \underline{\quad} \text{ m}$$
$$HL = 3 \text{ m, so } PR = \underline{\quad} \text{ m}$$

Find the missing measures.

1.

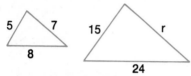

2.

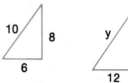

3.

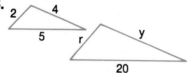

4.

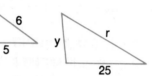

Solve these problems.

5. Debbie measured the height of a tree. She put a 4-foot stick next to the tree, and measured the shadow of the stick. Then she measured the shadow of the tree. What was the tree's height?

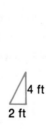

4 ft
2 ft

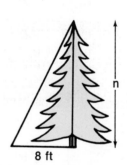

8 ft

6. Josh used the shadow method to find the height of a house. How high is it?

★7. At the same time of day, Josh found the shadow of a nearby lamppost to be $2\frac{1}{2}$ meters long. How tall was the lamppost?

14 m
5 m

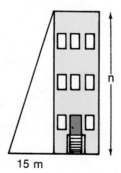

15 m

315

SCALE DRAWING

Here is a part of the map of Rowton City. The scale says that 1 centimeter represents 2 kilometers.

	Map Measurement	Actual Distance
Downtown To Motel	1 cm	2 km
Downtown To Park	2 cm	4 km
Downtown to University	3 cm	6 km

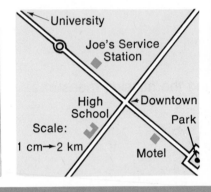

University
Joe's Service Station
High School — Downtown
Park
Scale: 1 cm → 2 km
Motel

1. Here is a part of a road map.

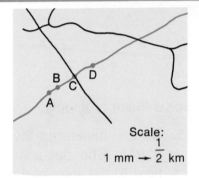

B D
C
A
Scale: 1 mm → $\frac{1}{2}$ km

a. It is 3 mm from *A* to *B*. How many kilometers is this?

b. How many kilometers is it from *A* to *C*?

c. How many kilometers is it from *A* to *D*?

2. Architects make scale drawings.

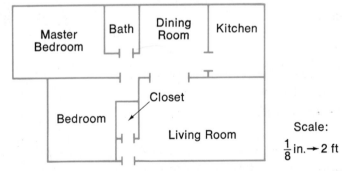

Master Bedroom
Bath
Dining Room
Kitchen
Closet
Bedroom
Living Room
Scale: $\frac{1}{8}$ in. → 2 ft

a. In the drawing, the master bedroom is 1 in. long and $\frac{6}{8}$ in. wide. What is its actual size?

b. Measure the length and width of the living room. What is its actual size?

c. Measure the length and width of the second bedroom. What is its actual size?

SOME PROJECTS

1. Bring a road map of your town, city, county, or state to class. Find the scale on the map. Check distances between two cities or between two streets by measuring and using the map scale.

2. Find an architect's drawing. (Often you can find some in popular magazines.) If a scale is given, use it and your ruler to find room dimensions. If the scale is not given, make up one which seems reasonable.

3. Make your own house drawing. Give your scale.

4. On a sunny day, you can measure the height of a tree or another tall object in the school yard or near your home. (See Exercises 5 and 6 on page 315.) Hold a stick upright. Measure its shadow. Measure the stick. Measure the tree's shadow. Now calculate the height of the tree using this ratio.

$$\frac{\text{height of stick}}{\text{length of stick's shadow}} = \frac{\text{height of tree}}{\text{length of tree's shadow}}$$

5. Measure a large object in your classroom or in your home like a window, a chalkboard, a bulletin board, or a door. Make a scale drawing of the object. A good scale might be 1 centimeter represents 1 meter (100 cm).

6. Make a scale drawing of a plot of land, or a court for a sports game. For example, you can make a scale drawing of a football field or a basketball court or a tennis court. You can find the regulation dimensions in an encyclopedia.

317

CHAPTER REVIEW

Find the areas.

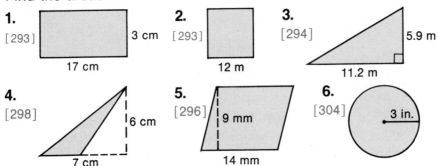

1. [293] 3 cm / 17 cm

2. [293] 12 m

3. [294] 5.9 m / 11.2 m

4. [298] 6 cm / 7 cm

5. [296] 9 mm / 14 mm

6. [304] 3 in.

7. Find the perimeter of the rectangle in Item 1.
[292]

8. Find the circumference of the circle in Item 6.
[302]

Which is a model of a rectangular prism? cylinder? sphere? cone? [306]

9. Box   **10.** Ball   **11.** Tin can   **12.** Funnel

Find the volumes. Find the surface areas. [310, 312]

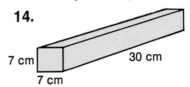

13. 3 mm / 5 mm / 7 mm

14. 7 cm / 7 cm / 30 cm

Find the missing measures. [314]

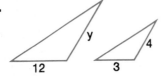

15. y / 12 / 4 / 3

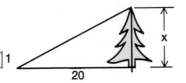

16. x / 1 / 2 / 20

17. On this map, what is the
[316] distance from the library to
the town hall?

Scale: 1 mm = 20 meters

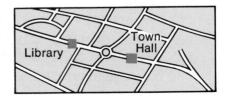

CHAPTER TEST

Find the areas.

1.
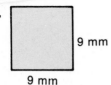
9 mm

9 mm

2.
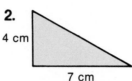
4 cm

7 cm

3.
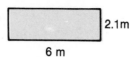
2.1m

6 m

4.
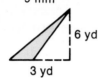
6 yd

3 yd

5.
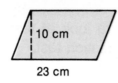
10 cm

23 cm

6.

2 mm

7. Find the perimeter of the square in Item 1.

8. Find the circumference of the circle in Item 6.

9. Find the volume.
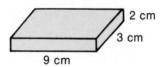
2 cm

3 cm

9 cm

10. Find the surface area.
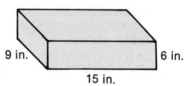
9 in.

6 in.

15 in.

Which is a model of a rectangular prism? cylinder? sphere? cone?

11. Sipping straw

12. Dunce cap

13. Globe of the earth

14. Shoe box

15. Find the height of the flagpole.
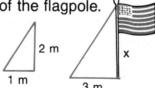
2 m

1 m

x

3 m

16. On this architect's drawing, what is the actual size of the room?

1 mm = 20 cm

1. Copy and complete the table.

PUPPET SHOW SALES

Mon: Gr 7: $6, Gr 6: $2, Gr 5: $10
Tues: Gr 7: $7, Gr 6: $7, Gr 5: $10
Wed: Gr 7: $6, Gr 6: $12, Gr 5: $10
Thurs: Gr 7: $21, Gr 6: $34, Gr 5: $11
Fri: Gr 7: $5, Gr 6: $19, Gr 5: $12

PUPPET SHOW SALES

Grade	M	T	W	Th	F	Total
7						
6						
5						
Total						

2. On which day did Grade 7 sell the most? Grade 6? Grade 5?

3. On which day were the sales the greatest? the least?

4. On which day did Grade 7 do worst? Grade 6? Grade 5?

5. Which grade sold more on Friday than any other day?

Here is some more information for a table.

6. The school principal kept track of how many pupils were absent each day in each grade. Make up a table for these facts. Give a weekly total for each grade, a daily total for all the grades, and the total absent for all grades for the whole week.

Mon: Grade 5: 10, Grade 6: 6, Grade 7: 9.
Tues: Grade 5: 11, Grade 6: 9, Grade 7: 9.
Wed: Grade 5: 5, Grade 6: 8, Grade 7: 10.
Thurs: Grade 5: 4, Grade 6: 0, Grade 7: 2.
Fri: Grade 5: 1, Grade 6: 3, Grade 7: 3.

SOLVING PROBLEMS USING A TABLE

CALORIES AND VITAMINS OF SELECTED FOODS

Food	Calories	Vitamin A (units)	Vitamin B₁ (mg)	Vitamin C (mg)
1 apple	70	50	.04	3
1 banana	119	190	.05	10
1 hamburger	330	50	.05	0
1 cup carrots	50	15,520	.04	5.6
1 ear corn	100	400	.09	10
1 egg	80	550	.4	0
1 orange	75	300	.08	72
1 cookie	109	0	.007	0
1 dish ice cream	290	750	.04	.9
1 glass milk	166	400	.06	2.8
1 glass cola	75	0	0	0
1 cup spinach	40	14,580	.03	50

Solve these problems using the table.

1. For lunch Maria had a hamburger, a glass of milk, and a cookie. How many calories was that?

2. Chip debated whether he would have a dish of ice cream or a cookie for desert.

   a. Which desert has more calories? How much more?

   b. Which is higher in Vitamin B_1? How much higher?

3. Which food has $\frac{1}{2}$ as much Vitamin C as a cup of carrots?

4. Vitamin C is said to be good for colds. Name the two foods in the table which are highest in Vitamin C.

5. Both spinach and carrots are high in Vitamin A. Compare these two vegetables. Which is higher in Vitamin B_1? How much higher?

6. Gloria's daily requirement for Vitamin C is 80 mg. What part of her daily requirement is 1 cup of spinach?

323

PICTOGRAPHS

Often we use pictures in graphs. Such graphs are called **pictographs**.

Data

SCHOOL ENROLLMENT IN VALLEY CITY

Brook School: 500   Hill School: 350
Fairhaven School: 400   Park School: 275

Pictograph

SCHOOL ENROLLMENT IN VALLEY CITY

School	Number
Brook	☺ ☺ ☺ ☺ ☺
Fairhaven	☺ ☺ ☺ ☺
Hill	☺ ☺ ☺ ◖
Park	☺ ☺ ◖

Key: ☺ = 100 students

1. The symbol ☺ stands for 100 students. ◖ is $\frac{3}{4}$ of a face, so it stands for 75 students.

   a. ◖ is $\frac{1}{2}$ of a face. It stands for how many students?

   b. River School: ☺ ☺ ◖ How many students attend that school?

   c. Terrace School has 250 students. Draw pictures to show this number.

2. Here is some more data. Copy and complete the pictograph.

   Game One: 1,000
   Game Two: 500
   Game Three: 2,000
   Game Four: 2,500
   Key: ● = 1,000 spectators

   ATTENDANCE AT CITY HIGH SCHOOL FOOTBALL GAMES

Game	Spectators
One	
Two	
Three	
Four	

324

Consider this pictograph.

1. How many children were absent each day?

2. What was the total number of children absent that week?

3. On which day were 24% of the week's absences?

SCHOOL ABSENCES

Day	Number
Monday	☺
Tuesday	☺ ☺
Wednesday	☺ ◖
Thursday	☺ ◄
Friday	◖

Key: ☺ = 4 children

4. Here is some data for sales in the school candy sale. Copy and complete the pictograph.

   Grade 5: 300 boxes
   Grade 6: 200 boxes
   Grade 7: 250 boxes
   Grade 8: 350 boxes

SCHOOL CANDY SALE

Grade	Boxes Sold
Grade 5	
Grade 6	
Grade 7	
Grade 8	

Key: ☐ = 100 boxes

5. Make a pictograph to show the number of children in your class who have birthdays in each month. Use the symbol ⚲ to stand for one person. Which month has the most birthdays? Is there a month in which no one in your class has a birthday?

6. Make a pictograph to show the number of pupils in your class who have red, blond, black, and brown hair. Use ⚲ to stand for two persons. Use ⚴ to stand for one person. Which is the most common color hair in your class? least common?

7. Classify each person in your class as having blue or brown eyes. Make a pictograph to show the number of pupils having each kind. Use ● to stand for 4 persons, ◔ to stand for 3 persons, ◖ to stand for 2 persons, and ◄ to stand for one person. Which eye color is more common?

325

BAR GRAPH

Sometimes we use a **bar graph** in order to compare data.

CLASS ELECTION

Candidate	Number of Votes
Paul	7
Bob	1
Susan	3
Jeff	4
Joanne	5

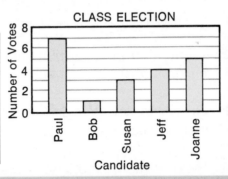

CLASS ELECTION

1. Study this bar graph. The average temperature for Boston on January 1 is 36°.

   a. Give the average temperature for Chicago.

   b. Give the average temperature for New York.

   c. Give the average temperature for San Francisco.

   d. How many degrees colder is the average January 1 temperature in Chicago than it is in New York?

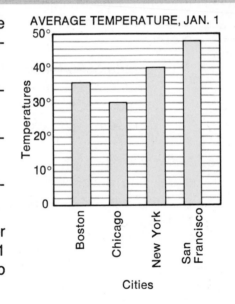

AVERAGE TEMPERATURE, JAN. 1

2. Fargo County had a Fight Pollution Campaign.

   Madison: $8,000
   Notch: $10,000
   Fargo: $14,000
   Edison: $8,500

   Copy and complete the graph.

   FARGO COUNTY POLLUTION CAMPAIGN

   Madison
   Notch
   Fargo
   Edison

   0   2   4   6   8   10   12   14
   Thousands of Dollars Contributed

Answer these questions about the graph at the right.

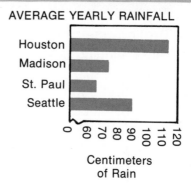

1. Which city has the most rain? the least rain?

2. Houston has an average yearly rainfall of 115 cm. What about each of the other cities?

3. Here is some data for a bar graph to show speeds of some well-known airplanes.

(1909) Signal Corps: 50 mph
(1919) D. H. 9C: 100 mph
(1936) DC-3: 200 mph
(1946) Lockheed Constellation: 300 mph
(1958) Boeing 707: 550 mph
(1965) VC 10: 600 mph
(1975) SST: 2,000 mph

Copy and complete the bar graph.

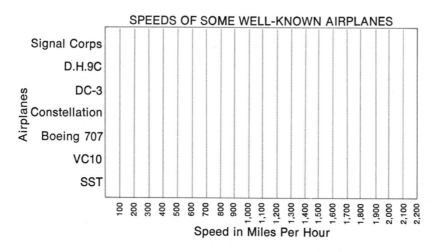

4. Make a bar graph to show this data of life expectancy.

man: 70 years   cat: 15 years
lion: 25 years   dog: 15 years
bear: 20 years   monkey: 15 years

327

BROKEN-LINE GRAPH

Broken-line graphs are often used to show change of facts with changing time.

1950: 1,000
1955: 6,000
1960: 6,000
1965: 16,000
1970: 13,000
1975: 13,000

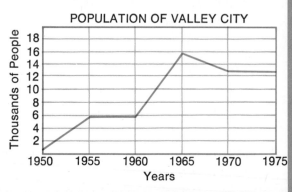

POPULATION OF VALLEY CITY

1. Look at the graph above. What was the increase in population from 1950 to 1955?

2. In which 5-year period was the increase the greatest?

3. In which 5-year period did the population decrease?

Here is some data on the average temperature in San Francisco for certain months.

February: 11°
April: 13°
June: 15°
August: 15°
October: 16°
December: 11°

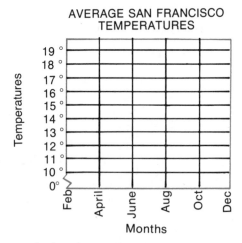

AVERAGE SAN FRANCISCO TEMPERATURES

4. Copy and complete the graph.

5. During which two 2-month periods does the temperature increase the same?

6. During which periods does it decrease? By how much?

Consider this broken-line graph about John's 6-month diet.

1. John recorded his weight on the first day of each month he dieted. What was his weight each month?

2. In which three months did John lose the same amount of weight?

3. John got tired of dieting one month and ate more than he should have. He didn't lose weight. What month was that?

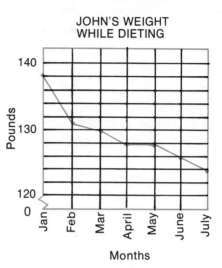

JOHN'S WEIGHT WHILE DIETING

4. Suppose he kept dieting and lost the same amount of weight from July 1 to August 1 as he did from June 1 to July 1. How much would he have weighed August 1?

Here is some information about California population, rounded to the nearest million.

> 1930: 6,000,000
> 1940: 7,000,000
> 1950: 11,000,000
> 1960: 16,000,000
> 1970: 20,000,000

5. Copy and complete the graph.

6. During what 10-year period did the population increase the most? the least?

7. In which two 10-year periods did the population increase the same?

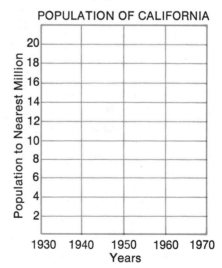

POPULATION OF CALIFORNIA

329

8. Make a broken-line graph to show this data.

BERTHA'S GROWTH IN HEIGHT OVER A 5-YEAR PERIOD

Jan 1, 1974	145 centimeters
Jan 1, 1975	150 centimeters
Jan 1, 1976	160 centimeters
Jan 1, 1977	165 centimeters
Jan 1, 1978	170 centimeters

9. Make a broken-line graph to show the change in Ralph's earnings for cutting grass.

April	$5
May	$8
June	$13
July	$13
August	$12

Brainteaser

Pia thought she saw a pattern in the numerals for numbers divisible by 4. She started with 152, the first number divisible by 4 and larger than 150.

$$152 \longrightarrow 52 \div 4 = 13$$
$$156 \longrightarrow 56 \div 4 = 14$$
$$160 \longrightarrow 60 \div 4 = 15$$
$$164 \longrightarrow 64 \div 4 = 16$$

Is it possible that if a number is divisible by 4, then the number named by the last two digits is divisible by 4?

Try some numbers greater than 1,000.

Check

$$1,524 \longrightarrow 24 \div 4 = 6 \qquad 4\overline{)1,524} \quad 381$$

It seems to work! Try some more. Can you tell why Pia's rule works?

Here's a crossnumber puzzle to solve.

ACROSS

1. $9 \times 40{,}321$

8. 10×843.5

10. $342 \div 6$

12. the 9th prime number

13. 5^2

14. eight centuries

15. 12^2

16. $8^2 + (7 \times 2)$

17. 31% of 200

19. $28 \div .5$

20. the number of meters in 5.225 kilometers

22. 147,863 rounded to the nearest ten

DOWN

2. 32% of 212.5

3. 50% of 484

4. $\frac{1}{4} \times 3{,}332$

5. 20% of 425

7. $5^2 \times 1{,}435$

9. $\frac{2}{5} \times 63{,}650$

11. 10% of 7,080

13. $2{,}712 - 2{,}467$

17. $18.81 \div .03$

18. the number of inches in 19 feet

20. $2\frac{1}{4} \times 24$

21. $9^2 - 5^2$

CIRCLE GRAPHS

We can also use a **circle graph** to compare facts.

North America has 43% of all the world's TV sets.

Europe has 37% of the world's TV sets.

PERCENT OF ALL TELEVISIONS IN WORLD BY REGION

North America 43%

Europe 37%

Rest of World 20%

There were 300,000,000 TV sets in the world in 1970. Here is how we find the number in North America.

$$43\% \times 300{,}000{,}000 = n$$
$$.43 \times 300{,}000{,}000 = n$$
$$= 129{,}000{,}000$$

Mr. Nilak used a circle graph to help plan his budget.

NILAK FAMILY BUDGET

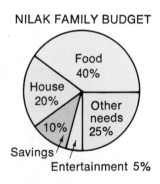

Food 40%

House 20%

Other needs 25%

10%

Savings

Entertainment 5%

1. He was paid $800 a month. How much did he plan to spend on each item?

2. Mr. Nilak got a raise to $900 a month. How much would he now spend for each item?

332

Toni's class had a newsletter. They made a circle graph to show the budget. Complete this table to find the amount of money they could spend on each item if they had $200 to spend.

	Item	Amount
1.	Paper	
2.	Printing	
3.	Supplies	
4.	Postage	
	Total	$200

NEWSLETTER BUDGET

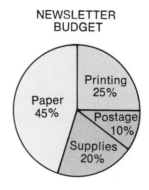

Here is a circle graph for a baseball player's record one season. Complete this table to find the number of hits, walks, outs, etc. that he had that season.

	Item	Number
5.	Hits	
6.	Walks	
7.	Strike outs	
8.	Other	
	Total	500

BATTING RECORD

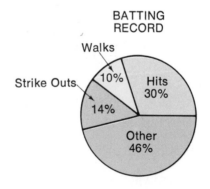

Brainteaser

You can tell if a number is divisible by 2 by the last digit. You can tell if a number is divisible by 4 by the last two digits. Do you think that if a number is divisible by 8, then you can tell by its last three digits? Check it out.

1,368   22,468   14,235   357,904

Lucia and Bill are playing a card game.

Card	Meaning	Integer	Read
+5	gain of 5 points	+5	positive five
-3	loss of 3 points	-3	negative three

1. Complete the table.

	Card	Meaning	Integer	Read
a.	+4		+4	positive four
b.	-2		-2	

2. Lucia drew a +3 and then a +7. This is the same as having a +10 in his hand.

   a. Is +10 a gain or a loss? of how much?

   b. Drawing a +4 and a +3 is the same as drawing what one card?

3. Bill draws a -2 and then a -6. This is the same as having a -8 in his hand.

   a. Is this a loss or a gain? of how much?

   b. Is drawing a -4 and then a -5 a loss or a gain? of how much?

4. You can use -5 to describe many things.

   loss of 5 yards   5° below zero

   Describe each with an integer.

   a. Gain of 10 meters   **b.** 6° below zero

   c. 7° above zero   **d.** 2 km above sea level

   e. Profit of $10   **f.** 5 sec before blast off

Write a word name for each integer.

1. ⁻8   **2.** ⁺12   **3.** ⁻27   **4.** ⁺15

Describe each with an integer.

5. 12° above zero   **6.** 1 km below sea level

7. Loss of ten meters   **8.** Gain of 23 yards

9. 3° below zero   **10.** 298 ft above sea level

11. Profit of $100   **12.** Two min after blast off

13. Loss of 5 pounds   **14.** Loss of $17

What one card would replace these two cards in Lucia's and Bill's card game?

15. ⁺2   ⁺3   **16.** ⁻4   ⁻6   **17.** ⁻2   ⁻4

18. ⁺7   ⁺8   **19.** ⁻10   ⁻6   **20.** ⁻3   ⁻9

★ What one card would replace these cards?

21. ⁺4   ⁻3   **22.** ⁻4   ⁺3   **23.** ⁺3   ⁻4   ⁻6

ACTIVITY

Graph your class!

Think of some questions for everyone in the class to answer. Some examples: How many brothers do you have? sisters? Are you the oldest? youngest? How many minutes a day do you read? watch television? What's your favorite magazine? television program? radio program? music? animal? After you have chosen your questions, you must decide how to get answers from everyone. It would be best to write each question on a piece of paper and pass that paper to each classmate. What other questions would you like to ask about things that are important to you?

INTEGERS ON THE NUMBER LINE

A number line helps to show the order of the integers.

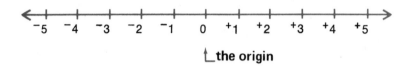

⌞ the origin

On the number line, the smaller numbers are to the left of the larger numbers.

⁺3 < ⁺5   ⁻4 < ⁺1   ⁻6 < ⁻2

⌞ read: "is less than"

These are also true sentences.

⁺4 > ⁺1   ⁺1 > ⁻3   ⁻2 > ⁻4

⌞ read: "is greater than"

1. Complete. Use < or >. Think of the number line.

   a. ⁻7 ▤ ⁻5   **b.** ⁻12 ▤ 0   **c.** ⁻3 ▤ ⁻17

   d. ⁺8 ▤ 0   **e.** ⁺6 ▤ ⁺4   **f.** ⁻10 ▤ ⁺5

   g. ⁻10 ▤ ⁺3   **h.** ⁻17 ▤ ⁻1   **i.** ⁺1 ▤ ⁻2

2. Look at the integer number line.

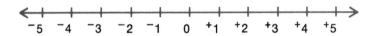

⁺4 is four units from the origin.
⁻4 is four units from the origin.

How far is each from the origin?

   a. ⁺5   **b.** ⁻1   **c.** ⁺3   **d.** ⁻5

   e. ⁻4   **f.** ⁺1   **g.** ⁻3   **h.** ⁺2

336

A thermometer is like an integer number line. Look at the thermometer at the right. Compare these temperatures. Use < or >.

1. $^+7° \equiv {}^+10°$ **2.** $^-2° \equiv {}^-17°$

3. $^+8° \equiv 0°$ **4.** $^-13° \equiv {}^-1°$

5. $^-29° \equiv {}^-15°$ **6.** $^+8° \equiv {}^-3°$

7. $^-20° \equiv {}^-10°$ **8.** $^+32° \equiv {}^-1°$

9. $^-42° \equiv {}^-37°$ **10.** $^+25° \equiv {}^+60°$

11. $^-6° \equiv 0°$ **12.** $^+14° \equiv {}^-10°$

13. $^+2° \equiv {}^-16°$ **14.** $^-7° \equiv {}^+4°$

15. $^-13° \equiv {}^-20°$ **16.** $^+6° \equiv {}^-42°$

True or false.

17. $^-8 < {}^-4$ **18.** $^-3 < {}^-12$

19. $^+2 > {}^-21$ **20.** $^+12 < {}^+5$

21. $^-18 > {}^-28$ **22.** $^+12 < {}^+10$

23. $^-20 > {}^+10$ **24.** $^+25 > {}^+26$

Tell what integers are between each pair.

25. $^+1$ and $^+6$ **26.** $^-6$ and $^-1$

27. $^-3$ and $^+3$ **28.** $^-23$ and $^-18$

29. $^-1$ and $^-4$ **30.** $^+7$ and $^-6$

How far is each integer from the origin?

31. $^-7$ **32.** $^+7$ **33.** $^+10$ **34.** $^-2$

ADDING TWO INTEGERS

We can show the addition of ⁺3 and ⁺4 on the number line.

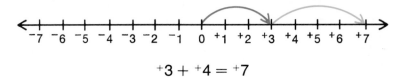

$$^+3 + {}^+4 = {}^+7$$

To add ⁻3 and ⁻4 we start at 0 and move left 3 units, then left 4 more units.

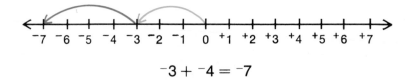

$$^-3 + {}^-4 = {}^-7$$

1. Use the number line to find the sum.

   a. ⁺2 + ⁺6
   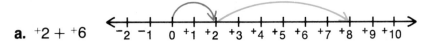

   b. ⁻1 + ⁻3
   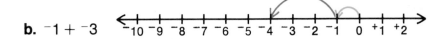

2. What additions are shown?

   a.
   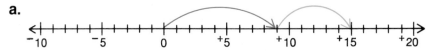

   b.
   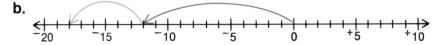

3. Think of the card game again. If you picked up a ⁻4 and then a ⁻8, this would be the same as a loss of twelve points, or ⁻12 points.

338

Add.

a. $^-7$
   $+ {}^-9$

b. $^+4$
   $+ {}^+6$

c. $^-21$
   $+ {}^-4$

d. $^+98$
   $+ {}^+47$

Add.

1. $^+9 + {}^+7$

2. $^-8 + {}^-3$

3. $^-4 + {}^-9$

4. $^+5 + {}^+8$

5. $^+6 + {}^+9$

6. $^-4 + {}^-10$

7. $^-3 + {}^-2$

8. $^+5 + {}^+6$

9. $^-7 + {}^-2$

10. $^-1 + {}^-4$

11. $^-8 + {}^-2$

12. $^+5 + {}^+9$

13. $^-10 + {}^-6$

14. $^+7 + {}^+7$

15. $^-2 + {}^-12$

16. $^-20 + {}^-40$

17. $^+25 + {}^+2$

18. $^-18 + {}^-2$

19. $^+23 + {}^+4$

20. $^-41 + {}^-6$

21. $^+70 + {}^+30$

22. $^-37 + {}^-21$

23. $^-48 + {}^-26$

24. $^+64 + {}^+52$

25. $^+70 + {}^+32$

26. $^-123 + {}^-241$

27. $^-829 + {}^-136$

Solve these problems.

28. The temperature was 19° above zero by 8:00 am. By noon it had risen 12°. What was the temperature at noon? Give the answer as an integer.

29. John took a picture of a space ship 10 seconds before lift off, then another picture 5 seconds after lift off. How many seconds apart were his two pictures?

★30. Agnes drew a $\boxed{^-51}$ as her first card in a card game. After drawing a second card, she ended up with a total of $^-72$ points. What was her second card?

339

FILE CLERKS

1. Ali Harris can file 120 memos in 4 hours. What is her average rate per hour?

2. Sally O'Hare worked in an office where the files filled up one whole wall. The wall was 50 meters 27 centimeters wide. To save space, the company threw out some old files. They left 39 meters of files along the wall. How much less space do the files occupy now?

3. When she started, Ms. O'Hare was able to do one kind of filing in $31\frac{3}{4}$ hours. Now it takes her $27\frac{1}{2}$ hours. How much less time does it take her now?

4. Amy Testa had the job of organizing 3,000 documents into files. She used only 8 files. On the average, how many documents did she put in each file?

5. Last year, Howard Tanaka's company used a system that put 180 lines of print on 1 centimeter of microfilm. This year's new system puts 1,800 lines on 1 centimeter. How many more lines of print can the new system fit on 1 centimeter?

6. Vic Leonard can file 140 memos in 5 hours. How many memos would he file in a 40-hour week?

OPPOSITES

To make up a loss of 4 points, $\boxed{^-4}$, Steve knew he must draw a gain of 4 points, $\boxed{^+4}$. We can show this on the number line.

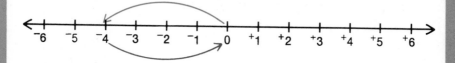

$$^-4 + {}^+4 = 0$$

We say that $^+4$ is the **opposite** of $^-4$, and $^-4$ is the opposite of $^+4$.

1. Add.

    a. $^-7 + {}^+7$ **b.** $^+9 + {}^-9$ **c.** $^-12 + {}^+12$

2. Find the opposites.

    a. $^-7$ **b.** $^+7$ **c.** $^-9$ **d.** $^-12$

Find the opposites.

1. $^-3$ **2.** $^+5$ **3.** $^+1$ **4.** $^-20$

5. $^-21$ **6.** $^+30$ **7.** $^+12$ **8.** $^-17$

9. $^+4$ **10.** $^-24$ **11.** $^-6$ **12.** $^+9$

Solve.

13. $^-2 + n = 0$ **14.** $^+6 + n = 0$ **15.** $n + {}^-10 = 0$

16. $n + {}^+20 = 0$ **17.** $^-13 + n = 0$ **18.** $n + {}^+19 = 0$

19. $^-6 + n = 0$ **20.** $^+7 + {}^-7 = n$ **21.** $^-4 + {}^+4 = n$

ADDING POSITIVES AND NEGATIVES

In the card game, suppose you drew these two cards: ⎡‾3⎤ and ⎡⁺5⎤. A loss of 3 points, followed by a gain of 5 points gives a total gain of 2 points. The number line shows this.

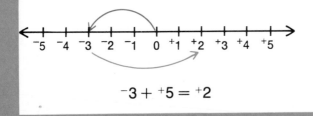

$$^-3 + {}^+5 = {}^+2$$

1. Let's add: $^-5 + {}^+3$.

   a. Think: does a loss of 5 points followed by a gain of 3 points give a loss, or a gain? of how much?

   b. Complete: $^-5 + {}^+3 = $ _____ .

2. Use the number lines to find the sums.

   a. $^+4 + {}^-7 = n$

   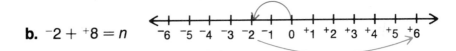

   b. $^-2 + {}^+8 = n$

   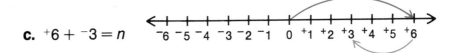

   c. $^+6 + {}^-3 = n$

3. Add.

   a. $^-9 + {}^+7$ b. $^+9 + {}^-7$ c. $^-8 + {}^+3$

   d. $^+8 + {}^-3$ e. $^+2 + {}^-10$ f. $^-12 + {}^+4$

342

Add.

1. ⁻6 + ⁺1   2. ⁻6 + ⁺5   3. ⁻4 + ⁺7

4. ⁻4 + ⁺8   5. ⁺2 + ⁻7   6. ⁺6 + ⁻8

7. ⁻2 + ⁺1   8. ⁺6 + ⁻1   9. ⁺1 + ⁻9

10. ⁻3 + ⁺5   11. ⁺8 + ⁻3   12. ⁻5 + ⁺7

13. ⁻1 + ⁺8   14. ⁺5 + ⁻4   15. ⁺10 + ⁻1

16. ⁻10 + ⁺3   17. ⁻12 + ⁺4   18. ⁺13 + ⁻13

19. ⁺6 + ⁻12   20. ⁻12 + ⁺13   21. ⁺2 + ⁻11

22. ⁺9 + ⁻13   23. ⁻15 + ⁺10   24. ⁺10 + ⁻12

25. ⁺8 + ⁻15   26. ⁻11 + ⁺12   27. ⁺6 + ⁻14

28. ⁻14 + ⁺15   29. ⁻19 + ⁺20   30. ⁻1 + ⁺17

31. ⁺5 + ⁻15   32. ⁺3 + ⁻14   33. ⁻20 + ⁺21

34. ⁻12 + ⁺20   35. ⁻20 + ⁺25   36. ⁺7 + ⁻21

37. ⁺48 + ⁻24   38. ⁺60 + ⁻30   39. ⁺50 + ⁻25

40. ⁺60 + ⁻40   41. ⁺100 + ⁻90   42. ⁻91 + ⁺67

★ **43.** ⁺17 + ⁻20 + ⁺3   ★ **44.** ⁻40 + ⁺50 + ⁻17

Solve this problem.

45. Playing a game of shuffle-board, Kate got 8 points, and then lost 10 points. Did Kate gain or lose points? How many?

SUBTRACTING

Mike used the card game to explain subtraction.

> TAKING AWAY A GAIN CARD DOES THE SAME TO YOUR SCORE AS DRAWING A LOSS CARD.

1. Let's think about what Mike said.

Jane drew a ⊡+5, a 5-point gain. The referee took away a 4-point gain. She then had only a 1-point gain.
$$^+5 - ^+4 = ^+1$$

Charlie drew ⊡+5, a 5-point gain. He then drew a ⊡−4, a 4-point loss. He then had only a 1-point gain.
$$^+5 + ^-4 = ^+1$$

Was it a tie between Jane and Charlie?

Subtracting an integer is the same as adding its opposite.
$$^+5 - ^+4 = ^+1$$
$$^+5 + ^-4 = ^+1$$

2. Subtract an integer by adding its opposite.

$$^-8 - ^+6 = ^-8 + ^-6$$
$$= ^-14$$

$$^+7 - ^-3 = ^+7 + ^+3$$
$$= ^+10$$

Complete.

a. $^+7 - ^+2 = ^+7 + ^-2$
$$= \underline{\quad}$$

b. $^-10 - ^+3 = ^-10 + ^-3$
$$= \underline{\quad}$$

c. $^+9 - ^-6 = ^+9 + \underline{\quad}$
$$= \underline{\quad}$$

d. $^-8 - ^-7 = ^-8 + \underline{\quad}$
$$= \underline{\quad}$$

344

3. Write as additions. Solve.

a. $^+8 - ^-4$ **b.** $^+2 - ^-8$ **c.** $^-6 - ^+2$

d. $^-6 - ^-9$ **e.** $^-5 - ^-6$ **f.** $^-9 - ^-3$

Subtract.

1. $^-1 - ^+5$ **2.** $^+1 - ^-5$ **3.** $^+9 - ^-2$

4. $^-7 - ^+6$ **5.** $^-8 - ^+10$ **6.** $^-9 - ^+2$

7. $^+5 - ^+2$ **8.** $^-6 - ^+4$ **9.** $^-8 - ^-1$

10. $^-10 - ^+6$ **11.** $^-3 - ^+7$ **12.** $^+2 - ^-8$

13. $^-6 - ^+6$ **14.** $^+4 - ^-8$ **15.** $^+6 - ^-3$

16. $^-1 - ^+8$ **17.** $0 - ^-5$ **18.** $^+7 - ^+4$

19. $^+9 - ^-6$ **20.** $^-10 - ^+3$ **21.** $^+5 - ^+2$

22. $^-12 - ^+10$ **23.** $^-15 - ^-5$ **24.** $^+6 - ^+8$

25. $^+12 - ^-3$ **26.** $^-15 - ^+2$ **27.** $^-28 - ^+12$

28. $^+35 - ^-14$ **29.** $^+50 - ^-25$ **30.** $^-42 - ^+15$

31. $^-55 - ^+10$ **32.** $^+22 - ^-18$ **33.** $^-40 - ^+25$

Solve these mini-problems.

34. Temperature $^-5°$F.
Rose 11°.
New temperature

35. Hike.
Started 15 m below sea level.
Climbed 75 m up mountain.
How far above sea level now?

36. Drew $\boxed{^-6}$.
What card needed
for 3-pt gain.

37. Temperature $^-3°$C.
What degree rise needed to
be $^+10°$C?

345

Mr. Richards showed his class five drawings. He asked each student to vote for his favorite one. Here are the results.

Picture	No. of Votes	Number Pairs
1	5	→ (1, 5)
2	4	→ (2, 4)
3	4	→ (3, 4)
4	2	→ (4, 2)
5	3	→ (5, 3)

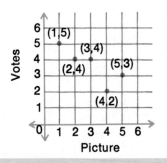

1. We call (2, 4) a **number pair**. To graph a number pair, (2, 4), go to the right 2 units, then up 4 units. Use graph paper. Graph these number pairs.

   a. (3, 4)   **b.** (4, 2)   **c.** (5, 3)

2. The number pair for a point is called its **coordinates**. Look at the graph below. The coordinates of point B are (4, 3). What are the coordinates of these points?

   a. A   **b.** C   **c.** D

   d. X   **e.** Y   **f.** M

   g. L   **h.** Q   **i.** R

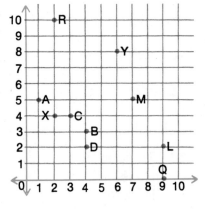

3. Use graph paper. Mark points with these coordinates.

   a. A(1, 2)   **b.** B(2, 5)   **c.** C(4, 0)   **d.** D(0, 3)

   e. E(4, 3)   **f.** F(0, 5)   **g.** G(2, 1)   **h.** H(3, 2)

346

Study this graph. What are the coordinates of these points?

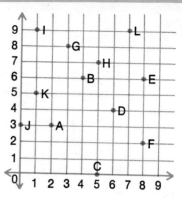

1. A
2. B
3. C

4. D
5. E
6. F

7. G
8. H
9. I

10. J
11. K
12. L

Use graph paper. Mark points with these coordinates.

13. $A(2, 1)$
14. $B(3, 6)$
15. $C(4, 0)$
16. $D(5, 5)$

17. $E(5, 6)$
18. $F(0, 3)$
19. $G(0, 0)$
20. $H(1, 2)$

21. $I(0, 4)$
22. $J(8, 4)$
23. $K(6, 8)$
24. $L(0, 7)$

Study this table.

25. Write six number pairs from this table. The first number will be the score. The second number will be the number of pupils making that score. Then graph the number pairs.

TEST RESULTS

Score	No. of Pupils
0	3
1	0
2	1
3	2
4	7
5	3

26. Freda kept track of the temperatures on a cold afternoon in Alaska. The first number shows the hour, and the second number shows the temperature. Write five number pairs. Then graph the number pairs.

SOME TEMPERATURES IN ALASKA

Hour	Temperature
1 pm	6°
2 pm	8°
3 pm	7°
4 pm	1°
6 pm	0°

347

We can graph pairs of integers also.

Point	Coordinates
A	($^-$3, $^+$2)
B	($^-$4, $^-$3)
C	($^-$1, 0)
D	(0, $^+$3)
E	($^+$3, $^-$3)
F	($^+$2, 0)

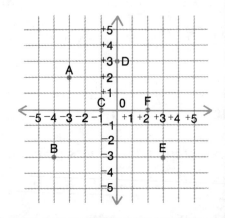

1. To graph ($^+$2, $^-$4) we count 2 units to the right and then 4 units down. On this graph ($^+$2, $^-$4) is named *T*.

Here are some coordinates. What letter names do they have on the graph?

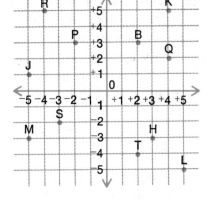

   a. ($^+$4, $^+$2)   **b.** ($^+$3, $^-$3)

   c. ($^-$2, $^+$3)   **d.** ($^-$3, $^-$2)

2. What are the coordinates of these points?

   a. *B*   **b.** *J*   **c.** *K*

   d. *L*   **e.** *M*   **f.** *R*

3. Use graph paper. Mark points for these coordinates.

   a. *A*(0, $^+$3)   **b.** *B*($^+$3, 0)   **c.** *C*($^+$2, $^-$4)

   d. *D*($^-$2, $^-$5)   **e.** *E*($^-$4, $^+$2)   **f.** *F*($^+$5, $^+$1)

   g. *G*($^-$6, $^-$2)   **h.** *H*($^+$8, $^-$1)   **i.** *I*(0, $^-$7)

Study this graph. What are the coordinates of these points?

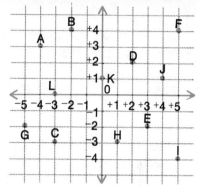

1. A   **2.** B   **3.** C

4. D   **5.** E   **6.** F

7. G   **8.** H   **9.** I

10. J   **11.** K   **12.** L

Use graph paper to mark points with these coordinates.

13. $A(^+1, ^+4)$ **14.** $B(^+1, ^-4)$ **15.** $C(^+2, 0)$ **16.** $D(0, ^+2)$

17. $E(^-1, ^+4)$ **18.** $F(^-2, ^-3)$ **19.** $G(^-5, 0)$ **20.** $H(^+3, ^-6)$

21. $I(0, ^+6)$ **22.** $J(^-1, ^+3)$ **23.** $K(^+5, ^-2)$ **24.** $L(^-3, ^-5)$

25. $M(0, ^-5)$ **26.** $N(^+6, ^-2)$ **27.** $P(^-3, ^+1)$ **28.** $Q(0, ^-6)$

ACTIVITY

Graph each point in order. Connect the points with line segments as you graph. See what figure you get.

1. $(^+1, ^-2)$; $(^+6, ^-2)$; $(^+5, ^-4)$; $(^-5, ^-4)$; $(^-6, ^-2)$; $(^-1, ^-2)$; $(^-1, ^+11)$; $(0, ^+12)$; $(^-1, ^+13)$; $(0, ^+15)$; $(^+1, ^+14)$; $(0, ^+12)$; $(^+1, ^+13)$; $(^+1, ^-2)$

2. $(0, 0)$; $(^+7, 0)$; $(^+9, ^-1)$; $(^+8, ^-2)$; $(^+7, ^-2)$; $(^+6, ^-3)$; $(^+5, ^-2)$; $(^-5, ^-2)$; $(^-6, ^-3)$; $(^-7, ^-2)$; $(^-10, ^-2)$; $(^-10, ^-1)$; $(^-8, 0)$; $(^-6, ^+1)$; $(^-2, ^+1)$; $(0, 0)$

3. $(^-12, ^+8)$; $(^+3, ^+8)$; $(^+2, ^+7)$; $(^+5, ^+7)$; $(^+5, ^+4)$; $(^+6, ^+7)$; $(^+7, ^+7)$; $(^+7, ^+5)$; $(^+8, ^+5)$; $(^+12, ^+7)$; $(^+13, ^+8)$; $(^+14, ^+8)$; $(^+15, ^+6)$; $(^+13, ^+5)$; $(^+12, ^+3)$; $(^+11, ^+3)$; $(^+11, ^-1)$; $(^+9, ^-3)$; $(^+9, ^-5)$; $(^+10, ^-8)$; $(^+9, ^-8)$; $(^+7, ^-5)$; $(^+6, ^-5)$; $(^+4, ^-6)$; $(^+1, ^-6)$; $(^-1, ^-9)$; $(^-3, ^-6)$; $(^-5, ^-6)$; $(^-9, ^-4)$; $(^-12, ^-3)$; $(^-14, ^+1)$; $(^-14, ^+3)$; $(^-13, ^+6)$; $(^-12, ^+8)$

A function machine gives number pairs. Let's work with the whole numbers again.

Input n	Output n + 2
0	2
1	3
2	4
3	5
4	6

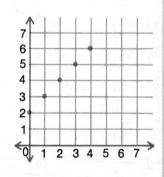

1. Copy and complete both the table and the graph.

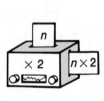

n	n × 2
0	0
1	2
2	4
3	
4	

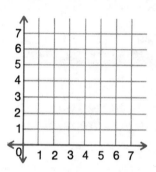

2. What pattern do you see in the graph in Item 1?

3. Complete this table. Graph the number pairs. Do you see the same type of pattern as in Item 1?

n	n − 3
3	0
4	1
5	
7	
8	
10	

350

1. Copy and complete both the table and the graph.

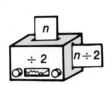

n	n ÷ 2
0	0
2	1
4	
6	
8	

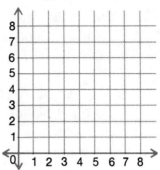

Complete the tables. Make graphs from the tables.

2.

n	n + 3
0	3
1	4
2	
3	
4	
5	

3.

n	n − 2
2	0
3	
4	2
5	
6	4
7	

4.

n	3 × n
0	
1	
2	6
3	
4	
5	15

Make tables from these function machines. Graph the number pair from the tables. Choose six inputs for each.

5.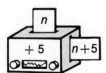

6.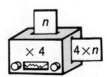

7.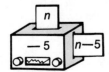

8.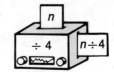

CHAPTER REVIEW

Study this broken-line graph. [328]

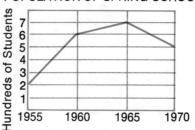

POPULATION OF SPRING SCHOOL

1. What was the population of Spring School in 1955? in 1965? in 1970?

2. During what 5-year period did the population decrease?

3. Draw a bar graph to show this data. [326]

WEEKLY SCHOOL LUNCHES

Mon: 50, Tues: 100, Wed: 150, Thurs: 125, Fri: 75.

Consider this circle graph. [332]

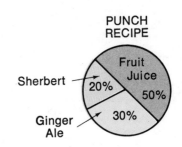

PUNCH RECIPE

4. Betsy is making 5 gallons of punch. How many gallons of ginger ale should she use?

5. How much fruit juice should she use?

Complete. Use < or >. [336]

6. $^-8 \equiv {}^-3$ 7. $^+8 \equiv {}^+3$ 8. $^-9 \equiv {}^+6$

Add. [338, 342]

9. $^+4 + {}^+8$ 10. $^-5 + {}^-6$ 11. $^-3 + {}^+9$ 12. $^-7 + {}^+2$

Use graph paper. Mark points for these coordinates. [348]

13. $D(^+8, {}^+2)$ 14. $E(^+7, {}^-4)$ 15. $F(^-3, {}^-6)$

16. Complete the table. [350]

17. Make a graph using the number pairs. [350]

n	$n - 6$
7	1
8	
10	
12	

352

CHAPTER TEST

Study this broken-line graph.

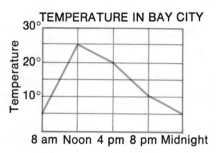

1. What was the temperature at 4 pm?

2. Between 8 am and midnight, when was it warmest?

3. Draw a bar graph to show this data.

HEIGHTS OF THE MEMBERS OF THE SMITH FAMILY

Mother, 165 cm   Lisa, 150 cm
Father, 175 cm   Alan, 130 cm

Consider this circle graph. Fred's allowance is $5 per week.

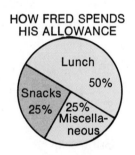

4. How much does Fred spend on lunches?

5. How much does he spend on snacks?

Complete. Use < or >.

6. $^-7 \equiv {}^+3$ **7.** $^-2 \equiv {}^-5$ **8.** $^-4 \equiv 0$

Add.

9. $^+7 + {}^+3$ **10.** $^-4 + {}^-5$ **11.** $^-8 + {}^+10$ **12.** $^-6 + {}^+4$

Use graph paper. Mark points for these coordinates.

13. $A(^+3, {}^+7)$ **14.** $B(^+5, {}^-3)$ **15.** $C(^-4, {}^+6)$

16. Complete the table.

17. Make a graph using the number pairs.

n	$n + 4$
0	4
1	
2	
3	

353

PRACTICE EXERCISES

Add.

1. $1 + 3$	**2.** $2 + 4$	**3.** $6 + 0$	**4.** $3 + 3$
5. $5 + 2$	**6.** $1 + 7$	**7.** $2 + 2$	**8.** $6 + 2$
9. $7 + 4$	**10.** $3 + 7$	**11.** $8 + 8$	**12.** $7 + 5$
13. $4 + 1$	**14.** $5 + 4$	**15.** $1 + 9$	**16.** $4 + 3$
17. $3 + 2$	**18.** $6 + 4$	**19.** $9 + 6$	**20.** $2 + 8$
21. $3 + 5$	**22.** $5 + 7$	**23.** $7 + 9$	**24.** $1 + 8$
25. $8 + 5$	**26.** $5 + 5$	**27.** $9 + 5$	**28.** $7 + 2$
29. $7 + 6$	**30.** $8 + 7$	**31.** $5 + 6$	**32.** $6 + 8$
33. $9 + 9$	**34.** $3 + 9$	**35.** $9 + 8$	**36.** $6 + 6$

Subtract.

1. $13 - 5$	**2.** $9 - 7$	**3.** $4 - 3$	**4.** $10 - 9$
5. $8 - 5$	**6.** $13 - 4$	**7.** $11 - 8$	**8.** $5 - 3$
9. $10 - 5$	**10.** $4 - 1$	**11.** $8 - 1$	**12.** $11 - 7$
13. $3 - 0$	**14.** $12 - 9$	**15.** $13 - 6$	**16.** $14 - 5$
17. $15 - 7$	**18.** $7 - 3$	**19.** $12 - 3$	**20.** $8 - 6$
21. $5 - 2$	**22.** $10 - 6$	**23.** $6 - 6$	**24.** $14 - 7$
25. $11 - 2$	**26.** $16 - 8$	**27.** $9 - 6$	**28.** $12 - 5$
29. $17 - 9$	**30.** $15 - 8$	**31.** $12 - 6$	**32.** $14 - 9$
33. $9 - 2$	**34.** $9 - 1$	**35.** $15 - 9$	**36.** $11 - 5$

Multiply.

1. 1×3	**2.** 2×2	**3.** 4×2	**4.** 4×9
5. 7×4	**6.** 5×1	**7.** 8×9	**8.** 6×2
9. 8×0	**10.** 7×2	**11.** 3×9	**12.** 8×5
13. 5×3	**14.** 9×8	**15.** 3×3	**16.** 2×4
17. 9×5	**18.** 4×6	**19.** 6×3	**20.** 5×4
21. 8×7	**22.** 1×7	**23.** 0×4	**24.** 6×4
25. 2×8	**26.** 1×1	**27.** 9×7	**28.** 7×8
29. 6×6	**30.** 5×6	**31.** 5×9	**32.** 4×8
33. 3×0	**34.** 6×7	**35.** 9×6	**36.** 6×8
37. 9×9	**38.** 0×5	**39.** 2×6	**40.** 4×4
41. 5×2	**42.** 5×5	**43.** 4×7	**44.** 6×7
45. 7×7	**46.** 6×0	**47.** 7×6	**48.** 3×2
49. 9×4	**50.** 8×8	**51.** 7×5	**52.** 9×8
53. 2×1	**54.** 7×9	**55.** 5×8	**56.** 2×9
57. 4×5	**58.** 3×6	**59.** 9×7	**60.** 1×8
61. 8×4	**62.** 6×6	**63.** 8×1	**64.** 6×9
65. 9×3	**66.** 7×3	**67.** 3×4	**68.** 8×7
69. 0×7	**70.** 3×7	**71.** 0×6	**72.** 7×6
73. 3×8	**74.** 5×8	**75.** 1×2	**76.** 5×7
77. 4×3	**78.** 8×9	**79.** 8×3	**80.** 4×1

Divide.

1. $10 \div 5$　　**2.** $0 \div 8$　　**3.** $54 \div 6$　　**4.** $6 \div 2$

5. $0 \div 4$　　**6.** $35 \div 7$　　**7.** $3 \div 3$　　**8.** $16 \div 8$

9. $42 \div 6$　　**10.** $20 \div 5$　　**11.** $16 \div 4$　　**12.** $81 \div 9$

13. $10 \div 2$　　**14.** $8 \div 4$　　**15.** $45 \div 9$　　**16.** $0 \div 9$

17. $9 \div 3$　　**18.** $48 \div 6$　　**19.** $42 \div 7$　　**20.** $36 \div 4$

21. $63 \div 9$　　**22.** $56 \div 8$　　**23.** $25 \div 5$　　**24.** $24 \div 4$

25. $40 \div 5$　　**26.** $72 \div 9$　　**27.** $12 \div 2$　　**28.** $36 \div 9$

29. $28 \div 4$　　**30.** $15 \div 3$　　**31.** $36 \div 6$　　**32.** $56 \div 7$

33. $27 \div 3$　　**34.** $27 \div 9$　　**35.** $12 \div 4$　　**36.** $45 \div 5$

37. $3 \div 1$　　**38.** $40 \div 8$　　**39.** $49 \div 7$　　**40.** $28 \div 7$

41. $16 \div 2$　　**42.** $21 \div 7$　　**43.** $35 \div 5$　　**44.** $32 \div 4$

45. $12 \div 6$　　**46.** $20 \div 4$　　**47.** $8 \div 1$　　**48.** $15 \div 3$

49. $54 \div 6$　　**50.** $24 \div 3$　　**51.** $0 \div 7$　　**52.** $20 \div 4$

53. $15 \div 5$　　**54.** $18 \div 2$　　**55.** $12 \div 3$　　**56.** $27 \div 3$

57. $54 \div 9$　　**58.** $18 \div 6$　　**59.** $8 \div 2$　　**60.** $72 \div 9$

61. $72 \div 8$　　**62.** $14 \div 7$　　**63.** $54 \div 6$　　**64.** $64 \div 8$

65. $30 \div 6$　　**66.** $24 \div 8$　　**67.** $63 \div 9$　　**68.** $30 \div 5$

69. $18 \div 3$　　**70.** $81 \div 9$　　**71.** $32 \div 8$　　**72.** $49 \div 7$

73. $14 \div 2$　　**74.** $63 \div 7$　　**75.** $18 \div 9$　　**76.** $21 \div 3$

77. $24 \div 6$　　**78.** $48 \div 8$　　**79.** $40 \div 5$　　**80.** $9 \div 3$

(vi) Write standard numerals.

1. 200 + 40 + 7

2. (6 · 100) + (0 · 10) + (9 · 1)

3. 8,000 + 600 + 9

4. (5 · 100) + (3 · 10) + (8 · 1)

5. 3,000,000 + 800,000 + 40,000 + 6,000 + 30 + 2

6. (9 · 1,000,000) + (6 · 100,000) + (3 · 10,000) +
(7 · 1,000) + (3 · 100) + (2 · 10) + (7 · 1)

Write two expanded numerals for each.

7. 724   **8.** 2,030   **9.** 625,310

Tell the value of the underlined digit.

10. 8,6<u>3</u>7   **11.** <u>5</u>3,278   **12.** 246,<u>8</u>07

13. 9,<u>5</u>32,012   **14.** 123,4<u>0</u>6   **15.** 8,436,7<u>9</u>5

(8) Round to the nearest ten.

1. 34   **2.** 65   **3.** 482   **4.** 691

5. 489   **6.** 2,374   **7.** 24,538   **8.** 73,622

Round to the nearest hundred.

9. 879   **10.** 450   **11.** 4,527   **12.** 6,918

13. 44,500   **14.** 96,439   **15.** 233,649   **16.** 863,281

Round to the nearest thousand.

17. 8,451   **18.** 3,562   **19.** 94,448   **20.** 62,811

21. 238,501   **22.** 942,399   **23.** 703,486   **24.** 3,542,298

Round to the nearest million.

25. 73,532,009   **26.** 36,200,022   **27.** 81,618,493

28. 41,163,277   **29.** 55,267,999   **30.** 28,673,221

(30) Add.

1. 23 + 41	**2.** 56 + 30	**3.** 29 + 47	**4.** 38 + 29
5. 284 + 542	**6.** 532 + 397	**7.** 498 + 967	**8.** 764 + 888
9. 3,241 + 5,543	**10.** 8,647 + 2,294	**11.** 6,487 + 3,953	**12.** 8,296 + 2,904
13. 8,598 + 6,743	**14.** 27,095 + 29,782	**15.** 78,349 + 24,673	**16.** 498,673 + 432,039
17. 29 35 14 + 76	**18.** 234 794 567 + 135	**19.** 1,470 3,692 5,813 + 5,791	**20.** 26,048 37,159 49,506 + 17,283

(35) Subtract.

1. 96 − 41	**2.** 83 − 52	**3.** 675 − 123	**4.** 9,876 − 2,805
5. 73 − 29	**6.** 87 − 38	**7.** 784 − 237	**8.** 456 − 196
9. 5,532 − 3,215	**10.** 3,750 − 1,118	**11.** 6,413 − 4,290	**12.** 17,325 − 2,199
13. 7,913 − 6,913	**14.** 5,814 − 2,819	**15.** 87,152 − 28,654	**16.** 69,124 − 52,669

(37) Subtract.

1. 403 − 256	**2.** 904 − 397	**3.** 7,002 − 6,227	**4.** 6,005 − 2,599
5. 6,003 − 123	**6.** 8,802 − 489	**7.** 6,003 − 85	**8.** 80,404 − 669
9. 90,056 − 27,894	**10.** 80,004 − 54,325	**11.** 70,043 − 54,248	**12.** 60,007 − 15,328

(58) Multiply.

1. 23
  × 6

2. 81
  × 7

3. 35
  × 5

4. 76
  × 8

5. 217
  × 4

6. 417
  × 8

7. 310
  × 9

8. 947
  × 3

9. 2,071
  × 5

10. 3,957
  × 6

11. 4,675
  × 7

12. 9,005
  × 3

13. 24,638
  × 6

14. 58,009
  × 7

15. 35,061
  × 8

16. 328,008
  × 4

17. 431,903
  × 6

18. 371,234
  × 9

(62) Multiply.

1. 34
  × 23

2. 79
  × 35

3. 81
  × 57

4. 65
  × 73

5. 278
  × 46

6. 345
  × 78

7. 409
  × 28

8. 673
  × 37

9. 940
  × 81

10. 747
  × 28

11. 248
  × 123

12. 893
  × 249

13. 428
  × 297

14. 508
  × 603

15. 378
  × 206

16. 913
  × 572

(65) Multiply.

1. 3,827
  × 1,458

2. 4,678
  × 2,037

3. 6,708
  × 2,457

4. 3,009
  × 2,408

5. 6,725
  × 3,007

6. 34,567
  × 4,895

7. 13,579
  × 2,463

8. 68,005
  × 1,426

9. 78,257
  × 8,009

10. 25,893
  × 3,311

11. 72,346
  × 1,908

12. 57,827
  × 5,050

(84) Divide.

1. 4$\overline{)182}$ **2.** 5$\overline{)393}$ **3.** 6$\overline{)254}$

4. 7$\overline{)591}$ **5.** 8$\overline{)773}$ **6.** 9$\overline{)1,461}$

7. 5$\overline{)3,465}$ **8.** 6$\overline{)4,456}$ **9.** 7$\overline{)3,953}$

10. 8$\overline{)4,379}$ **11.** 9$\overline{)21,976}$ **12.** 8$\overline{)6,917}$

13. 8$\overline{)47,951}$ **14.** 9$\overline{)62,094}$ **15.** 7$\overline{)32,633}$

(86) Divide.

1. 3$\overline{)1,223}$ **2.** 6$\overline{)4,384}$ **3.** 9$\overline{)5,451}$

4. 2$\overline{)960}$ **5.** 5$\overline{)4,513}$ **6.** 8$\overline{)5,601}$

7. 4$\overline{)28,026}$ **8.** 8$\overline{)40,279}$ **9.** 2$\overline{)12,415}$

10. 6$\overline{)43,925}$ **11.** 5$\overline{)32,502}$ **12.** 9$\overline{)63,548}$

(92) Divide.

1. 40$\overline{)2,684}$ **2.** 90$\overline{)753}$ **3.** 70$\overline{)4,862}$

4. 30$\overline{)1,945}$ **5.** 80$\overline{)16,491}$ **6.** 50$\overline{)24,372}$

7. 60$\overline{)37,284}$ **8.** 40$\overline{)82,963}$ **9.** 80$\overline{)94,281}$

(94) Divide.

1. 71$\overline{)289}$ **2.** 63$\overline{)327}$ **3.** 32$\overline{)766}$

4. 41$\overline{)3,022}$ **5.** 24$\overline{)571}$ **6.** 61$\overline{)5,134}$

7. 62$\overline{)3,986}$ **8.** 51$\overline{)4,811}$ **9.** 22$\overline{)4,895}$

10. 21$\overline{)4,566}$ **11.** 82$\overline{)34,037}$ **12.** 31$\overline{)28,657}$

13. 92$\overline{)28,877}$ **14.** 33$\overline{)13,977}$ **15.** 21$\overline{)18,852}$

16. 36$\overline{)40,361}$ **17.** 42$\overline{)98,328}$ **18.** 21$\overline{)67,461}$

360

(96) **Divide.**

1. 82$\overline{)4,941}$ **2.** 73$\overline{)2,194}$ **3.** 52$\overline{)20,938}$

4. 61$\overline{)36,652}$ **5.** 92$\overline{)28,363}$ **6.** 33$\overline{)19,944}$

7. 41$\overline{)24,639}$ **8.** 31$\overline{)27,998}$ **9.** 83$\overline{)58,924}$

(98) **Divide.**

1. 67$\overline{)333}$ **2.** 78$\overline{)571}$ **3.** 66$\overline{)6,150}$

4. 37$\overline{)1,737}$ **5.** 76$\overline{)299}$ **6.** 69$\overline{)3,212}$

7. 79$\overline{)38,332}$ **8.** 39$\overline{)12,032}$ **9.** 27$\overline{)2,425}$

10. 19$\overline{)308}$ **11.** 38$\overline{)2,189}$ **12.** 49$\overline{)23,695}$

13. 57$\overline{)49,955}$ **14.** 49$\overline{)24,401}$ **15.** 28$\overline{)2,265}$

16. 58$\overline{)21,162}$ **17.** 98$\overline{)36,152}$ **18.** 89$\overline{)41,012}$

(100) **Divide.**

1. 300$\overline{)19,863}$ **2.** 500$\overline{)43,298}$ **3.** 700$\overline{)58,462}$

4. 200$\overline{)14,647}$ **5.** 600$\overline{)74,532}$ **6.** 400$\overline{)568,641}$

7. 900$\overline{)847,321}$ **8.** 800$\overline{)532,069}$ **9.** 300$\overline{)297,248}$

(102) **Divide.**

1. 416$\overline{)29,987}$ **2.** 325$\overline{)6,849}$ **3.** 241$\overline{)17,845}$

4. 632$\overline{)48,032}$ **5.** 246$\overline{)20,479}$ **6.** 708$\overline{)85,779}$

7. 237$\overline{)20,944}$ **8.** 428$\overline{)86,461}$ **9.** 847$\overline{)46,011}$

10. 294$\overline{)180,435}$ **11.** 586$\overline{)234,400}$ **12.** 237$\overline{)78,738}$

13. 311$\overline{)126,778}$ **14.** 419$\overline{)247,237}$ **15.** 532$\overline{)425,625}$

(142) Draw factor trees to find prime factorizations.

1. 18 **2.** 24 **3** 36 **4.** 54 **5.** 45

6. 84 **7.** 64 **8.** 72 **9.** 110 **10.** 132

(146) Find the greatest common factor of each pair.

1. 6 and 9 **2.** 9 and 12 **3.** 6 and 8

4. 8 and 12 **5.** 8 and 18 **6.** 12 and 18

7. 10 and 9 **8.** 6 and 18 **9.** 4 and 12

10. 5 and 20 **11.** 4 and 18 **12.** 6 and 15

(150) Find the least common multiple of each pair.

1. 4 and 6 **2.** 4 and 8 **3.** 4 and 9

4. 6 and 12 **5.** 6 and 10 **6.** 7 and 9

7. 7 and 10 **8.** 9 and 10 **9.** 9 and 12

10. 2 and 3 **11.** 2 and 4 **12.** 3 and 4

(158) Compare. Use $<$, $=$, or $>$.

1. $\frac{3}{4} \equiv \frac{1}{4}$ **2.** $\frac{5}{8} \equiv \frac{6}{8}$ **3.** $\frac{1}{3} \equiv \frac{2}{3}$ **4.** $\frac{6}{9} \equiv \frac{7}{9}$

5. $\frac{2}{3} \equiv \frac{3}{5}$ **6.** $\frac{3}{4} \equiv \frac{5}{8}$ **7.** $\frac{2}{3} \equiv \frac{7}{9}$ **8.** $\frac{1}{2} \equiv \frac{3}{5}$

9. $\frac{5}{6} \equiv \frac{3}{4}$ **10.** $\frac{3}{5} \equiv \frac{3}{4}$ **11.** $\frac{5}{7} \equiv \frac{2}{3}$ **12.** $\frac{7}{9} \equiv \frac{5}{6}$

(164) Simplify.

1. $\frac{3}{6}$ **2.** $\frac{4}{10}$ **3.** $\frac{3}{12}$ **4.** $\frac{9}{12}$ **5.** $\frac{4}{6}$

6. $\frac{5}{10}$ **7.** $\frac{3}{15}$ **8.** $\frac{8}{12}$ **9.** $\frac{12}{18}$ **10.** $\frac{16}{20}$

11. $\frac{10}{15}$ **12.** $\frac{2}{4}$ **13.** $\frac{16}{18}$ **14.** $\frac{6}{12}$ **15.** $\frac{5}{15}$

(166) **Add. Simplify if possible.**

1. $\frac{1}{3} + \frac{1}{3}$ **2.** $\frac{1}{4} + \frac{1}{4}$ **3.** $\frac{1}{12} + \frac{5}{12}$ **4.** $\frac{5}{12} + \frac{4}{12}$

5. $\frac{2}{5} + \frac{2}{5}$ **6.** $\frac{3}{12} + \frac{5}{12}$ **7.** $\frac{1}{6} + \frac{3}{6}$ **8.** $\frac{2}{6} + \frac{3}{6}$

9. $\frac{1}{8} + \frac{3}{8}$ **10.** $\frac{1}{9} + \frac{2}{9}$ **11.** $\frac{3}{8} + \frac{3}{8}$ **12.** $\frac{2}{9} + \frac{4}{9}$

(168) **Add. Simplify if possible.**

1. $\frac{1}{3}$ $+\frac{1}{4}$ **2.** $\frac{1}{6}$ $+\frac{1}{4}$ **3.** $\frac{1}{2}$ $+\frac{1}{4}$ **4.** $\frac{2}{5}$ $+\frac{1}{3}$ **5.** $\frac{1}{4}$ $+\frac{2}{3}$

6. $\frac{3}{4}$ $+\frac{1}{6}$ **7.** $\frac{1}{4}$ $+\frac{5}{12}$ **8.** $\frac{3}{8}$ $+\frac{1}{12}$ **9.** $\frac{1}{6}$ $+\frac{2}{3}$ **10.** $\frac{1}{3}$ $+\frac{1}{6}$

11. $\frac{3}{4}$ $+\frac{1}{5}$ **12.** $\frac{2}{3}$ $+\frac{2}{9}$ **13.** $\frac{1}{4}$ $+\frac{5}{8}$ **14.** $\frac{1}{3}$ $+\frac{5}{12}$ **15.** $\frac{3}{4}$ $+\frac{2}{9}$

(170) **Subtract. Simplify if possible.**

1. $\frac{4}{5} - \frac{1}{5}$ **2.** $\frac{7}{8} - \frac{5}{8}$ **3.** $\frac{5}{6} - \frac{1}{6}$ **4.** $\frac{2}{3} - \frac{1}{3}$

5. $\frac{2}{6} - \frac{1}{6}$ **6.** $\frac{11}{12} - \frac{1}{12}$ **7.** $\frac{13}{17} - \frac{5}{17}$ **8.** $\frac{13}{24} - \frac{5}{24}$

9. $\frac{9}{10}$ $-\frac{3}{5}$ **10.** $\frac{3}{4}$ $-\frac{1}{2}$ **11.** $\frac{11}{12}$ $-\frac{3}{4}$ **12.** $\frac{7}{12}$ $-\frac{3}{8}$ **13.** $\frac{3}{4}$ $-\frac{3}{8}$

14. $\frac{2}{3}$ $-\frac{2}{5}$ **15.** $\frac{1}{4}$ $-\frac{1}{6}$ **16.** $\frac{4}{5}$ $-\frac{3}{10}$ **17.** $\frac{3}{8}$ $-\frac{1}{10}$ **18.** $\frac{1}{2}$ $-\frac{1}{4}$

19. $\frac{2}{3}$ $-\frac{1}{7}$ **20.** $\frac{5}{8}$ $-\frac{1}{3}$ **21.** $\frac{7}{9}$ $-\frac{1}{6}$ **22.** $\frac{1}{2}$ $-\frac{3}{10}$ **23.** $\frac{3}{4}$ $-\frac{1}{3}$

363

(177) Add. Simplify if possible.

1. $2\frac{2}{5}$
   $+3\frac{1}{5}$

2. $13\frac{1}{4}$
   $+45\frac{1}{4}$

3. $6\frac{3}{10}$
   $+3\frac{2}{10}$

4. $9\frac{3}{12}$
   $+7\frac{5}{12}$

5. $8\frac{1}{3}$
   $+6$

6. $5\frac{4}{5}$
   $+2\frac{3}{5}$

7. $29\frac{1}{3}$
   $+78\frac{1}{3}$

8. $34\frac{2}{3}$
   $+69\frac{2}{3}$

9. $7\frac{3}{7}$
   $+7\frac{4}{7}$

10. $3\frac{1}{4}$
    $+8\frac{1}{6}$

11. $5\frac{1}{3}$
    $+7\frac{1}{6}$

12. $5\frac{2}{3}$
    $+7\frac{5}{6}$

13. $7\frac{7}{8}$
    $+2\frac{1}{4}$

14. $13\frac{3}{8}$
    $+24\frac{1}{5}$

15. $8\frac{2}{9}$
    $+7\frac{1}{6}$

16. $29\frac{3}{4}$
    $+35\frac{5}{6}$

17. $15\frac{3}{5}$
    $+24\frac{2}{3}$

18. $26\frac{5}{8}$
    $+39\frac{5}{6}$

19. $48\frac{4}{5}$
    $+19\frac{5}{6}$

20. $36\frac{7}{9}$
    $+34\frac{2}{3}$

(179) Subtract.

1. $8\frac{3}{7}$
   $-5\frac{1}{7}$

2. $11\frac{5}{8}$
   $-8\frac{3}{8}$

3. $19\frac{4}{6}$
   $-9\frac{1}{6}$

4. $24\frac{4}{5}$
   $-15\frac{2}{5}$

5. $38\frac{7}{12}$
   $-25\frac{1}{6}$

6. $45\frac{5}{12}$
   $-27\frac{1}{8}$

7. $17\frac{3}{4}$
   $-8\frac{1}{6}$

8. $27\frac{3}{4}$
   $-12\frac{1}{3}$

9. $5\frac{1}{5}$
   $-2\frac{4}{5}$

10. $48\frac{5}{12}$
    $-21\frac{7}{12}$

11. 36
    $-9\frac{2}{3}$

12. $22\frac{3}{8}$
    $-15\frac{7}{8}$

13. $9\frac{2}{3}$
    $-5\frac{3}{4}$

14. $8\frac{2}{5}$
    $-4\frac{5}{6}$

15. $35\frac{1}{6}$
    $-7\frac{3}{8}$

16. $15\frac{2}{3}$
    $-9\frac{3}{4}$

17. $17\frac{1}{10}$
    $-12\frac{4}{5}$

18. $98\frac{1}{8}$
    $-23\frac{5}{6}$

19. $82\frac{1}{8}$
    $-32\frac{1}{4}$

20. $72\frac{1}{6}$
    $-35\frac{1}{4}$

364

(186) Multiply.

1. $\frac{4}{5} \times \frac{1}{6}$ 2. $\frac{2}{3} \times \frac{9}{5}$ 3. $\frac{5}{7} \times \frac{7}{12}$ 4. $\frac{7}{9} \times \frac{5}{6}$

5. $\frac{8}{13} \times \frac{5}{12}$ 6. $\frac{1}{4} \times \frac{10}{11}$ 7. $\frac{7}{8} \times \frac{8}{7}$ 8. $\frac{12}{25} \times \frac{5}{18}$

9. $\frac{8}{9} \times \frac{10}{11}$ 10. $\frac{1}{24} \times 12$ 11. $\frac{1}{12} \times 24$ 12. $1\frac{1}{2} \times 2\frac{1}{3}$

13. $1\frac{1}{3} \times \frac{9}{12}$ 14. $1\frac{2}{3} \times 1\frac{2}{5}$ 15. $1\frac{2}{3} \times \frac{3}{5}$ 16. $6\frac{2}{7} \times 4\frac{2}{3}$

(194) Divide.

1. $4 \div \frac{1}{3}$ 2. $\frac{3}{4} \div 4$ 3. $6 \div \frac{1}{2}$ 4. $\frac{2}{3} \div \frac{1}{3}$

5. $\frac{6}{7} \div \frac{3}{7}$ 6. $\frac{1}{2} \div \frac{1}{3}$ 7. $\frac{5}{8} \div \frac{3}{2}$ 8. $\frac{8}{9} \div \frac{2}{3}$

9. $\frac{8}{9} \div \frac{6}{7}$ 10. $\frac{7}{10} \div \frac{14}{15}$ 11. $\frac{12}{7} \div \frac{3}{5}$ 12. $\frac{6}{11} \div \frac{6}{7}$

13. $\frac{6}{7} \div \frac{6}{11}$ 14. $\frac{3}{5} \div \frac{3}{5}$ 15. $\frac{4}{9} \div 18$ 16. $5 \div \frac{25}{4}$

(195) Divide. Simplify if possible.

1. $1\frac{1}{2} \div \frac{3}{4}$ 2. $2\frac{1}{3} \div \frac{5}{6}$ 3. $6 \div 1\frac{1}{2}$ 4. $12 \div 1\frac{5}{7}$

5. $1\frac{2}{3} \div 2\frac{1}{5}$ 6. $3\frac{1}{3} \div 3\frac{1}{3}$ 7. $4\frac{2}{3} \div \frac{7}{9}$ 8. $2\frac{1}{4} \div 1\frac{1}{9}$

9. $5 \div 2\frac{1}{2}$ 10. $2\frac{1}{2} \div 5$ 11. $3\frac{1}{5} \div 8$ 12. $8 \div 3\frac{1}{5}$

(212) Write in fractional form.

1. .2   2. .03   3. .80   4. .83

5. 7.4   6. .123   7. .100   8. .020

9. .003   10. .4527   11. .4000   12. .0500

13. .0020   14. .0007   15. .0034   16. .0521

365

(212) Write in decimal form.

1. $\frac{7}{10}$ 2. $\frac{23}{100}$ 3. $\frac{3}{100}$ 4. $\frac{20}{100}$

5. $4\frac{3}{10}$ 6. $5\frac{8}{100}$ 7. $\frac{412}{1,000}$ 8. $\frac{87}{1,000}$

9. $\frac{503}{1,000}$ 10. $\frac{720}{1,000}$ 11. $\frac{9,876}{10,000}$ 12. $\frac{925}{10,000}$

13. $\frac{83}{10,000}$ 14. $\frac{7}{10,000}$ 15. $\frac{300}{10,000}$ 16. $\frac{4,000}{10,000}$

(218) Compare. Use $<$, $>$, or $=$.

1. .8 ≡ .96 2. .9 ≡ .86 3. .7 ≡ .70

4. .222 ≡ .3 5. .314 ≡ .0976 6. .4 ≡ .3987

7. .088 ≡ .200 8. .270 ≡ .27 9. .83 ≡ .831

10. .360 ≡ .036 11. .333 ≡ .0444 12. .7100 ≡ .71

(220) Write in decimal form.

1. $\frac{3}{8}$ 2. $\frac{4}{25}$ 3. $\frac{3}{50}$ 4. $\frac{9}{25}$ 5. $\frac{11}{50}$

6. $\frac{7}{40}$ 7. $\frac{3}{80}$ 8. $\frac{18}{25}$ 9. $\frac{17}{80}$ 10. $\frac{21}{40}$

11. $\frac{5}{8}$ 12. $\frac{27}{80}$ 13. $\frac{17}{500}$ 14. $\frac{7}{8}$ 15. $\frac{31}{50}$

(224) Add.

1. .6
   +.3

2. .51
   +.34

3. .59
   +.34

4. .30
   +.42

5. .07
   +.06

6. .567
   +.123

7. .683
   +.142

8. .364
   +.187

9. .486
   +.937

10. .1234
   +.8765

11. .8327
   +.6378

12. .9876
   +.8765

(226) **Add.**

1. .2 + .54

2. 8.4 + .59

3. .84 + 6.3

4. 3.51 + 4.9

5. .664 + .25

6. 77.21 + .345

7. 9.8 + .93

8. .34 + 5.4391

9. 82.6 + 4.25

10. .51 + .8723

11. 5.64 + .349

12. .486 + 5.5

(228) **Subtract.**

1. .8 − .4

2. .78 − .45

3. .82 − .39

4. .306 − .004

5. 1.598 − .405

6. .485 − .127

7. .3782 − .1111

8. .0041 − .0014

9. .8200 − .0500

10. 2.4897 − .39

11. .48 − .1

12. .479 − .3

13. 8.3 − .5

14. 7.7 − .93

15. 11.3 − .84

(230) **Multiply.**

1. .9
   ×7

2. .09
   ×7

3. .009
   ×7

4. .325
   ×8

5. .0043
   ×6

6. .713
   ×4

7. .0635
   ×9

8. 3.497
   ×3

9. 1.345
   ×6

10. .07
   ×48

11. .24
   ×37

12. .73
   ×25

(232) **Multiply.**

1. .8 × .6

2. .09 × .3

3. .8 × .57

4. .64 × .37

5. .23 × .19

6. .7 × .473

7. .024 × .64

8. 52.9 × .48

9. .0016 × .94

10. 34.91 × .063

11. 9.42 × .0634

12. 5.673 × .98

367

(236) Divide.

1. $3\overline{)2.1}$ 2. $4\overline{).32}$ 3. $2\overline{).46}$

4. $5\overline{)9.5}$ 5. $3\overline{)7.02}$ 6. $6\overline{).054}$

7. $7\overline{).511}$ 8. $8\overline{)1.008}$ 9. $4\overline{)5.368}$

10. $9\overline{)41.13}$ 11. $5\overline{)20.615}$ 12. $2\overline{).0352}$

13. $6\overline{)1.4202}$ 14. $7\overline{)63.245}$ 15. $8\overline{)98.80}$

16. $5\overline{)34.945}$ 17. $9\overline{)5.9814}$ 18. $3\overline{)42.81}$

(238) Divide.

1. $.3\overline{)2.7}$ 2. $.04\overline{)1.936}$ 3. $.007\overline{).035}$

4. $1.2\overline{)1.32}$ 5. $.006\overline{).0108}$ 6. $.31\overline{).16244}$

7. $1.2\overline{)36}$ 8. $.23\overline{)20.7}$ 9. $.042\overline{).294}$

10. $1.7\overline{)2.38}$ 11. $.27\overline{)299.7}$ 12. $.18\overline{).00576}$

13. $1.1\overline{)6.82}$ 14. $.33\overline{).561}$ 15. $1.5\overline{)171}$

16. $.59\overline{)85.55}$ 17. $3.7\overline{).4625}$ 18. $.75\overline{)393}$

19. $.83\overline{).9545}$ 20. $5.2\overline{)8.736}$ 21. $4.8\overline{)571.2}$

(242) Write decimals.

1. $\frac{3}{8}$ 2. $\frac{7}{20}$ 3. $\frac{3}{5}$ 4. $\frac{4}{25}$ 5. $\frac{3}{4}$

6. $\frac{5}{16}$ 7. $\frac{9}{20}$ 8. $\frac{5}{8}$ 9. $\frac{7}{16}$ 10. $\frac{1}{8}$

11. $\frac{3}{16}$ 12. $\frac{9}{16}$ 13. $\frac{11}{80}$ 14. $\frac{13}{16}$ 15. $\frac{15}{16}$

16. $\frac{17}{20}$ 17. $\frac{1}{40}$ 18. $\frac{3}{40}$ 19. $\frac{19}{20}$ 20. $\frac{13}{25}$

368

(276) Write percents.

1. $\frac{49}{100}$ 2. $\frac{52}{100}$ 3. $\frac{7}{100}$ 4. $\frac{4}{5}$ 5. $\frac{17}{50}$

6. $\frac{3}{4}$ 7. $\frac{1}{2}$ 8. $\frac{2}{5}$ 9. $\frac{9}{10}$ 10. $\frac{9}{25}$

11. $\frac{97}{100}$ 12. $\frac{6}{10}$ 13. $\frac{6}{100}$ 14. $\frac{60}{100}$ 15. $\frac{66}{100}$

16. $\frac{1}{10}$ 17. $\frac{19}{50}$ 18. $\frac{19}{25}$ 19. $\frac{19}{20}$ 20. $\frac{11}{20}$

21. .07   22. .17   23. .81   24. .10   25. .01

26. .75   27. .55   28. .50   29. .05   30. .99

31. .08   32. .64   33. .49   34. .80   35. .53

(278) Write percents.

1. $\frac{13}{20}$ 2. $\frac{12}{40}$ 3. $\frac{3}{4}$ 4. $\frac{3}{5}$ 5. $\frac{3}{6}$

6. $\frac{6}{8}$ 7. $\frac{6}{15}$ 8. $\frac{51}{60}$ 9. $\frac{9}{45}$ 10. $\frac{21}{35}$

11. $\frac{6}{75}$ 12. $\frac{9}{12}$ 13. $\frac{35}{125}$ 14. $\frac{85}{500}$ 15. $\frac{21}{140}$

(279) Write fractional percents.

1. $\frac{1}{3}$ 2. $\frac{2}{3}$ 3. $\frac{1}{6}$ 4. $\frac{5}{6}$ 5. $\frac{3}{7}$

6. $\frac{3}{8}$ 7. $\frac{5}{8}$ 8. $\frac{7}{8}$ 9. $\frac{1}{9}$ 10. $\frac{2}{9}$

(280) Write as a ratio, as a simplified fraction, and a decimal.

1. 13%   2. 12%   3. 32%   4. 40%   5. 10%

6. 25%   7. 46%   8. 17%   9. 15%   10. 1%

11. 50%   12. 75%   13. 68%   14. 35%   15. 90%

(282) Compute.

1. 24% of 46   **2.** 25% of 62   **3.** 85% of 40

4. 76% of 35   **5.** 44% of 87   **6.** 53% of 42

7. 91% of 306   **8.** 15% of 847   **9.** 30% of 692

10. 18% of 222   **11.** 78% of 521   **12.** 30% of 147

(286) Find the interest on each year's deposit. The annual interest rate is 5%.

1. $200   **2.** $800   **3.** $900   **4.** $940

5. $6,000   **6.** $300   **7.** $70   **8.** $4

9. $6,300   **10.** $6,070   **11.** $6,370   **12.** $6,374

(338) Add.

1. $^+8 + {}^+6$ **2.** $^-3 + {}^-5$ **3.** $^-7 + {}^-9$

4. $^+9 + {}^+12$ **5.** $^+8 + {}^+21$ **6.** $^-5 + {}^-10$

7. $0 + {}^+8$ **8.** $0 + {}^-8$ **9.** $^-30 + {}^-40$

10. $^-15 + {}^-8$ **11.** $^+22 + {}^+18$ **12.** $^+45 + {}^+31$

13. $^-39 + {}^-58$ **14.** $^+231 + {}^+735$ **15.** $^-287 + {}^-396$

(342) Add.

1. $^-7 + {}^+2$ **2.** $^-7 + {}^+6$ **3.** $^-7 + {}^+8$

4. $^-7 + {}^+7$ **5.** $^+1 + {}^-8$ **6.** $^-10 + {}^+4$

7. $^-12 + {}^+8$ **8.** $^+10 + {}^-6$ **9.** $^+13 + {}^-7$

10. $^-12 + {}^+13$ **11.** $^+17 + {}^-14$ **12.** $^+23 + {}^-27$

13. $^-24 + {}^+37$ **14.** $^-91 + {}^+76$ **15.** $^+84 + {}^-26$

(38) Solve these problems.

1. Mr. Anderson, a grocer, had 56 cans of tuna, 34 cans of salmon and 21 cans of shrimp. How many cans of seafood did he have in all?

2. An automobile factory produced 235 cars in one day. The next day, a breakdown caused the factory to close early. Only 179 cars were produced. How many more cars were produced the first day?

3. George Washington was born in 1732. When he died, he was 67 years old. In what year did he die?

4. The space ship Explorer 17 made one orbit of the Earth, a distance of 18,634 miles. Then it traveled 243,167 miles to the moon. How many miles did it travel in all?

5. Mt. Everest is 29,028 feet high. In 1971, a team of climbers reached a height of 27,149 feet. How many more feet did they have to go to reach the top?

(68) Solve these problems.

1. Marie wants to buy skis which cost $124.95 and boots which cost $49.50. How much will she spend in all?

2. A factory packs pencils by the gross, or 144 pencils to a box. How many pencils are in 25 gross?

3. Leonard's restaurant produces about 28 kilograms of garbage a day. How many kilograms of garbage would it produce in a year?

4. On Saturday 8,643 people attended a baseball game. On Sunday 10,624 people attended a baseball game. How many more people attended on Sunday?

5. Mr. Redfeather bought 8 tires for his trucks. Each tire cost $44.95. How much did he spend in all?

(91) Solve these problems.

1. Mrs. Miller spent 69 dollars on shoes for her 3 children. Each pair of shoes cost the same amount of money. How much did she spend for each pair?

2. Mr. Oliveri and Mr. O'Leary both ran for mayor. Mr. Oliveri got 86,431 votes. Mr. O'Leary got 76,729 votes. How many people voted in all?

3. A playground in the shape of a square has 392 meters of fencing around it. How long is each side of the playground?

4. The Alston Hotel needs 36 square meters of carpeting for each of its 24 rooms. How many square meters of carpeting are needed in all?

5. There were 306 pairs of scissors to be divided equally among 9 classrooms. How many pairs of scissors would each classroom receive?

(139) Write a mini-problem. Solve.

1. Sam had a birthday party. It cost his mother $17 for refreshments, $9 for a present, and $18 for decorations. How much did she spend for the party?

2. Sam's mother paid $3.89 for the birthday cake. She gave the bakery clerk a $10 bill. How much money did she get back?

3. His mother drove 5 miles to the bakery. Then she drove 3 miles to the grocery. Before she got home, she had to drive 11 more miles. How many miles did she drive in all?

4. At the grocery, she bought 3 gallons of ice cream at $3.49 each, 4 cans of peaches at 39 cents each, and 4 bottles of juice at 49 cents each. What was the total cost?

5. Sam's mother filled the car's gas tank. The gas cost $.17 a liter. She needed 68 liters. How much did she spend for gas?

372

(172) Solve these problems.

1. David walks $\frac{1}{2}$ kilometer on his paper route each day except Sunday. On Sunday, he walks $\frac{3}{4}$ kilometer. How much farther does he walk on Sunday?

2. An average flea is $\frac{1}{32}$ inch long. An average ant is $\frac{3}{4}$ inch long. How much longer is the average ant?

3. Jim ran the race in $\frac{3}{5}$ minute. Jeff ran the race in $\frac{5}{6}$ minute. How much slower was Jeff?

4. José made a cone with $\frac{1}{3}$ of a pint of chocolate ice cream and $\frac{2}{5}$ of a pint of mint ice cream. How much ice cream did he use in his cone?

5. Rick gave $\frac{1}{6}$ of a candy bar to his brother Bill. He gave another $\frac{1}{6}$ to his friend Nick. Then he ate $\frac{1}{2}$ of it himself. How much of the candy bar was gone?

(181) Solve these problems.

1. Jane bought 2 bottles of cola for 23 cents each. She gave the clerk a dollar. How much money did she get back?

2. Mrs. Baskin paid $2.52 for 3 dozen cookies. How much did each cookie cost?

3. Jason bought 5 baseballs for $3.59 each. How much change should be receive from a $20 bill?

4. Richard works part-time. He earns $2 an hour. One week he worked $10\frac{1}{4}$ hours. The next week he worked $9\frac{3}{4}$ hours. What did he earn those two weeks?

5. Ed bought a record album for $5.95 and shampoo for $1.98. How much change should he receive from a $10 bill?

373

(196) Solve these problems.

1. Al spent $\frac{1}{2}$ hour preparing for each of his classes. He studied for $2\frac{1}{2}$ hours. How many classes does he have?

2. The Blanchard family used $\frac{2}{3}$ of a dozen eggs for breakfast. How many eggs did they use?

3. Claire can mow $1\frac{1}{3}$ lawns in an hour. How many lawns can she mow in $5\frac{1}{2}$ hours?

4. One U.S. dollar was worth about $4\frac{1}{6}$ German marks in 1950. How many marks would you have gotten for three dollars?

5. Jodi used $3\frac{1}{2}$ pounds of hamburger to make 2 meat loaves of the same size. How many pounds of hamburger were in each?

(207) Solve. If there is not enough information, write "not enough information". If there is extra information, tell what it is.

1. Catherine went fishing. She caught a 2-kilogram bass, a 3-kilogram pike, and a 5-kilogram old tire. How many kilograms of fish did she catch?

2. The playground at River School is shaped like a rectangle. It is 30 meters long. What is the area of the playground?

3. Carmen takes 20 minutes for breakfast. She walks for 10 minutes to the bus stop then takes a bus for 15 minutes to school. How long does it take her to reach school?

4. Mr. Lewis is making 10 shelves. How many boards 3 meters long will he use to make the shelves?

5. Len made 3 touchdowns and kicked 2 field goals in a football game. A touchdown is 6 points and a field goal is 3 points. How many touchdown points did he score?

374

(241) Solve these problems.

1. You have just crossed the Atlantic Ocean in a rowboat. It took you 56.7 days. The world record for such a trip is 48.61 days How much longer did your trip take?

2. Mrs. Johnson has a diamond that weighs 2.3 grams. What is the size of the diamond in carats? Hint: 1 carat = .2 grams.

3. It is 5.8 kilometers from Kingsboro to Ralfson and 9.6 kilometers from Ralfson to Egton. How far is it from Kingsboro to Egton?

4. Mrs. Alverez bought 2 kilograms of chicken for $.98 a kilogram. How much did she pay in all?

5. Mr. Rosen weighed 178.5 pounds before his diet. After his diet he weighed 159 pounds. How much did he lose?

(288) Solve these problems.

1. In a recent study, 90%, of the doctors questioned, recommended aspirin over other leading pain relievers. If 400 doctors were questioned, how many recommended aspirin?

2. Mr. Jameson deposited $124.75 in a bank that pays 5% interest per year. How much interest did he receive after a year?

3. Jane bought a new dress marked $30.95, a new hat marked $14.29 and shoes marked $25.16. Since she was a store employee, she received a 25% discount. How much did she pay for the clothes?

4. Mrs. Daley sells used cars. She receives 18% of the cost of each car she sells. One month she sold cars totaling $9,375. How much did she make that month?

5. Philip deposited $36.45 in a bank which pays 4% interest per year. How much interest did he earn after a year?

375

TABLE OF MEASURES

Length

1 centimeter (cm) = 10 millimeters (mm)
1 decimeter (dm) = 10 centimeters
1 meter (m) = 10 decimeters
1 dekameter (dam) = 10 meters
1 hectometer (hm) = 100 meters
1 kilometer (km) = 1,000 meters

Liquid

1 liter (L) = 1,000 milliliters (mL)

Weight

1 gram (g) = 1,000 milligrams (mg)
1 kilogram (kg) = 1,000 grams

Time

1 minute = 60 seconds
1 hour = 60 minutes
1 day = 24 hours
1 week = 7 days
1 year = 12 months
1 decade = 10 years
1 century = 100 years

GLOSSARY

This glossary contains an example, an illustration, or a brief description of important terms used in this book.

Acute angle   Any angle whose measure is less than 90°.

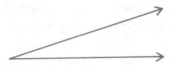

Altitude   A segment with one endpoint at a vertex of a triangle or quadrilateral and its other endpoint on the opposite side, so that it is perpendicular to that side.

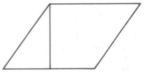

Angle   The union of two rays with a common endpoint.
Arc   Part of a circle.

Area   The number of unit squares that cover a region. The area of this rectangle is 6 square centimeters.

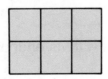

Associative property of addition   When three numbers are added, the sum is the same, no matter which two are added first.
Example $(20 + 3) + 4 = 20 + (3 + 4)$

377

Associative property of multiplication When three numbers are multiplied, the product is the same, no matter which two are multiplied first.

Example $2 \times (3 \times 10) = (2 \times 3) \times 10$

Average The average of 2, 3, 3, 4, 8 is 4, because it is the quotient of the sum of the numbers divided by the number of addends.

Bank interest The number of dollars paid by a bank to a person leaving money (the principal) in the bank.

Base of a numeration system The value of the place to the left of the ones place in a numeration system.

Base of a triangle or parallelogram The side of the figure to which the altitude is drawn. Its length is used to calculate the area.

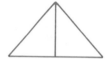 

Bisect The midpoint of a line segment bisects the segment. Also, $\overrightarrow{AD}$ bisects angle *BAC* in this figure.

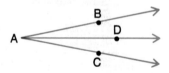

Central angle An angle whose vertex is the center of a circle.

Chord Any line segment with its endpoints on a circle.

Circle The set of all points in a plane that are the same distance from a given point called the center.

378

Circumference   The distance around a circle.

Common factor   2 is a common factor of 6 and 8 because it is a factor of both numbers.

Common multiple   24 is a common multiple of 6 and 8 because it is a multiple of both numbers.

Commutative property of addition   The sum is the same no matter in which order two numbers are added.
Example $2 + 3 = 3 + 2$

Commutative property of multiplication   The product is the same no matter in which order two numbers are multiplied.
Example $2 \times 3 = 3 \times 2$

Composite number   A number with more than two factors.
Example   6 is a composite number.

Cone   A three-dimensional figure.

Congruent   If a figure is exactly the same as another figure as shown by a turn, a slide, or a flip, then the two figures are congruent.

Coordinates   Coordinates are numbered pairs for a point. They are used in making graphs.

Corresponding sides   Sides of equal length in congruent triangles and those in proportion in similar triangles.

Counting numbers   Any of these numbers: 1, 2, 3, . . .

Cylinder   A three-dimensional figure.

Decimal   A number shown with a decimal point.
  Example   .54, .2525

Degree   A unit used to measure circles and angles. There are 360° in a complete circle Also, a measure of temperature.

Denominator   In $\frac{3}{4}$, the denominator is 4.

Diagonal   Any line segment whose endpoints are nonconsecutive vertices of a polygon. $\overline{AX}$ and $\overline{BX}$ are diagonals.

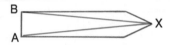

Diameter   Any segment having its endpoints on a circle and containing the center.

Digit   Any of the individual symbols used to show a number less than the base of the numeration system. In the base-ten system, the digits are 0, 1, 2, 3, 4, 5, 6, 7, 8, 9.

Distributive property   A property that relates addition and multiplication.
  Example $2 \times (30 + 4) = (2 \times 30) + (2 \times 4)$

Divisible   A whole number is divisible by a counting number if the remainder is 0.
  Example   8 is divisible by 4, but is not divisible by 5.

Equation   A mathematical sentence with an equals sign.

Equivalent fractional numerals   Two or more names (numerals) for the same fraction.
  Example $\frac{3}{4} = \frac{6}{8}$

Even number   A number with a factor of 2.

380

Expanded numeral A numeral that shows the value of each place in a standard numeral.
  Example $234 = 200 + 30 + 4$ or $(2 \cdot 100) + (3 \cdot 10) + (4 \cdot 1)$

Exponent The 2 in 5^2, which specifies that 5 is to be used as a factor 2 times: $5^2 = 5 \times 5$.

Factor Each of the numbers to be multiplied.
  Example   The 2, 3, and 5 in $2 \times 3 \times 5 = 30$

Factor tree A form used for showing the prime factorization of a number.
  Example

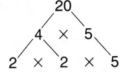

Finite A set with a definite number of members.

Flip The figures below are flips in geometry. The figure does not change shape or size.

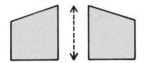   

Fraction Any number named by a numeral such as $\frac{1}{2}$ or $\frac{3}{4}$.

Fractional numeral A fraction's name such as $\frac{1}{2}$ or $\frac{3}{4}$.

Greatest common factor The largest of the common factors of a pair of numbers.
  Example   For 12 and 8, 4 is the greatest common factor.

Greatest possible error In measuring a length, the largest error, which is $\frac{1}{2}$ the unit of measure.

Height The length of an altitude of a triangle or parallelogram.

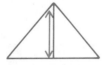   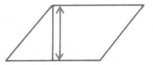

Inequality A number sentence that contains $<$, $>$, or $\neq$.

Infinite A set with an unending number of members.

Integer Any of these numbers: . . . $^-3$, $^-2$, $^-1$, 0, $^+1$, $^+2$, . . .

Interest rate The percent used to figure out how much interest is paid for a given amount.

Inverse operations Multiplication and division are inverse operations. Addition and subtraction are inverse operations.

Least common denominator The least common multiple of the denominators of two or more fractions.

Least common multiple The smallest of the common multiples of two or more numbers.

Example For 4 and 6, 12 is the least common multiple.

Line A set of points going straight in two directions and having no end.

Line segment The set of all points consisting of two points on a line together with the points between them.

Mixed numeral A numeral such as $2\frac{1}{2}$, $8\frac{3}{4}$.

Multiple A multiple of a whole number is the product of that number and any counting number.

Example 6 is a multiple of 3.

Number line The result of matching the points of a line with numbers.

Number sentence An equation or inequality.

Examples $n + 7 = 29$ $2 \times 3 < 7$ $3 + 5 > 7$

Numeral A name for a number.

Numerator In $\frac{3}{4}$, the numerator is 3.

Obtuse angle An angle whose measure is greater than 90°.

Odd number A counting number that is not even.

Open number sentence   A number sentence that is neither true nor false.

Parallel lines   Two or more lines in the same plane that do not intersect.

Parallelogram   A quadrilateral with both pairs of opposite sides parallel.

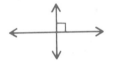

Percent   A ratio in which the second number is 100, but shown by using the % symbol.
Example   27% instead of 27 out of 100

Perimeter   The sum of the measures of the sides of a polygon.

Perpendicular lines   Two lines that intersect so that each angle they form measures 90°.

Pi   The ratio of the circumference of any circle to its diameter. It is about $3\frac{1}{7}$ or 3.14.

Plane   A set of points in space such that a line joining any two of its points lies entirely in the set.

Polygon   A simple closed curve made up entirely of line segments.

Prime factor   A factor that is a prime number.
Example   2 is a prime factor of 8.

Prime factorization Thinking of a number as the product of prime factors only.

Example $2 \times 2 \times 3$ is a prime factorization of 12.

Prime number A number that has exactly two factors, itself and 1.

Probability The quotient found by dividing the number of favorable outcomes by the total number of all possible outcomes.

Product The answer when two numbers are multiplied.

Property of zero for addition The sum of zero and any number is the number itself.

Property of zero for multiplication The product of zero and any number is zero.

Property of one for multiplication The product of 1 and any number is that number.

Protractor A device for measuring angles.

Quadrilateral A polygon of four sides.

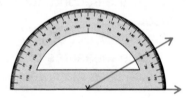

Quotient The answer when one number is divided by another.

Radius A line segment with one endpoint at the center of the circle and the other endpoint on the circle.

Ratio The comparison of two numbers by division.

Ray A set of points forming a straight path that has one endpoint and extends indefinitely in one direction.

Reciprocal Two numbers are reciprocals of each other if their product is 1.

Example $\frac{2}{3}$ and $\frac{3}{2}$ are reciprocals.

Rectangle A parallelogram with four right angles.

Rectangular prism A prism with rectangular faces. A good model is a box.

Rectangular region A rectangle together with its interior.

Relatively prime Two numbers are relatively prime when their greatest common factor is 1.

Example 3 and 7 are relatively prime.

Repeating decimal The result of dividing the numerator of a fraction by the denominator when the division does not terminate.

Example $.\overline{6}$ is the repeating decimal for $\frac{2}{3}$.

Replacements Numbers used to replace the variable in a mathematical open sentence.

Rhombus A parallelogram with all sides equal in measure.

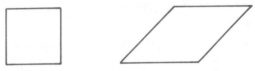

Right angle An angle whose measure is 90°.

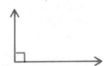

Right triangle A triangle with a right angle.

Similar triangles Two triangles whose corresponding angles are equal in measure and whose corresponding sides are in proportion.

Simple closed curve A curve that ends where it begins and never crosses itself.

Slide   The figures below are slides in geometry. They do not change shape or size.

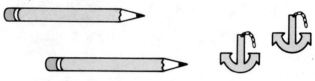

Solution   A number that makes a sentence true.

Sphere   A sphere is a set of points in space where every point is the same distance from one point called the center of the sphere. A ball is a sphere.

Square   A rectangle with all sides equal in measure. Also, the product of a number multiplied by itself.

Square root   One number is the square root of a second number if the second number is the square of the first. 3 is the square root of 9 because 9 is the square of 3.

Standard numeral   The common symbol for a numeral. The standard numeral for 20 + 3 is 23.

Trapezoid   Any quadrilateral that has at least one pair of parallel sides.

Triangle   A polygon that is the union of three line segments.

Turn   The figures below are turns in geometry. They do not change shape or size.

Variable   The letter, frame, or other abstract symbol that is replaced by the name of a number.

Vertex   The common endpoint of the sides of an angle or the common endpoint of two sides of a polygon.

Volume   The measure of the interior of a space figure.

Whole Number   Any of these numbers: 0, 1, 2, 3 . . .

SYMBOL LIST

		Page
$5 \cdot 8$	five times eight	2
10^4	ten to the fourth power	6
$\doteq$	is about equal to	8
34_5	three, four, base five	16
$>$	is greater than	46
$<$	is less than	46
$\neq$	is not equal to	160
$\sqrt{}$	square root	67
$\overleftrightarrow{AB}$	line AB	108
$\overline{AB}$	line segment AB	108
$\overrightarrow{AB}$	ray AB	108
$\angle ABC$	angle ABC	110
$120°$	120 degrees	112
$m\angle A$	measurement of $\angle A$	112
$\overleftrightarrow{AB} \parallel \overleftrightarrow{CD}$	$\overleftrightarrow{AB}$ is parallel to $\overleftrightarrow{CD}$	118
$\overleftrightarrow{AB} \perp \overleftrightarrow{CD}$	$\overleftrightarrow{AB}$ is perpendicular to $\overleftrightarrow{CD}$	118
$\cong$	is congruent to	246
50%	fifty percent	274
π	pi (about 3.14)	302
$^+5$	positive 5	334
$^-5$	negative 5	334

INDEX

division of, 236–240 •
multiplication of, 230–234 •
subtraction of, 228–229

Fractions, addition of, 166–169 •
division of, 192–195 •
multiplication of, 184–187 •
subtraction of, 170–181

Whole numbers, addition facts, 27
• addition of, 30–31 • division
facts, 75 • division of 76–80,
82–87, 92–103 • multiplication
facts, 51 • multiplication of,
58–63, 65 • subtraction facts,
34 • subtraction of, 35–37

Cone, 306–307
Congruence, 129
Coordinates, 346–347
Cross multiplication, 160
Cubic centimeter, 310
Cup, 268–269
Curve(s)
exterior of, 124 • interior of, 124
• simple closed, 124–125
Customary measure(s)
changing, 266–271 • of capacity,
268–269 • of length, 264–267 •
of weight, 270–271
Cylinder, 306–307

D

Decimal(s)
addition of, 224–227 • as
divisors, 238–240 • comparing,
218–219 • divison of, 236–240 •
fractions and, 220–221, 242 •
moving decimal point in division,
240 • multiplication by a power
of ten, 234 • multiplication of,
230–235 • percents and, 276–278
• repeating, 243 • subtraction of,
228–229 • terminating, 242
Decimal numeral(s)
equivalent, 216–217 • expanded
form, 214–215 • fractional form
for, 210–213 • place value in,

214–215 • word names for,
210–213
Decimeter, 250–251
Degree
of an angle, 112–113 • of
temperature, 261
Dekameter, 250–251
Denominator, 154
Diameter, 301–302
Distributive property, 55, 190
Divisibility
by five, 137 • by nine, 138 • by
ten, 137 • by three, 138 • by
two, 136–137
Division
as opposite operation of
multiplication, 74–75 • basic
facts, 75 • by multiples of one
hundred, 100–101 • by multiples
of ten, 92–93 • by one-digit
divisor, 82–87 • by three-digit
divisor, 102–103 • by two-digit
divisor, 92–99 • by zero, 77 •
checking, 80, 82, 84 • estimates
too large in, 98–99 • long form
for, 84–85 • mixed numerals and,
176 • of decimals, 236–240 •
of fractions, 192–195 • of whole
numbers, 74–89, 92–103 • one
in, 76 • patterns in, 78–79, 88–89
• remainders in, 80 • short form
in, 84, 92, 94, 100, 102 • with
mixed numerals, 195 • with
money, 97 • zero in, 76–77 •
zero in the quotient, 86–87, 96

E

Egyptian numeral(s), 12–13
Endpoint, 109
Equation(s)
graphing solution for, 42–43 •
replacements for, 42–43 •
solutions for, 42–43 • true, 44–45
• using a variable twice in, 44–45
• variable in, 42–43

machines, 350–351 • of integer pairs, 348–349 • of number pairs, 346–347 • of solution for equation, 42–43 • of solutions for inequalities, 46–47 • pictograph, 324–325

Greatest common factor (GCF), 146–147

Greatest possible error, 256, 264–265

H

Hectometer, 250–251
Hexagon, 124–125
Hindu-Arabic system of numeration, 12–13

I

Inch, 264–267
Inequality(ies)
graphing solution for, 46–47 • meaning of, 46–47 • replacements for, 46–47 • solutions for, 46–47

Input-output tables, 26, 69–70
Integer(s)
addition of, 338–339, 342–343 • comparing, 336–337 • meaning of, 334–335 • on the number line, 336–337 • subtraction of, 344–345

Interest, 286–287

K

Keeping Fit(s), 45, 57, 89, 90, 111, 122, 147, 148, 165, 197, 219, 222, 263, 285, 300, 313, 331

Kilogram, 259–260
Kilometer, 250–251

L

Least common denominator, 158–159, 168

Least common multiple (LCM), 150–151

Line(s)
intersecting, 118–119 • meaning of, 108 • parallel, 118–119 • perpendicular, 118–119

Line of symmetry, 128
Line segment(s)
bisecting, 132–133 • congruent, 246 • copying, 130–131 • meaning of, 108

Liter, 257–258

M

Measure(s)
addition with, 256–258, 267, 269, 271 • congruent, 246 • customary system of, 264–271 • greatest possible error of, 255, 264–265 • metric system of, 250–261 • of capacity, 257–258, 268–269 • of length, 250–253, 264–267 • of temperature, 261 • of time, 262 • of weight, 259–260, 270–271 • precision of, 254–255, 264–265 • subtraction with, 256–258, 267, 269, 271 • to the nearest unit, 247–248, 264–265

Meter, 250–253
Metric measure(s)
changing, 252–253, 259–260 • in problem solving, 11, 54, 68, 81, 91, 123, 181, 241, 249, 295, 340 • of capacity, 257–258 • of length, 250–253 • of temperature, 261

Mile, 266–267
Milligram, 259–260
Milliliter, 257–258
Millimeter, 250–253
Missing factor, 235
Mixed numeral(s)
addition with, 177–178 • division and, 176 • division with, 195 • fractional numerals and, 174–175 • meaning of, 174–175 •

391

Sentence(s)
closed, 40–41 • false, 40–41 •
open, 40–41 • related, 33, 74–75
• true, 40–41

Set(s)
finite, 10 • infinite, 10 • of whole
numbers, 10

Set notation, 10

Similar figure(s), 314–315

Slide, 126–127

Sphere, 306–307

Square, 124–125

Square root, 67

Subtraction
as opposite of addition, 33 •
basic facts, 34 • of decimals,
228–229 • of fractions, 170–172
• of integers, 344–345 • of whole
numbers, 33–39 • regrouping in,
35–36 • with measures, 256–258,
267, 269, 271 • with mixed
numerals, 179–180 • with money,
35, 39 • zero in, 37

Surface area, 312–313

Symbol(s)
is approximately equal to, 6 • is
equal to, 42 • is greater than, 46
• is less than, 46 • is not equal
to, 160

Symmetry, 128

T

Tablespoon, 268–269

Time zones, 262

Ton, 270–271

Trapezoid, 124–125

Triangle
area of, 294, 298–299 • as
polygon, 124–125 • right, 294 •
similar, 314–315 • sum of the
measures of the angles, 120

True sentence, 40–41

Turn, 126–127

V

Variables, 42–45

Vertex
of an angle, 110–111

Volume, 309–311

Y

Yard, 266–267

Z

Zero
in division, 76–77 • in
subtraction, 37 • in the quotient,
86–87, 96 • property for addition,
26–27 • property for
multiplication, 53

ANSWERS

This section contains answers to developmental items only.

CHAPTER 1 • PAGES vi–1

1.a. $400 + 30 + 7$ or $(4 \cdot 100) + (3 \cdot 10) + (7 \cdot 1)$ **b.** $900 + 80 + 6$ or $(9 \cdot 100) + (8 \cdot 10) + (6 \cdot 1)$ **c.** $700 + 20 + 1$ or $(7 \cdot 100) + (2 \cdot 10) + (1 \cdot 1)$ **d.** $1,000 + 400 + 20 + 1$ or $(1 \cdot 1,000) + (4 \cdot 100) + (2 \cdot 10) + (1 \cdot 1)$

2.a. $3,000,000 + 100,000 + 20,000 + 5,000 + 600 + 40 + 3$ or $(3 \cdot 1,000,000) + (1 \cdot 100,000) + (2 \cdot 10,000) + (5 \cdot 1,000) + (6 \cdot 100) + (4 \cdot 10) + (3 \cdot 1)$ **b.** $4,000,000 + 300,000 + 0 + 6,000 + 200 + 50 + 7$ or $(4 \cdot 1,000,000) + (3 \cdot 100,000) + (0 \cdot 10,000) + (6 \cdot 1,000) + (2 \cdot 100) + (5 \cdot 10) + (7 \cdot 1)$ **c.** $400,000,000,000 + 80,000,000,000 + 1,000,000,000 + 500,000,000 + 10,000,000 + 7,000,000 + 800,000 + 30,000 + 2,000 + 0 + 0 + 4$ or $(4 \cdot 100,000,000,000) + (8 \cdot 10,000,000,000) + (1 \cdot 1,000,000,000) + (5 \cdot 100,000,000) + (1 \cdot 10,000,000) + (7 \cdot 1,000,000) + (8 \cdot 100,000) + (3 \cdot 10,000) + (2 \cdot 1,000) + (0 \cdot 100) + (0 \cdot 10) + (4 \cdot 1)$

3.a. $5 \cdot 10$ **b.** $4 \cdot 100$ **c.** $2 \cdot 1,000$; $8 \cdot 10$ **d.** $5 \cdot 10,000,000,000$; $0 \cdot 10,000$

PAGE 2

1. $1,000,000,000$ days; no   **2.a.** 940   **b.** 76   **c.** 12

3.a. Twelve trillion, eight hundred five billion, seventy-six million, nine hundred forty thousand, nine hundred forty-seven

b. Twenty-seven million, four hundred twenty-five thousand, eight hundred sixty-two   **c.** Eight hundred forty-three billion, five hundred sixty-two million, forty-five thousand, six hundred sixty-six   **d.** Two hundred fifty-seven billion, four million, five hundred twenty-nine thousand, four hundred sixty-three

e. Nine hundred ninety-nine trillion, nine hundred ninety-nine billion, nine hundred ninety-nine million, nine hundred ninety-nine thousand, nine hundred ninety-nine   **f.** Eight hundred twenty-one million, five hundred sixty-two thousand, two hundred eighty-seven

PAGE 4

1. 2   **2.a.** $10 \cdot 10$; 2   **b.** $10 \cdot 10 \cdot 10$; 3   **c.** $10 \cdot 10 \cdot 10 \cdot 10$; 4   **d.** $10 \cdot 10 \cdot 10 \cdot 10 \cdot 10$; 5   **e.** $10 \cdot 10 \cdot 10 \cdot 10 \cdot 10 \cdot 10$; 6

3.a. $(1 \cdot 10^2) + (4 \cdot 10^1) + 5$ **b.** $(2 \cdot 10^3) + (7 \cdot 10^2) + (4 \cdot 10^1) + 5$ **c.** $(1 \cdot 10^4) + (2 \cdot 10^3) + (4 \cdot 10^2) + (6 \cdot 10^1) + 3$ **d.** $(2 \cdot 10^5) + (3 \cdot 10^4) + (4 \cdot 10^3) + (4 \cdot 10^2) + (3 \cdot 10^1) + 2$

PAGES 6–7

1.a. 40   **b.** 30   **c.** 80   **d.** 30   **2.a.** 20   **b.** 50   **c.** 90   **d.** 10   **3.a.** 600   **b.** 800   **c.** 300   **d.** 400   **4.a.** 3,000   **b.** 2,000   **c.** 6,000   **d.** 7,000

PAGES 6–7 (Continued)

5.a. 40,000 **b.** 70,000 **c.** 80,000 **d.** 80,000
6.a. 500,000 **b.** 400,000 **c.** 500,000 **7.a.** 50¢ **b.** 70¢
c. 90¢ **d.** 60¢

PAGE 9

2.b. yes **c.** 39,000

PAGE 10

1.a. 0, 1, 2, 3, . . . 20 **b.** 46, 47, 48, . . . 75
2.a. 7 **b.** 15 **3.a.** finite **b.** infinite

PAGE 12

1.a. 5 **b.** 40 **c.** 400 **d.** 4,000,000

2.a. ||||||| **b.** ∩∩∩∩∩ **c.** 999 **d.** /////

3.a. 1,232 **b.** (Mayan/Egyptian numerals)

c. (Egyptian numerals) **d.** 3,210,213

e. (Egyptian numerals)

PAGE 14

1.a. 23 **b.** 71 **c.** 1,312 **d.** 1,752 **2.a.** 408 **b.** 44 **c.** 94
d. 921 **3.a.** 1,000,000 **b.** 2,000,000 **c.** 90,000
d. 32,114

PAGES 16–17

1.a. 3 **b.** 2 **2.a.** 4 **b.** 0 **3.a.** 23_{five} **b.** 41_{five}
c. 110_{five} **4.** 2, 3, 4, 2, 75, 20, 2, 347
5.a. 69 **b.** 108 **c.** 222 **d.** 188

PAGE 18

1.a. 3 **c.** 23; 4 **e.** 3 **f.** 343_{five} **2.a.** 33_{five}
b. 122_{five} **c.** 222_{five} **d.** 321_{five} **e.** 212_{five}
f. 332_{five} **g.** 143_{five} **h.** 41_{five}

PAGE 20

1.a. 16 **b.** 207 **c.** 349 **d.** 691

PAGE 21

1.a. multiply by 3 **b.** 81 **2.a.** 13, 16, 19, 22
b. 16, 8, 4, 2

CHAPTER 2 • PAGES 26–27

1.a. 31; 32; 39; 40; 70 **b.** yes **2.a.** 9; 90; 16; 160 **b.** yes
3.a. 0; 1; 2; 9; 10; 40 **b.** They are the same.
4.a. 7 **b.** 0 **c.** 0

PAGES 28–29

1.a. 4 **b.** 19 **c.** 6 **d.** 19 **2.a.** 9 **b.** 2

    3.a. $(7 + 3) + 9 = 19$

      b. $(15 + 5) + 21 = 41$

      c. $(17 + 3) + 4 = 24$

      d. $(25 + 75) + 72 = 172$

PAGE 30

    1.a. 49   **b.** 96   **c.** 79   **d.** 95   **2.** 7; 60; 70; 7

    3.a. 7   **b.** 9, 8   **c.** 138, 3

    4.a. 92   **b.** 430   **c.** 651   **d.** 16,231

      e. 103,076   **f.** 16,606

PAGE 33

    1.a. $9 - 6 = n$; 3   **b.** $x + 6 = 9$; 3   **c.** $7 - 2 = p$; 5

    2.a. 1   **b.** 2   **c.** 13

    3.a. $6 - 5 = x$; 1   **b.** $10 - 4 = n$; 6

      c. $12 - 5 = c$; 7   **d.** $9 - 7 = n$; 2

      e. $3 + 5 = x$; 8   **f.** $2 + 4 = x$; 6

PAGE 35

    1.a. 23   **b.** 432   **c.** 706   **d.** 4,427   **2.a.** 569   **b.** 863,228

      c. 325,356

PAGE 37

    1.a. 12   **b.** 14   **c.** 89   **d.** 29   **2.a.** 387   **b.** 3,068   **c.** 4,244   **d.** 433

PAGE 40

    1.a. open   **b.** closed   **c.** open

    2.a. false   **b.** true   **c.** open   **d.** open   **e.** false   **f.** true

      g. open   **h.** false   **i.** open   **3.** Answers may vary.

PAGES 42–43

    1.a. no   **b.** no   **c.** yes   **d.** no   **2.a.** 4   **b.** 4   **c.** 2

    3.a. 5   (number line: dot at 5; labeled 1 2 3 4 5 6)

      b. 8   (number line: dot at 8; labeled 1 2 3 4 5 6 7 8 9)

      c. 4   (number line: dot at 4; labeled 1 2 3 4 5 6)

    4.a. no solution   **b.** no solution   **c.** 13

PAGES 44–45

    1.a. yes   **b.** 3

    2.a. no   **b.** no solution

    3.a. yes   **b.** commutative

    4.a. no   **b.** There is no number that makes the equation true.

PAGES 46–47

    1.a. $<$ **b.** $<$ **c.** $>$ **d.** $=$ **e.** $>$ **f.** $>$

    2.a. true   **b.** false

      c. false   **d.** false   **e.** false   **f.** true

    3.a. $1 + 6 < 10$; $3 + 6 < 10$; $2 + 6 < 10$

      b. It is not one of the replacements.

4.a. $7 + 3 > 8$; $6 + 3 > 8$; $8 + 3 > 8$ **b.** $\{6, 7, 8\}$

4.b. ⟵+—+—+—+—+—•—•—•—⟶
　　　　1　2　3　4　5　6　7　8

5.a. ⟵+—+—•—•—•—•—•—•—+—+—⟶
　　　　1　2　3　4　5　6　7　8　9　10

b. ⟵+—+—+—+—+—•—•—•—+—+—⟶
　　　1　2　3　4　5　6　7　8　9　10

c. ⟵+—+—•—•—•—•—•—•—+—+—⟶
　　　1　2　3　4　5　6　7　8　9　10

CHAPTER 3 • PAGE 50
　1. $15　**2.** 6 beans　　**3.** 12 desks
PAGES 52–53
　1.a. 83　　**b.** 47　　**2.a.** $9 \times (2 \times 5)$　　**b.** $(5 \times 2) \times 7$
　3.a. 0　**b.** 17　**c.** 39　**d.** 0　**4.a.** 1　**b.** 0　**c.** 48
PAGE 55
　1.a. 5　　**b.** 7; 6　　**2.a.** 68　　**b.** 96　　**c.** 48
PAGE 56
　1.a. the price of 5 cans of soup　　**b.** $5z = 95¢$
　2.a. a number of cupcakes plus 5　　**b.** $c + 5 = 17$　　**3.** $n - 3 = 18$
PAGE 58
　1. 3; 40; 9; 729　　**2.a.** 1,286　　**b.** 1,251　　**c.** 612　　**d.** 9,774
　3. yes; $4 \times 29 = 116$　　**4.a.** $3 \times 60 = 180$　　**b.** $5 \times 60 = 300$
　　c. $7 \times 40 = 280$
PAGE 60
　1. 9,810; 98,100　　**2.a.** 9,360　　**b.** 93,600　　**c.** 936,000
　3.a. 252,780　　**b.** 2,527,800　　**c.** 25,278,000　　**4.a.** 1,530
　　b. 359,100　　**c.** 246,800　　**d.** 7,203,000
PAGES 62–63
　1.a. 1,512　**b.** 513　**c.** 24,288　**d.** 127,092　**2.a.** 95,816; 95,816
　　b. They are the same.　**3.a.** 191,016　　**b.** 120,098　**c.** 275,114
　4. 207,132
PAGE 64
　1.a. Open it.　**b.** Each answer for the decision block has two separate
　　sets of steps.
PAGE 65
　1.a. 33,001,872; 33,001,872　**b.** They are the same.　**2.a.** 4,891,172
　　b. 10,646,757　　**c.** 24,150,216
PAGE 67
　1.a. $6 \times 6 = 36$　**b.** $7 \times 7 = 49$　**c.** $8 \times 8 = 64$　**d.** $4 \times 4 \times 4 = 64$
　2.a. 4　　**b.** 7　　**c.** 5　　**d.** 2
PAGES 69–70
　1. 6; 9; 12; 33; 36; 7; 17; 22; 37; 62
　2. 1; 3; 6; 11; 1; 2; 4; 9

1.a. 9 **b.** 8 **c.** 42 **2.a.** $7 \times 5 = m$; 35 **b.** $9 \times 8 = y$; 72
c. $7 \times 5 = n$; 35 **d.** $36 \div 4 = n$; 9 **e.** $28 \div 7 = y$; 4 **f.** $56 \div 7 = x$; 8

PAGE 76
1.a. 4 **b.** 15 **c.** 0 **d.** 1 **e.** 30 **f.** 0 **g.** 0 **h.** 1 **2.a.** 1
b. 1 **c.** 8 **d.** 12 **e.** 0 **f.** 0

PAGE 77
1.a. None will work. **b.** no **c.** no
2.a. Any number works. **b.** no

PAGE 78
1.a. 8; 80; 800; 8,000 **b.** 4; 40; 400; 4,000 **c.** 3; 30; 300; 3,000
d. 7; 70; 700; 7,000 **2.a.** 20 **b.** 50 **c.** 700 **d.** 50 **e.** 400
f. 800 **g.** $60 **h.** $500 **i.** 400

PAGE 80
1.a. 7 r 3 **b.** 6 r 2 **c.** 9 r 3 **d.** 7 r 7
2.a. 5 r 2 **b.** 4 r 3 **c.** 5 r 4 **d.** 8 r 2

PAGES 82–83
1.a. 100 **b.** 900 **c.** 20 **d.** 927 **e.** $927 \times 2 = 1,854$
2.a. 86 **b.** 328 **c.** 866 r 2

PAGES 84–85
1.a. 6 **b.** 3 **c.** 63; 2 **d.** 443
2.a. 976; 1 **b.** $976 \times 2 = 1,952$; $1,952 + 1 = 1,953$ **3.a.** 57 r 3
b. 87 r 4 **c.** 263 r 1 **d.** 331 r 1

PAGE 86
1.a. 309 r 1 **b.** 407 r 1 **c.** 903 r 3 **d.** 230 r 3 **e.** 450 r 4 **f.** 720 r 7
2.a. 406 **b.** 702 r 4 **c.** 407

PAGE 88
1.a. 4 **b.** 6 **c.** 4 **d.** 3 **2.a.** 2 **b.** 5 **c.** 7 **d.** 8 **e.** 4
f. 7 **g.** 3 **h.** 2 **i.** 6

PAGES 92–93
1.a. 6 **b.** 7 **c.** 67; 17 **d.** 1,357
2.a. 484; 25 **b.** $484 \times 40 + 25 = 19,385$; $19,360 + 25 = 19,385$
3.a. 85 r 47 **b.** 78 r 34 **c.** 168 r 50 **d.** 72 r 3 **e.** 935 r 31 **f.** 799 r 52

PAGES 94–95
1.a. 6 **b.** 4 **c.** 64; 13 **d.** 1,357
2.a. 71 r 50 **b.** 42 r 51 **c.** 51 r 2
3.a. 726 r 14 **b.** 776 r 21 **c.** 952 r 3

PAGE 96
1.a. 6 **b.** 0 **c.** 18 **2.a.** 40 r 37 **b.** 205 r 17

PAGE 98

```
      71 r 4
1. 28)1,992      2.a. 62      b. 319 r 2      c. 381 r 1
      1 96
        32
        28
         4
```

1.a. 7   **b.** 2   **c.** 6   **d.**

$$\begin{array}{r} 726 \text{ r } 137 \\ 400\overline{)290{,}537} \\ \underline{280\ 0} \\ 10\ 53 \\ \underline{8\ 00} \\ 2\ 537 \\ \underline{2\ 400} \\ 137 \end{array}$$

    e. $726 \times 400 = 290{,}400$
290,400 + 137 = 290,537
2.a. 31 r 239   **b.** 69 r 493   **c.** 26 r 98

1.a. 3   **b.** 2   **c.** 4   **d.**

$$\begin{array}{r} 324 \text{ r } 501 \\ 712\overline{)231{,}189} \\ \underline{213\ 6} \\ 17\ 58 \\ \underline{14\ 24} \\ 3\ 349 \\ \underline{2\ 848} \\ 501 \end{array}$$

    e. $324 \times 712 = 230{,}688$
230,688 + 501 = 231,189

2.a. 69 r 20   **b.** 162 r 268   **c.** 288 r 72

1.a. 12; 16; 52; 13   **b.** 204; 2; 102   **2.a.** 93   **b.** $25

CHAPTER 5 • PAGE 108
1. A line has no end.   **2.** no   **3.** yes; yes; an infinite number

1.d. $\angle XFY$, $\angle YFX$, $\angle F$ **e.** $\overrightarrow{FX}$ and $\overrightarrow{FY}$ **2.a.** smaller   **b.** larger
3.a. obtuse   **b.** acute   **c.** right

1.a. 10°   **b.** 60°   **c.** 30°   **d.** 140°   **e.** 90°   **f.** 130°   **2.** $\angle COH$
3.c. 90°

1.a. 90°   **b.** 56°   **c.** 107°
2.a. acute   **b.** 76

1.a. one   **b.** one   **c.** yes; one   **2.a.** yes; yes
   b. $\overleftrightarrow{AC} \parallel \overleftrightarrow{BD}$, $\overleftrightarrow{DE} \parallel \overleftrightarrow{BF}$, or $\overleftrightarrow{DB} \parallel \overleftrightarrow{EF}$ or $\overleftrightarrow{CA} \parallel \overleftrightarrow{EF}$
3. 90°   **4.a.** Answers may vary.

1.a. 80°   **b.** 180°   **2.d.** They lie along a line. The measure
of the angle formed is 180°.
3.a. 60°   **b.** 30°   **c.** 85°

PAGES 124–125
 1. none; c; none; b
 2.a. Both pairs of opposite sides are parallel.   **b.** It has no right angles.
 3.a. Its opposite sides are parallel.   **b.** The sides do not all have the
   same measure.

PAGE 126
 1.a. yes   **b.** yes   **c.** no
 2.a. no   **b.** yes   **c.** yes
 3.a. yes   **b.** no   **c.** yes

PAGE 128
 1.b. two lines   **c.** four lines

PAGE 129
 1.a. yes   **b.** no   **c.** yes   **d.** no

PAGE 132
 1. Measure $\overline{AC}$ and $\overline{CB}$. They should have the same measure.

CHAPTER 6 • PAGES 136–137
 1.a. yes; no   **b.** no; yes
 2.a. Answers may vary.   **b.** Answers may vary.
 3.a. 35, 40, 45, 50, 55   **b.** 70, 80, 90, 100, 110

PAGE 138
 1.a. no   **b.** yes   **c.** yes   **2.a.** no   **b.** yes   **c.** yes

PAGE 140
 1. 1, 2, 4, 7, 14, 28   **2.a.** 1, 2, 3, 6, 9, 18   **b.** 1, 19
 c. 1, 2, 4, 5, 10, 20   **d.** 1, 2, 3, 4, 6, 8, 12, 24   **e.** 1, 2, 4, 8, 16
 3.a. no **b.** yes **c.** yes **d.** no **e.** no **4.a.** composite **b.** composite
 c. prime   **d.** prime   **e.** composite

PAGE 142
 1.a. $2 \times 3 \times 3$ **2.b.** $2 \times 2 \times 2 \times 3$ **3.a.** 3, 2, 2   **b.** 24, 2, 2; 2
 4.a.   36   **b.** 32   **c.** 40

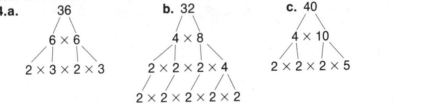

PAGE 145
 1. 1; 3   **2.a.** 1; 2; 4; 8; 16; 32   **b.** 1; 2; 4; 5; 10; 20   **c.** 1; 2; 4
PAGE 146
 1. 2   **2.a.** 1; 2; 3; 6   **b.** 6   **3.a.** 1; 2; 4; 8   **b.** 8   **c.** no   **d.** 4
 e. yes
PAGE 149
 1.a. 8, 16, 24, 32, . . .   **b.** 10, 20, 30, 40, . . .   **c.** 40, 80, 120, . . .
 2.a. 14, 28, 42, . . .   **b.** 12, 24, 36, . . .   **c.** 20, 40, 60, . . .
PAGE 150
 1. 10   **2.** 12   **3.a.** 35   **b.** 12   **c.** 9   **d.** 12   **e.** 30   **f.** 24

1. 7; 10   **2.** $\frac{1}{3}$ **3.** $\frac{3}{10}$

PAGES 155–156

1.a. $\frac{3}{4}$ **b.** $\frac{6}{8}$ **c.** 6   **2.** $\frac{15}{20}$

3.a. 10   **b.** 6   **c.** 14

PAGE 157

1. $\frac{24}{3}$; $\frac{32}{4}$; $\frac{40}{5}$; $\frac{48}{6}$ **2.** $\frac{6}{6}$; $\frac{7}{7}$; $\frac{8}{8}$; $\frac{9}{9}$

PAGES 158–159

1.a. $<$ **b.** $>$ **c.** $>$

2.b. 21; 20   **c.** $>$

3.a. $<$ **b.** $<$ **c.** $>$ **d.** $<$ **e.** $<$ **f.** $<$

4.a. 4   **b.** 3   **c.** $\frac{1}{3}$ **5.a.** $<$ **b.** $>$ **c.** $>$

PAGE 160

1.a. 20; 20   **b.** yes   **2.a.** $=$ **b.** $=$ **c.** $\neq$

PAGE 162

1.a. 1, 2, 3, 4, 6, 12   **b.** 1, 2, 4, 8, 16   **c.** 4   **d.** $\frac{3}{4}$

e. Yes; the GCF of the numerator and the denominator is 1.   **2.** $\frac{5}{6}$

PAGE 164

1.a. $\frac{5}{6}$ **b.** $\frac{3}{4}$ **c.** $\frac{1}{2}$ **d.** $\frac{2}{3}$ **2.a.** $\frac{3}{4}$ **b.** $\frac{4}{5}$ **c.** $\frac{4}{5}$ **d.** $\frac{2}{3}$

PAGE 166

1. $\frac{5}{8}$ **2.a.** $\frac{4}{5}$ **b.** $\frac{11}{12}$ **c.** $\frac{6}{8}$ **3.a.** $\frac{1}{2}$ **b.** $\frac{2}{3}$ **c.** $\frac{4}{5}$ **4.a.** $\frac{3}{4}$ **b.** $\frac{7}{10}$

PAGES 168–169

1.a. 12   **b.** 8; 3   **c.** 11   **2.b.** 24   **c.** 9; 4; 13

3.a. $\frac{9}{10}$ **b.** $\frac{13}{15}$ **c.** $\frac{7}{10}$ **d.** $\frac{11}{12}$

PAGE 170

1.a. $\frac{2}{9}$ **b.** $\frac{1}{10}$ **c.** $\frac{6}{17}$ **2.b.** 9; 4   **c.** 5   **3.a.** $\frac{1}{6}$ **b.** $\frac{7}{12}$ **c.** $\frac{7}{15}$ **d.** $\frac{1}{8}$

PAGE 173

1.a. $\frac{3}{4}$ **b.** $\frac{7}{12}$ **c.** $\frac{5}{6}$ **2.a.** $\frac{3}{7}$ **b.** $\frac{2}{3}$

PAGES 174–175

1.a. $4\frac{2}{3}$ **b.** $5\frac{3}{4}$ **c.** $7\frac{2}{3}$ **2.a.** $4+\frac{2}{3}$ **b.** $5+\frac{3}{8}$ **c.** $8+\frac{5}{6}$ **3.a.** $\frac{19}{3}$ **b.** 20; $\frac{21}{5}$

c. $\frac{25}{5}$; $\frac{28}{5}$

4.a. $\frac{14}{3}$ **b.** $\frac{43}{8}$ **c.** $\frac{53}{6}$

PAGE 176

1.a. $7 \div 3$ **b.** $8 \div 5$ **c.** $9 \div 4$ **c.** $10 \div 7$ **2.a.** $2\frac{2}{5}$ **b.** $7\frac{1}{3}$ **c.** $9\frac{1}{4}$ **d.** $5\frac{4}{5}$

PAGE 177

1. 1; $\frac{1}{3}$; $3\frac{2}{3}$; $3\frac{2}{3}$ **2.a.** 8; 3   **b.** $6\frac{11}{12}$ **3.** $15\frac{2}{3}$

PAGE 179

1.a. $2\frac{1}{3}$ **b.** $1\frac{1}{6}$ **c.** $4\frac{4}{21}$ **d.** $3\frac{1}{8}$ **2.a.** $4\frac{3}{5}$ **b.** $15\frac{1}{4}$ **c.** $2\frac{11}{12}$ **d.** $3\frac{7}{24}$

1.a. $\frac{1}{3}$ **b.** $\frac{3}{16}$ **c.** $\frac{3}{10}$ **2.a.** $3\frac{5}{7}$ **b.** $2\frac{1}{10}$ **c.** $3\frac{1}{3}$

3.a. $\frac{4}{7}$ **b.** $1\frac{1}{5}$ **c.** 6

PAGE 186

1.a. $\frac{4}{9}$ **b.** $\frac{8}{31}$ **c.** 3   **2.a.** $\frac{2}{5}$ **b.** $\frac{2}{9}$ **c.** $\frac{3}{16}$

PAGE 189

1.a. $\frac{1}{7}$ **b.** $\frac{3}{5}$ **c.** $\frac{2}{3}$ **d.** $\frac{1}{10}$ **2.a.** $\frac{17}{19}$ **b.** $\frac{17}{19}$ **c.** $\frac{17}{19}$ **d.** $\frac{17}{19}$; yes

PAGE 190

1. $9\frac{2}{3}$ **2.a.** $6\frac{2}{5}$ **b.** $12\frac{6}{7}$ **c.** $32\frac{6}{7}$

PAGE 191

1.a. 1   **b.** 1   **c.** $\frac{1}{6}$ **2.a.** $\frac{8}{3}$ **b.** $\frac{7}{5}$ **c.** 4   **d.** $\frac{1}{3}$

PAGES 192–193

1.a. 8 **b.** $\frac{12}{3}$, or 4 **c.** 20 **2.a.** 2 **b.** 5 **c.** 4 **3.** 6; 4; 1; 6; 4; 1

4.a. 16   **b.** 12   **c.** 12   **d.** 4   **5.a.** $\frac{18}{25}$ **b.** 18   **c.** $\frac{24}{35}$

PAGE 194

1.a. $\frac{1}{4}$ **b.** $\frac{1}{3}$ **c.** $\frac{3}{4}$ **2.a.** $1\frac{7}{8}$ **b.** $1\frac{1}{5}$ **c.** $1\frac{1}{5}$

PAGE 195

1.a. $\frac{3}{4}$ **b.** $4\frac{8}{9}$ **c.** $\frac{5}{6}$ **2.a.** $3\frac{1}{2}$ **b.** $\frac{3}{5}$ **c.** $2\frac{1}{4}$

PAGE 198

1. 28   **2.a.** 40   **b.** 10   **c.** 45   **3.a.** yes   **b.** yes   **c.** no   **d.** yes
e. yes   **f.** no

PAGE 201

1. $\frac{15}{2} = 7\frac{1}{2}, \frac{25}{3} = 8\frac{1}{3}$ **2.** $\frac{15}{2} < \frac{25}{3}$

PAGES 202–203

1.a. 1 **b.** 5 **c.** $\frac{1}{5}$ **2.a.** 3 **b.** 5 **c.** $\frac{3}{5}$ **3.a.** 2 **b.** 6 **c.** $\frac{2}{6}$, or $\frac{1}{3}$

d. $\frac{3}{6}$, or $\frac{1}{2}$; $\frac{1}{6}$

4.a. no   **b.** 1, or $\frac{6}{6}$

PAGE 204

1.a. 1 on red, 5 on blue   **b.** 2 on red, 5 on blue   **c.** 3 on red, 4 on blue

2.a. 9   **b.** $\frac{1}{9}$; $\frac{1}{9}$ **3.** (1, 6) (2, 5) (3, 4); $\frac{2}{9}$; (2, 6) (2, 5) (2, 4); $\frac{3}{9}$ or $\frac{1}{3}$;

(2, 6) (2, 4); $\frac{2}{9}$; Both numbers are odd; (1, 5) (2, 5) (3, 5); $\frac{3}{9}$ or $\frac{1}{3}$

1.a. three tenths   **b.** seven tenths   **c.** six hundredths
d. five hundredths   **e.** ninety-three hundredths   **f.** two and seven tenths
g. forty-two hundredths   **h.** five and eight tenths

PAGE 210 (Continued)

    i. seven and twenty-one hundredths   **j.** three and nine hundredths

    2.a. $\frac{9}{10}$ **b.** $\frac{9}{100}$ **c.** $\frac{48}{100}$ **d.** $\frac{8}{100}$ **d.** $5\frac{7}{10}$ **3.a.** .4 **b.** .04 **c.** 3.1

    d. .31   **e.** 5.37

PAGE 212

    2.a. $\frac{635}{1,000}$ **b.** $\frac{71}{1,000}$ **c.** $\frac{4,256}{10,000}$ **d.** $\frac{37}{10,000}$ **3.a.** .002   **b.** .523

    c. .2135   **d.** .0071

PAGE 214

    1.a. 3   **b.** 600; 20; 3; 6   **c.** 3; 2; 4   **d.** 20; 4; 9; 6; 3

    2.a. $900 + 20 + 7 + \frac{6}{10} + \frac{7}{100}$ **b.** $400 + 30 + 9 + \frac{9}{10} + \frac{2}{100} + \frac{6}{1,000}$

    c. $70 + 5 + \frac{8}{10} + \frac{9}{100} + \frac{2}{1,000} + \frac{4}{10,000}$ **3.a.** $\frac{327}{100}$

    b. $\frac{14,038}{1,000}$ **c.** $\frac{192,075}{10,000}$ **4.a.** 7 tenths   **b.** 2 hundredths

    c. 3 thousandths   **d.** 6 ten thousandths   **e.** 4 thousandths

    f. 1 hundredth

PAGE 216

    1.a. 70; 7   **b.** 10; 60   **2.a.** .6   **b.** .4   **c.** .9   **d.** 1.2   **3.a.** .70

    b. .20   **c.** .50   **d.** 2.30   **4.a.** .60; .6   **b.** .40; .4   **c.** .50; .5

    d. .90; .9   **e.** .600   **f.** .700   **g.** .400   **h.** .020

PAGE 218

    1.a. <   **b.** >   **c.** <   **2.a.** >   **b.** <   **c.** =

PAGES 220–221

    1.a. .2 **b.** .4 **c.** .8 **d.** 1.5 **e.** 1.2 **2.a.** .24 **b.** .44 **c.** .25 **d.** .06

    e. 1.25   **3.a.** .125   **b.** .375   **c.** .075   **d.** .875   **e.** .175

PAGE 224

    1.a. .8   **b.** .7   **c.** 1.5   **2.a.** .78   **b.** .63

    c. .70   **3.a.** .007   **b.** .175   **c.** .549

PAGE 226

    1.a. $2\frac{9}{10}$; 2.9   **b.** $4\frac{1}{2}$; 4.5   **c.** $5\frac{87}{100}$; 5.87   **d.** $9\frac{12}{100}$; 9.12   **2.a.** .92

    b. .39   **c.** .451   **d.** 6.91   **e.** 83.69   **f.** 36.431

PAGES 228–229

    1.a. .2   **b.** .34   **c.** .894   **2.a.** .38   **b.** .172   **c.** .4592

    3.a. .016   **b.** .113   **c.** 4.6126

PAGE 230

    1.a. 1.38   **b.** 1.428   **c.** 10.3443   **2.a.** .6   **b.** 1.75

    c. 2.4756   **3.a.** 14.8   **b.** 203.2   **c.** 168.82

PAGES 232–233

    1.a. $\frac{8}{100}$; .08   **b.** $\frac{16}{100}$; .16   **c.** $\frac{42}{100}$; .42   **d.** $\frac{15}{100}$; .15

    2.a. $\frac{8}{1,000}$; .008   **b.** $\frac{12}{1,000}$; .012   **c.** $\frac{42}{1,000}$; .042   **d.** $\frac{75}{1,000}$; .075

    3. 2; 1, 1; 1, 3; 3, 2   **4.a.** .91   **b.** .2163   **c.** .2336

PAGE 234

    1.a. 25   **b.** .36   **c.** 13.4   **3.a.** 25   **b.** 36   **c.** 75.6

PAGE 235

    1.a. 4   **b.** 40   **c.** 5   **d.** .5   **2.a.** 10   **b.** 10   **c.** 100   **d.** 100

1.a. .6   **b.** 3.6   **c.** 4.32   **d.** .009
2. The decimal points in the dividend and the quotient are aligned.
3.a. .7   **b.** .74   **c.** 2.75   **4.a.** 2.38   **b.** 5.43   **c.** 2.346

PAGES 238–239

1.a. 100   **b.** 6.3   **c.** .3   **d.** $.21 \times .3 = .063$ **2.a.** 6.1   **b.** .7   **c.** 12
3.a. .6   **b.** .81   **c.** 3.4   **d.** 4.2   **e.** 3.2   **f.** .73   **4.a.** 50   **b.** 315   **c.** 90
   d. 210   **e.** 360   **f.** 460   **5.a.** 5.2   **b.** 18   **c.** 15   **d.** 190   **e.** 238

PAGE 242

1.a. .5   **b.** .6   **c.** .8   **d.** .5   **2.** .375

PAGE 243

1.a. 6; 6   **b.** no   **2.a.** $\overline{.45}$ **b.** $.\overline{7}$ **c.** $.\overline{142857}$

CHAPTER 10 • PAGE 246

1.a. 3 cm   **b.** 5 cm   **c.** 8 cm   **2.** none of them

PAGE 247

1. 2 cm   **2.** 34 mm   **3.** Answers may vary.

PAGES 250–251

1.c. 10; 100   **d.** 10; 1,000
2.a. Answers may vary.   **b.** Answers may vary.   **c.** Answers may vary.

PAGES 252–253

1.a. 100   **b.** 10   **c.** 1,000   **d.** 2   **e.** 5   **f.** 40
2.a. 400   **b.** 60   **c.** 1,000; 9,000   **d.** 10; 120
3.a. 6   **b.** 7   **c.** .01; 4   **d.** .001; .05

PAGE 254

1.a. 8 cm; 81 mm   **b.** 4 cm; 36 mm   **c.** 10 cm; 103 mm   **d.** 6 cm; 60 mm
  e. 9 cm; 93 mm   **f.** 5 cm; 48 mm
2. Answers may vary.   **3.a.** $\frac{1}{2}$ cm   **b.** $\frac{1}{4}$ cm

PAGE 256

1.a. 7   **b.** 39   **2.a.** 6; 6   **b.** 2; 61

PAGES 257–258

1.a. 3,000 mL   **b.** 5,000 mL   **c.** 7,000 mL   **d.** 6 L   **e.** 4 L   **f.** 10 L
2. eye dropper–2 milliliters; glass of milk–200 milliliters;
    bucket of water–20 liters   **3.** 3
4.a. 6 L 65 mL   **b.** 11 L 521 mL   **5.** 840

PAGE 259

1.a. g   **b.** kg   **c.** mg   **2.a.** 4,000 g   **b.** 5,700 g   **c.** 5 kg
  d. 6.825 kg   **3.a.** 5,000 mg   **b.** 6,480 mg   **c.** 6 g   **d.** 7.9 g

PAGE 261

1.a. 16°   **b.** ⁻6°   **c.** 28°   **2.a.** 20°C   **b.** 8°C   **c.** 11°C

PAGES 264–265

1. $1\frac{1}{2}$ in.   **2.** $2\frac{1}{4}$ in.   **3.** $1\frac{5}{8}$ in.   **4.** $\frac{1}{8}$ inch; $\frac{1}{4}$ inch
5.a. $\frac{1}{2}$ inch   **b.** $\frac{1}{4}$ inch   **6.** $\overline{EF} = 1\frac{5}{16}$; $\overline{CD} = \frac{11}{16}$; $\overline{AB} = 1\frac{1}{16}$ **7.** $\frac{1}{32}$ inch

1.a. 6; $\frac{1}{2}$ **b.** 2; 24   **2.a.** $\frac{2}{3}$ **b.** $1\frac{1}{2}$ **c.** 3 ft   **d.** 36 in.
e. 60 in.   **f.** 24 in.   **3.a.** 6; 18   **b.** 6; 2   **4.a.** 6 ft   **b.** 36 ft
c. 39 ft   **d.** 4 yd   **e.** 8 yd   **f.** 16 yd   **5.a.** 21,120 ft
b. 26,400 ft   **c.** 52,800 ft
6.a. 9 ft 4 in.   **b.** 12 ft 2 in.   **7.a.** 3 ft 8 in.   **b.** 2 ft 7 in.

1.a. 6; 3   **b.** 6; 12   **2.a.** 2 pt   **b.** 4 pt   **c.** 10 pt   **3.a.** 4; 2
b. 4; 16   **4.a.** 3 qt   **b.** $4\frac{1}{2}$ qt   **c.** 20 qt   **5.a.** 8   **b.** 4; 8
6.a. 6 tbs   **b.** 12 tbs   **c.** 14 tbs   **d.** 6 cups   **e.** 12 cups   **f.** 14 cups
7.a. 10 gal   **b.** 5 pt   **8.a.** 2 cups 5 fl oz   **b.** 2 gal 2 qt

1.a. 4; 64   **b.** 4; $\frac{1}{4}$ **2.a.** 32 oz   **b.** 48 oz   **c.** 192 oz   **d.** $\frac{1}{8}$ lb
e. $\frac{3}{4}$ lb   **f.** 2 lb   **3.a.** 2; 4,000   **b.** $\frac{1}{4}$ **4.a.** 8,000 lb
b. 16,000 lb   **c.** 20,000 lb   **d.** $\frac{1}{2}$ ton   **e.** $\frac{3}{4}$ ton   **f.** 2 ton
5.a. 9   **b.** 29   **6.a.** 2; 14   **b.** 7; 13

CHAPTER 11 • PAGE 274

1.a. yes   **b.** yes   **c.** yes   **d.** no; Tom answered 88% of the questions correctly.   **2.a.** 90 out of 100, or $\frac{90}{100}$ **b.** 42 out of 100, or $\frac{42}{100}$
c. 17 out of 100, or $\frac{17}{100}$ **3.** 3rd

1.a. 43%   **b.** 66%   **c.** 36%   **d.** 90%   **2.a.** 37%   **b.** 20%   **c.** 98%
d. 50%   **3.a.** $\frac{14}{20} = 70\%$ $\frac{19}{25} = 76\%$ **b.** $\frac{9}{10} = 90\%$ $\frac{4}{5} = 80\%$

1. 40%   **2.a.** 40%   **b.** 50%   **c.** 75%   **d.** 60%

1. $12\frac{1}{2}\%$ **2.** $37\frac{1}{2}\%$ **3.** $62\frac{1}{2}\%$ **4.** $16\frac{2}{3}\%$ **5.** $8\frac{1}{3}\%$

1.a. 35 out of 100   **b.** 7 out of 100   **c.** 40 out of 100   **2.a.** $\frac{43}{100}$
b. $\frac{2}{5}$ **c.** $\frac{1}{25}$ **3.a.** .24   **b.** .07   **c.** .70

1. 20   **2.a.** $.10 \times 40 = n$ **b.** $4

PAGE 284

1.a. $2.50   **b.** $3   **c.** $1.25   **2.** $22.50   **3.a.** $28   **b.** $35
c. $15.89   **d.** $44.94   **e.** $12.53   **f.** $36.40

PAGE 286

1.a. $15   **b.** $12.50   **c.** $120
2.a. $24   **b.** $15.60   **c.** $108

CHAPTER 12 ● PAGE 292

1. 42 yd   **2.a.** 12 mm   **b.** 24 cm   **c.** 16 in.

PAGE 293

1.a. 54 cm²   **b.** 70 m²   **2.** 49 cm²

PAGE 294

1. 20; 20   **2.a.** 12 m²   **b.** 3 cm²   **c.** 4.5 mm²

PAGE 296

1.d. rectangle   **e.** yes   **2.a.** 25 cm²   **b.** 28 m²

PAGE 298

1.e. half   **f.** half   **2.a.** 28 in.²   **b.** 14 in.²   **3.a.** 20 cm²
b. 36 mm²   **c.** 14 in.²

PAGE 301

1.a. blue   **b.** red   **2.** Check students' drawings. The length of a diameter is twice that of a radius.

PAGE 303

2. 12.56; 12.56   **3.** 37.68; 37.68 cm

PAGES 304–305

1. 200.96; 200.96   **2.a.** r **b.** πr **c.** r; r; r
3.a. 78.5 in.²   **b.** 4.5216 cm²

PAGES 306–307

2. 8; 12   **3.** cereal box, desk drawer   **4.** Answers may vary.
5. air

PAGE 309

1. A **2.** B has a larger volume.   **3.** yes

PAGES 310–311

1. the volume of a cube measuring 1 cm on each edge; the volume of a cube measuring 1 inch on each edge
2.a. 18   **b.** 2   **c.** 36; 36 cubic units
3.a. 3 cm; 7 cm   **b.** 84 cm³   **c.** 84   **d.** yes
4.a. 16 ft³   **b.** 16 m³

PAGES 312–313

1.a. 10; 3   **b.** 10; 4   **c.** 4; 3   **d.** 164 in.²   **2.** Answers may vary.
3. Answers may vary.

PAGES 314–315

1. $\overline{EF}$; $\overline{DF}$ **2.a.** $\overline{MR}$; $\overline{MP}$; $\overline{PR}$ **b.** 8; 6

1.a. $1\frac{1}{2}$ km   **b.** 4 km   **c.** 7 km   **2.a.** 16 ft by 12 ft

b. 22 ft by 14 ft   **c.** 14 ft by 12 ft

CHAPTER 13 • PAGE 320

1. 7   **2.** 90%   **3.** 4   **4.** 6

5.a. 20   **b.** $\frac{4}{20}$, or $\frac{1}{5}$ **c.** 20%

6.a. $\frac{3}{20}$ **b.** 15%

PAGE 321

1. Tom: $5, $6, $15; $36, $4, $66
Ed: $7, $8, $16, $16, $19, $66
Rita: $16, $11, $21, $17, $15, $80
Totals: $28, $25, $52, $69, $38, $212

2. Thursday; Friday; Wednesday

3. Thursday   **4.** yes

PAGE 324

1.a. 50   **b.** 225   **c.** ☺ ☺ ☹

2.

One	🏈		
Two	◁		
Three	🏈	🏈	
Four	🏈	🏈	◁

PAGE 326

1.a. 30°   **b.** 40°   **c.** 48°   **d.** 10°

2.

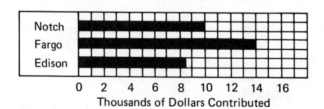

Thousands of Dollars Contributed

PAGE 328

    1. 5,000   **2.** 1960 to 1965   **3.** 1965 to 1970

    5. February–April and April–June   **6.** October–December; 5°

PAGE 332

    1. Food: $320, House: $160, Savings: $80, Entertainment: $40,
    Other needs: $200   **2.** Food: $360, House: $180, Savings: $90,
    Entertainment: $45, Other needs: $225

PAGE 334

    1.a. gain of 4 points   **b.** loss of 2 points; negative two

    2.a. gain; 10 points **b.** $^+7$ **3.a.** loss; 8 points **b.** loss; 9 points

    4.a. $^+10$ **b.** $^-6$ **c.** $^+7°$ **d.** $^+2$ km   **e.** $^+10$ **f.** $^-5$

PAGE 336

    1.a. $<$ **b.** $<$ **c.** $>$ **d.** $>$ **e.** $>$ **f.** $<$ **g.** $<$ **h.** $<$ **i.** $>$

    2.a. 5 units   **b.** 1 unit   **c.** 3 units   **d.** 5 units   **e.** 4 units

    f. 1 unit   **g.** 3 units   **h.** 2 units

PAGES 338–339

    1.a. $^+8$ **b.** $^-4$ **2.a.** $^+9 + {}^+6$ **b.** $^-12 + {}^-6$

    3.a. $^-16$ **b.** $^+10$ **c.** $^-25$ **d.** $^+145$

PAGE 341

    1.a. 0   **b.** 0   **c.** 0   **2.a.** $^+7$ **b.** $^-7$ **c.** $^+9$ **c.** $^+12$

PAGE 342

    1.a. loss; 2 points   **b.** $^-2$ **2.a.** $^-3$ **b.** $^+6$ **c.** $^+3$ **3.a.** $^-2$

    b. $^+2$ **c.** $^-5$ **d.** $^+5$ **e.** $^-8$ **f.** $^-8$

PAGES 344–345

    1. yes   **2.a.** $^+5$ **b.** $^-13$ **c.** $^+6; {}^+15$ **d.** $^+7; {}^-1$

    3.a. $^+12$ **b.** $^+10$ **c.** $^-8$ **d.** $^+3$ **e.** $^+1$ **f.** $^-6$

PAGE 346

1.a.–c.

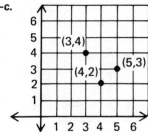

3.a.–h.

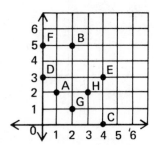

409

   2.a. (1, 5)   **b.** (3, 4)   **c.** (4, 2)   **d.** (2, 4)   **e.** (6, 8)

    f. (7, 5)   **g.** (9, 2)   **h.** (9, 0)   **i.** (2, 10)

PAGE 348

   1.a. Q **b.** H **c.** P **d.** S **2.a.** ($^{+}2, ^{+}3$)   **b.** ($^{-}5, ^{+}1$)

   c. ($^{+}4, ^{+}5$)   **d.** ($^{+}5, ^{-}5$)   **e.** ($^{-}5, ^{-}3$)   **f.** ($^{-}4, ^{+}5$)

3.a.–i.

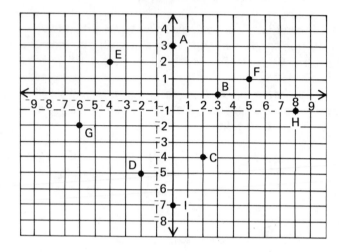

PAGE 350

   1. 6; 8   **3.** 2, 4, 5, 7; yes

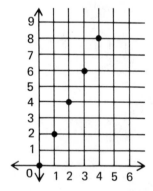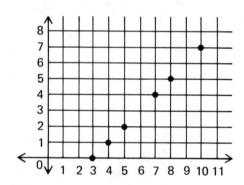

  2. The points lie along a straight line.

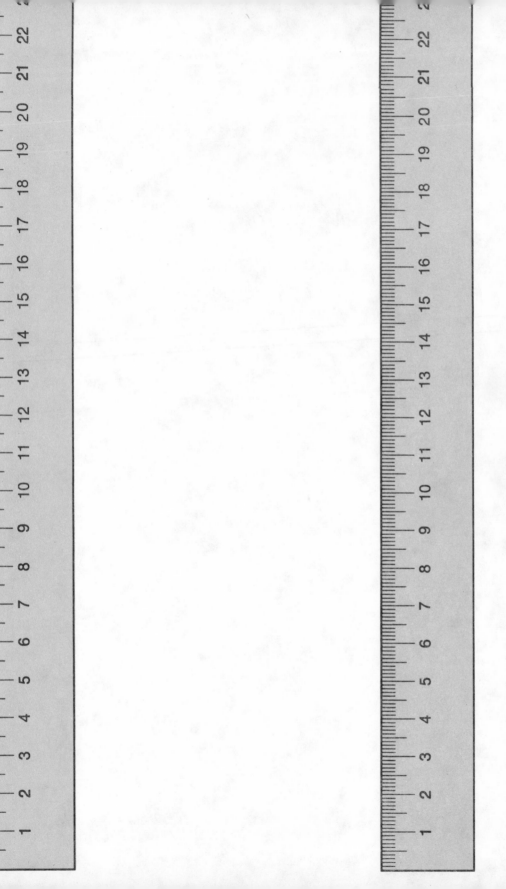